17.50

D1263891

World Population Crisis

Phyllis Tilson Piotrow
foreword by
George H. Bush, Jr.,
U.S. Representative to the UN

World Population Crisis
The United States Response

PRAEGER SPECIAL STUDIES IN INTERNATIONAL ECONOMICS AND DEVELOPMENT

Praeger Publishers   New York   Washington   London

LAW AND POPULATION BOOK SERIES No. 4

Law and Population Program
Fletcher School of Law and Diplomacy

The Law and Population Program is sponsored, in
part, by the Agency for International Development

PRAEGER PUBLISHERS
111 Fourth Avenue, New York, N.Y. 10003, U.S.A.
5, Cromwell Place, London S.W.7, England

Published in the United States of America in 1973
by Praeger Publishers, Inc.

Second printing, 1974

Library of Congress Catalog Card Number: 72-79545

Printed in the United States of America

To my parents

Few issues in the world have undergone such a rapid shift in public attitudes and government policies over the last decade as the problems of population growth and fertility control.

My own first awareness of birth control as a public policy issue came with a jolt in 1950 when my father was running for the United States Senate in Connecticut. Drew Pearson, on the Sunday before Election Day, "revealed" that my father was involved with Planned Parenthood. My father lost that election by a few hundred out of close to a million votes. Many political observers felt a sufficient number of voters were swayed by his alleged contacts with the birth controllers to cost him the election. The subject was taboo—not only because of religious opposition but because at that time a lot of people were unwilling to discuss in public what they considered a private matter.

Today, the population problem is no longer a private matter. In a world of nearly 4 billion people increasing by 2 percent, or 80 million more, every year, population growth and how to restrain it are public concerns that command the attention of national and international leaders. The per capita income gap between the developed and the developing countries is increasing, in large part the result of higher birth rates in the poorer countries.

World Population Crisis: The United States Response recounts and analyzes the events which mobilized the United States leaders to action. Dr. Piotrow presents a story of determined and sometimes disruptive advocates, of conscientious, careful scientists, of political leaders striving to reach a new consensus, of vigorous officials building action programs. It is, above all, a story of individuals and institutions struggling to solve a new kind of worldwide problem within the framework of individual choice and responsible government.

The population problem does not have easy answers. As a member of the U.S. House of Representatives in the late 1960s, I remember very well how disturbed and perplexed my colleagues and I were by this issue. Famine in India, unwanted babies in the United States, poverty that seemed to form an unbreakable chain for millions of people—how should we tackle these problems? I served on the House Ways and Means Committee. As we amended and updated the Social Security Act in 1967 I was impressed by the sensible approach of Alan Guttmacher the obstetrician who served as president of Planned Parenthood. It was ridiculous, he told the committee, to blame mothers on welfare for having too many children when the clinics and hospitals they used were absolutely prohibited from saying a word about birth control. So we took the lead in Congress in providing money and urging—in fact, even requiring—that in the United States family planning services be available for every woman, not just the private patient with her own gynecologist.

I remember another bill before the Ways and Means Committee. This one successfully repealed the prohibition against mailing information about birth control devices or sending the devices themselves through the mails. Until 1970 the mailing of this information had been heaped in with the mailing of "pornographic" material.

As chairman of the special Republican Task Force on Population and Earth Resources, I was impressed by the arguments of William H. Draper, Jr. that economic development overseas would be a miserable failure unless the developing countries had the knowledge and supplies their families needed to control fertility. Congress constantly pressed the rather nervous federal agencies to get on with the job. General Draper continues to lead through his tireless work for the UN Population Fund.

Congressional interest and support in population problems was remarkably bipartisan—including Jim Scheuer, Ernest Gruening, Bob Taft, Bill Fulbright, Joe Tydings, Bob Packwood, Alan Cranston, and many others from both parties and every section of the country. Presidents Johnson and Nixon both were seriously concerned about the problem, too. In fact, early in 1969 President Nixon delivered an official Message on Population to Congress. In the federal agencies there were at first only a few determined individuals like R. T. Ravenholt in AID and Philander P. Claxton, Jr. in the State Department who were willing to urge their superiors ahead. Now the recommendations of the Commission on Population Growth and the American Future, chaired by John D. Rockefeller 3rd, have urged many agencies to take on a larger role and have called for the U.S. government to adopt a national population policy.

When I moved to the United Nations in 1971 as United States Ambassador, I found that the population problem was high on the international agenda, though lacking some of the urgency the matter deserves. The General Assembly had designated 1974 as World Population Year with a major conference of governments scheduled. The UN Fund for Population Activities, which has raised some $50 million, now stands ready to help agencies and governments develop appropriate programs. It is quite clear that one of the major challenges of the 1970s, the Second United Nations Development Decade, will be to curb the world's fertility.

The United Nations population program, including the Fund and specialized agencies, stands today at the threshold of international impact. The problem has been recognized; the organizations exist; the resources are at hand. But policy making on the international level no less than on the national one is an educational process. In developing the programs needed, the public as well as government leaders learn from one another. New technologies lead to new policies and laws, new public and private values, new insights into our own problems as well as those of others. We all proceed by trial and error. Will we learn fast enough from one another and with one another how to defuse the population bomb?

One fact is clear: in a world of nearly 4 billion people, with some 150 independent governments, myriad races, religions, tribes and other organizations, major world problems like population and environmental protection will have to be handled by large and complex organizations representing many nations and many different points of view. How well we and the rest of the world can make the policies and programs of the United Nations responsive to the needs of the people will be the test of success in the population field.

Success in the population field, under United Nations leadership, may, in turn, determine whether we can resolve successfully the other great questions of peace, prosperity, and individual rights that face the world.

Dr. Piotrow's study of evolving population policy, in the United States and in the United Nations, is necessarily a story without an ending. It is not a blueprint for the future, but rather a search for the meaning of the past, an exploration of the means, the arguments, the individuals and the events which did, in fact, influence U.S. policy making over the last decade and a half. But the lessons suggested here—about leadership, about innovation, about national and international organizations—surely have continuing application for the future. Dr. Piotrow was in a unique position to observe and even participate in many of the actions taken.

I worked with Phyllis Piotrow on some of these issues. This book is far too modest about her own efforts, for she has contributed significantly herself to public understanding and support of population activities through her work with the Population Crisis Committee. Certainly the private organizations, like the Population Crisis Committee, Planned Parenthood—national and international—, the Population Council, the Population Reference Bureau, the Population Institute, Zero Population Growth, and others, have played a major role in assisting government policy makers and in mobilizing the United States response to the world population challenge that is described in this volume.

George Bush
U.S. Representative to the United Nations

In December 1959 President Dwight D. Eisenhower declared that "birth control . . . is not our business. I cannot imagine anything more emphatically a subject that is not a proper political or governmental activity or function or responsibility."

Ten years later, in July 1969, President Richard Nixon issued the first presidential message on population. After discussing U.S. and world population growth and the need for family planning, he stated that "this Administration does accept a clear responsibility to provide essential leadership."

The U.S. government had moved in barely a decade from complete repudiation to promotion and subsidizing of birth control services in the United States and overseas. By 1969, in fact, the U.S. government was the principal source of funding for family planning programs throughout the world. Yet three years later, in 1972, President Nixon, like President Eisenhower, rejected the recommendations of the carefully selected Commission of Population Growth and the American Future, for legalized abortion and contraceptive services to minors. No sooner was birth control and population planning officially endorsed in one form than the issue advanced again, beyond the pale of political acceptance, toward new formulations and policies to meet continuing problems.

The purpose of this study is to trace and analyze the metamorphosis of U.S. government policy toward the problems of rapid population growth and toward birth control as a solution to those problems. The development of any policy is, as Charles Lindblom suggests, "an extremely complex analytical and political process to which there is no beginning or end and the boundaries of which are most uncertain."[1] Basically a policy is a government response to a perceived problem. When that response includes funds and personnel allocated to carry out specific objectives, a program is created.

The formation of a government population policy and program is all the more complex because population problems have no fixed dimensions. Certainly if population is regarded in the demographic sense as the cumulative impact of human births and deaths, virtually every aspect of government activity can influence the number and distribution of population. By some, this impact is perceived as no problem at all; others see increasing numbers as an apocalyptic threat to the human race. Therefore the proposed policy solutions have ranged from continued general economic development to compulsory sterilization and celestial emigration.

This study will concentrate on the making of a State Department and foreign aid policy to meet the challenge posed by the very high rates of postwar population growth in the underdeveloped countries. The principal element of this policy through the 1960s was the support of voluntary birth control programs. The considerable efforts undertaken by the private population organizations during this period will be touched upon mainly to the extent that they influenced State Department and foreign aid actions, as will the development of government policy for the United States within the Department of Health, Education, and Welfare, the Office of Economic Opportunity, and the Commission on Population Growth and the American Future. This account will not deal with such issues as taxation, housing, agriculture, education, social security, military service, interest rates, employment, and other government activities that may in the long run have a greater impact on population change than do family planning measures. What are now considered "hidden population policies" were not perceived or evaluated as such by U.S. government policy makers except at the end of the decade.

Instead, by focusing attention in detail on the various steps by which government policy toward birth control was reversed and a substantial foreign aid program established in an area originally considered too controversial for government, this book will try to illuminate some of the avenues for innovation in policy, from both inside and outside the agencies concerned. Furthermore, since voluntary birth control services may represent the first move toward more extensive population policy, the evolution of this issue offers useful insight for the development of other areas of population policy.

As Bernard Berelson pointed out, issues have a "life history" in their course across the political stage, the events and needs of society pushing certain proposals into, through, and beyond the political gateway of decision with the actions of individuals, organizations, and political parties influencing "not so much the final decision as the speed of acceptance."[2] This study traces the life history of U.S. government policy on birth control as the issue grew from a controversial crusade initiated almost singlehandedly by one determined woman into a recognized and established government program. The process is clearly an incremental one that can best be analyzed in chronological format because at any given moment the best predictors of the next event are the actors' perceptions and rationalizations of previous events. In the simplest terms, "Innovation begins with the disruption of an existing consensus by those proposing a new program. It is the process by which the unfamiliar becomes the accepted."[3]

The life history of the birth control issue, policy, and program is broken down here into three broad, often overlapping phases. As seen from the standpoint of government policy the first phase, lasting until 1959, was nonpolicy. Birth control was irrelevant to any accepted government objectives not only because the U.S. government had limited social responsibilities but also because birth control itself was an issue of moral and religious disagreement. This issue had "two major adversaries. One is the taboo, imbedded a little bit in us all against the open factual discussion of matters connected with sex. The other is the abiding opposition of a powerful church."[4]

After World War II rapid worldwide population growth became a measurable, publicly documented, economically defined problem reaching its most extreme proportions in the underdeveloped countries. That phenomenon was increasingly relevant to the goals of the U.S. government. Therefore, the first stage in policy making was to focus public attention on the issue, to disrupt the national agenda that excluded consideration of the problem. Proving birth control relevant required arguing down and defeating both the silent and the articulate opposition. Publicity—to achieve recognition and concern—was necessary. Private organizations, both those favoring and those opposing birth control, often deliberately generated conflict in a bid for public backing. Government policy makers remained conspicuously silent. By the end of this period, however, birth control had reached a peak of controversy and passed its most crucial political threshold.

After a decade of skirmishes the recommendations of the Draper Committee in 1959, the attack of the Catholic bishops, the repudiation by President Eisenhower, and the election of a Catholic president in 1960 finally made the issue nationally and politically relevant. Despite the evasive tactics of politicians birth control did become an appropriate subject for public policy debate after 1960.

The second phase, extending from 1961 to 1965, might be termed the development of government policy. Within the government the issue to be resolved was no longer relevance but feasibility. What in the light of political and technological constraints was a feasible policy for the U.S. government to undertake or support? Assigning a few staff, gathering information, participating in meetings—these were the first initiatives that could in fact be taken. The early 1960s was a period of trailblazing speeches by high-level government officials matched by little visible funding or action. Speeches seemed feasible; programs seemed not. It was also a period of conciliation and accommodation, of efforts to look for common ground and to mute somewhat a level of controversy that had finally proved embarrassing even to ardent advocates. Feasibility was established not by positive programs for birth control but rather by the removal of impediments against it, including the declining official Catholic opposition. As the impediments fell, action programs became possible.

During this period the United States responded formally and favorably to initiatives from the United Nations. President Kennedy gave lukewarm consent to a wider research and information program. Family planners and Catholics did try to agree on general principles. The Agency for International Development (AID) began to study the problem. In the Alliance for Progress, active policy and program leaders initiated an acceptable program of population research and education. The third and—for this study—final phase of government policy is the implementation of a program, which took place primarily between 1966 and 1972. Marked not by speeches but by personnel and funding levels, program implementation depends essentially on priorities and timing. In government funding, priorities are determined by those who have the financial or personnel power to resolve competition among all the causes, offices, and professions that always seek a larger share of an always limited federal budget.

Priority and the closely related factor of timing are often influenced by extraneous events dramatizing a need that may have existed before but was not vividly perceived. When priority and timing are established, positive new programs are initiated that go beyond the mere repeal of prohibitions. The presence of funds and the lack of time become catalysts in the organizational structure, breaking administrative restrictions and crossing professional and jurisdictional boundaries. At this stage, conciliation of opponents may give way to rivalry among former allies. Much of this struggle, however, is fought within bureaucratic confines and professional publications. It does not always reach public awareness.

Program implementation in the foreign aid framework was delayed not by the original controversies but rather by personnel shifts, organizational incapacities, and budgetary stringencies. Only under the pressure of encroachment by other agencies was a separate office in AID established in 1967. Only under the statutory demands of ear-marked funding by Congress was a substantial program undertaken. Finally, under a determined and convinced director, the program won a secure base in the agency. Similarly in the United Nations a special voluntary fund, operating apart from previously institutionalized activities, was necessary for program leadership.

A three-step process therefore forms the basic chronology: first the establishment of relevance, achieved by conflict and controversy and marked by increasing public awareness; second the development of policy, achieved by conciliation and compromise and marked by identification of feasible actions; and third the expansion of program, achieved by outside events and top-level decisions and marked by fiscal and personnel priorities.

Throughout this changing pattern, as initiative gradually shifted from individuals to organizations to Congress to the executive branch, and ultimately perhaps to the United Nations—five themes will be stressed:

1. the defining of the issue,
2. the influence of technology,
3. the behavior and relations of the activists and the professionals,
4. the role of Congress, and
5. the extent of individual leadership in accelerating the process.

Critical to any policy is the perception of the problem. During the 1950s and 1960s the question was refined and rephrased as each side vied for public support. When government officials were in effect asked, "Should public funds be expended for a program regarded as immoral by 25 percent of the population?" they avoided the issue. When, on the other hand, they were asked, "Should the poor be denied access to family planning because government-supported health facilities do not now provide it?" their answer was more sympathetic. Similarly, the intensity and certainty of the opposition was also shaken by new emphasis on freedom of information and an end to discrimination against the poor. A comparable shift took place later in the definition of abortion legislation.

Secondly, the role of technology is crucial in developing government policy as in influencing individual behavior. Where technology is totally inadequate to the task, a government policy is rarely considered. Where technology is readily available and easily applied by the individual, a government policy is not needed. A government policy becomes feasible only as technology reaches the stage to make a program possible but yet is so difficult as to remain beyond the resources of individual or commercial effort. Although it would be wrong to regard birth control or population policy during the 1950s and 1960s as primarily a scientific or technological issue—since it was viewed by policy makers almost exclusively in a practical, political framework—nevertheless changes in birth control technology clearly changed the speed and direction of policy. Even in the religious sphere, it was the pill more than the pope that influenced Catholic morality.

A third line of emphasis will be the relationships between the professionals and the activists. Every profession tends to define and then try to solve problems with the techniques in its own professional arsenal. Every profession looks with suspicion on the popularizer, the huckster who bids for public attention by oversimplification.

Demographers, physicians, economists, sociologists, technologists, administrators, educators, and ecologists have all contributed, in concert and in cacophony, to the definition and development of a population policy. In twentieth-century America, feminists were the first obvious clientele for a birth control program designed, as Margaret Sanger put it, "to help women own their own bodies" by preventing unwanted pregnancy. But they needed the skills and the authority of the medical profession to satisfy their demand. The physicians had the techniques but were not fully convinced that aggressive promotion of birth control fell within medical norms. Therefore, while the demographers defined the "what" of a population problem and the health professions controlled the "how" of modern birth control, it was the economists who developed the "why" to justify government allocation of resources for a specific program.

The sociologists—professional students of family, community, and cultural structure—doubted that any important changes could be achieved merely by promoting birth control methods but, however articulate, they were at first unable to propose other policies sufficiently sure, discreet, and acceptable to win government favor. By the end of the decade ecologists and biologists began to challenge the economic and social science theories of growth with an ecological theory of stabilization.

At virtually every stage of the policy process the pressures of the activists—expanding, exaggerating, and often distorting the issues—were added to the interplay of these disciplines. Whether they are businessmen or women's liberationists, activists tend to be expansionary, inclusive, trying to subsume all problems and convert all people to a single point of view. "Whatever your cause, it's a lost cause unless we control population" is the very epitome of an active publicist slogan. The professions on the other hand are restrictive, exclusive, tending to bar the unqualified and limit the boundaries of technical competence. The publicists aim at immediate impact and wide audience. The professions seek an institutional base and the longevity of established organizations. In the population field the rivalry between the two is intensified by the fact that success cannot be achieved in the laboratory alone but only by actually reaching and convincing millions of other people. The very tensions generated by this interdisciplinary and extradisciplinary competition have been an important stimulant in the life history of the population issue.

A fourth determining element in this account is the role played by Congress in forcing the attention of the executive agencies of government upon a population policy. Paradoxically, this nettle of an issue, which few in the executive branch were anxious to handle even with the president's blessing, was grasped with determination by the legislative branch. It was Congress that, through lengthy hearings, delineated the terms upon which the birth control issue was debated. It was Congress that enacted, against the firm and continuing opposition of the executive agencies, the legislation that decisively established policy and priority for these programs, that is, Title X of the Foreign Assistance Act of 1961.

The leadership of Congress on the population issue—contrasted with the virtual abdication of responsibility by high officials in the executive branch—can be seen at its most effective level in the field where Congress has traditionally exercised greatest power—funding. Congressional leadership has, so far, been least effective in the area of administrative or structural change, where executive agencies have most vigorously resisted initiatives from Congress.

At the same time the difficulties and lags in the acceptance of new programs by established organizations are also an important factor. Although innovation entirely from within a government agency rarely occurs, innovation forced from outside, even by Congress, is dependent upon the ability, commitment, and determination of officials within the agency for its ultimate success. The gradual conversion of a large segment of AID personnel from resistance to grudging acceptance to genuine support for family planning was basically the result of congressional insistence, but it occurred slowly, through the mediating influence of AID's internal procedures and an originally very small cadre of supporters. A similar pattern emerged in the United Nations where a few member governments and the secretary-general pushed the program forward despite the reluctance of well-established agencies.

Finally, this study is also an account of those individuals who took the initiative to influence policy, deliberately creating, shaping, and trying to direct organizations to specific ends. Given the facts of population increase, an eventual government policy promoting voluntary birth control was probably inevitable. Nevertheless, the manner in which the policy developed, the programs that flourished, and equally the programs that foundered, reflect the impact of individual leadership. Leadership can be defined, as it can be exercised, in many different ways. For the purpose of policy development the leaders are those whose eyes are fixed upon the problem itself, the challenge to be met, and not simply upon the piecemeal activities that can most readily be performed by existing organizations or professions. The dichotomy between those who looked at the problem and those who looked at the existing institutional possibilities may represent in part the often-remarked differences between the charismatic leader and the organizer, the fanatic and the bureaucrat. Yet the population issue was perhaps remarkable in attracting the concern of a number of people who were simultaneously able to look at the problem and to shape new institutions to deal with it.

Among those individuals who committed their time, talent, and resources to the development of an effective government policy during this period, several stand out—John D. Rockefeller 3rd, Hugh Moore, and William H. Draper, Jr.—for although they worked in different ways all three were determined that governmental policy makers should take account of the issue. Birth control was not their job; it was their mission. In Congress, Senators

Fulbright, Gruening, Clark, Tydings, Taft, Packwood, and Cranston, and also Congressmen Morgan, Hays, Findley, Scheuer, Bush, and DuPont took the initiative without regard to immediate political benefit or constituent pressures. Reflecting their own convictions, they used their innovative powers in Congress, through the committee system, to promote meaningful policy. And ultimately within AID and the Department of State a small group, including an assistant administrator of AID, two deputy assistant secretaries of state, the director of the office of population, and the special assistant to the secretary for population matters struggled through the full gamut of bureaucratic obstacles to develop a purposive new program, not just to add incrementally to existing projects.

This account then is a record of individuals and organizations, private and governmental, consciously trying to change the attitudes and behavior of their fellow citizens and the policies of their government. Throughout the policy process they made decisions and took actions that at one point or another decisively influenced the outcomes in government policy. At the same time, of course, they and others made negative or nondecisions about taking actions that, if taken, might have led to very different results, for instance, the nondecision to develop a population program in the National Institutes of Health (NIH) in the early and mid-1960s.

The process itself can be seen then as three different phases—public awareness, policy development, and program implementation—through which can be traced several major themes: defining and redefining the problem, giving it professional status and public notice, relating it to existing technology, guiding it through the emerging pattern of legislative innovation and executive resistance, with individual intervention at various stages seeking and often able to determine the resulting action.

The basic purpose of this study is not to prove definitively any specific hypotheses but rather to provide a fairly detailed account of what actually happened, indicating how the events differed in certain critical respects from official retrospective accounts and highlighting the initiatives that had a critical impact. The last chapter will identify some of the points or hypotheses emerging from this account that may have either a wider validity for policy studies in general or a unique significance for the further development of population policy. These hypotheses may then be useful as points of departure for further testing or application in other countries or under other circumstances.

It also seems appropriate to acknowledge at this point that no one approaches population or birth control policies from wholly neutral ground. Although I have tried to deal objectively with the data, undoubtedly my own biases are evident. I believe that population growth threatens not only present values and institutions but also the opportunity for billions of people, born and unborn, to live with peace, prosperity, and dignity in years to come. I believe, therefore, that private and public, national and international programs to limit population growth are desirable, necessary and ultimately inevitable. I believe also that the more rapidly and effectively fertility control programs are undertaken on a voluntary basis, the more likely they are to succeed in reducing population growth without either coercion or substantial increases in mortality.

This study does not try to answer the question of how effective present programs may actually be in reducing fertility. It concentrates on the development of the central funding institutions and policies that now support population and family planning work, particularly in the U.S. Agency for International Development. What these institutions have achieved in the field is and will surely continue to be the subject of many books.

I would like to acknowledge with thanks the generous assistance received from many of the individuals and organizations which are referred to throughout this study—particularly the Ford Foundation which provided a fellowship that initiated the study; the Population Crisis Committee which offered continuing support and encouragement; the Law and Population Programme of the Fletcher School of Law and Diplomacy, Tufts University which has included this book in their international series; Planned Parenthood-World Population, the International Planned Parenthood Federation, the Population Council, the Population Reference Bureau, and other national and international agencies which provided helpful material. To the many busy people who took time to answer my questions and to comment on portions of the manuscript, I am particularly grateful. It should be added that, while generous with time and available information, none of the government agencies referred to provided any financial support for the research and writing of this study and the opinions expressed herein are entirely—perhaps in some cases exclusively— my own.

My special thanks go to Professors Francis Rourke, John Kantner, Milton Cummings, and Robert Peabody at the Johns Hopkins University for their many useful suggestions. I am grateful also for the help and sympathy of my husband and two children and for the untiring editorial and clerical assistance of Joy Chiles, Milton Fairfax, and Xenia Mesernisky.

NOTES

1. Charles S. Lindblom, *The Policy Making Process*, Foundations of Modern Political Science Series (Englewood Cliffs, N.J.: Prentice-Hall 1968), p. 4.

2. Bernard Berelson *et al.*, *Voting* (Chicago: University of Chicago Press, 1956), p. 204.

3. Samuel P. Huntington, *The Common Defense* (New York: Columbia University Press, 1961), p. 293.

4. Planned Parenthood, "The Anatomy of a Victory" (mimeo., New York, 1959), p. ii.

CONTENTS

LIST OF TABLES

LIST OF CHARTS

"NOT THE GOVERNMENT'S BUSINESS," 1945-60

1

THE
POPULATION
EXPLOSION

A NEW PROBLEM

Human population growth in the last half of the twentieth century is proving different in degree, if not in kind, from any previous population trends. Although the number of people on earth has multiplied from 250 million persons estimated to be alive at the time of Christ to nearly 4 billion in 1972, more than one third of that increase has occurred since World War II. (See Chart 1.1.)

Moreover, before 1950 population growth took place primarily in those portions of Europe, North America, Asia, and Africa settled by Europeans. Since 1950, however, approximately 80 percent of world population growth has taken place in Asia, Africa, and Latin America. Population increase in those regions has jumped from a decennial rate of about 12 percent in the 1930s and 1940s to 20 percent in the 1950s and 22 percent in the 1960s.[1]

To describe the full impact of this phenomenon, even the sober, dispassionate reports of the UN Population Division seem at a loss for words:

> If the speed-up appearing in the more developed regions after 1950 can be called a "revolution," a more forceful term seems appropriate to describe the far greater acceleration, since about 1950, in the population trend of less developed regions. In fact, so strong a word as "population explosion" has gained much currency, and this should be no cause for surprise because the unprecedented magnitude of this new phenomenon is indeed baffling,[2]

Basically, population increase represents the difference between births and deaths. Throughout most of recorded history, human birth and death rates have been high, often in the range of 40 to 50 per 1,000. But at various times and most consistently beginning in the eighteenth century in Europe, death rates declined. Life expectancy, estimated to be 20 years at the fall of the

3

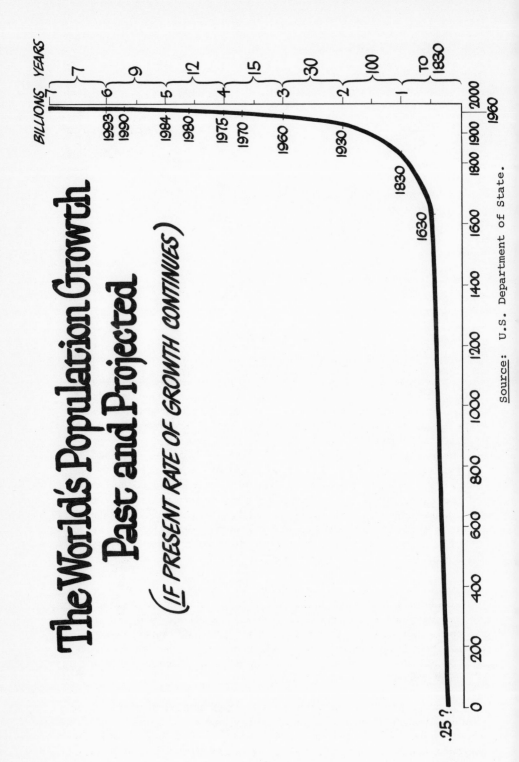

The World's Population Growth Past and Projected

(IF PRESENT RATE OF GROWTH CONTINUES)

Source: U.S. Department of State.

4

Roman Empire, probably did not exceed 40 years until the nineteenth century. In other words, over the last two and a half centuries, influenced by a combination of factors—better nutrition, reduction of epidemic disease, better sanitation, potable water, improved public health measures, immunization, and finally antibiotics—death rates gradually fell to a point where life expectancy in the United States and most of Europe is now close to 70 years.[3]

Similarly, but usually after a time lag of several generations, birth rates also have declined. By 1970, birth rates in the developed countries ranged from about 10 to 20 per 1,000, whereas death rates had fallen to about eight to ten per 1,000. Whatever specific factors were the most influential in this long-term demographic transition, there is no dispute that—except in Japan—the dual decline of death and birth rates was the product of European culture, influenced by economic and social change within those societies and carried out in accordance with indigenous attitudes and technology.

Postwar population growth, however, although equally a result of declining death rates and therefore greater life expectancy, was not equally an indigenous product of the peoples affected. The techniques—ranging from DDT and penicillin to massive shipments of food and fertilizer—that conquered many epidemic diseases and mitigated the impact of famine and malnutrition in Asia, Africa, and Latin America were not the result of slow local development and adjustment but rather represented a windfall of foreign largesse. Although death rates responded, often with astonishing speed, to this externally supplied technology, birth rates, still the result of individual action and decision, did not. (See Chart 1.2.)

In a notable early (1945) discussion of the approaching postwar situation, Frank Notestein wrote:

> The more rapid response of mortality than of fertility to the forces of modernization is probably inevitable. The reduction of mortality is a universally acceptable goal and faces no substantial social obstacles. But the reduction of fertility requires a shift in social goals from those directed toward the survival of the group to those directed toward the welfare and development of the individual. This change, both of goals and of social equipment by which they are achieved, is at best a slow process. As a result, the period of modernization is virtually certain to yield rapid population increase.[4]

In strictly demographic terms the postwar population problem was easily defined as a temporary imbalance in birth and death rates, most acute in Asia but potentially serious in all the underdeveloped areas. Historical and statistical research had by the end of World War II further established that the declines in European fertility resulted not from any physiological changes in human reproduction but rather from deliberate fertility control—primitive methods of contraception, abortion, and even infanticide. In his classic *Medical History of Contraception*, Norman Himes offers evidence through virtually all times and cultures of a strong desire to control childbirth and an extraordinary variety of measures to do so.[5]

The Demographic Transition

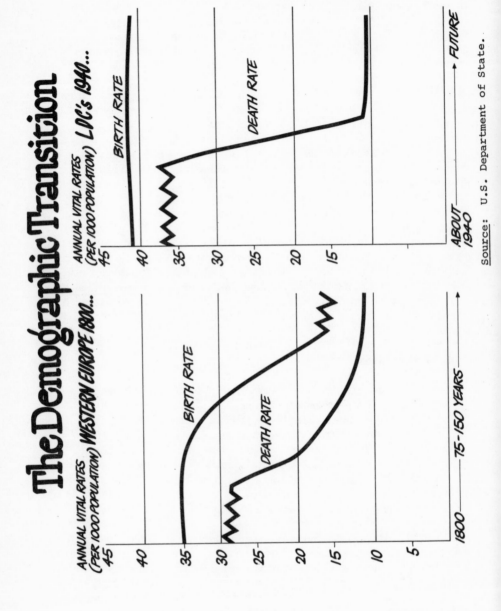

ANNUAL VITAL RATES
(PER 1000 POPULATION) WESTERN EUROPE 1800...

45
40
35
30
25
20
15
10
5

BIRTH RATE

DEATH RATE

1800 ———— 75-150 YEARS ————→

ANNUAL VITAL RATES
(PER 1000 POPULATION) LDC's 1940...

45
40
35
30
25
20
15

BIRTH RATE

DEATH RATE

ABOUT 1940 ——→ FUTURE

Source: U.S. Department of State.

6

THE BACKGROUND OF U.S. CONCERN

Nevertheless, despite the widespread private use of various birth control techniques a public policy of disseminating birth control information was not a welcome topic for debate in the United States. As the scientist Harrison Brown, writing in the mid-1950s, pointed out, "The extent to which human beings avoid discussing conception control is truly incredible."[6] Not only was birth control intimately involved with sexual practices and religious beliefs—neither considered appropriate for government concern—but also, in the words of one sympathetic official, "The high emotionalism necessary to get this issue going as a social reform worked for a long time against the willingness of government to undertake it."[7]

Two very different elements were involved, almost from the start, in the promotion of birth control and population as issues of U.S. public policy. On the one hand the activist line of birth control promotion was symbolized in the career of Margaret Sanger, who literally invented the term, who publicized the issue in the United States, and who for many years determined the way in which birth control advocates would approach the government and challenge their adversaries.[8] On the other hand the professionals—physicians, scientists, demographers—wanted to study the implications of the issue quietly in terms of their own professional values without becoming embroiled in public controversy. The activists needed the theoretical base and factual data of the scientists to make their case. They needed the support of the professionals to give them legitimacy. The scientists, on their side, benefited from the increased public interest that led to a greater demand for their technical output, even as they sometimes shuddered at the uses to which it was put.

In a relationship somewhat like Gresham's Law in reverse, the wide dissemination of bad data stimulated the search for good data. Similarly, the spread of inadequate theories and poor contraceptives by nonprofessionals promoted the search for better approaches by those technically competent to develop them. In many ways the story of the development of birth control policy is a story of the professionalization of the activists and the activation of the professionals. In the prewar years, however, the gap between the two was still wide and sharp.

On the activist side, Margaret Sanger founded most of the birth control clinics and educational groups now combined in Planned Parenthood. Her legacies, many of them still controversial, include a determined feminism, an emphasis upon birth control as a panacea for virtually all sexual, social, and ecomonic ills, and an unrelenting struggle to eliminate legal barriers blocking access to birth control. She also had "an unfailing instinct for showmanship and newsmaking."[9] Time and time again, by vividly defining her own role as support for maternal and child health, for freedom of information, freedom of speech, freedom of religion, and privacy of medical records she forced her opponents into a position that most Americans could not easily support. This confrontation technique was valuable to the birth control movement, as it has been to other social reformers who have tried to alter community attitudes.

But it was a double-edged weapon that could also cut its most effective wielders out of any role as conciliators of professional opinion or participants in government policy making.

In fact, despite Margaret Sanger's claim that "the Birth Control Movement has allied itself with science and no small part of its present propaganda is to awaken the interest of scientists to the pivotal importance to civilization of this instrument,"[10] doctors and demographers both held aloof from her activities. The physicians, newly imbued with a sense of their own professional standards, were suspicious of lay medicine. Not until 1937 did the American Medical Association endorse birth control at all and then only for therapeutic reasons. Most medical journals avoided the subject.

But the publicity that Margaret Sanger aroused did in fact force medical attention upon the question. Certainly an important factor in the 1937 resolution of the American Medical Association approving birth control was the desire of the doctors to check the proliferation and widespread advertising of useless and even harmful birth control techniques that had developed to meet the growing public demand. As she had predicted, "Just as supply and demand are related to all ëconomic questions, so is propaganda a related part of scientific research in the realms of sex psychology. The medical profession will ultimately meet the issue on the demands of public opinion."[11]

The demographers and others concerned with population on a large scale were at first no more eager than the physicians to take "Sangerism" seriously; many were reluctant even to mention birth control. When in 1927 Margaret Sanger initiated, organized, and largely funded the first World Population Conference in Geneva for scientists of international repute in order to impress the League of Nations with the importance of the population issue, the scientists were uneasy. Delegates to the conference—mainly statisticians, biologists, and economists—disputed the use of her name on the program, "granted her no official recognition, and barred the topic of contraception from the agenda."[12] Despite lively discussions and complete freedom in the exchange of ideas and information, one of the demographers present recounts that "the scholars at this conference deemed it inappropriate to form a continuing organization under the sponsorship of a proponent of action in a controversial field, and they arranged to meet for this purpose privately in Paris the following year. The International Union for the Scientific Study of Population Problems (I.U.S.S.P.) was organized there in 1928."[13]

The most eagerly sought and acknowledged funding for professional and scientific activities in the field of population came from the foundations. Through the Scripps Foundation for the Study of Population, established in 1922 at Miami University in Ohio, Warren Thompson and P. C. Whelpton became virtually the first academic demographers in the United States, joining the very limited number of population analysts in the Census Bureau and life insurance firms. The Milbank Memorial Fund was encouraged by a determined board member to look at the impact of birth control in a public health context and in 1936 provided funds for an Office of Population Research at Princeton University, under Frank Notestein. The first large foundations to make grants in the population field were the Rockefeller Foundation and the Carnegie Foundation. Influenced by the strong interest of one or two trustees, both foundations supported professional organizations and research but avoided a large direct role.

But even though the researchers and foundations tried to keep at arm's length from Margaret Sanger and her crusade for birth control, they could not avoid some of the same liabilities. Research on sexual problems still carried an aura of witchcraft and was hardly a prestigious scientific field. Catholic opposition remained a perennial source of embarrassment. Frank Notestein recalls friends shaking their heads and wondering how he would ever be able to make a living in such a new and precarious field.[14]

The low status of population activists and scientists alike was reflected in their minimal impact on national government policy. The activists, with Margaret Sanger in the lead, vigorously urged and organized for repeal of the federal "Comstock laws" that barred mailing, shipping in interstate commerce, and importing contraceptives. They tried to amend state laws to permit the operation of birth control clinics. But even with medical support, state legislatures and the U.S. Congress refused to act.

Judicial action brought the first changes in government policy. Lawyers and physicians united in a series of cases to urge the removal of arbitrary, outmoded restrictions upon the prescription of contraceptives for health and welfare. In the critical decision, Judge Augustus Hand ruled that none of the existing Comstock laws should be construed "to prevent the importation, sale, or carriage by mail of things which might intelligently be employed by conscientious and competent physicians for the purpose of saving life or promoting well-being of their patients."[15] Thus only in the courts, where the activists and the professionals could cooperate and, above all, where the political pressures were reduced, was government action possible.

Two other elements weakened the position of those involved in birth control or population work in the immediate prewar and postwar years. First, the state of technology was clearly inadequate. The birth control methods in common use—coitus interruptus, condoms, diaphragms, douching, and various jellies—were not considered effective, esthetic, acceptable, or even safe. They were least practical for those people and nations that most needed help to reduce fertility. Furthermore, because of their immediate link with sexual relations, the methods did not lend themselves readily to public discussion.

Secondly, the Great Depression had a curious and complex influence upon birth control and population studies in the United States. Economic conditions during the 1930s persuaded many couples to have smaller families. As a result the practice of birth control increased even without fully satisfactory methods. Yet as birth rates remained low, especially in better-educated and higher-income families, many demographers forecasted a declining quantity and quality of population for the United States and Western Europe. Such predictions hardly encouraged government enthusiasm for birth control as a national policy.

THE OPPOSITION TO BIRTH CONTROL

The most conspicuous barrier to government policy in the birth control field, however, lay not in the differences between activists and professionals, nor in the temporary exigencies of economics, but rather in the opposition of the Roman Catholic Church. The sexual orientation of Christianity was historically hostile to onanism or birth control, but in the whole compendium of Christian writings up to the nineteenth century, contraception had actually occupied little more than a footnote.[16] Organized, articulate opposition to birth control, characteristic of Protestant churches in the nineteenth century and the Catholic Church in the twentieth, was, like population growth, a relatively new phenomenon.

Birth rates had been declining in Western Europe for centuries. That decline was widely recognized and publicized during the late nineteenth century at the very time when the birth control advocates issued their first public appeals. The various national bishops, not the Vatican, responded first to the challenge. From France, after defeat in the Franco-Prussian War, came objections on patriotic as well as moral grounds to a practice that seemed to be depleting French armies as well as endangering French souls. The first theological work devoted exclusively to the subject appeared in France in 1876.[17] Contraception and declining birth rates seemed to be associated with declining power.

In the United States, too, the militancy of Catholic opposition to birth control had political and ethnic overtones. By 1900, just as the birth control movement was beginning, millions of poor, ignorant, but prolific Irish had immigrated to Massachusetts and other northeastern states. Then came the Italians. By force of numbers and political machines the Irish dispossessed their Anglo-Saxon predecessors. Not altogether welcome in their new home and led by priests and bishops who equated English origins with Irish subjection, the Irish were Catholic in culture and politics as well as in religion. When the ladies of Planned Parenthood tried to offer help, the Black Irish reaction was "What business do those thin-lipped Boston Brahmins have telling us how to behave in bed?" When Harvard graduates argued for repeal of the nineteenth-century Massachusetts and Connecticut Comstock laws in order to propagate birth control, the Irish and Italian Catholics voted "No" at the polls even if they practiced a measure of birth control at home. The emotional revulsion that contraception aroused among Catholics[18] was often an ethnic revulsion against the people who were promoting it. As Father John Ryan put it in testimony against one of the Sanger bills, "We simply cannot subscribe to the idea that the poor, . . . instead of getting justice from the Government and more rational social order, are to be required to reduce their numbers. . . . That is Toryism."[19] At the same time Ryan was perfectly willing to cooperate behind the scenes in drafting legislation that would place control of contraception more fully in medical hands.[20]

The tactics that the Catholic Church in America used to fight against birth control were ambivalent. As a religious institution the church was fighting heresy; error had no rights and did not deserve a hearing. But in the political environment of U.S. government policymaking the right to equal time and the principle of majority rule could not be dismissed as heresy. As the Catholic Church and American Catholic politicians began to demand their share of national resources and their turn at national leadership, they were increasingly compelled to abide by political rules.

When Margaret Sanger began her educational campaign, the Catholic Church had tried to cut off all public discussion. Hotels, meeting halls, even political leaders were threatened with boycotts and reprisals if they offered a public forum. But measures such as these only provided confrontations Margaret Sanger needed to publicize her cause. "Hostility aroused against the Roman Catholic community by these tactics," one Catholic complained, "would be hard to overestimate. In proportion to their ill effect their good effect is small."[21]

Meanwhile, Protestant churches were beginning to break away from their traditional prohibitions on birth control. The 1930 Lambeth Conference of Anglican bishops hestitantly proposed that "where there is a clearly felt moral obligation to limit or avoid parenthood, the method must be decided on Christian principles."[22] As the issue in the United States shifted from a conflict between birth control and religion to an internal skirmish among different religions, the Catholic hierarchy was increasingly isolated.

By the late 1930s the Catholic Church was already looking for a way to accommodate its blanket prohibition with the exceptions required by political, professional, economic, and individual circumstances. Doctrinally, the encyclical *Casti Connubii* issued by Pope Pius XI on December 31, 1930, had denounced contraception and the permissive Anglican bishops in no uncertain terms; yet at the same time it declared sexual relations licit "even though, through natural causes either of time or of certain defects, new life cannot thence result."[23] Though the research that would establish a fair degree of reliability for the "rhythm method" was not yet publicized, the pope's brief reference opened for married couples a doctrinal escape route that soon became a well-travelled highway.

Despite the efforts of Margaret Sanger to promote it and the Roman Catholic Church to prohibit it, birth control before World War II was basically a private practice, not a social issue. Most of those who practiced it were not prepared to preach it. The success of the lawyers in drawing the sting from federal statutes removed rather than stimulated the need for legislative action. The U.S. government even during the Great Depression had few economic and social responsibilities at home and fewer still overseas. Birth control was not relevant to any immediate objective. Even those directly involved were very far from agreement in their definition of the issue. Activists like Margaret Sanger saw birth control as a panacea for social, economic, and sexual ills. Doctors and demographers wanted to consider it only as a single, narrow substratum of their larger fields. On the other side, the Catholic Church was publicly determined to exercise the broadest moral and religious prerogatives that were politically feasible. For a government caught among these currents, the only prudent policy was no policy at all.

After the Second World War, victory overseas and world power, tempered only by continuing cold war competition, replaced the pessimism of the depression. A new U.S. prosperity was fueled by consumers who wanted more of everything, including children. In the immediate postwar years, birth control had little appeal for those who had been waiting to start or continue their families. Without a pressing social need, with women returning happily to home and cradle, the birth control movement in the United States lost what little momentum it had.

THE SCIENTIFIC APPROACH

Nevertheless, the professionals in the field of population study had an initial advantage over the activists in the postwar era. They possessed the technical skills necessary to identify the new overseas population problem and a recognized institutional base (the Office of Population Research at Princeton) under qualified leadership (Frank Notestein). When in 1946 the Economic and Social Council of the United Nations established a Population Commission representing member governments, a Population Division also was set up in the UN Secretariat under Notestein's direction. The first UN demographic yearbook appeared in 1949 and was followed almost annually by volumes summarizing census data and studying specific problems in detail. Influential for their public impact were the UN projections of future population growth. In 1952, for example, a world population of 3.6 billion by 1980 was forecasted.[1] By 1957, the projection for 1980 was revised upward to 4.2 billion; the median estimate for the year 2000 was 6.3 billion.[2]

As a rough measure of the low public attention and interest in world population growth, the *New York Times* index entries for population and vital statistics increased from barely one inch in 1950 to a little over two inches in

1958, but about one half of the total coverage was directly or indirectly related to UN statistical reports and meetings.[3] (See Chapter 3.)

A high point in UN concern during the 1950s was the 1954 World Population Conference in Rome, jointly sponsored by the International Union for the Scientific Study of Population and UN specialized agencies and attended by some 600 participants from nearly 40 countries. The largest scientific meeting on population held to date, the Rome conference also considered relationships between population and economic development, but Catholics and communists together blocked recommendations for action.[4] In 1955 when Dag Hammarskjold succeeded Trygve Lie as secretary-general, population and other research-oriented activities of the United Nations were cut back. The UN Population Division was downgraded to a Population Branch for the next decade.

Apart from the statistical work at the United Nations, the principal boost for increased scientific and professional attention to the population problem in the 1950s came from John D. Rockefeller 3rd. Returning from the Far East in 1948 very much concerned about population growth, especially in Japan, and not satisfied with the token support provided by the Rockefeller Foundation, he arranged for a four-member team—including a public health physician, a social scientist, and two demographers— to report on the status of public health and demography in Asia. Emphasizing the difficulty of reducing birth rates, the complexity of social change, the threat of political upheaval, and the need for better contraceptive techniques, their report recommended "study rather than action in the years immediately ahead."[5] They cautiously observed that "the role of the private agencies lies in encouraging teaching, research, experiment and demonstration to increase knowledge and ultimately to foster its wide dissemination."[6] Yet the Rockefeller Foundation hesitated to make interdisciplinary population studies a major program. Private soundings indicated continuing Catholic disapproval; the foundation's institutional biases were toward public health and agriculture; conservative lawyers feared to jeopardize its far-flung work by entering such a controversial field; and most of the board of directors did not share Rockefeller's feeling of urgency.

In June 1952 at the suggestion of Rockefeller and under the sponsorship of the National Academy of Sciences, a high-level group of experts in public health, conservation, planned parenthood, agriculture, nutrition, demography, and the social sciences was convened in Williamsburg, Virginia. The conference recommended establishment of an international council to concern itself exclusively with the scientific study of population in all its related aspects. In November 1952 the Population Council was organized with Rockefeller as chairman of the board and Frederick Osborn as executive vice-president. Its stated purposes were:

To study the problems presented by the increasing population of the world; to encourage and support research and to disseminate as appropriate the knowledge resulting from such research; to serve generally as a center for the collection and expansion of facts and information on the population questions; to cooperate with individuals and institutions in the development of programs; and to

take the initiative in the broad fields which in the aggregate constitute the population problem.[7]

The founding of the Population Council was a significant start in
mobilizing the professionals for action. For the first decade or so, its activities
were largely research and training, channelled through a relatively small
academic community. The universities and the professions both needed this
kind of moral and financial encouragement to take up a sensitive multidisciplin-
ary issue. The Population Council provided a heretofore-lacking respectable
base from which to influence professional and academic norms and to finance a
more specifically problem-oriented approach to population.

The difference the Population Council made in helping to reorient professional behavior can be seen in the case of the National Committee on
Maternal Health, headed by Dr. Chris Tietze. The committee had refused in the
late 1940s to become openly associated with Planned Parenthood's work, but
by 1957 the committee accepted a considerable grant from the Population
Council "to undertake under the best medical auspices an important program
of research to evaluate the effectiveness, acceptability, safety, and cost of
various methods and materials of fertility control."[8] By January 1967 the
committee's staff and activities were transferred to the Bio-Medical Division of
the council—a classic example of professional cooptation.

Yet despite the insistence, as late as 1965, that "the scientific and
technical fields are those in which our kind of organization can be most
effective,"[9] the Population Council was drawn very quickly into a more active
role, mainly because its professionals were among those best qualified to advise
developing countries on what action to take. The Indian government, spurred
on by the newly opened Ford Foundation office, asked for help from the
Population Council. Frank Notestein and Dr. Leona Baumgartner, then New
York City Health Commissioner, visited India in the fall of 1955. They
recommended to the government an interdisciplinary program— emphasizing a
public health approach, including contraceptives—with strong demographic
support from a national center. Marshall Balfour of the council participated in
a second technical assistance mission to Pakistan in 1959, to help General Ayub
Khan establish a government birth control program. Notestein hoped to
develop university-centered public health advisory units and Balfour was
accompanied to Pakistan by Dr. Paul Harper of the Johns Hopkins School of
Hygiene and Public Health.

During 1955, 1956, and 1957 the Population Council sponsored a series
of meetings that included Planned Parenthood officials as well as physical and
social scientists to develop and define general principles for promoting birth control overseas. The importance of indigenous leadership, the need for economic
planning as an approach to the elite, and the use of public health programs as an
approach to the masses were emphasized.[10] These guidelines were to influence
not only the programs of the Population Council but also the policy advice given
to foreign governments and eventually to the government of the United States.

Another project, encouraged by Notestein at Princeton and partially
supported by the council in the 1950s, was influential in later government
policy making. Economists like Joseph Spengler and Harvey Leibenstein were

developing a theoretical framework to show that population growth, usually considered an impetus to economic growth in the industrial age, could be an impediment in underdeveloped countries.[11] The demographer Ansley Coale and the economist Edgar Hoover applied these arguments explicitly to India to demonstrate that expenditures on family planning would, over various periods, increase per capita income more than any other type of government investment.[12] The heart of their argument was applicable to all developing countries: namely, that a reduced rate of population growth would always mean additional funds for capital investment because it would produce fewer dependents and smaller expenditures for consumption and social needs. This approach turned attention away from the troublesome questions of population size or density (where European history always disproved the Malthusian argument) and focussed the spotlight instead on population growth rates in the developing countries as barriers to economic growth rates. The Coale-Hoover thesis eventually provided the justification for birth control as a part of U.S. foreign aid policy.

The creation of the Population Council had a further impact in the philanthropic area. As an avowedly professional scientific organization that sought to avoid and not to provoke controversy, it was more acceptable for foundation support than were the active birth controllers. The first two Ford Foundation grants of over $500,000 were to the Population Council, which received nearly 80 percent of all Ford population grants in the 1950s.

Ultimately, as both a grant-making and an operating foundation, the Ford Foundation was to develop population into a major program under Oscar Harkavy, an economist. But at first, and until 1959, support was only for demographic and educational activities and the Population Council was the preferred intermediary.

Thus the activity and funding channels in the field of population spread from a few individuals and universities before the war to smaller foundations, and from smaller foundations to larger foundations (with the former often acting as retailers and the latter as wholesalers).[13] By the late 1950s, although no solutions to the population problem were in sight the professional and scientific community had developed a base of expertise and funding to react independently of U.S. government policy to the problem of population growth overseas.

At the same time the implicit justification for organized philanthropy in the United States was not to solve economic and social problems but rather to act as a catalytic agent, providing seed money for innovative projects until such time as others, most frequently governments, would assume responsibility.[14] Only the government could provide to researchers, laboratories, and universities the continuing support they needed after initial foundation grants had expired. Despite a deliberate refusal to seek any direct influence upon U.S. government programs, the foundations were an indirect but powerful force impelling the American government toward recognition of the population problem.

THE ACTIVISTS ORGANIZE

The institutional base for the birth control activists was the Planned Parenthood Federation of America, formed by the merger of the American

16

WORLD POPULATION CRISISWORLD POPULATION CRISIS

Birth Control Federation and the Clinical Research Bureau in 1939 and given its present name in 1942. But it was considerably weaker than its professional and scientific counterparts. In fact, the organization had fewer field workers, fewer patients at the main New York clinic, and fewer affiliated local groups in 1959 than in 1939.[15] The transition from a one-woman social reform crusade to a community-based, professional service organization—the classic "routinization of charisma" process—was clearly difficult for Planned Parenthood.

During the 1950s the principal aim of Planned Parenthood was to win acceptance—acceptance from the medical profession, from prospective donors, from community leaders, from the mass media, and from the general public. A staff member who joined in 1955 described the whole first decade of his Planned Parenthood work as "trying to persuade people that the roof will not fall in on them if they mention or support birth control."[16] Trying to live down its radical, feminist reputation, Planned Parenthood wooed men, doctors, Protestant and Jewish clergy, and business leaders.

One element of Margaret Sanger's special concern that remained strong was the search for better contraceptives. Diaphragms and the medical, clinical, female-oriented approach that they required were not entirely satisfactory for low-income patients. Condoms depended on male motivation and were associated with prostitution and venereal disease. Margaret Sanger personally and later the Planned Parenthood Federation actively encouraged the search for "the pill." In 1951 the federation provided a small grant to Drs. Gregory Pincus and M. C. Chang at the Worcester Foundation for Experimental Biology to study hormonal contraception and later helped to arrange additional private funding, not available from foundations or the National Institutes of Health. In 1958, with the pill only two years away, Dr. Alan Guttmacher, president of Planned Parenthood, predicted "We are on the threshhold of a new era in birth control."[17]

The main public attention the movement received during this period stemmed from confrontation and conflict as, for example, when various state laws were challenged or when in 1953 Catholic agencies resigned from the New York City Welfare and Health Council because Planned Parenthood was elected to membership.[18]

A confrontation that Margaret Sanger herself could not have designed better came in New York City in 1958. Unwritten city policy prevented the otherwise-legal prescription of contraceptives for indigent patients in municipal hospitals. Dr. Louis Hellman in Kings County Hospital directly challenged the policy, which had been publicized by the New York Post. When ordered by the commissioner of hospitals not to fit a diaphragm for a diabetic woman, he called reporters. The controversy raged and received full coverage in New York papers for six months. Planned Parenthood, working behind the scenes, lined up near-unanimous religious and medical support from the non-Catholic community. The issues were carefully and repeatedly defined: medical judgment in a life-threatening situation was being arbitrarily overrruled by a religious minority; freedom of medical practice, freedom of religion, freedom of information, even majority rule were threatened. Administrators and elected officials tried to evade the issue but could not. Planned Parenthood and its supporters would not compromise (despite urgings from embarrassed friends).

When the smoke of battle cleared, by late 1958, New York City had a new policy of providing birth control through health and welfare departments. City officials had a different sense of the balance of power on birth control; Planned Parenthood had a renewed confidence in standing up for its position. Perhaps most important, many Catholics specifically redefined their public and political role as a result of that confrontation. "It should be clear," a *Commonweal* article lamented,

> that there are many sound and compelling reasons why Catholics should not generally strive for legislation and directives which clash with the beliefs of a large portion of society. In doing so, they not only strain the limits of the community and actually lessen the persuasive force of their teachings but they almost inevitably strengthen in the minds of non-Catholics the already present worries about Catholic power.[19]

The success of the 1958 confrontation resulted in part from the increased professionalization of the national Planned Parenthood headquarters. In contrast to many local affiliates, where the part-time volunteer board members (and physicians) were unwilling to risk their community and social status over an awkward controversy for Planned Parenthood,[20] the national staff was fully committed to the cause of birth control and extremely skillful in developing and defining the issue.[21] They deliberately forced the conflict to an unexpectedly successful conclusion.

Planned Parenthood's main effort and also in the long run its greatest impact on U.S. governmental policy, both domestic and overseas, was through its work in the United States. Nevertheless, the massive growth of population in the developing countries was not ignored by Planned Parenthood speakers and publications.

The United Nations was an early target for the internationally minded birth control activists, as it was for the demographers. As early as 1948, voices were raised suggesting that birth control be included in the activities of the World Health Organization (WHO).[22] The government of India, also much concerned about population growth, asked for UN assistance. Dr. Brock Chisholm, first director-general of WHO and a Canadian, wanted to respond to India's request for technical help. A Norwegian resolution to study the relationship of health and population growth was dropped, however, after a number of Catholic states threatened to boycott the organization if any such work were undertaken.[23] Under Catholic pressure, WHO's role was restricted to sponsoring a study of the rhythm system. Several Planned Parenthood consultants were dispatched to India but even by the mid-1950s it was clear that the rhythm system, birth control without contraceptives, would not work there.[24]

Margaret Sanger, who was not always at ease with the more cautious U.S. groups she had organized, saw the drama of the world situation. In 1952 at the third conference of the International Committee on Planned Parenthood in Bombay she helped to organize the International Planned Parenthood Federation (IPPF) to link birth control groups now springing up in a number of countries. An IPPF conference in Stockholm in 1953, a regional one in Puerto Rico in 1955, and a large and well-publized conference in Tokyo in 1955 attracted increasing publicity as well as the participation of an international contingent od doctors, demographers, and sociologists. By 1958 nearly 500 foreign visitors a year were coming to the Planned Parenthood offices in New York to see what kind of help was available for overseas work.[25]

From a political point of view, however, Planned Parenthood activists remained voices in the wilderness. In February 1955 IPPF's application for membership as a consultative organization with the UN Economic and Social Council was voted down with seven abstentions (including the United States), two negative votes, and no votes in favor.[26] From a financial point of view Planned Parenthood resources were minimal. The headquarters U.S. Planned Parenthood budget in 1959 was only $340,000; the International Planned Parenthood Federation budget, only $35,000. But every year brought more public attention to the issue and more converts to the cause.

An important recruit to the activist ranks in the 1950s was Hugh Moore. The enterprising and successful founder of the Dixie Cup company, he had established the Hugh Moore Fund in 1944 to promote world peace. Overpopulation, he concluded, was the greatest threat to world peace. His initial strategy was to alert businessmen to the crisis. A deliberately provocative pamphlet entitled *The Population Bomb* was distributed to 10,000 American leaders whose names were taken from *Who's Who*. Letters, dinners, and meetings were organized to win over influential people by a polite equivalent of shock tactics.

Demographers and others who wished to approach the problem quietly and scientifically were appalled. Frederick Osborn of the Population Council, for instance, wanted to prevent distribution of *The Population Bomb*. But Moore was not deterred. As he told one irate demographer, "You've been raised in academic halls. I've been raised in the market place. I'm used to presenting facts dramatically. Students of demography have talked for years and nobody listened.[27]

A controversial figure whom most of the large, professionally oriented foundations were reluctant to assist, Moore "spun-off" half a dozen important organizations or activities that eventually played a role in the establishment of government policy. In each case he would seize an issue or opportunity before it was respectable, then fund, encourage, and promote it to a legitimate status. Then just as his flamboyant methods began to embarrass his own organizational protégés he would move on to something else. In the 1950s his influence was a first step in lining up business support and contributions for Planned Parenthood; his attention to the International Planned Parenthood Federation provided staff and the first serious fund-raising campaign; his interest in the Population Reference Bureau, a small information service in Washington, was a catalyst in expanding its horizons. Later he supported voluntary sterilization, birth control advertising campaigns, and the beginnings of the environmental issue.

Unique in his salesmanship, Moore was in other respects typical of a new breed of activists in the population movement. Male, active in the business world, and more concerned with economics than biology,[28] the new activists included men like John Nuveen, Eugene Black, John Cowles, Cass Canfield, Lammot DuPont Copeland, and William H. Draper, Jr. The experience of the war and European recovery increased their basic confidence, as it had that of many Americans, that most problems are soluble. Economic development was the solution to poverty and communism in Asia, Africa, and Latin America just as the Marshall Plan had been the solution in Europe. However, as economic development lagged and as increasingly persuasive statistics suggested that population growth was a reason for the lag, a few of these internationally minded businessmen and bankers began to speak out.

They, like the Planned Parenthood activists, were distinguished from the professionals—both medical and demographic—by wanting, above all, a solution. The lowering of birth rates, in other words, was a definite project to be undertaken, like winning the war or rebuilding Europe; it could be achieved by the appropriate application of the right resources. Rockefeller saw these resources in the form of professional skills, new technology, and scientific data to be developed; Moore saw the resources more in terms of public awareness and federal expenditures; Draper saw them particularly in the form of leadership and government priority. More organizationally oriented than the Planned Parenthood volunteers, these men thought in terms of building new institutions to extend continuing pressure.

The activists, male and female both, wanted to solve a problem and knew that they needed the help of professionals to do so. The professionals on their part refused to be harnessed so easily to someone else's project. Essentially, to be a professional is to seek and value complex professional outputs for their own sake, not just as a means to some other end. To be an activist, on the other hand, is to look for the simplest, most direct means to the specified goal and to apply it as quickly as possible. To the professionals the problem of high birth rates called for definition, study, research, and knowledge or practice for its own sake. To the activists, the population problem was much more likely to call for money, good management, and removal of the most obvious bottlenecks.

3

What impact did the studies and practice of the professionals plus the agitation of the activists have on public opinion and government policy? What difference did the opposition of the Catholic Church make? What was the reaction, in terms of public awareness, private practice, and government action, to the new issue that was developing?

Measured by press and periodical coverage—a rough measure, at best—concern for the national or international issue was not great during the 1950s. Periodical coverage reached a peak in the early 1930s, receded through the 1940s and 1950s, and did not exceed the level of the early 1930s until after 1960.

During the 1950s the *New York Times* had a most sympathetic editorial policy and covered local city disputes thoroughly in 1953 and 1958. Excluding these, however, even the *New York Times* averaged only 15 stories, letters, or editorials annually on birth control from 1950 through 1958 and of these only three were on page one. Under the index heading "population" the *New York Times* carried an average of 17 stories annually and of these four (relating mainly to U.S. growth) were on page one. Between 1950 and 1958 inclusive, the *Readers' Guide* listed an average of 13 periodical articles per year on birth control and contraception, or slightly more than one per month. By any reckoning, the amount of publicity before 1959, although rising gradually, was not very great. (See Charts 3.1 and 3.2.)

Public attitudes and opinions are reflected in the available poll data. However, between March 1947 and December 1959 no nationwide polls included any question directly on birth control or population—in itself, a measure of public indifference.[1] A Gallup Poll in November 1945 asked, "Should the United Nations organization educate the (German) (Japanese) people in birth control methods?" Responses were as follows:[2]

	Should	Should Not	No Opinion
German people	39%	34%	27%
Japanese people	47	29	24

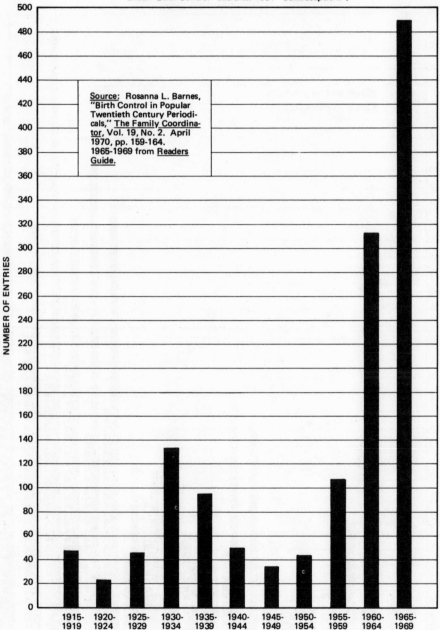

CHART 3.1

Periodical Coverage of Birth Control, 1915-69
(as measured by number of entries in Readers Guide
under "Birth Control" and after 1951 "Contraception.")

Source: Rosanna L. Barnes,
"Birth Control in Popular
Twentieth Century Periodicals," The Family Coordinator, Vol. 19, No. 2. April
1970, pp. 159-164.
1965-1969 from Readers
Guide.

NUMBER OF ENTRIES

| | 1915-1919 | 1920-1924 | 1925-1929 | 1930-1934 | 1935-1939 | 1940-1944 | 1945-1949 | 1950-1954 | 1955-1959 | 1960-1964 | 1965-1969 |

CHART 3.2

New York Times Coverage of Birth Control and Population, 1950-70

(number of inches in <u>Index</u>)

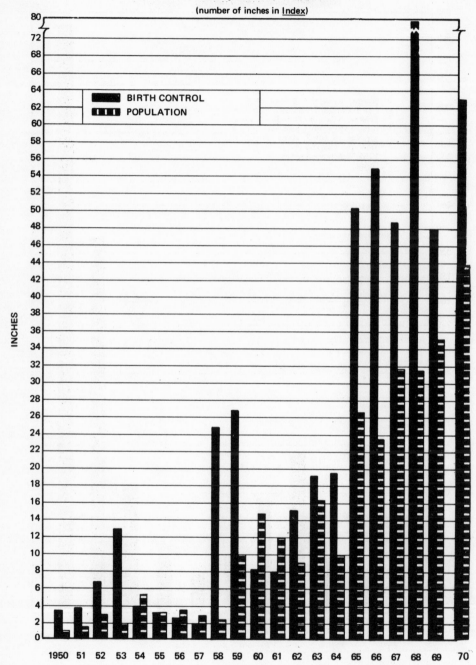

The question, referring only to the defeated enemies, indicates that overpopulation was seen mainly as a cause for aggression and not as a factor in economic stagnation.

To the question, "Would you approve or disapprove of having government health clinics furnish birth control information to married people in this country who want it?" the following answers were given:[3]

		Yes, Approve	No, Disapprove	No Opinion
December	1939	71%	18%	11%
January	1940	69	20	11
December	1943	61	23	16
November	1945	61	23	16
March	1947	64	23	13
December	1959	72	14	14

These figures indicate a slight decline in support for birth control after the 1930s, but nonetheless about two thirds of the respondents regularly favored making birth control information available to married persons who wanted it—a sizable popular majority.

The actual practice of birth control in the United States during the 1950s was consistent with the opinions expressed in polls. The nationwide studies of the growth of American families surveyed family planning practices of married white women, ages 18 to 39, in 1955, 1960, and 1965 (also nonwhites in 1960 and 1965). In 1955, 70 percent of the white wives had used contraception and another 9 percent expected to.[4] By 1960, 81 percent had used contraception and another 6 percent expected to do so. In 1960, when nonwhites were surveyed, 59 percent had used contraception and another 17 percent expected to.[5] Although combined use and expectation of use were higher for non-Catholics and for upper socioeconomic levels in both years, the increase in use and expectation of use was greater among Catholics and women of lower socioeconomic status.[6] (See Chart 3.3)

With respect to the type of contraception used, approximately half of the Catholic wives practicing birth control had used prohibited methods and half had not at the times of both surveys. But by 1960, 38 percent of all Catholic wives had used prohibited methods compared with 30 percent in 1955. To put it the other way around, the percentage of Catholic wives conforming to church teachings declined from 70 percent to 62 percent between 1955 and 1960.[7] Yet despite the increasing use of contraception and of methods condemned by the Catholic Church, even by Catholics, public policy lagged behind both private practice and public opinion.

The poll evidence, plus the advantages of hindsight, suggests that one barrier to more rapid development of a birth control policy during the 1950s was the inhibitions of birth control supporters in not forcing the issue to national attention sooner. Agnes Meyer, one of the bolder voices, may have been at least partially correct in 1955 when she told a Planned Parenthood meeting:

> The Catholic Church has the right to defend and promulgate its ideas
> on birth control as much as any other group. If non-Catholics were as

CHART 3.3

Attitudes toward Making Birth Control Information
Available, National Polls in Selected Years, 1936-71

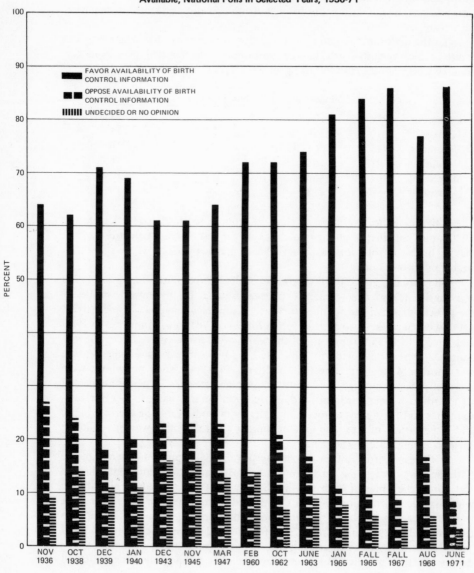

Note: All polls charted are nationwide surveys conducted by the American Institute of Public Opinion (AIPO), Princeton, New Jersey. Although these polls give a general overview of American attitudes toward making birth control information available, they are not precisely comparable because the question asked was rarely asked in exactly the same form as before. The questions asked at each date were as follows:

November 1936: Should the distribution of birth control information be made legal?

October 1938: Would you like to see a government agency furnish birth control information to married people who want it?

December 1939 to March 1947: Would you approve or disapprove of having governmental health clinics furnish birth control information to married people who want it (in this country)?

February 1960 to January 1965 and August 1968: Do you think birth control information should be available to anyone who wants it or not?

Fall 1965 and 1967: Do you believe that information about birth control ought to be easily available to any married person who wants it?

June 1971: Do you think that information about birth control should or should not be made available by the government to all men and women who want it?

Sources: November 1936: Gallup press release (AIPO), January 5, 1965. October 1938 to January 1965: Hazel Gaudet Erskine, "The Polls: The Population Explosion, Birth Control and Sex Education," *Public Opinion Quarterly*, XXX, 3 (Fall 1960), 490-95. Fall 1965 and Fall 1967: John F. Kantner, "American Attitudes on Population Policy: Recent Trends," *Studies in Family Planning*, No. 30 (May 1968), p. 6. August 1968: AIPO Poll No. 766, Ropner Public Opinion Research Center, Williamstown, Massachusetts. June 1971: U.S. Commission on Population Growth and the American Future, *Research Papers* (in press).

honest and forthright in advancing their theories, the influence of the Catholic Church would be confined to its own members and the fog of obscurity, vacillation, and cowardice which surround the need for a nationwide contraceptive program would be dissolved.[8]

CHANGES IN ATTITUDES AND PRACTICE IN THE 1960s

During the 1960s, as might have been expected, the principal shifts in opinion took place among Catholics rather than Protestants. (See Tables 3.1 and 3.2.) Protestant approval remained consistently high through the 1960s, at about 80 percent.

TABLE 3.1

Attitudes of Catholics Toward Making Birth Control Information Available, National Polls in Selected Years, 1936-71
(in percent)

		Approve	Disapprove	No Opinion or Don't Know
	1936[a]	43	45	12
December	1959[b]	58	29	13
August	1962[a]	56	38	6
April	1963[a]	53	39	8
January	1965[a]	78	14	8
June	1965[a]	60	28	12
Fall	1965[c]	81	—	—
Fall	1967[c]	83	—	—
August	1968[d]	77	15	8
June	1971[e]	83	12	5

Notes to Chart 3.3 give the exact wording of the questions.

Sources: [a]Hazel Gaudet Erskine, "The Polls: The Population Explosion, Birth Control and Sex Education," *Public Opinion Quarterly*, XXX, 3 (Fall 1966), 495

[b]American Institute of Public Opinion, Poll No. 621, question 39

[c]John F. Kantner, "American Attitudes on Population Policy: Recent Trends," *Studies in Family Planning*, No. 39 (May 1968), p. 6 (question restricted to availability for married persons)

[d]American Institute of Public Opinion, Poll No. 766, question 18

[e]National Public Opinion Survey, U.S. Commission on Population Growth and the American Future, question 35.

TABLE 3.2

Attitude of Protestants Toward Making Birth Control Information Available,
National Polls in Selected Years, 1959-71
(in percent)

		Approve	Disapprove	No Opinion or Don't Know
December	1959b	77	9	13
August	1962a	77	16	7
April	1963a	80	11	9
January	1965a	82	10	8
Fall	1965c	86	—	—
Fall	1967c	88	—	—
August	1968d	76	18	6
June	1971e	86	9	4

Notes to Chart 3.3 give the exact wording of the questions.

Sources: aHazel Gaudet Erskine, "The Polls: The Population Explosion, Birth Control and Sex Education," *Public Opinion Quarterly*, XXX, 3 (Fall 1966), 495

bAmerican Institute of Public Opinion, Poll No. 621, question 30

cJohn F. Kantner, "American Attitudes on Population Policy: Recent Trends," *Studies in Family Planning*, No. 30 (May 1968), p, 6 (question restricted to availability for married persons; all non-Catholics included in Protestants)

dAmerican Institute of Public Opinion, Poll No. 766, question 18

eNational Public Opinion Survey, U.S. Commission on Population Growth and the American Future, question 35.

By May-June 1971, in the poll conducted for the U.S. Commission on Population Growth and the American Future, 87 percent of the weighted sample agreed that information about birth control should be made available by the government to all men and women who want it—the same percentage as in 1967 favored having birth control information "easily available to any married person who wants it" (with no reference to the government). (See Chart 3.4.)

During the 1960s Catholic attitudes shifted in two directions, according to Gallup poll data. Between December 1959 and April 1963 (the actual dates the questions were asked), Catholic approval declined by 5 percentage points and Catholic disapproval increased by 10 percentage points, even though the question was asked in the identical manner. This shift suggests that Catholic

CHART 3.4

Percentages of Married Couples Who Have Used or Expect To Use Contraception, 1955, 1960, and 1965

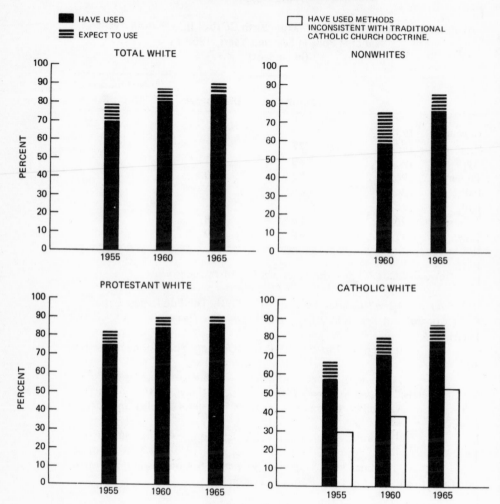

SOURCE: CHARLES F. WESTOFF AND NORMAN N. RYDER "RECENT TRENDS IN ATTITUDES TOWARD FERTILITY CONTROL AND THE PRACTICE OF CONTRACEPTION IN THE UNITED STATES," FERTILITY AND FAMILY PLANNING: A WORLD VIEW, UNIVERSITY OF MICHIGAN, ANN ARBOR, 1969; WESTOFF AND RYDER "UNITED STATES: METHODS OF FERTILITY CONTROL, 1955, 1960, AND 1965," STUDIES IN FAMILY PLANNING, NO. 17, FEBRUARY 1967, p.5.

antagonism toward birth control increased during the administration of President Kennedy, who was clearly not a birth control enthusiast. By late November 1964, however, Catholic approval for making birth control available increased by 25 percentage points over the April 1963 figure and disapproval declined by the same amount. Whether these shifts reflected personal habits, events in Washington, indecision in Rome, or a combination, they were permanent and left the church as an institution out of step with many individual Catholics.

With respect to foreign aid and U.S. support either through the United Nations or in response to requests from other governments, the sparse and not fully comparable data suggest a similar and substantial increase in support from 1959 to 1968. The major change again was in Catholic attitudes. Catholic backing increased from 40 percent in December 1959, when a plurality of Catholics were opposed, to 69 percent in August 1968 despite the papal condemnation. By 1968 Protestant and Catholic views hardly differed in this area either. (See Tables 3.3 and 3.4.)

TABLE 3.3

Attitudes Toward Birth Control and Foreign Aid, National Polls in Selected Years, 1959-68 (in percent)

		Approve	Disapprove	No Opinion or Don't Know
December	1959[b]	54	29	17
April	1963[a]	65	21	14
Fall	1965[c]	58	34	8
Fall	1967[c]	64	30	6
August	1968[d]	72	20	8

Sources: [a]Hazel Gaudet Erskine, "The Polls: The Population Explosion, Birth Control and Sex Education," *Public Opinion Quarterly*, XXX, 3 (Fall 1966), 495. Question: It has been suggested that the United Nations organization supply information on all birth control methods to the people who want this information. Favor or oppose?

[b]American Institute of Public Opinion, Poll No. 621, question 30. Same question as directly above.

[c]John F. Kantner, "American Attitudes on Population Policy: Recent Trends," *Studies in Family Planning*, No. 30 (May 1968), p. 6. Question: Do you think our government should help other countries with their birth control programs if they ask us?

[d]American Institute of Public Opinion, Poll No. 766, question 18. Question: Are you in favor of the U.S. government helping other nations who ask our aid in their birth control programs?

TABLE 3.4

Attitudes of Catholics and Protestants Toward Birth Control and Foreign Aid,
National Polls in Selected Years, 1959-68
(in percent)

		Approve	Disapprove	No Opinion or Don't Know
		Catholic		
December	1959b	40	48	11
April	1963a	42	44	14
Fall	1965c	55	—	—
Fall	1967c	56	—	—
August	1968d	69	21	10
		Protestant		
December	1959b	58	24	18
April	1963a	72	15	13
Fall	1965c	59	—	—
Fall	1967c	66	—	—
August	1968d	71	22	7

Sources: aHazel Gaudet Erskine, "The Polls: The Population Explosion, Birth Control and Sex Education," *Public Opinion Quarterly*, XXX, 3 (Fall 1966), 495. Question: It has been suggested that the United Nations organization supply information on all birth control methods to the people who want this information. Favor or oppose?

bAmerican Institute of Public Opinion, Poll No. 621, question 30. Same question as directly above.

cJohn F. Kantner, "American Attitudes on Population Policy: Recent Trends," *Studies in Family Planning*, No. 30 (May 1968), p. 6. All non-Catholic included in Protestant. Question: Do you think our government should help other countries with their birth control programs if they ask us?

dAmerican Institute of Public Opinion, Poll No. 766, question ·18. Question: Are you in favor of the U.S. government helping other nations who ask our aid in their birth control programs?

Even more notable than the shifts in attitude during the 1960s, among men and women of all ages, was the shift in contraceptive behavior, most notably by younger women. Between 1960 and 1965 the oral contraceptive became "the most popular method of contraception used by American couples."[9] By 1965, although the pill was only five years old, 29 percent of non-Catholic women (married, living with husbands) and 21 percent of Catholic women under age 45 had used oral contraceptives.[10] More than half of the women under 30 with some college education had, by 1965, used pills, and nearly 60 percent of those who had ever used them were still doing so.[11] By 1969 more Catholic women using some form of birth control were using oral contraceptives than the rhythm system, and twice as many were not using rhythm as were using it even after the papal condemnation of all other methods.[12]

Apart from oral contraceptives specifically, the percentage of fecund couples who had used some form of contraception (including the rhythm method) increased from 83 percent in 1955 to 89 percent in 1960 to 93 percent in 1965. Including also those who *expected* to use contraception later the percentages increased from 91 percent in 1955 to 96 percent in 1960 to 97 percent by 1965.[13] "Where two established and institutionalized religious groups support opposing moral norms," it has been observed, "the less demanding norm tends to win the less committed members of both groups."[14] That is what seemed to be happening in contraceptive practice during the 1950s and 1960s.

NONRESPONSE BY THE GOVERNMENT, 1930-59

The response of the U.S. government, to the widespread acceptance of birth control in the United States, to the facts of world population growth, to the studies of the professionals, to the agitation of the activists, and to the continued resistance of the Roman Catholic Church, was essentially a non-response. Within the United States, Margaret Sanger's work and the Supreme Court decision of 1936 had stopped any deliberate federal effort to prohibit private birth control activities. Yet Surgeon-General Parran's permissive policy of 1942 had little effect in promoting state-sponsored birth control activities because resources were limited. State legislation, medical regulations, and municipal agreements hampered operations of clinics. The climate of government disapproval often prevented publicity or accurate records even where birth control services were available. Congress avoided the subject.

Toward population problems overseas beyond the continental United States, particularly those prominent enough to attract any public notice, the government response was even more negative. In Puerto Rico, for example, the federal government had direct responsibility for a crowded, poverty-stricken island where birth rates were double the continental level. In 1936 Ernest Gruening, director of the Division of Territories and Island Possessions of the Department of the Interior, tried to include family planning in the maternal and child health programs of the Puerto Rican Reconstruction Administration.

He sought—and believed he had won—the approval of the Catholic bishop in Puerto Rico for a quiet beginning. But the objections of Cardinal Spellman in New York, relayed privately to Democratic National Committee Chairman James A. Farley in the midst of the presidential election campaign, forced Gruening to sever all official support for birth control. As Gruening later commented, "Who was I to jeopardize F.D.R.'s campaign for reelection? The following November he would carry only 46 out of 48 states."[15]

In spite of the Catholic Church, the Puerto Rican legislature in 1937 legalized birth control, which was then provided through the maternal health clinics until 1946, when the Department of Health downgraded birth control.[16] Meanwhile, the Puerto Ricans were developing their own solution to the problem. Female sterilization in hospitals following delivery was promoted by private physicians on a fee basis and well publicized by Catholic pastoral letters (of condemnation). It was relatively cheap, effective, and involved only a single "sinful" action.[17] By 1965, when federal funding for family planning resumed, one third of Puerto Rican mothers 20 to 49 years of age had already had "la operacion," two thirds of them while still in their twenties.[18] By a method that was acceptable to Puerto Rican women and profitable to Puerto Rican physicians, birth control prevailed in Puerto Rico. As in Western Europe and America, however, the process represented a default of timely government action and a deliberate defiance of church doctrine.

The situation in Japan immediately after World War II was not dissimilar.[19] The Supreme Allied Commander in the Pacific General Douglas MacArthur (SCAP) had broad responsibility for demilitarization and demobilization of the country. Very soon it was evident that population increase, caused by return of 7 million Japanese to the islands and lower mortality as well as by higher birth rates, would strain employment opportunities and resources. Demographers Warren Thompson and P. K. Whelpton were invited by SCAP to serve as consultants to the Natural Resources Section on demographic factors. Margaret Sanger, however, who tried to visit Japan in 1949, was refused a military permit because of Catholic opposition.[20] At that time, MacArthur issued a statement declaring,

> The Supreme Commander wishes it understood that he is not engaged in any consideration of the problem of Japanese population control. Such matter does not fall within the prescribed scope of the Occupation, and decisions thereon rest entirely with the Japanese themselves.[21]

A SCAP-planned survey of attitudes toward the population problem was promptly cancelled. In 1950 several sentences in a SCAP study, *Japan's Natural Resources*, about balancing population and resources through reduced birth rates were deleted as a result of protests from the American Catholic Women's Club of the Tokyo-Yokohama area, which consisted largely of U.S. Army wives.

Meanwhile, as early as 1946 the Japanese government and press began to study the population problem for themselves. While councils, institutes, foundations, Cabinet committees, and news bureaus were pondering and publicizing the issue, the Japanese Diet in 1948 revised the 1940 Eugenics Protection Law to allow induced abortion for eugenic and health reasons. In 1949 and 1952 the law, which also legalized sterilization and contraception, was further amended to permit abortion for economic reasons and under simplified procedures. Although the importation of supplies for producing contraceptives was allowed, neither SCAP nor the Japanese government provided funds for a national contraceptive program. Still, the birth rate fell from 34.3 per 1,000 in 1947 down to 17.2 in 1957, a 50 percent reduction in a single decade.[22] The decline was unprecedented in demographic history. Induced abortion, condemned by demographic, public health, medical, government, civic, and religious leaders as the least desirable birth control technique, was the principal method used. Only later, after 1952, was contraception specifically fostered to reduce the incidence of abortion. Then contraception was depicted as, in Irene Taeuber's words, "a public health activity, a program to lessen the harm presumably caused by abortions whose performance was presumably permitted to protect health."[23]

In Japan as in Puerto Rico the reluctance of U.S. government policy makers to endorse or finance contraceptive programs was undoubtedly a factor in turning people toward a private sector method, profitable to the medical profession, acceptable to the population, and requiring no initial funding, supplies, or government support other than legality. Thus in both cases the U.S. government's susceptibility to Catholic protests may well have stimulated sterilization and abortion, although both were less acceptable to Catholic as well as non-Catholic leaders than other means of family planning.

The Japanese case was important not only as another example of U.S. policy default but also because of the widely perceived link between reducing birth rates and speeding economic progress. For example, in 1962 Chikao Honda noted, "It is an important fact to observe that the economic boom in Japan today owes much to the efforts of the people in general to rationalize and modernize their family life on the basis of planned parenthood."[24]

Despite the unwillingness of the U.S. government to acknowledge it, the overseas population problem was hard to avoid. An agricultural mission to China in 1946 recommended reducing population pressure on the land as a necessary alternative to famine.[25] A 1953 Citizens Advisory Committee, composed primarily of educators and economists, urged Mutual Security Administrator Harold Stassen to take "real steps in the direction of conscious promotion of population limitation." Although the report did not use the words "birth control" it warned that the task of economic development would be taken over by the communists if, because of population growth, "the rising expectations of the people have been disappointed."[26]

On Taiwan, the Joint Committee on Rural Reconstruction tried to promote birth control as early as 1950. More than a million copies of a JCRR booklet entitled *The Happy Family*, which advocated family planning by the rhythm method, were distributed. But the brochure was condemned by the Chinese in Taiwan as "a communist plot" to deplete Nationalist armies and as contrary to the teachings of Sun Yat-sen.[27] In 1954, after a demographic study sponsored by the Rockefeller Foundation and Princeton University, the China Family Planning Association was formed and government involvement began.

"To avoid misunderstanding by the military," birth control was introduced "as a patriotic measure" in the context of "training in first-aid for women of childbearing ages in military dependents' villages and rural areas to prepare for possible enemy air raids."[28] This unusual approach proved effective.

The U.S. government provided support until 1957 when a Catholic program officer of the International Cooperation Administration Mission tried to block it. The U.S. mission chief intervened. Upon assurance of no publicity and no Chinese religious opposition, he overruled the program officer but renamed the program "pre-pregnancy health" instead of "reduction of wasteful deaths."[29] Health was always the acknowledged aim of the program, which was not officially identified as family planning or population control until 1969.

In Ceylon in the late 1950s when government officials approached the U.S. foreign aid mission for help in checking population growth they were referred to the Swedish government, which was just beginning to offer technical assistance in birth control. To mobilize a change in U.S. policy would be too long and arduous a task, the Ceylonese were told, to be worth the small amount of help that could be provided.[30]

The case of India might have been a potent influence on U.S. policy makers and undoubtedly was an indirect influence on public opinion. The very image of "Mother India" was synonymous with overpopulation and poverty. Yet even though the Indian government was the first to adopt a national family planning policy in the 1950s, the program was vague and the requirements uncertain. Mahatma Gandhi's opposition to contraceptives, reflected by succeeding ministers of health and Nehru's concentration on industrialization and capital investment, kept the birth control program from achieving real priority until the 1960s.[31] Funding for construction of a drug-manufacturing facility that would also have been able to produce contraceptives was cancelled by a wary Draper Committee staff man upon arrival on assignment in India.[32]

On the whole, until 1959 the State Department and foreign aid administrators were not pressed by foreign governments or by internal staff to take any action on the controversial problem. In the field, in places like Taiwan where U.S. aid missions did encourage family planning, those most eager to provide birth control help did so—quietly and indirectly. They went out of their way to avoid high-level review and policy decisions lest the repercussions kill off their own projects. In this way, small beginnings were protected but larger considerations were postponed.

During this period the professionals in population and birth control, who were unsure themselves what approach the U.S. government could take overseas, made little effort to convince government officials to take action. Whereas they kept at arm's length from the government, the government itself kept at arm's length from activists like Margaret Sanger. Thus the considerable private use of birth control in the United States was not automatically translated into approval for public programs—or indeed even for public discussion. The victories Planned Parenthood won, in New York City for example under a Catholic mayor or in Japan where Margaret Sanger was later honored, were seen by U.S. government officials not as triumphs for a good cause but rather as embarrassments to be avoided. At the government level the institutional voice of the Catholic Church remained many times louder and stronger than the pleas of the ardent activists or the studies of the professionals in the population field.

4

THE DRAPER COMMITTEE
SPOTLIGHTS THE ISSUE,
1959

The Draper Committee, formally known as The President's Committee to Study the United States Military Assistance Program, was not the first advisory body to take note of the population problem but it was the first to spell it out in detail and to recommend specific action. Why did this unlikely panel of high officials—all men, most with some military background, none previously involved in any "birth control cause"—advocate government-supported birth control?

The committee was created to look at a wholly different issue. In August 1958 eight influential senators on the Foreign Relations Committee complained to President Eisenhower that too much emphasis was being placed on military aid and not enough on economic assistance. They called for an immediate presidential review of foreign aid priorities.[1]

U.S. foreign assistance had been born as an emergency relief operation in Europe right after World War II. The Marshall Plan was originally designed to accelerate the economic reconstruction of Europe, but very quickly, under Soviet pressure, it was transformed into a military and economic defense against communism. During the 1950s the worldwide Mutual Security Program was justified to Congress and the country as an efficient way to subsidize foreign armies instead of sending American soldiers overseas again. At the same time the Point IV program of technical assistance, initiated by President Truman, provided a small start toward technical assistance and development aid in Asia, Africa and Latin America.[2]

Support for military assistance remained consistently strong in the House of Representatives. In the Senate on the other hand, and among an increasing number of government officials, support was growing for economic aid on a longer-term basis to counter new Soviet tactics of trade, aid, and friendship with the developing countries.

Tracy Vorhees, a New York attorney who served with several voluntary groups to promote public support for foreign assistance, suggested to Sherman Adams, then President Eisenhower's chief aide, that General William H. Draper, Jr., be appointed to head the high-level review.[3]

Draper was a New York investment banker who had served as economic adviser to General Lucius Clay during the German occupation and in a civilian capacity as the U.S. special representative in Europe directing the European Recovery Program.[4] He was in 1958 chairman of the Mexican Light and Power Co., Ltd., and thus combined a record in European economic recovery with experience in a developing country.

Compared with other presidential committees or commissions, the 10-member group was noteworthy because it consisted entirely of men who had previously served at high levels of government with considerable military or economic responsibility. There was no attempt to obtain broad representation either of interest groups such as labor, Negroes, universities, or business per se, or of academic experts (except in staff roles). The emphasis was on practical experience in high government posts.

The Draper Committee included the following: Dillon Anderson, attorney, who had recently served as President Eisenhower's special assistant for national security affairs; Joseph M. Dodge, businessman and banker, who had served as financial adviser in Germany and Japan and as director of the Bureau of the Budget; General Alfred M. Gruenther, who had recently served as supreme Allied commander in Europe and was then president of the Red Cross; Marx Leva, attorney, who had been assistant secretary of defense and chairman of a Senate foreign aid review panel; John J. McCloy, attorney and banker, who had formerly been president of the World Bank and U.S. high commissioner for Germany and was then chairman of the board of the Chase Manhattan Bank and the Ford Foundation; George McGhee, oil producer, who had served as assistant secretary of state and ambassador to Turkey; General Joseph T. McNarney, an air force general who had been commander of U.S. forces in Europe and was then president of Convair; Admiral Arthur W. Radford, who had commanded the Pacific Fleet and served as chairman of the Joint Chiefs of Staff; and James E. Webb, who had served as director of the Bureau of the Budget and under secretary of State.

Just before Thanksgiving the White House announced formation of the panel under Draper's chairmanship "to undertake a completely independent, objective, and nonpartisan analysis of the military assistance aspects of our Mutual Security Program" and to determine "the relative emphasis which should be given to military and economic programs, particularly in the less developed areas."[5]

Although Senator J. William Fulbright (D.-Ark.) praised Draper as "a first rate chairman," several others suggested that the president's committee was "top heavy with military men."[6]

THE POPULATION ISSUE IS RAISED

The question of population had not occurred to anyone as being relevant until the day after the committee was established, when the chairman received a long wire addressed to him personally. It concluded with the words, "If your committee does not look into the impact and implications

of the population explosion, you will be derelict in your duty." The wire
was from Hugh Moore.

Draper read the lengthy wire to assembled committee members, who
reacted with chuckles. Draper chuckled, too, but he also quietly called in
Robert C. Cook, president of the Population Reference Bureau, to provide the
committee members with background materials on the population question.

At approximately the same time—early December 1958—Draper was
nudged from another direction to consider the impact of population growth.
President Eisenhower himself raised the issue even though he later repudiated
the committee's recommendation. Draper had been invited to a National
Security Council meeting on December 3 to discuss the study which the
committee would make. In the middle of his briefing the president turned to
Draper and commented, "And Bill, don't forget the population problem
because that is very serious in some of these countries."[7]

Draper did not forget either the president's words or Hugh Moore's wire.
As early as December 29, 1958, the minutes of the committee record that the
chairman "also reviewed the problem caused by the population explosion in
the less-developed countries of the non-Communist world." On the same date
the committee secretary was instructed to send to committee members a
booklet on population growth (Hugh Moore's *Population Bomb*).

In mid-February, Tyler Wood the economic study coordinator made this
note, with obvious lack of enthusiasm:

> The question of the relation of the "population explosion" is
> brought up frequently in discussions with the chairman and other
> members of the committee. It would therefore seem necessary to
> have a staff paper prepared containing the pertinent facts and certain
> indicated conclusions which are regarded as relevant to the work of
> the committee.[8]

Meanwhile, after what one committee member described as "considerable
internal discussion and some shadow-boxing with State Department personnel
and the White House staff,"[9] the committee expanded its review to cover
economic aid more comprehensively. Like many such commissions, it wanted a
wider scope of reference. More attention to economic aid meant very naturally
more attention to the forces stimulating or impeding economic growth. By
1959 it was increasingly difficult to ignore population growth as a factor that
in one way or another could strongly influence economic development.

During the first half of the committee's study, which included visits to
Japan, Taiwan, and Korea, Draper became personally convinced that too-rapid
population growth would undermine economic development. Previously, as
under-secretary of the army, Draper had been aware of the postwar population
crisis in Japan. He had visited Japan in 1947 and 1948 and discussed population as well as economic problems. Then in 1959 he observed at first hand how,
with legalized abortion and considerable publicity, the Japanese people had
sharply reduced birth rates and achieved their "economic miracle." The example of Japan influenced Draper as it did Rockefeller and others. Encouraged
as he thought by the president, urged on by Hugh Moore and Robert Cook,

convinced by the mounting impact of UN statistics, and undoubtedly stimulated by the realization that others agreed but were fearful of speaking out, Draper grew determined to bring the issue of rapid population growth directly into the light of public policy debate.

He gave the first public expression of this strong concern in his testimony before the Senate Committee on Foreign Relations on May 18, 1959. When Senator George Aiken (R.-Vt.) asked pointedly whether all U.S. assistance was not still failing to prevent a decline in per capita income in some developing countries, Draper replied, "The population problem, I'm afraid, is the greatest bar to our whole economic aid program and to the progress of the world."[10] No one contradicted him.

The other members of the president's committee had not taken a comparable interest in the population issue. There was some feeling that any recommendations on population were beyond the committee's jurisdiction and might even be regarded as intervening in the internal affairs of foreign governments. Others thought that it was difficult enough to build support for foreign aid without antagonizing the Catholic Church, and that attention should not be distracted from the committee's major recommendations on foreign aid funding and organization.

Moreover, the committee members were far closer in background and outlook to the officials they were advising than to either the activists or the professionals in birth control and population. Unlike social reformers they were not in the habit of "rocking the boat" to put their views across; they relied on persuasion, negotiation or, if necessary, command. Most wanted to help, not to embarrass, the administration. Public confrontation on a difficult issue was against their experience and inclination.

Yet Draper was stubborn, and the facts were undeniable. Many of the committee members had considerable experience in economic recovery and development. They were familiar with the sense of "uphill struggle" in their efforts. As McCloy put it, "There were always more mouths the following year than you had planned for the year before."[11] Whatever were the views of the others as to the political wisdom of mentioning population, they could not rebut Draper's arguments. Furthermore, they stood as independent advisers to the president, not as implementers. If such a recommendation did not originate from impartial outside advisers how could it possibly come from administrators in more sensitive operational roles? Draper's clinching argument was: how could the population problem be ignored when President Eisenhower had specifically asked them to consider it?

Nevertheless, two centers of opposition remained. Most important was General Gruenther, a devout Catholic who was unwilling to sign a report that the church might condemn. With considerable difficulty Draper persuaded Gruenther that the subject of population growth could not be ignored. Then Draper worked closely with Gruenther to prepare language that would not be offensive to Catholics. Gruenther took the drafts and conferred privately with Catholic lawyers and experts to ensure their acceptability. The oblique reference to "maternal and child health services" as an immediate way to deal with the population problem testifies to Gruenther's influence on the final statement. After this and similar changes were made the committee hoped that the report would not be strongly criticized by Catholic leaders. Gruenther, after his reluctant agreement, hoped that these recommendations, buried in the larger report, would not receive a great deal of public attention. Both expectations proved wrong—to the committee's chagrin and Gruenther's embarrassment.

Also opposed to any reference to the population dilemma was the committee staff. From the top echelon—Tracy Vorhees, as general counsel, George Lincoln the staff director, and Tyler Wood—right down to at least one of the secretaries who reportedly refused to type a research paper that discussed contraceptives, many of the staff were apprehensive or hostile. Staff opposition, in the days before any agency had staff people directly assigned to population, was typical. Draper's deputies, like Rockefeller's and Moore's before them, saw many good reasons to protect their agencies or organizations from such a sensitive subject.

MAKING A RECOMMENDATION

The various drafts of the report show Draper's increasing personal attention to the subject. The first specific references to population growth in the studies by the staff and consultants were brief and fatalistic. For example, a memorandum dated February 20 on India from Max Millikan stated, "Since population growth can be expected in the neighborhood of 2 per cent a year . . . output must grow significantly faster if the average individual is to have a sense of progress."[12]

The next version, based on a background memorandum submitted by Robert Adams, Gruenther's modifications, and considerable negotiation with committee members and staff, was much more conciliatory. There was no reference to "birth control" or "pre-conditions" of aid. It explained the rapid population growth in developing areas as the result of decreasing mortality caused by public health measures and indicated that to assist the "normal adjustment" toward lower fertility, government birth control programs had been established "with broad acceptance."[13] An additional paragraph about food shortages was subsequently added. In a move he later regretted, George Lincoln also had a map prepared to illustrate the demographic data. Lincoln was by that time resigned to Draper's decision but still hoped to keep the language brief.

After nearly a dozen drafts, the statement stressed food shortages, public health involvement, assistance only upon the request of another country, and maternal and child welfare. These were the committee's final recommendations:

We Recommend: That, in order to meet more effectively the problems of economic development, the United States (1) assist those countries with which it is cooperating in economic aid programs, on request, in the formulation of their plans designed to deal with the problem of rapid population growth, (2) increase its assistance to local programs relating to maternal and child welfare in recognition of the immediate problem created by rapid population growth, and

(3) strongly support studies and appropriate research as a part of its own Mutual Security Program, within the United Nations and elsewhere, leading to the availability of relevant information in a form most useful to individual countries in the formulation of practical programs to meet the serious challenge posed by rapidly expanding populations.[14]

The most significant point omitted from the committee's recommendation, even though it was developed at considerable length in the staff study, was the call for U.S. government support of "expanded medical research relating to the physiology of human reproduction," and implicitly aimed at development of better birth control methods.[15] That suggestion, although much stressed a few years later, then seemed quite irrelevant to foreign aid efforts and too directly related to the still unmentionable aspects of birth control for Gruenther and the others on the committee to accept.

To publicize the committee's far-reaching economic proposals—which called for an economic assistance agency independent of the Department of State[16]—a press conference was arranged for Draper July 23 in the White House office of Jim Haggerty, Eisenhower's press secretary.

Reporters immediately perceived the implications of birth control as a political issue, especially since one of the emerging Democratic contenders for the presidency, John F. Kennedy, was Catholic. Pressed by questioners, Draper first responded that the committee was thinking primarily of "demographic information" but finally conceded that birth control information might be included, depending "on the way the program is carried out."[17] While Haggerty looked on in silence and his own staff in dismay, Draper held up for the photographers the map showing population growth. Both during the press conference and afterward on the White House porch for television, Draper discoursed at some length on the population problem. He emphasized that assistance would be given only on request and that no specific legislation would be necessary. "We simply wanted to air for public discussion a problem which has for too long been kept under the rug," he pointed out, then and later.

The problem was indeed aired. The photograph of Draper pointing to a map of world population growth and urging action was reproduced around the world. Several U.S. newspapers, including the *Washington Post* and *New York Times*, ran lengthy background articles on the demographic situation. Gruenther was furious that Draper had deliberately emphasized the issue. Monsignor George Higgins director of the Social Action Department of the National Catholic Welfare Conference expressed the immediate reaction of Catholic officialdom by praising the report generally but calling the population recommendations "extremely disturbing, to say the least." He declared that "The population problem in many parts of the world admittedly is very serious at the present time. But to advocate a program of artificial birth control as a solution to the problem is not only immoral, it is also a counsel of defeatism and despair."[18]

The Draper Committee report did not cause an immediate explosion. President Eisenhower submitted it to Congress without recommendation, urging only careful study. As Arthur Krock observed in the *New York Times*:

This recommendation caused a one-day flurry. . . . But the politicians and the people generally paid little heed to the incident. The President made no adverse comment and the sensation was confined to Draper committee members who had hoped the item would not be pinpointed and to the ever-nervous State Department.[19]

CHANGE ON OTHER FRONTS

But in 1959 while the Draper Committee was moving toward new ground those in the population field had not been standing still either. On the activist side the International Planned Parenthood Federation's Sixth International Conference in New Delhi, including some 750 delegates from 27 countries, heard Indian Prime Minister Nehru warn of "a tremendous crisis" if population growth were not checked. A unanimous resolution was dispatched to Dag Hammarskjold the UN secretary-general, urging that family planning be made an integral part of UN programs and be considered "a basic human right."[20]

Professional support of a particularly welcome nature came in October when the World Council of Churches approved for circulation a report prepared by the Reverend Richard Fagley strongly justifying all birth control methods used "in Christian conscience."[21] During the year, four major religious groups in the United States endorsed family planning: the United Presbyterian Church, the Union of American Hebrew Congregations, and the American Baptist Convention.[22]

The long-sought backing of public health professionals was won in November 1959 when the American Public Health Association not only endorsed birth control but also recommended that it be made an integral part of health programs and that scientific research in the whole field be greatly expanded. Dr. Leona Baumgartner, still recalling the impact of the New York City fight of 1958, was influential as president of the APHA in working for compromise language that all could accept.

Even within the government voices were being raised that reinforced the Draper Committee report. A State Department review of world population trends completed in July and released in November warned, "Rapid population growth may prove to be one of the greatest obstacles to economic and social progress and to maintenance of political stability in many of the less developed areas of the world."[23] A study by Stanford Research Institute, commissioned by the Senate Committee on Foreign Relations, pointed out even more bluntly that "in certain parts of the world population control is already a necessity."[24] The institute reported on progress with the new orals and recommended an international research program to develop and test new contraceptives.[25]

These developments, together with the Draper Committee report which went directly to the president and Congress, could be compared to a critical mass, large enough to generate a strong reaction, too large to be ignored.

CHAPTER

5

BIRTH CONTROL
AND THE 1960
ELECTION

Birth control as an issue of public policy emerged from the dim light of crusading, professional, and specialized interest into the full glare of national publicity in the last two months of 1959. As one columnist observed, "Not in our lifetime—never again maybe—will the problem go back on the shelf."[1]

CATHOLIC CONFRONTATION

What really attracted national and top-level attention were not the reports and studies of birth control advocates but, as it often was in the past, the criticism of birth control opponents. By November 1959 the Catholic Church could hold its fire no longer. The Catholic bishops of the United States declared in a statement released from Washington, November 25, 1959:

> United States Catholics believe that the promotion of artificial birth control is a morally, humanly, psychologically and politically disasterous approach to the population problem. . . . They will not support any public assistance, either at home or abroad, to promote artificial birth prevention, abortion or sterilization, whether through direct aid or by means of international organizations.[2]

Where the promoters of birth control had once seen a "conspiracy of silence" the Catholic prelates now discerned a "campaign of propaganda" and denounced "the recently coined terror technique phrase 'population explosion.' " The national effect of the bishops' statement, as Arthur Krock pointed out, was to move "the topic from the areas of private morals and theology into the realm of public discussion of political action . . . a result which organizations and individuals concerned . . . had been unable to achieve in years of dedication."[3]

On the political side, the emerging issue of the 1960 presidential campaign added fuel to the conflagration. For the first time since Al Smith's defeat in 1928 a Catholic candidate, Senator John F. Kennedy of Massachusetts, was seeking the presidency. To the consternation of both parties, the Catholic bishops' warning on birth control precipitated not only the usual Planned Parenthood denunciations but also a provocative political question from Episcopal Bishop James Pike of California: "Was the policy laid down by the Bishops binding on Roman Catholic candidates for office?"[4]

The question was aimed at Kennedy. In an immediate telephone interview with James Reston of the *New York Times*, Kennedy responded to the substantive question of birth control. It would be a "mean paternalism," the Massachusetts senator replied, and "not in the national interest" for the United States to promote birth control overseas. "It is a decision for the countries concerned to make for themselves," he declared, adding, "I think it would be the greatest psychological mistake for us to appear to advocate limitation of the black or brown or yellow peoples whose population is increasing no faster than in the United States."[5] Upon the overriding political question of the bishops' right to speak for him, Kennedy was equally decisive. He had held these views for some time, he said, and was "not influenced by the Bishops' statement." Moreover, he would certainly not refuse to give other assistance to a country simply because it was carrying out birth control programs.[6] In other words, Kennedy's answer was "no"—but his reason was not religion or morality. It was reluctance to force birth control upon foreign peoples.

The notion that the U.S. government might coerce other nations to practice birth control was not, of course, the recommendation of the Draper Committee. Coercion was a straw man that all candidates could safely attack while evading the real question of aid on request. When Kennedy was pressed during the campaign about how he might react as president if India or Pakistan asked the United States for help in curbing population growth or if Congress passed legislation providing funds for birth control, his emphasis shifted gradually from a negative assessment of birth control aid to a positive affirmation that he would act solely on the criterion of national interest.[7] For instance, this is what Kennedy told the American Society of Newspaper Editors in April 1960.

> The prospects of any President ever receiving for his signature a bill providing foreign aid funds for birth control are very remote indeed.[*] It is hardly the major issue some have suggested. Nevertheless, I have made it clear that I would neither veto nor sign such a bill on any basis except what I considered to be the public interest, without regard to my private religious views.[8]

Again, in addressing the greater Houston Ministerial Association in September, Kennedy declared, "I do not speak for my church on public

---

*Actually, President Johnson signed the first such bill, the *Foreign Assistance Act of 1963* (Public Law 88-205) on December 16, 1963, less than a month after Kennedy's assassination.

matters—and the Church does not speak for me." On birth control as on other issues, "I will make my decision," he asserted, "in accordance with what my conscience tells me to be in the national interest and without regard to outside religious pressure or dictate."[9]

For the other Catholic candidates, late in 1959, the question seemed even more difficult. California Governor Edmund (Pat) Brown was at first "not prepared to answer a question of regulation of births" but quickly shifted to Kennedy's line.[10] So did New York Mayor Robert Wagner, who had remained neutral during the 1958 New York City dispute; but he added sharply, we have "no right to enforce our will on any people. The Roman Catholic position is the view of the Church, period."[11]

Non-Catholics were equally uneasy in their first public comment on an issue never before considered important enough or appropriate for national attention. Like Kennedy, most of the candidates denounced coercion and tried to avoid the real questions. The only positive approval for birth control aid came from Senator Stuart Symington of Missouri, who acclaimed it as a useful way to combat poverty, disease, and communism.[12] Vice President Richard Nixon did not comment until April 1960, when he guardedly declared that "if underprivileged countries reach a decision that they want to limit population at a certain point and come to us for assistance, we should give it to them."[13]

EISENHOWER'S VIEWS

But long before April 1960 the question had been somewhat defused by President Eisenhower. Asked at a press conference in December 1959 for his reactions to the Draper recommendations on birth control, Eisenhower declared with his unusual bluntness, "I cannot imagine anything more emphatically a subject that is not a proper political or governmental activity or function or responsibility." Terming it "a religious tenet" in Catholic doctrine, he said that if other governments want "to do something about what is admittedly a very difficult question and an explosive question . . . they will go unquestionably to private groups, not to governments." He concluded, "This government will not, as long as I am here, have a positive political doctrine in its program that has to do with the problem of birth control. That's not our business."[14] To the dismay of birth control supporters, President Eisenhower had followed the line of the Catholic bishops—that birth control was basically a religious matter and therefore not a legitimate subject for national policy.

Actually, President Eisenhower's comments were determined by political and not substantive considerations. Eisenhower *was* worried about population growth, especially as it might nullify the effects of the foreign aid program. There is considerable evidence of his concern. As early as the fall of 1958 he surprised officials of the International Cooperation Administration (ICA) by devoting most of a National Security Council meeting on foreign aid to population growth. How can foreign aid succeed if population keeps increasing at the present rate, he wanted to know. Agency officials, particularly James Grant (then special assistant to ICA Director James Smith), pointed out that the technical know-how to make birth control programs work in countries like India was still lacking, that much more research by government, foundations, and others was necessary to develop better methods before any U.S. government input would be effective. In the meantime, one more controversy added to the existing unpopularity of the foreign aid program might be the straw that would break the camel's back. At the end of the discussion, Eisenhower commented that he would actually be willing to take on a pubic battle over the issue if he were convinced that U.S. government aid would make a difference; but he, too, hesitated to add a new note of discord to the program without greater promise for success.[15]

Draper several years later asked Eisenhower why he had rejected the committee's recommendation. Eisenhower told Draper somewhat apologetically that birth control had become a divisive issue and that he did not want to split the nation more deeply on the eve of a sensitive election.[16]

Early in 1960 Ambassador James Riddleberger, then director of the International Cooperation Administration, went to considerable lengths to persuade Eisenhower to allow ICA quietly to support birth control programs in India and Pakistan. After Eisenhower had turned down a confidential memorandum submitted by Riddleberger arguing the economic importance of reducing birth rates, Riddleberger asked him privately whether he disagreed with the analysis.

Eisenhower replied, "No, Jimmy, I suspect you are right, but I can't do it. If Kennedy is nominated and elected, he could do something about it, but I can't."[17]

Eisenhower wanted to avoid the bitterness of the 1928 Al Smith campaign, but only three years later he wrote in the *Saturday Evening Post*:

> When I was President, I opposed the use of Federal funds to provide birth control information to countries we were aiding because I felt this would violate the deepest religious convictions of large groups of taxpayers. As I now look back, it may be that I carried that conviction too far. I still believe that as a national policy we should not make birth control programs a condition to our foreign aid, but we should tell receiving nations how population growth threatens them and what can be done about it.[18]

Subsequently in serving as honorary chairman of Planned Parenthood and in making a number of public statements Eisenhower expressed unusually strong concern about the population explosion and endorsed federal support for family planning. Like a number of other high government officials his backing for such programs increased as his official capacity to implement them declined.

Eisenhower's comments reflect a characteristic pattern of American political life—"the tacit understanding not to raise issues certain to be disruptive and beyond solution."[19] Philip Converse, analyzing the 1960 election in depth, observes among political elites "a remarkable show of consensus in an attempt to stifle religion as an issue in the campaign."[20] That meant also to stifle birth control as an issue, since it aroused dissension between religions. In this sense the early treatment of birth control on the national level provides a good example of the exercise of "non-decision-making power," that considerable power, which Peter Bachrach and Morton Baratz describe, of "creating or reinforcing social and political values and institutional practices that limit the scope of the political process to public consideration of only those issues which are comparatively innocuous."[21]

KENNEDY'S POSITION

If Eisenhower dodged around the issue of birth control for the sake of national unity, Kennedy had equally good reason for not wanting it raised. Scion of a large Irish Catholic family, raised in Massachusetts where birth control was synonomous with the worst Catholic-Protestant feuding and where birth control meant Republican and antibirth control meant Democratic, and reelected to Congress in 1948 during a vitriolic birth control referendum campaign,[22] Kennedy did not have much enthusiasm for the issue or most of its supporters. He once commented that most people think "it is other people's families that provide the population explosion."[23] Although he occasionally referred, in speeches prepared by Sorenson or others, to the population explosion and twice in the television debates with Nixon mentioned India's "population pressures," there is no evidence that Kennedy himself ever took any initiative in promoting birth control policy as an answer to such pressures.

Furthermore, Kennedy's slogan in 1960 was the forceful appeal, "Let's get America moving again." In an achievement-oriented campaign that stressed competition with the Soviet Union, the missile gap, the sputnik scare and, above all, the need for great economic growth, the very idea of population control had a pessimistic, negative ring that was inconsistent with his larger political design. As far as foreign aid was concerned Kennedy's goal was more aid—to promote economic development, to enlarge the size of the pie, not to reduce the number of people to be fed. Like Eisenhower he feared that introducing birth control would jeopardize an already unpopular program— "you will get neither foreign aid nor birth control."[24]

But in 1959 and 1960, for Kennedy as for Eisenhower, it was not personal inclination or economic orientation that was decisive but rather the more pressing political need to prove to Protestant and Jewish voters that a candidate who was Catholic had loyalties no different from those of any other American. Unfortunately for Kennedy the bishops' statement dramatized church involvement in public policy along lines that most non-Catholics could not accept. Despite his reasoned response Kennedy was "sharply irritated that so sensitive and divisive an issue had been needlessly dragged into the headlines on the eve of his official campaign."[25] Sophisticated observers like James Reston might argue that the bishops' intervention was proof that the Catholic Church was *not* trying to get Kennedy elected,[26] but to nervous Protestants the bishops seemed to be flexing their political muscles.

Kennedy's aim, like Eisenhower's, was to deflate the birth control issue. But where Protestant Republican Eisenhower tried to remove the political sting by agreeing with the Catholic bishops, Kennedy tried to remove the religious sting by insisting that it was *not* religious but a valid political question to be decided on the basis of the national interest. Eisenhower's was the more traditional approach; the loyal old-line Democratic politicians, anxious to help Kennedy, lined up with Eisenhower to agree that birth control was religious, irrelevant, a distraction. Even Mrs. Roosevelt, an early supporter of birth control, put politics ahead of policy and reversed her previous position.[27] Kennedy's frontal approach, his willingness to discuss what others called "the religious issue" was new, but it was basic to his campaign. He had to demonstrate publicly that there were no "religious issues" that could influence his judgment as president.

THE ROLE OF THE MEDIA

Nevertheless, in spite of the politicians' consensus that birth control should not be on the political agenda the combined impact of the Draper Committee report, the Catholic bishops' denunciation, and the 1960 campaign convinced the press, often the strongest ally of a new movement trying to be heard, that a relevant public policy issue was involved. What Michael Lipsky calls the "awakening of the communications media" meant that the issue of birth control was finally on the news agenda for coverage, beyond the power of the Catholic Church to silence or boycott.[28]

Newspapers from Boston to San Francisco, from Minneapolis to Miami, suggested, like the *St. Louis Post Dispatch*, that "the question deserves to be seriously considered in other than political terms."[29] Even after the subject dropped from political news on page one it was vigorously debated elsewhere. For example, the *Readers' Guide to Periodical Literature* lists 13 articles under the headings "birth control" and "contraceptives" in the six months preceding the bishops' statements as compared with 36 articles in the three months following. These included not only factual accounts of population growth and a cover story in *Life* but also, significantly for the future, a number of studies in Catholic publications like the liberal, lay-edited *Commonweal* and the Jesuit weekly *America*, in which Catholics began to question their church's role in the birth control controversy. Perhaps Catholics should give up the struggle for prohibitive legislation;[30] perhaps the church should encourage scientific research to make the rhythm method more effective;[31] perhaps a Catholic president could permit public funds to support birth control programs.[32]

The "publicity explosion" included television. *CBS Reports* daringly featured an hour-long documentary November 11, 1959, on the population problem in India. Beginning somewhat cautiously with an apology for the use of "certain brief phrases pertaining to procreation," moderator Howard K. Smith insisted that "not talking about the problem because it's controversial or uncomfortable is a luxury that we, as leaders of the Free World, cannot afford."[33] The show was rebroadcasted on January 14, 1960 with an additional half-hour of much sharper debate relating to economic development. Some 9 million people saw the first presentation; 9.5 million saw the second,[34] a new

record in public exposure and a serious effort to look at the issue from many
points of view, not exclusively religious or political.

Even after the first flurry of political excitement had died, birth control
and the population problem kept coming up. Apart from any political motivation, for instance, leaders of all faiths felt obliged to clarify their churches'
positions. Geoffrey Fisher, archbishop of Canterbury, declared that "family
planning is a positive, Christian duty."[35] Richard Fagley of the World Council
of Churches offered a strong moral rationale for birth control in his book *The
Population Explosion and Christian Responsibility.*[36] Pope John XXIII, on the
other hand, told Catholics not to fear but to welcome all the children God
might send them.[37]

Meanwhile the birth control and population activists, although dismayed
by Eisenhower's position, were more active than ever. Restrictive state laws
were challenged in the courts not only in Massachusetts and Connecticut but
elsewhere as well. The American Civil Liberties Union called them unconstitu-
tional.[38] In May 1960 at a National Conference on the Population Crisis
co-sponsored by the Dallas Council on World Affairs and *Newsweek* magazine,
John D. Rockefeller 3rd made a plea that was to be repeated many times in the
decade ahead:

> The problems of population are so great, so important, so ramified
> and so immediate that only government, supported and inspired by
> private initiative, can attack them on the scale required. It is for the
> citizens to convince their political leaders of the need for imaginative
> and courageous action—action which may sometimes mean political
> and economic opposition.[39]

At the same time Hugh Moore began to organize the World Population
Emergency Campaign to raise funds from businessmen for family planning overseas and hopefully to transform the International Planned Parenthood Federation
from what he called a "debating society" into a powerful force. The campaign was
headed by Lammot Copeland, then vice-president of the DuPont company, and,
at Moore's insistence, by William H. Draper, Jr. Draper was being drawn more and
more into the birth control field. As Congressman Albert Quie (R.-Minn.) has
observed, "Recommendations of study groups never have much effect except on
those who make them."[40] Certainly one effect of the Draper Committee
recommendation—and its rejection by President Eisenhower—was to stiffen the
chairman's own determination to achieve what he had proposed. His first
objective, like Moore's, was to strengthen the private groups so that they could
play the leading role that Eisenhower had suggested for them.

Moreover, in spite of the politicians, questions about birth control policy
continued to come up even within the campaign. On October 21, barely two
weeks before the election, the three leading Catholic bishops of Puerto Rico
issued a pastoral letter instructing Catholics not to vote for the party of
popular Governor Munoz Marin because of his support for public schools and
birth control.[41]

From Kennedy's point of view the bishops' charge was "the cruelest
blow."[42] In spite of disclaimers by leading Catholic prelates in the continental

United States, the Puerto Rican bishops defended their stand and a week later threatened excommunication to anyone who voted for Munoz Marin. Such fireworks were not unusual in Puerto Rico where the Catholic Church had been denouncing birth control and liberal government unsuccessfully for decades, but they provoked a violent counterblast from Protestant clergymen to the north. Kennedy, caught between militant Catholicism and militant Protestantism, issued a statement calling it "wholly improper and alien to our domestic system for churchmen of any faith to tell the members of their church for whom to vote or for whom not to vote."[43] Nevertheless, Sorenson reports that "Senator Kennedy knew he had been hurt. 'If enough voters realize that Puerto Rico is American soil,' he remarked to me, 'this election is lost.' "[44]

THE IMPACT OF THE CAMPAIGN

On November 8 Kennedy was elected president by a margin of 118,550 popular votes out of 68,838,979 cast.[45] Survey data indicated that 56 percent of those who switched from Eisenhower in 1956 to Kennedy in 1960 were Catholic, whereas 81 percent of those who switched from Stevenson in 1956 to Nixon in 1960 were Protestant.[46] Second only to basic party identification, religious affiliation did apparently influence many voters. The pollster Lou Harris estimated that Kennedy lost 2 million votes in the last two weeks before the election as a result of the crescendo of literature, preaching, and publicity over the Puerto Rican bishops.[47] V. O. Key suggests that nearly 1 million of those who shifted from a Democratic vote in 1956 to a Republican vote in 1960 did so in the week preceding the election.[48]

Except as a factor in this powerful religious equation, birth control was not an election issue. Eisenhower had prevented it from dividing the two parties. In December 1959 only one out of every five people admitted to being "worried" about population increase.[49] Few voters were as single-minded as Margaret Sanger, who declared that she would leave the country if Kennedy were elected.[50] Simple group loyalty and personal impressions undoubtedly carried more weight than policy issues.

A liberal Catholic writer has suggested that if Kennedy had fitted the socioeconomic stereotype of "a typical American Catholic" from a middle-income family, graduate of a Catholic college, and married to a South Boston Irish girl, he could not have been elected.[51] But it may equally be that if Kennedy, even though he was a Harvard-educated ambassador's son, had meekly followed the judgment of the bishops on aid to education and birth control he would not have been elected either. Certainly Kennedy's political strategy of demonstrating to non-Catholic voters how rigidly he separated church and state in policy matters and of urging them to practice an equally rigid separation of church and state in voting matters made it easier for Protestants to support him. More than half of Kennedy's 34 million votes were cast by Protestants.[52]

Birth control as an issue in the 1960 election was more symbolic than substantive, more a test of religious attitudes than of demographic understanding, more significant to intellectual elites than to the masses. Probably, to the extent that birth control had any impact at all on the election, it did sharpen the sense of religious difference and of potential church-state conflict. Certainly it forced Kennedy to declare again and again that the national interest superseded church doctrine.

Clearly, the 1960 campaign and election did influence the development of birth control policy. The immediate effect was perceptible and negative. Right after the bishops' statement and even before Eisenhower's words, officials in the foreign aid program hastened to assure the press that the controversy was "academic." "Not one penny of foreign aid funds ever has been used for dissemination of birth control information and there are no plans to do so."[53] Because of the campaign, Riddleberger's private effort to persuade Eisenhower in 1960 had no greater success than Draper's public recommendation in 1959. Throughout 1960, administration witnesses emphatically assured congressional committees that birth control would not be included in foreign aid activities.[54] However, not until March 22, 1960, four months later, did ICA dispatch to its overseas missions the text of Eisenhower's statement, without any further comment or guidance as to support for such traditional areas of assistance as census-taking demography or maternal and child health.[55] Characteristically, perhaps, the extended bureaucracy that administered foreign aid was almost as reluctant to implement wholeheartedly the president's prohibition as it later would be to respond to presidential encouragement. Nevertheless, in the short run politics and the electoral process had set back what might have been the quiet beginnings of birth control assistance.

From a longer perspective, however, the possibilities for government support of birth control advanced. Controversy generated publicity, as we have noted. By mid-December 1959, 75 percent of the population had heard about the population increase—surprisingly a somewhat higher figure than in 1963 or 1965 (when there was even more publicity but less controversy).[56]

Furthermore, the stand that Kennedy took, although originally negative, could not in the long run prevent action. Kennedy had insisted so vigorously that he would make his decisions on the basis of national interest and not religion that religion ceased to be a publicly valid reason for avoiding the issue. For the first time a president had openly suggested that the population explosion and birth control were serious questions to be objectively analyzed in terms of the national interest.

Since a Catholic candidate could make this distinction between the teachings of the church and the national interest, so could millions of other Catholics. For many, Kennedy's election both symbolized and encouraged the increasingly vigorous and independent role of the lay Catholic man or woman, who often had views of sexual morality that differed from those of the priests.[57] Kennedy himself was not publicly anticlerical (after one struggle over aid to education he remarked privately, "Now I understand why Henry VIII set up his own Church").[58] However, like his contemporary, Pope John XXIII, Kennedy was not adverse to opening new windows on church or state doctrine.

Finally, too, the election of a Catholic president put strong pressure on those concerned about population growth and birth control to find a way to reconciliation and to marshall their serious arguments about population growth and national interests. Direct confrontation had made gains on the local scene and generated considerable publicity. But to confront or embarrass a Catholic president still further did not seem to be the best way to win government support. Maybe, as Eisenhowever had thought, a Catholic president could take political initiatives that a Protestant could not. After the sound and fury of the campaign, the election of America's first Catholic president provided a new incentive to search for accommodation on a problem that would no longer "go back on the shelf."

POLICY MAKING IN
THE EXECUTIVE BRANCH,
1961-65

6

THE STATE DEPARTMENT: CONSIDERING THE PROBLEM, 1961-62

Relevance, feasibility, priority, and urgency—these four qualities must be widely discussed and affirmed before any new government program is established. First, is the proposed new activity relevant to accepted national objectives? Second, is it feasible—politically, technically, financially? Third, how does it rank in importance with existing programs? And finally, how urgent is it timewise? The more favorably each of these questions is resolved—whether by the executive branch, by the legislative branch, or ultimately by the public—the more likely is an innovation in U.S. government to be adopted and fully supported.[1]

After the 1960 election the birth control policy debate began to shift from the question of relevance to the question of feasibility. Not only the press but gradually also the government admitted that population growth was directly—and adversely—relevant to economic development. In vain the Vatican and some economists and demographers might call this linkage "simplistic." As a practical formulation, it could no longer be ignored. So with some of the opposition outflanked a new series of questions began to be asked in the 1960s. What can actually be done to check population growth? What kind of policies are politically feasible? What kind of programs are technically feasible?

Proving the birth control issue relevant required not only data in the form of demographic statistics but also confrontation and controversy, a disruption of the existing consensus to add a new item to the national agenda. Proving that birth control assistance was feasible required something different. Political feasibility meant building the broadest possible support for any measures taken; it required conciliation, negotiation, and accommodation. Technical feasibility for a new field meant applying scientific and managerial skills. Both involved a lowering of the emotional tone that characterized birth control as an election issue and a new emphasis on practical possibilities.

An unexpected asset for the population movement that the Kennedy administration itself brought to Washington was an activist orientation toward government, embracing both foreign policy and social issues. Few issues of any

kind were considered "not the Government's business". Therefore, despite the
president's own hesitation on birth control some of his appointees were ready
to accept at face value the campaign comments that population growth and
birth control were "legitimate questions of public policy" to be judged calmly
in the light of "national interest." Thus a small group of advocates within the
State Department and the Agency for International Development joined the
scientists and activists outside of government in promoting a more active
policy. If these State and AID insiders seemed at times a small, conspiratorial
group, plotting with outsiders against their own bosses, they played an increasingly important role in the policy process, shaping the suggestions and
initiatives of the outsiders to conform with the more cautious context of
internal executive agency policy making.[2]

The first step toward a policy on population was taken by George
McGhee, a former assistant secretary of state, member of the Draper Committee, and husband of a Planned Parenthood volunteer. Appointed director of
the Policy Planning Council of the State Department in January 1961, McGhee
learned that a staff study on the foreign policy implications of the world
population explosion was already under way. (It had been initiated in 1960,
despite Eisenhower's ban, by Evan Wilson, a Foreign Service officer.) McGhee,
who had been exceedingly annoyed by Eisenhower's comments, took great
interest. The study was reviewed, expanded, printed, and circulated as an
official Policy Planning Council document.

The report concluded that the ability to control population growth was
"the single greatest determinant" of economic development; yet because of
religious, political, and social attitudes it was "not deemed feasible" for the
U.S. government to provide large or publicized assistance. Nevertheless, the
U.S. government could encourage research, dissemination of information, greater awareness, and more attention by private organizations and other governments to the population problem.[3]

After an initial negative reaction from Secretary of State Rusk, the final revised version of the report recommended half a dozen "minimum actions" that
the department should be taking. These included: a request to the National Institutes of Health to conduct a survey of research then under way in reproductive
physiology (toned down from the original request for a specific $10 million per
year fertility research program); appointment of a full-time State Department
population officer; encouragement of more population activities in the UN system; reversal of the still-standing Eisenhower ban on foreign aid for birth control;
more research by AID on the social and economic factors involved in population
growth; and quiet appeals to other governments to provide birth control aid.

The actions taken on those Policy Planning Council recommendations set in
motion the development of U.S. policy toward world population problems. Both
what was done and what was not done following the council report had major and
continuing repercussions.

THE RESEARCH CAMPAIGN

The proposal for an expanded research program at the National Institutes
of Health was the major specific recommendation of the Policy Planning

Council. It had not originated with the council but rather represented a long-term strategy developed and promoted by those outside government. Originally offered by Bishop Pike on CBS-TV in January 1960, the research strategy involved a crash program administered and financed by the National Institutes of Health to improve all techniques of birth control including the rhythm method.[4]

Planned Parenthood officials had long believed that a large-scale research effort could "hold the key both to substantial progress in dealing with the population problem—and to a lasting solution of the bitter religious dispute about contraception."[5] The research approach minimized Catholic opposition by stressing agreement on the principle of "responsible parenthood" or a legitimate "regulation of offspring" and not disagreement over specific methods. Despite the negative tone of *Casti Connubii* in 1931, Pius XI had endorsed the rhythm system in 1951 and specifically expressed hope that science could develop a more secure basis for its use.[6] Bishop Pike's proposal, framed as a response to that hope, was applauded by liberal Catholic scholars like Father John O'Brien at Notre Dame.

An expanded research program also minimized the differences within the birth control movement between activists and scientists, demographers and physicians. Everyone recognized the need for new and better birth control methods. Planned Parenthood and the Population Council had jointly sponsored a conference at West Point in 1959 to identify promising areas for research in reproductive physiology.[7] Although some wanted to go farther and faster, while others were dubious about a "crash program," no one within the population field was opposed to more research.

At the same time the 1950s had seen a tremendous and popular expansion of health research through the National Institutes of Health. Mary Lasker, president of the Albert and Mary Lasker Foundation and also a Planned Parenthood supporter, led the crusade to find a cure for cancer and to upgrade mental health activities at NIH. Her success encouraged the birth control activists to promote a similar campaign.

When McGhee undertook his policy review he conferred with Draper and Canfield. They urged the enlarged research program as a good starting point and the Policy Planning Council agreed. But Secretary of State Rusk did not approve their recommendation. First Rusk wanted to know exactly how the $10 million figure was arrived at. Then he implied that the population problem was far more complex than McGhee imagined. From his own experience as assistant secretary of State for Far Eastern affairs and later as president of the Rockefeller Foundation Rusk felt he understood the problem better than his advisers did.

In general, Rusk was reluctant for the State Department as he had been for the Rockefeller Foundation to push other nations—or agencies—forward in this field. The United States should wait for the developing nations to make their own requests. The State Department and AID should also not get too far ahead of U.S. domestic policies. In his judgment, knowledge and competent people were more important than money.

Nevertheless Rusk, like Eisenhower before him, could not wholly veto courses of action that his subordinates wanted to pursue. By late August 1961, when Rusk rejected even the watered-down proposal for a survey of research already under way, McGhee's aides had already approached NIH informally. Dr. David Price, deputy director of NIH, was asked to help defend the $10 million target figure which had been partly educated guesswork and partly an extrapolation from the costs of developing the Salk vaccine. Price was sympathetic. Without waiting for the formal request from Secretary Rusk—which never came—Dr. Errett Albritton, who had prepared a comparable summary in 1960, was assigned to compile an up-to-date report on actual and potential levels of research in human fertility.[8]

The initial version of the Albritton report listed U.S. research on fertility amounting to $5.7 million, of which NIH was funding $1.7 million, but concluded as follows: "Research and research support in the area of birth and population control are only a fraction of what they should be when measured by the urgency of the medical and public health problems."[9]

Furthermore the report, which had been prepared with the assistance of an outside advisory panel including representatives from Planned Parenthood, the Population Reference Bureau, and the Population Council, recommended annual NIH funding of nearly $17 million (plus $4 million in capital costs for eight population research institutes at various university and medical centers.)

The higher echelons of the Department of Health, Education, and Welfare (HEW) were alarmed by such obvious advocacy. HEW Secretary Abraham Ribicoff was planning to run for the Senate from Connecticut. The report circulated widely through HEW but was not released to the public.

News leaks about the "suppressed report" appeared in November 1961[10] and with greater detail in April 1962. The stories were ferreted out by David Broder, whom one official called "more help than Planned Parenthood." Rusk was then asked at a press conference whether HEW was holding up a State Department request for increased research in "population control methods." Calling the matter "a tempest in a teapot," Rusk stressed that population policy was "preeminently a question for each country to decide for itself, and as a practical matter something which each family must decide for itself." Avoiding the real question he nonetheless took a small policy step forward, saying,

> For us to be indifferent to population factors would be, I think, reckless on our part and we do take very seriously the population trends, the impact of population growth upon development plans and we shall continue to follow that problem.[11]

In September 1962 Dr. Luther Terry, surgeon-general of the Public Health Service, and Price, taking full responsibility on themselves, announced. that the report would not be released "because it might be misunderstood."[12] Within 24 hours, Congressman John Moss, chairman of the House Subcommittee on Foreign Operations and Government Information, announced that there would be an investigation; Pierre Salinger, White House press secretary, declared that President Kennedy was not involved; and the Secretary of HEW Anthony Celebrezze, who was to be embarrassed more than once by rumors of his antibirth control stand, ordered the report updated and released

by the year's end. Through this deliberate maneuver two birth control sym-
pathizers put themselves in an unfavorable light in order to force their un-
sympathetic boss to overrule them and release a report which he, not they,
would have preferred to shelve.

One of the first, though by no means the last, instances of combined
internal-external-press-congressional pressures on top officials, the effort had
mixed results. The revised report was released in December 1962 as a compilation of ongoing research. Father John C. Knott, director of the Family Life
Bureau of the National Catholic Welfare Conference, praised it as an excellent,
objective summary of basic research.

> The fact that such information could be used for what we, as
> Catholics, would consider immoral purposes should not prevent us
> from supporting those seeking the truth. Rather we as Catholics
> should positively encourage all efforts which have as a goal unlocking
> nature's secrets.[13]

But all the recommendations for additional research, crash programs, or
higher funding were deleted. The final version flatly stated the exact opposite
of what the Policy Planning Council had initially recommended:

> A research program to find new techniques which would be less
> expensive, or aesthetically, religiously, or culturally more acceptable
> or less prone to failure by reason of 'human error' is not an objective
> toward which NIH has a planned effort.[14]

Dr. Thomas Kennedy, assistant to the director of NIH, explained that the
original recommendations had been eliminated because they were "not
germane" and represented "special interests" rather than "the normal scientific
channels.[15] The incident was a sharp reminder that the birth control activists
were taking a risk whenever they forced the birth control issue up to the top
level. They could still be slapped down as "special interests," not fully
admitted to the scientific community. Yet if they did not take the risk they
were likely to be left out or suppressed anyway.

Thus McGhee's proposal for research, which Rusk never formally authorized and which subordinates at both the State Department and NIH promoted
beyond their explicit authority, resulted by early 1963 in little more than a
compilation of ongoing research, considerable tension between NIH and the
activists, and a strengthened desire at HEW to avoid the issue.

A POPULATION OFFICER FOR THE DEPARTMENT

Secretary Rusk approved McGhee's specific suggestion that a full-time
officer be assigned to the under-secretary for economic affairs, then George
Ball, "to maintain a continuing review of the foreign policy implications of the
world population problem and to take such actions as are called for in the

national interest." At the annual World Bank meeting in September 1961 Ball asserted more publicly than any other high official had to date that prevailing rates of population growth were a burden on economic development. Our goal, his speech concluded eloquently, is " a world in which every birth in accompanied by a birthright."[16]

Ball agreed that Rusk's decision should be implemented at once. Robert A. Barnett, a Foreign Service officer, then counselor in Brussels, was invited to become the department's first full-time population adviser.[17] Barnett, whose background was economics and Chinese affairs, was considered a better choice for such a sensitive post than any unpredictable outside demographer. In December 1961 Barnett joined the small undercover group in the State Department who were beginning to promote a positive U.S. government policy toward the population problem. The group included Robert Schaetzel, a Foreign Service officer on Ball's staff, William Nunley, also on Ball's staff, Leighton Van Nort, a demographic analyst in the research office, Blanche Bernstein in International Organization Affairs, Henry Owen of the Policy Planning Council, and Richard Gardner, deputy assistant secretary for international organization affairs.

"Talk about the problem all you can, but don't put anything in writing," Barnett was advised when he took over the new job. He obeyed the first instruction—talking so constantly about population in fact that some people began to avoid him in the elevators. But he soon perceived that conversations did not make policy. Gradually he developed his own strategy. It included, first, open discussion, to make sure that population was recognized as an appropriate issue in the context of economic development; second, active liaison with the private groups involved; third, tentative maneuvers to get his own superiors on record whenever possible, more and more publicly and at higher and higher levels, in favor of positive policies; and finally development, in the process, of a cautious definition of what the U.S. government was actually prepared to do.

A small breach had already been made in the official wall of silence when Ambassador T. P. Plimpton, deputy U.S. representative at the United Nations, spoke at a Planned Parenthood meeting in October 1961 but in a personal, not an official, capacity.[18] In December 1961 William Nunley, on Ball's staff, went a step further. At a National Conference on International Economic and Social Development he revealed publicly for the first time,

> We are thinking about population problems, talking about them,
> attempting to get other people to think and talk about these prob-
> lems—to stimulate individuals, organizations, and governments to add
> to the total store of knowledge on this subject.[19]

Robert Barnett's first achievement was clearance, all the way through the White House, of a new form letter, an explicit embodiment of the "openness" approach, repudiating what Barnett privately called the Eisenhower administration's "do-nothing and know-nothing" attitude. In reviewing all the old mail on the subject, Barnett had discovered less than five specific requests for assistance, but hundreds of complaints about the government's "no-policy policy."

Many of these were prompted by a full-page advertisement entitled "20¢ a day to live on," sponsored by the Hugh Moore Fund in August 1961 and signed by such notables as Eleanor Roosevelt, Elmo Roper, Ellsworth Bunker, Will Clayton, and David Lilienthal.[20]

In essence, this is what Barnett's revised form letter said:

> The United States during 1961 began to give attention to population problems as they are related to economic and social development. We are seeking to encourage scientific research and discussions by foundations, private organizations, and individuals, and to keep abreast of the results of such research and discussion . . . .
>
> We believe that the greatest contribution which the United States can make at this stage to the solution of the joint and important problems of population growth and economic development is to stimulate the acquisition of adequate and accurate knowledge. The United States is not prepared to advocate, much less to impose, any specific decisions or policies regarding population controls which other countries might, in due course, consider necessary.[21]

The formulation in the letter was important. Taking for granted the fact that population was relevant to economic growth, the letter explored what kind of government activity might actually be feasible. It shifted the focus of attention from "artificial birth control" (which was not politically feasible) to "acquisition of adequate and accurate knowledge" (which was becoming politically feasible). A good example of how policy may be made by answering the mail, the substance of the letter might well have been front page news if the secretary of State had included it in a speech, but as a routine form letter signed by a lower-level bureaucrat it was used in Washington and relayed overseas without attracting attention or criticism.

With equal lack of publicity, liaison between State Department officials and private organizations grew apace. Barnett conferred widely—with William H. Draper, Jr., and Cass Canfield, with Robert Cook of the Population Reference Bureau, with Fred Jaffe of Planned Parenthood, with Oscar Harkavy of the Ford Foundation, and with John D. Rockefeller 3rd. Barnett spoke to an off-the-record meeting at the Council on Foreign Relations in May 1962, warning that policy advances would be slow, quiet, and undramatic but adding that requests for assistance, especially information and training, would be considered.

Canfield and Draper made the Washington rounds a number of times, promoting various proposals. They recommended to Barnett, McGhee, Rusk, and Walt W. Rostow at the Policy Planning Council and to McGeorge Bundy at the White House that the president follow Dr. John Rock's suggestion and appoint a commission of experts in the social and biological sciences to study the problem. They called on Dr. James Shannon the director of NIH to plead for more research on fertility.

The highest-level interaction was a meeting between Secretary Rusk and the heads of some 30 large foundations in November 1962 in New York.

Draper and Canfield had proposed that Rusk speak privately to a gathering of foundation executives about how government and the foundations might collaborate in dealing with population problems. Rusk agreed to speak if Rockefeller would arrange the meeting. Rockefeller, who was much more sensitive than Canfield and Draper about twisting official arms, arranged the meeting. Such was the delicacy of the issue that Canfield, then president of Planned Parenthood, was asked not to attend.

Rusk's comments were disappointing to the activists. He did not urge the foundations to give high priority to population, though he said that government needed the stimulus of private ideas and research. He attributed the "explosion" of interest in population partly to the government shift toward longer-term foreign aid planning but he emphasized the need for the U.S. government to wait until other countries developed their own policies and requested aid. There were no simple, uniform solutions, he insisted, suggesting that rash experiment and subsequent disappointment could set back further progress for 20 or 30 years. The government cannot and should not crusade, he warned.

It was a very low-key approach, but the fact that the secretary came at all may have carried weight. The Ford and Rockefeller Foundations were already reassessing their small contributions to population work and were on their way toward the major program commitments that were announced in 1963. Other foundations also began to take an interest. Ironically, Rusk may have been more successful in spurring private groups to activity than they ever were in spurring him.

REVERSING THE FOREIGN AID BAN

The Policy Planning Council report included two specific recommendations for the foreign aid program:

First, that AID should "no longer consider itself restricted in the giving of information by its public health and other technicians, on request, on the various aspects of human reproduction"; and second, that AID take steps, including necessary preliminary studies, toward "bringing about social and economic changes which will assist countries in meeting a recognized population problem." Rusk approved the first, fairly straightforward proposal but did not press for any implementation. The second, rather vague proposal he did not approve.

Within the foreign aid agency, the most conspicuous obstacle was the airgram ICATO XA758 of March 20, 1960, which contained simply the text of Eisenhower's press conference statement. Henry Labouisse, Kennedy's first foreign aid administrator, agreed with McGhee that the Eisenhower message was no longer operative. But the real problem was how to communicate this shift in policy without developing a whole new policy or raising an issue that would embarrass the president. Labouisse once jokingly suggested that the missions simply be advised with reference to airgram ICATO XA758 that Eisenhower was no longer president.

A further obstacle was the massive 1961 review that eventually trans- formed the International Cooperation Administration into the Agency for International Development. During most of 1961 Labouisse was very much involved in planning and obtaining congressional support for the reorganiza- tion. Therefore although Labouisse was sympathetic he did not pay much attention to McGhee's report and he let McGhee know that he wanted no messages on the subject sent to the field. As a result only a handful of people in Washington knew that Eisenhower's blanket prohibition was no longer meant to apply.

The reorganization of the foreign aid program did not enhance the immediate prospects for action. The Kennedy administration was committed to systematic economic development that stressed comprehensive country plan- ning with long-term development loans rather than short-term technical assis- tance projects of the Point IV type. In the reorganized agency the four regional bureaus (Latin America, Africa, the Near East and South Asia, and East Asia) had more influence than the expert staff office (which was not even established on a comparable level until 1962). This shift sharply reduced AID assistance in the health field and put priority on government-directed income- and job- producing investments. In the long run, as Rusk observed, the change focussed attention on the economic impact of population growth but in the short run it downgraded the medical personnel who might have assisted in specific family planning projects.

At the same time the staff of the foreign aid agency through its many permutations lacked the continuity and experience of State Department officers. As Senator Gruening observed of AID administrators, "Most of them have suffered the fate of Henry VIII's wives—they haven't lasted very long."[22] After the reorganization Labouisse was succeeded in November 1961 by Fowler Hamilton, a law partner of George Ball, as the first administrator of the Agency for International Development. Hamilton was succeeded in December 1962 by David Bell, an economist and former director of the Bureau of the Budget. It was late 1961 or 1962 before many of the second-level personnel came into the agency, with its new administration and three directors in three years.

At the root of many of the bureaucratic problems in the foreign aid agency was, of course, the fact that the program had an uncertain base of support in the country and in Congress. AID officials had to face twice as many congressional committees for annual funding as did their State Department colleagues. They were therefore inclined to be twice as cautious about issues like birth control. This caution could only have been reinforced by Secretary Rusk's explicit warning when Fowler Hamilton took office that AID employees should avoid "errors" that could be "seized on by enemies" to diminish public support.[23]

Thus the activists in the State Department like McGhee, Barnett, Schaetzel, Gardner, and Van Nort were constantly frustrated during the early 1960s in their efforts to push AID ahead. When McGhee suggested in June 1961 new legislation to provide a secure base for action, AID officials im- mediately demurred. McGhee concluded in annoyance, "You have the author- ity but you don't intend to act."

Throughout the early 1960s Schaetzel and Barnett kept prodding AID to brief mission directors on population problems, to stimulate direct requests for aid from Taiwan and Korea where government-approved programs were already under way, to appoint full-time staff, to prepare a manual on outside organizations that could guide nations seeking help, to gather demographic data and relevant literature, and to promote population research. Yet without decisive backing from above, the Young Turks in the State Department could only propose and persuade. The power to initiate—or in 1961 and 1962, not to initiate—assistance programs remained with AID, despite its many internal handicaps.

In the summer of 1962, after Rusk's first public comment, Harry Krould, who became the new director of the AID health program and did favor birth control, obtained clearance through AID and the White House for a classified AID manual order that called demographic factors "of strategic importance." AID missions could therefore play two "significant roles"; one was to help with census-taking and demographic analysis—as had been done for nearly two decades; the other was to recommend on request other sources of information and help in dealing with population problems—including the United Nations, other governments, and "private foundations such as the Population Council, Inc., Planned Parenthood, and the Ford Foundation."[24]

Immediately the National Catholic Welfare Conference objected, through a Catholic senator, to any official U.S. endorsement of a contraceptive program for population control. This connotation was conveyed merely by mentioning the words "Planned Parenthood." Fowler Hamilton insisted on the responsibility of the agency to help nations that were looking for relevant data and tried to make a distinction between information and advocacy.[25] Nevertheless, the prompt Catholic protest did not reassure AID officials.

Early in the fall of 1962 Dr. Leona Baumgartner, Commisssioner of Health for the City of New York, joined the agency as assistant administrator for Human Resources and Social Development (HRSD, later renamed Technical Cooperation and Research, TCR). Her first AID contact with the population problem was, like Barnett's, answering the mail. Dr. Baumgartner had a long-standing interest in birth control, tempered somewhat by nine years in the political atmosphere of New York City, and a high reputation in health circles, having just served as president of the American Public Health Association. With Krould's encouragement she soon became a focal point for AID activities in population and was formally given that role in November 1962, when she accompanied Rusk to the meeting of foundations in New York. Her first act was to withdraw the contested manual order and promise further guidance shortly. But despite Rusk's approval she was not immediately successful in persuading either Frank Coffin the acting administrator or later David Bell to send a clarifying message out to the overseas posts.

Parallel to, but relatively independent of McGhee's, Barnett's, and Baumgartner's activities, Teodoro Moscoso, the assistant secretary in charge of the Alliance for Progress, also began in late 1961 to stimulate interest in population problems in the Latin American region. Having worked with Planned Parenthood in Puerto Rico, Moscoso had no great fear of the Catholic Church. In the summer of 1962 he asked Dr. Edgar Berman, a health consultant, to look into the population situation. Moscoso was convinced that without birth control Latin American economic and social progress would be impossible. As a result, operating through the nearly autonomous Alliance for Progress, Berman also began to investigate what might be done despite the supposed monolithic opposition of the Catholic Church in Latin America.

Thus in AID as in the State Department, but nearly a year later, the first important forward steps were the selection of personnel, who were partly assigned to the problem but partly operated on their own initiative. All distinctly able, ambitious, energetic, and somewhat competitive personalities, they constituted not so much a team as a group of friendly rivals, each trying to advance the same cause in a slightly different way through the tangle of what Nunley had first called "a jungle that is largely unexplored."[2][6]

7

THE UNITED NATIONS PRECIPITATES A DECISION, 1962

Of all the Policy Planning Council's recommendations, none came to more significant fruition than the brief reference to the United Nations. The secretary of state approved without hesitation McGhee's proposal that the United States "give maximum support consistent with avoiding undue publicity to work in the population field in the UN." With this endorsement and for other reasons, both institutional and personal, the United Nations became the forum for the first significant shift in U.S. government policy.

As an institution the United Nations moved at its own pace and set its own agenda. Unlike any private organization it could force governments to stand up and be counted on issues. In 1960 and 1961 the government of Sweden attempted to place and in 1962 finally succeeded in placing on the agenda of the General Assembly a resolution entitled "Population Growth and Economic Development." Richard Gardner and Robert Barnett obtained clearance not only from the secretary of state but also from the White House for the United States to support the resolution.

The crucial paragraph endorsed this view:

> . . . the view of the Population Commission that the United Nations should encourage and assist the Governments, especially of the less developed countries, in obtaining basic data and carrying out essential studies of the demographic aspects, as well as other aspects, of their economic and social development problems, and that the United Nations give technical assistance, as requested by governments, for national projects and programs dealing with the problems of population.[1]

The State Department's initial support was based on the argument that no new authority was involved. The United Nations already possessed the power to provide technical assistance in any area requested—an argument used many times in the next decade to justify both support and nonsupport of various measures. The White House accepted the argument, as eager as the rest of the U.S. government to let the United Nations lead.

The personal ingredient was provided by Richard N. Gardner, Harlan Cleveland's deputy assistant secretary for international organization affairs. Gardner, as a junior member of President Kennedy's Task Force on Foreign Assistance, had suggested in January 1961 that Kennedy's technical advisers should take the president at his word and review the population problem in the light of national interest. But he was overruled by Ball, Cleveland, Rostow, and the others who only replied, "Don't you know the President is Catholic?"[2] Just as some members of the Draper Committee had hestitated to embarrass Eisenhower by raising the issue, so Kennedy's advisers tried to shield him from it.

Gardner persisted. He volunteered to handle the Swedish resolution when it finally came before the United Nations in December 1962. Well-supplied with data plus the form letter and scraps of other approved statements, Gardner wanted to stress "the quality of life"—a new phrase at that time—and the need for discussion and a wider dissemination of knowledge. Julia Henderson, then director of the UN Bureau of Social Affairs, provided further help and encouragement in New York.

A gracefully executed "scissors and paste job," Gardner's speech gave the whole issue new stature and significance. At the core of the statement he transformed the cautious, negatively phrased form letter into a positive affirmation of the "great need for additional knowledge on population matters." For example, where the form letter stated that "the United States will not place obstacles in the way of other governments which . . . seek solutions to their population problems," Gardner declared, "The United States believes that obstacles should not be placed in the way of other governments." Whereas the form letter categorized UN research as "this valuable work that can cast significant light on the complex interrelationships," Gardner asserted, "It is the hope of the United States that these valuable efforts will be substantially expanded."[3]

At the last minute Gardner dispatched his draft by teletype from New York to Washington for clearance. Harlan Cleveland and Robert Barnett took the speech to Rusk. The secretary read it through from beginning to end. "It doesn't present any problems to me," Rusk said. "Let's go ahead." With the further approval of Ralph Dungan in the White House, Gardner proceeded.

The most controversial portion of the resolution was, as expected, the language authorizing technical assistance for national projects and programs. Originally Gardner had authority to vote in favor of the whole resolution. But before the vote specifically to delete that paragraph and those words, a spokesman from the National Catholic Welfare Conference came to Gardner and pointedly asked, "Are you going to support the paragraph about technical assistance?" In a manner that seemed very threatening, the Catholic visitor suggested that, if so, Catholics in the United States would withdraw their support from the United Nations and mobilize in opposition. It was the traditional Catholic threat of boycott. Gardner felt himself on rather thin ice with no clear line of support from above. Fearing that Catholic opposition could make the whole effort backfire, Gardner compromised. The United

States supported the resolution in its entirety when it was finally approved by a vote of 69 to 0 (with 27 abstentions). But the United States abstained in committee when that entire operative paragraph was barely retained by a vote of 32 to 30 (with 35 abstentions).[4] The United States also abstained on a much more critical vote in the General Assembly when the reference to technical assistance was deleted by a separate vote of 34 to 34 (with 32 abstentions). As it was an important question, a two-thirds majority was required. U.S. abstention on both votes was explained officially on the grounds that the United Nations already had full authority to provide technical assistance and that the paragraph "is therefore superfluous."[5] Thus the United States abstained publicly on the key votes for the very reason that had earlier been used internally to justify support for the resolution.

Gardner argues that:

Abstention on the controversial section—and its consequent defeat— was the price that had to be paid for achieving a broad consensus among the membership. It was also the price the United States and some other members had to pay for this first big step forward on population, given the uncertain state of domestic opinion.[6]

After the debate Gardner and his colleagues in the State Department waited apprehensively for criticism. None came, except a cable from a Planned Parenthood fan protesting U.S. abstention. Although it was the first General Assembly debate on population and the first official U.S. government statement, the press played it down. The *New York Times* was on strike at the time. Wire service reports indicated only that the United States had abstained on several votes but supported the resolution.

Nevertheless, Gardner's initiative was important, not because he said anything revolutionary, not because the UN resolution really conferred any additional authority, and not because the episode attracted wide attention at the time but rather because of the way it was used and interpreted afterward. Dr. Baumgartner in AID had not been consulted or even advised in advance of Gardner's move, but she was one of the first to see that here was a public banner under which AID policy could advance, even if high AID officials refused to clear AID cables. She and Gardner agreed that the speech and resolution should be reprinted as a pamphlet entiled "Population Growth: A World Problem" and subtitled "Statement of U.S. Policy." Under that imprimatur and financed by AID, the speech was dispatched to U.S. embassies and AID missions around the world. After three years, the ghost of Eisenhower's ban was finally exorcised from the State Department.

Furthermore, when no opposition developed other than a handful of Catholic editorials, Gardner and Baumgartner pressed further. In a not uncommon bureaucratic pattern, what had originally been depicted as a minimal decision was reinterpreted after the fact as a maximal one. By May 1963 Gardner was describing the UN action as "a turning point"[7] in world recognition of the population problem.

Throughout 1963 and 1964 Gardner used every occasion to confirm the importance and the official nature of the policy shift. President Kennedy personally had approved his statement, he said. No one contradicted him. Although at the top level McGhee, Labouisse, and Rusk had agreed among themselves as early as 1961 that Eisenhower's policy was no longer in effect, their private agreement made much less difference than a deputy assistant secretary's speech to an empty hall, because they deliberately refrained from communicating their decision and Gardner deliberately tried to communicate his. For Gardner had in fact indicated that "we can help other countries, upon request, to find potential sources of information and assistance on ways and means of dealing with population problems." No official of the U.S. government had ever said *that* in public before.

In the long run, the speech, the resolution, and the UN vote acquired significance because Gardner and birth control advocates believed that they were significant and spoke and acted vigorously upon that assumption. Two years of study and preparation, two years of behind-the-scenes work may have been necessary and helpful for government policy reorientation and to reassure nervous officials (although polls suggest that Catholic opposition to domestic birth control programs increased during this period of lesser publicity—See "Changes in Attitudes" in Chapter 3). But it was Gardner's speech at the United Nations and above all the later publicizing of it as a great leap forward that seemed to pull both government and public opinion toward a new policy consensus much more effectively than did the quiet off-the-record discussions that had occupied the previous two years.

8

The momentum that had been building up within the government, authorized by Rusk's decisions of August 1961 and precipitated by the UN debate in December 1962, did not develop in a vacuum. The environment outside the State Department was changing also. From the private organizations came a deluge of publicity and agitation. In addition to the making of repeated trips to Washington by notables like Draper and Canfield, Planned Parenthood for example circulated a "Statement of Conviction about Overpopulation." With signatures of 179 distinguished national and international figures from 19 nations, it was printed as an advertisement and presented to UN Secretary-General Dag Hammerskjold in late November 1960.[1] On the local level, state restrictions on birth control were contested, as in Connecticut, and state welfare policies were protested, as in Illinois.

Hugh Moore's World Population Emergency Campaign staged a lively symposium in May 1961 at which Catholics were openly criticized for their resistance to birth control. Marriner Eccles, former chairman of the Federal Reserve Board, called world population growth "more explosive than the atomic or hydrogen bomb."[2] In an editorial entitled "The World Population Explosion" the *New York Times* agreed.[3] Planned Parenthood files include nearly 50 editorials dated 1961 from all over the country urging government consideration of the population problem.

The International Union for the Scientific Study of Population, on the other hand, reacted against activist alarmism. Demographers derided the "emotional" phrase "population explosion." Dudley Kirk was quoted as saying, "The term is unfortunate and would not be used at a scientific meeting such as this. We are a scientific society and not a social movement."[4] Nevertheless, both the term and the idea were coming into common usage.

More conciliatory than Hugh Moore's meetings and advertisements was the November 1961 speech of John D. Rockefeller 3rd's in Rome to the UN Food and Agriculture Organization. He repeated his call for government involvement but urged study before action. Rockefeller wondered "whether the issue of birth control—only one of the facets of the population question—has not in some countries pushed the entire question beyond public discussion."[5] Tact was the new tactic.

On the professional side, the Population Council increased its budget from $1 million in 1959 to more than $5.5 million in 1963. Between November 1962 and April 1963 the council sponsored three overseas advisory missions—to Korea, Tunisia, and Turkey—and in 1964 established a new Division for Technical Assistance, reflecting the growing interest of other governments in population. The first experiments with the new intrauterine contraceptive device also provided "a basis for optimism" that a major breakthrough in contraceptive technology was at hand.[6]

Three important publications in 1961 and 1962 also stressed compromise and conciliation. An article by the Catholic physician John Rock, who had organized field trials for the first oral contraceptives at his infertility clinic, appeared in the July 1961 issue of *Good Housekeeping* under the politically appealing title, "We Can End the Battle Over Birth Control."[7] Senator Fulbright privately called Rock's article "the most sensible statement I have seen."[8] In October 1961 in an article in *Look*, Father John O'Brien of Notre Dame University also suggested, "Let's Take Birth Control Out of Politics."[9] The doctor and the priest both emphasized the wide areas of agreement between Catholic doctrine and other religions; both called for more dialogue on the issues and more scientific research on human reproduction.

From many sides and professions, the population problem was beginning to be redefined. *Does Overpopulation Mean Poverty?* was the suggestive title of a bright red pamphlet by Joseph Marion Jones, with an introduction by World Bank President Eugene Black. The brochure was issued in 1962 by the Center for International Economic Growth but was promoted, sponsored, financed, and distributed by the population organizations, with help from Mary Lasker.[10]

Important voices from overseas also raised the birth control question and prompted further U.S. editorial comment. General Ayub Khan, president of Pakistan, during his July 1961 visit bluntly told Americans to stop squabbling and spur their scientists to develop a cheap, simple pill. His appeals influenced Vice President Johnson considerably.[11] India's Prime Minister Jawaharlal Nehru also referred to the problem.[12] Yet the only government prepared to offer help was Sweden, which announced in 1962 that birth control would be a major part of its expanding foreign aid program.[13]

While Protestant and Jewish institutions became increasingly positive about the virtues of "responsible parenthood," the Catholic Church found itself under far greater pressures not only from the birth control movement but also from its own communicants. Pope John XXIII reaffirmed traditional Catholic doctrine on birth control in the encyclical *Mater et Magister* of July 15, 1961, but few were completely convinced that it was the last word. A new spirit was in the air. The once-radical proposal that Catholics should stop opposing the practice of birth control by others was gradually being supplanted by the far more revolutionary recognition that many Catholics did not themselves agree with the teachings of their church. By the end of 1962 the first rumors were circulating that Pope John had started to consult very seriously with physicians and demographers as well as bishops and theologians.[14] The slightest hint of doubt in the Vatican powerfully accelerated doubts elsewhere.

But in the United States the pressures that were building up for a change in policy on birth control were aimed at the White House far more than the Vatican. After 1962 the prize to be sought in Washington was no longer just a private meeting with the secretary of state or a speech by a representative at the United Nations but rather the public support of the president and the legislative backing of Congress. In terms of a power struggle, by 1963 the population activists had finally built a scientific and religious coalition strong enough to undermine the organized opposition and large enough to demand attention. In terms of intellectual progress, the 1962-63 *Report* of the Population Council announced:

> During ... 1962 and 1963, a turning point was passed in general public awareness of the problems of population growth. ... The views of scientists became the views of the people, at least of enough people to influence national decisions in enough nations to make an impact on the world. ... Concern with population problems and action on their solution now have come into the public domain.[15]

In more realistic terms the pro and con division of U.S. public opinion had not shifted toward birth control. On the contrary, the opposition of the Catholic man in the street may have increased. But government policy makers, *New York Times* editorial readers, and opinion leaders of various kinds had become much more accustomed to thinking and talking about population. Similarly the leaders of the Catholic opposition were more acutely aware that they could no longer speak with firm assurances of lay Catholic or Vatican support. The change in thinking in the early 1960s was more a subtle change on the part of opinion makers than a massive transformation of national attitudes.

PRESIDENT KENNEDY SPEAKS

For the first Catholic president of the United States, birth control lacked the political priority that he attached to parochial school aid and the international priority that he attached to an effective foreign assistance program. As a matter of principle Kennedy would not give blanket endorsement to Catholic Church doctrine and privately criticized the Catholic bishops. But as a matter of politics Kennedy and his aides still feared that birth control was dynamite. "Endorsing birth control was like endorsing the A.D.A., you lost fifty votes for every one you gained."[16] As a matter of policy, Kennedy and his contemporaries clearly preferred to think in more positive and invigorating terms. What Kennedy once called the "mean paternalism" of birth control was both intellectually unconvincing and emotionally unappealing to him as a shortcut to economic success. Or, as Lee Rainwater put it in his analysis of common pronatilist attitudes, "the good person in a good world has a large family."[17]

Kennedy's top policy aides shared much of his optimism about economic development and his skepticism about birth control as a panacea. Furthermore, McGeorge Bundy, Theodore Sorenson, David Bell, Robert Kennedy, and other associates did not want to embarrass the president by raising the question where it was not strictly necessary. Ralph Dungan, whom Schlesinger described as "a thoughtful Catholic of the John XXIII school,"[18] served as informal liaison with the Catholic Church and gradually became the keeper of the White House gate on birth control. Dungan recognized and sympathized with the liberal stirrings in the Catholic Church but he was more anxious for Kennedy to remain within the limits of Catholic consensus than to use the prestige of the White House to advance the frontiers of birth control.

Nevertheless, President Kennedy's desire for a strong and substantial foreign aid program made it almost impossible to ignore population. His very first Foreign Aid Message pointed out,

> The magnitude of the problem is staggering. In Latin America, for example, population growth is already threatening to outpace economic growth.[19]

But Kennedy deliberately refused to link economic development and birth control as the State Department was trying to do. In a 1961 press converence he observed,

> Population control is a matter which goes very much to the life of a country. It is a personal decision and a national decision which those nations must make. The problem is not altogether an economic one. We help countries which carry out different policies in this regard and it is a judgment in my opinion, which they should make.[20]

Kennedy gave the same answer again in 1962 when asked for his reaction to the Jones pamphlet.[21]

In the summer of 1962 President Kennedy asked Draper, whose views on birth control were then well known, to undertake a confidential mission to Brazil to assess the political and economic status of President Goulard's government. Draper found the situation in Brazil very serious. Robert Kennedy arranged for him to make a personal report to the president. After reporting fully and answering questions on the main purpose of the mission, Draper asked, "Do you have ten or fifteen minutes, Mr. President, to hear about the population problem which is especially serious in Northeast Brazil?" Kennedy replied with interest, "Yes indeed." So Draper described conditions in that area—where per capita income was not much higher than in India and where annual population growth rates of over 3 percent exceeded the annual increase in food and jobs. Kennedy listened attentively and raised several questions.

After Draper's presentation, the president asked, "Why doesn't the Ford Foundation concentrate all of its resources on the population problem around the world?"

Draper replied that the Ford Foundation had done more than any other organization, and that he too had asked John McCloy, then chairman of the board, why the foundation did not do more. McCloy's reply was that there were a lot of other problems to work on, too. A few minutes later, as Draper was leaving, Kennedy commented again at the door, "I just don't see why the Ford Foundation doesn't concentrate on this issue."[22]

The Ford Foundation was indeed expanding its commitments in population, partly because of Rusk's encouragement and partly because of the active campaign Draper and several trustees and staff members had been waging. But the foundation's leaders shared Rusk's fears that there were too few trained people in the field and too great a danger that "highly visible failures" might prejudice future efforts. Kennedy wanted the Ford Foundation to lead but the Ford Foundation's general policy in the early 1960s was that while it would support research and training it would not support action programs or public information (or propaganda) except where the government had first adopted a favorable policy.[23] Until then, Ford Foundation programs in the United States were discreetly directed at the very leaders who were waiting for the foundations to lead.

By the spring of 1963, however, other initiatives from government and private advocates forced the issue to national attention. First, on April 18, Dr. John Rock's book *The Time Has Come, A Catholic Doctor's Proposals to End the Battle Over Birth Control* appeared.[24] The subtitle carried the message. From the clinical professor emeritus of obstetrics and gynecology at Harvard came a plea for tolerance by American Catholics and non-Catholics alike. It was also a plea for research by the American government, and a plea for approval by the Vatican of the new oral contraceptives as a natural, physiological (not artificial) method of birth control. Richard Cardinal Cushing of Boston disagreed with Rock's argument about the pill but took the unusual step of commenting, "In this book there is much that is good."[25]

The very next day, with a timing that was coincidental but a common theme that was not, the National Academy of Sciences released a panel study entitled *The Growth of World Population*. Sponsored and personally supported by Dr. George Kistiakowsky, former science adviser to President Eisenhower, the report grew from his own frustrated recognition that the scientific community outside of government had to move first before the scientists inside government would be allowed to act. Every time Kistiakowsky had tried to urge Eisenhower to do something about population or to stimulate the National Science Foundation he had met great reluctance. Those he conferred with in the Kennedy administration during 1962 and 1963—from the State Department and AID to the White House—strongly encouraged his effort—but warned that if he mentioned their names they would have to deny everything.

Dr. William McElroy, chairman of the Biology Department of Johns Hopkins University, prepared the report including, at Kistiakowsky's insistence, a very specific section on biomedical research. The report did not mince any scholarly words. "Either the birth rate of the world must come down or the death rate must go back up."[26] Since high birth rates impeded economic development and since lower birth rates could be hastened with better, more acceptable contraceptives, the report called for increased government and private support of biomedical, demographic, and social research and training.[27] It was a wholehearted endorsement by the prestigious scientific community for the research approach to government population policy.

Two days later Richard Nixon, then a private citizen, added his voice, calling for a "critical reappraisal" of foreign aid and birth control. This "immensely controversial subject can no longer be swept under the carpet," he maintained. "The United States cannot justify spending billions of dollars for economic assistance for the purpose of raising living standards and discover year after year that population growth outruns growth of the economy.[28]

Planned Parenthood staff and others, including Barnett in the State Department, deliberately encouraged reporters to raise the population issue at the next presidential press conference. Barnett and Baumgartner drafted a sympathetic response for Kennedy. In response to a direct question about the NAS and Rock proposals, Kennedy hedged somewhat, then finally said:

> If your question is, can we do more, should we know more about the whole reproduction cycle, and should this information be made more available to the world so that everyone can make their own judgment, I would think it would be a matter which we could certainly support. . . . Whether we are going to support Dr. Rock's proposal, which is somewhat different, is another question.[29]

With these words President Kennedy gingerly opened the door halfway. He said just enough to legitimize and encourage what was already being said and done but not quite enough to support any significant new programs. He gave legitimacy to the research approach but he still did not touch upon the economic issue.

President Kennedy's last statement on population, on June 5, 1963, came closer than any other to acknowledging the Malthusian implications of population growth. Addressing the World Food Congress in Washington, D.C., he declared:

> Population increases have become a serious concern. . . . The Population growth rate is too often the highest, where hunger is already the most prevalent.[30]

Within the next few months two other former political rivals of President Kennedy added their support for birth control. Adlai Stevenson, then ambassador to the United Nations, spoke to Planned Parenthood in October 1963 about the urgency of the population problem.[31] In a *Saturday Evening Post* article, General Eisenhower candidly admitted he had been wrong in barring government programs and that regardless of religious differences the population problem was too important to be ignored.[32] Other private organizations like the American Assembly endorsed and expanded on the need for more research and for technical assistance, as requested, overseas.[33]

The momentum for support of birth control was clearly building up. Even Kennedy's limited approval of more research and greater access to it was widely hailed by scientists and activists alike. The spring meeting of Planned Parenthood, a symposium on "Man's Future," provided the scenario for coming action. Dr. John Rock urged a massive "Manhattan Project" in medical research to find acceptable means of fertility control. Draper praised Kennedy's "wise leadership" and affirmed that "this is a big milestone passed." Then, with what one observer calls "his ratchet-like tendency" to check any backsliding by immediately moving on to the next step, Draper urged Congress to take up the issue. Draper suggested that if the National Institutes of Health did not have any mandate to conduct applied research—as NIH director Shannon still implied—then Congress should provide a "direct authorization" for a massive, coordinated research and development effort. He further proposed that the money the Clay Committee had just recommended cutting from foreign aid programs be applied instead to educate the world about the population problem.[34]

That was the first direct public appeal to Congress for specific action. Until then, most of the population activists, including Draper, had tiptoed around Congress trying not to stir up opposition and hoping for progress within the less-exposed atmosphere of the executive agencies.[35] But after April 1963 the endorsement of a Catholic president provided protection for more overt moves elsewhere.

Draper was extremely impatient with what he called the "skittishness" of lower-level federal employees who "exaggerated the seriousness" of Catholic opposition.[36] He had talked with Dr. Shannon several times but always came away with the feeling that NIH did not consider contraceptive development its responsibility. He was not satisfied with the usual NIH response that no good applications for research on fertility were ever turned down. He thought NIH should be deliberately stimulating more proposals.[37] He had talked with Secretary of State Rusk and other State and AID officials but he did not agree with the State and AID position that other nations had to move first. He thought the U.S. government could exercise leadership.

In short, at a time when officials in both agencies were still thinking in terms of how to respond to outside initiatives, Draper was advocating a directed research program in NIH and an action program in AID. Fully convinced of the relevance and feasibility of such a course, he was already pressing for higher priority, more resources, and faster timing. Not surprisingly, some officials began to dread his visits. So Draper went directly to Congress.

CONGRESS ACTS

Actually, Congress had not ignored the population problem. Senator J. William Fulbright, (D.-Ark.), chairman of the Foreign Relations Committee, told foreign aid officials in India in 1958 that they certainly should be doing something about population growth even if they did not report it to Congress.[38] Questions came up with increasing frequency at congressional hearings. By 1961 when the Kennedy administration requested $4.3 billion for foreign aid and defended the request by pointing to vast underdeveloped and impoverished populations, Fulbright began to raise even more pointed questions. He asked Under-Secretary of State George Ball whether "more direct action" might not be required to reduce population growth.[39] He privately suggested to the horrified Secretary of the Treasury Douglas Dillon that the population question should be discussed with Latin American nations at the 1961 Montevideo Conference.[40] This frustrating exchange with Wymberley Coerr, acting assistant secretary for Latin America in 1961, explains Fulbright's mounting impatience:

> Fulbright: You say that economic growth of these countries is slower than population growth. Could I conclude that you are concerned about population growth? You think, perhaps, something ought to be done about it?
> Coerr: I would rather not pronounce on the population growth.
> Fulbright: You would not?
> Coerr: I would rather not make any recommendation about the population growth itself.
> Fulbright: Why not? It is no secret.
> Coerr: No, it certainly is no secret . . .
> Fulbright: A large part of this has been brought about by your program because you are working on health conditions in these countries.
> Coerr: That is right, improving their health.
> Fulbright: You talk about health. Why don't you talk about population control? Why is that forbidden to you?
> Coerr: I think you are right, sir, probably it should not be forbidden to me. I just recognize it as a politically sensitive subject.
> Fulbright: I know it is. . . . This is one of the things, among others, that causes me a sense of complete helplessness or hopelessness.[41]

But the largest cuts in the increasingly embattled foreign aid program in 1961, 1962, and 1963 were made in the House of Representatives, not in the Senate. The House Committee on Foreign Affairs included at least three members, Clement Zablocki (D.-Wisc.), Edna Kelly (D.-N.Y.), and James Fulton (R.-Pa.), whose support was needed for the foreign aid bill as a whole but who were openly opposed to birth control. As Fulton put it in 1960:

> I think that a U.S. foreign aid program of economic and military assistance has nothing whatever to do with the population of a country, and especially when birth control cuts across religious views that are strongly held. . . . We in the United States should stay out of sex problems of foreign countries.[42]

A not uncommon view, perhaps, was that of Congressman Barratt O'Hara (D.-Ill.), who projected the official views of the Catholic Church upon the whole country:

> I think the great majority of our Americans, regardless of religion, would be against birth control. There is something in the thought of

birth control that just isn't American, and yet population pressure is
a serious problem.[43]

The administration was clearly more alarmed by the possibility of a
Catholic revolt against foreign aid in the House than by Fulbright's sense of
"helplessness or hopelessness," especially since the Arkansas senator had almost
no Catholic constituents. Rusk continued to deny that the population problem
was merely numbers, emphasizing instead that good health, training, and
technology would make the same numbers of people an asset rather than a
liability.[44]

In the spring of 1963 Draper went to see Senator Fulbright, whom he had
known from Marshall Plan days. He suggested that Fulbright simply include
language in the bill to convince "skittish" bureaucrats that Congress did want
action.

On July 20, 1963, the Senate Foreign Relations Committee, without
opposition, added an amendment offered by Senator Fulbright specifically
authorizing "research into the problems of controlling population growth" and
"technical assistance to cooperating countries in carrying out programs of
population control."[45] This "explicit authority" was provided, the committee
report pointed out, because of the "profound impact of population growth on
economic development."[46]

In the Agency for International Development Dr. Baumgartner thought
the amendment was "fine." Nevertheless the official AID position (described in
a memorandum to the White House on November 25 while Baumgartner was
out of the country) remained "neutral." "The language would convey no
authority not now in the legislation. House conferees are likely to oppose the
provision. The executive branch has been, and we believe should remain
neutral."[47]

In conference with the House of Representatives Zablocki, as expected,
raised objections and the reference to "technical assistance" was dropped. In its
final form, the amendment read: "Funds made available to carry out this
section may be used to conduct research into the problems of population
growth."[48] As Fulbright later told Baumgartner the text "should not be read
legalistically, but . . . should be interpreted as a broad mandate to the administration."[49]

The foreign aid authorization, with Fulbright's amendment, was signed
into law by President Johnson December 16, 1963. What Kennedy had once
considered "remote" had occurred, partly as a result of his own actions, partly
as a result of his administration's apparent inaction.

Three weeks after Fulbright quietly offered his amendment, two other
senators, Joseph S. Clark (D.-Pa.) and Ernest S. Greuning (D.-Alaska), introduced
a formal resolution (S. Con. Res. 56) to increase NIH research and to encourage a
Presidential Commission on Population. In the first postwar speech on the Senate
floor about population, Clark emphasized Dr. Rock's reasoning and appealed to
the National Institutes of Health to "spare but $2 or $3 million a year for fertility
research out of a budget of close to $900 million."[50] "I am confident," Clark
concluded, "that we in Congress can play our part in the solution of one of the
most difficult problems today confronting the human race."

Senator Fulbright's action applied what were basically the policy-setting and administrative oversight powers of the Congress directly to legislation under his own committee's jurisdiction. As committee chairman he required neither outside publicity nor public pressure to get the amendment adopted. Nor was there any statutory need for congressional action at all. Fulbright and AID officials both agreed that AID already possessed full legal power to do everything in the amendment and more besides, but there was a hortatory purpose to be served by specific congressional endorsement in such a sensitive area. Then, as later, AID's refusal to support the amendment confirmed Fulbright's conviction that additional pressure was necessary.

The action of Senators Clark and Gruening, on the other hand, was a call for debate rather than for immediate legislation. Even though it was referred to the Committee on Labor and Public Welfare of which Clark was a senior member, the resolution was not expected to pass in the form introduced. It was primarily a vehicle for hearings and discussion, the first step in making a case for legislation or appropriations. It was an example of Congress, acting in its very broad educational role, trying to air important issues even when no clear solutions were yet in sight. Both of these congressional initiatives were made politically possible by Kennedy's support, prompted specifically by Draper's suggestions but undertaken only because of the long-standing concern of each of the senators involved. Both went beyond any previous executive agency action.

Although the assassination of President Kennedy, the inauguration of the new Johnson administration, and the election campaign of 1964 pushed the issue of birth control out of political sight until 1965, the initiatives taken in 1963 remained on the record. Kennedy had acquiesced in the need for more research. Congress had gone still further in asserting the relevance, feasibility, and increasing importance of a more active U.S. government role. In the foreign aid field the responsibility for implementing such a program clearly rested on AID.

Within AID had anyone suggested in January 1963 that by the end of the year President Kennedy would have endorsed more population research and Congress would have passed new legislation directing AID to move ahead, most officials would have been incredulous. Although Baumgartner did succeed in circulating Gardner's speech, all the other signs were negative. She could not get clearance within AID for the instructions needed by the overseas missions. Moreover in late 1962 Barnett became deputy assistant secretary of State for Far Eastern affairs, under Averell Harriman, leaving no one in the State Department with full-time responsibility for population until 1966.

Even in his new post Barnett tried to press AID officials to be as forthright in their congressional testimony as Gardner had been at the United Nations. In a memorandum signed by Harriman, Barnett cited the "apparent timidity" of AID missions and concluded with the warning:

> General William Draper is but one of those saying privately that
> unless the Administration takes account of the population problem
> in planning its programs of economic assistance, the time will soon
> come when the Congress will consider prolongation of our aid
> activities to be irrational.[1]

Bell did not appreciate this State Department intervention. Three days later, on March 11, the regional assistant secretaries of State met and decided, on Bell's insistence, that future strategy, tactics, and timing on population issues should be left to him, possibly in consultation with the White House. Bell would decide when and whether to use Gardner's still-unpublicized statement or to issue a further clarification. For three and a half months, drafts and revisions of proposed testimony for Congress circulated through AID until the issue finally became academic because half a dozen State Department and AID witnesses, including Rusk, had already answered a variety of questions in a variety of different ways.

ARTICULATING AID POLICY

It was not until late April, after Dr. Rock's book, after the National Academy of Sciences report, and, above all, after President Kennedy's statement, that Baumgartner finally succeeded in sending to the field the explanatory airgram that had been promised in December. Referring to the new "focus of public attention" on population, the AID airgram affirmed that AID was now interested in the subject of population but indicated that any real assistance would have to come from other sources. Specifically, the message identified Baumgartner's office as the focal point for population in AID-Washington; listed U.S. support for various UN activities including a proposed $500,000 contribution which was later made to the World Health Organization for research on human reproduction; expressed willingness to consider requests to support "research activities" or to build "research institutions" for social science, demography, and census work; and asked that Washington be notified of requests for help. On the other hand, after quoting President Kennedy on "socio-biological aspects" the airgram pointed out that since AID had "no specialized professional competence in this area" requests would be referred to private institutions, and in the U.S. government to the Public Health Service and Children's Bureau.[2]

President Kennedy's statement and the lack of public opposition encouraged the State Department to advance. Gardner obtained first departmental and then White House clearance for an amplifying policy statement to be made at an American Assembly meeting on population on May 4. There he announced more specifically that the United States would support international cooperation in demography, medical research on reproduction, and the establishment of general health services (which could provide the necessary infrastructure for family planning).[3] The impact of Kennedy's statement was also reflected in the difference between Secretary Rusk's equivocating response to the House Committee on Foreign Affairs on April 5 and his strong affirmation to the Senate committee on June 11 that Gardner's latest words were "officially spoken on behalf of the Department." In fact, he assured Fulbright that if countries "asked for assistance in terms of information, in terms of technical assistance, in terms of building up their medical centers, their population research centers, and things of that sort, yes, I think we would."[4]

AID also became bolder. During the 12 months following, two more airgrams were dispatched to all AID missions overseas. AIDTO Circular A-44 (August 10, 1963) was a follow-up to the UN secretary-general's demographic questionnaire. AID-Washington asked whether the host country was able to respond to the inquiry; whether demographic assistance had been requested; and, if not, why not, or if so, with what results. A second airgram, AIDTO Circular XA-1149 (April 17, 1964), included a list of books, articles, and other educational materials on population that AID could supply on request. Together they represented a small start toward an information program.

In mid-April 1963 Baumgartner's office was reorganized and expanded somewhat. Dr. Philip Lee was recruited to replace Dr. Eugene Campbell, a birth

control opponent who had directed AID health programs. The affable Philip
Lee got along better with David Bell than did dynamic, talkative Leona
Baumgartner, but he did not push as hard. Later Dr. Edward O'Rourke and Dr.
Bruce Jessup also joined Human Resources and Social Development and in
December 1963 the noted demographer Irene Taeuber became a regular consultant. Although Draper's suggestions that full-time population officers be
appointed "in every country where population is expanding at an excessive
rate" was not taken very seriously by Lee or Baumgartner—nor were funds
available—a Population Reference and Research Branch was officially established within HRSD in June 1964.

Events overseas also were pushing AID toward a bolder posture. The First
Asian Population Conference was held in late 1963 in New Delhi under the
auspices of the Economic Commission for Asia and the Far East. The conference, which was by, for, and about governments, concluded with a government appeal to all UN agencies to provide technical assistance on request for
research and action "in all aspects of population problems."[5] At the Asian
conference, for the first time Communist hostility to birth control was somewhat muted. Baumgartner was an active participant. She reassured the Catholic
Philippines that "natural" methods of birth control were also included.[6] The
Asian governments (five of which already had programs) were well ahead of the
rest of the world in the specifics of birth control work. "The Asian Population
Conference," Baumgartner pointed out, "marks the great divide between de-
liberation and the dedication to decision, plan and program."[7]

In Washington, too, a lesser divide seemed to have been passed after
Kennedy's statement in 1963. At Bell's suggestion Baumgartner and Gardner
began to touch congressional bases. Senators Fulbright and Humphrey urged
AID to move ahead "quietly."[8] Congressman Otto Passman, generally considered the scourge of AID, expressed his private approval for both research
and technical assistance, since population growth might otherwise "eat up
everything we had poured into the foreign aid program."[9] Even Congressman
Zablocki indicated that he would not object to family planning research and
study as long as it was not overemphasized. All the congressional reactions
turned out to be much more favorable than expected.

Yet when Baumgartner tried to send a further summary of developments
and another policy statement to the field in 1964, no one, from Stevenson,
Bell, and Rusk to Dungan and Bundy in the White House seemed to feel that it
was necessary. The subject had already been talked to death, they thought. It
was "a dead issue," a boring question already settled, she was told.

Indeed, after nearly three years of off-the-record consultation, trial-
balloon public statements, and conciliatory dialogues about "our pluralistic
society," an acceptable formulation of public policy had been reached. As
Leona Baumgartner put it in a 1964 speech at the Johns Hopkins University:

> First of all, what we do and say must be based on a concern for
> human well-being and on facts uncovered by studies of the relations
> of population growth to economic and social development as well as
> on results of biomedical research programs now under way. . . .

Second. . . . There is no one solution. . . . A balanced program to raise the plans of economic, social, and family relationships is needed both at home and abroad.

Third, it is recognized that the decisions as to population policies and their implementation in other countries are to be made by individual countries and families in accord with their own needs and values. . . . The U.S. government feels it desirable that all health facilities supported by public funds shall provide such freedom of choice, so that persons of all faiths are given equal opportunities to exercise their choice without offense to their consciences. . . .

And, finally, in accord with our government's support of the United Nations, its regional commisions, and specialized agenices, as well as the tradition of governmental co-operation with private groups and friendly governments, we stand ready to work cooperatively with such groups.[10]

Protected in such humanitarian generalities, AID population policy did not indeed present much of a target for political attack or even a subject for discussion. For the moment the great bogey of coercion was thoroughly dissolved. At the same time there were no specific AID projects to criticize. Moreover, AID and State Department officials had already made a considerable concession to Catholic opinion. Vastly relieved as they had been to find that Catholics would not really oppose research and information programs, the policy makers on their part had leaned over backward to assure Catholic spokesmen that the U.S. government would not become directly involved in the contraceptive business. Contraceptives had been on the prohibited list for commodity assistance since 1948. Senators Fulbright and Humphrey had both indicated, when pressed, that the only AID actions that might be embarrassing to Congress were large shipments of "already manufactured" contraceptives.[11] Gardner conceded therefore in his May 4 speech, with Baumgartner's agreement, that the implementation of family planning programs remained an area where major disagreements "exist or will continue to exist for the foreseeable future." He concluded, "The provision of materials for this purpose can best be done by those governments whose citizens are not divided on this question, by private foundations and by business firms."[12]

This prohibition was, like many AID restrictions, erected into an even higher barrier within the agency than the senators had intended. For instance, when Barnett urged AID in May 1964 to provide an investment guarantee to a U.S. firm for construction of a contraceptive manufacturing facility in India at the Indian government's request, Bell and his deputy William Gaud both drew back. "It is not clear to me," Gaud wrote, "why the government of India has to use our rupees rather than its own to support its population planning activities."[13] In 1964, he and Bell did not want anything to do with contraceptives.

But the peculiar anomaly of a talked-to-death policy combined with no program at all was beginning to be recognized. Baumgartner, Lee, and Jessup knew they had first to convince the economists who dominated AID that population programs would make some difference. They began during 1964, in contracts with universities and research groups and a series of policy meetings, to build up the economic arguments and to specify exactly what help AID could provide. Slowly, carefully, and quietly they began to consider how the new AID policy could be translated into feasible projects.

DEVELOPING A LATIN AMERICAN PROGRAM

While Baumgartner and her colleagues struggled over the relationship between an articulated policy and a feasible program, elsewhere in AID another population program was proceeding unexpectedly fast without regard for any policy statements. In the Alliance for Progress, Moscoso had asked Dr. Edgar Berman in 1962 to take a look at the Latin American population problem. Berman was not a bureaucrat. He insisted on serving independently in a consultant capacity. He wanted direct access to Moscoso, to Dungan in the White House, and to friends on the Hill. Baumgartner was apprehensive about a second population effort but Dungan as well as Moscoso wanted Berman to make a start, even if no meaningful results could be achieved for some time. So in the region where opposition to birth control seemed strongest Berman moved forward where angels feared to tread.

First he made contacts in the United States. The Latin American Science Board of the National Academy of Sciences agreed to serve in an advisory capacity for AID. Meetings with the Milbank Memorial Fund, Population Council, Population Reference Bureau, and Planned Parenthood showed Berman what a small but enthusiastic start had been made by the private organizations. With Dungan's help Berman sought out Catholic leaders. He conferred with Monsignor James Gremillion and others at the Catholic Relief Services; he discovered that Dr. Benedict Duffy wanted to start a research center on the rhythm method at Georgetown University (which the Ford Foundation later financed while Duffy joined Berman's AID staff); and he learned that Notre Dame had a Latin American family study project. Berman was surprised to find out that some of these U.S. Catholic groups wanted his help as badly as he wanted theirs—and that some of the population organizations were much more reluctant than Catholics to accept AID support.

After a number of meetings with most of the private and government agencies involved, in January 1964 a Population Office was formally established in the Alliance for Progress— the first in the agency.[14] Then Berman turned to Latin America. In the first six months of 1964 he visited seven Latin American countries, trying to see heads of state, finance ministers, planning commissions, medical leaders, and then the highest representatives of the Catholic Church. To his further surprise, most of the Latin Americans were eager to talk to him about population, but even more eager to find out from him what their own colleagues had said. The issues that Berman discussed with them—the economic, social, and health hazards of rapid population growth—most of then had never discussed with one another.[15]

After that indication of interest, Moscoso and Berman obtained the quiet approval of the Senate Foreign Relations Committee for two grants in fiscal year 1964. They represented the first Washington-funded, U.S.-dollar support for population work by AID.[16] These grants went to CELADE in Chile, a UN-sponsored demographic training center ($100,000) and to the Pan American Health Organization for a feasibility study on research training programs ($40,000).

This activity was not unnoticed in the House of Representatives. Zablocki complained to Assistant Secretary Thomas Mann (who replaced Moscoso in 1963) that "nowhere in this legislation has AID been given authority to promote control of population growth by scientific devices." Mann assured him that AID only supported "talk" and "private concerns that are largely engaged in an educational problem [sic]."[17] Ten days after the congressman's criticism, Mann's deputy William Rogers addressed a Puerto Rican meeting of the International Planned Parenthood Federation, which AID had helped to finance. Representatives, mostly governmental, attended from every country in Latin America.[18]

Barely a month later Berman and his assistant Lee Bullitt (wife of an assistant secretary of the treasury and as little intimidated by the AID bureaucracy as Berman) dispatched a five-page airgram to all the Latin American missions. Unusually forthright and positive, the airgram quoted President Kennedy and asserted:

AID is prepared to assist host governments as fully and effectively as possible in the areas of (a) information, (b) training, (c) research, and (d) institution-building. . . . We now have the opportunity to convert the broad principles of AID policy into meaningful programs for Latin America.[19]

The missions were instructed to "consider the population program as a priority area." Citing a number of specific proposals as "the product of intensive examination" by the prestigious National Academy of Sciences advisory group, the AID missions were further requested:

1. "to designate a high official to be responsible for population programs" in each mission;
2. to inform host governments that AID considers it "appropriate" further to develop population programs; and
3. to report promptly to AID-Washington "any indications of interest by host governments or activities by public or private organizations."[20]

Unlike Baumgartner, Berman did not clear his airgrams with Bell, Gaud, or four other bureaus. Less than a week after Bell had declined to discuss with Rusk or send to the field a much less forceful statement that Leona Baumgartner had been working on for months, AIDTO Circular LA-158 (May 11, 1964) entitled "Action Program—Population" was dispatched to Latin America.

Even Draper and Canfield, who were beginning to be regarded in Washington as population fanatics, expressed astonishment at Berman's activities. Canfield predicted that he would soon be fired. In fact, Berman (with

Moscoso's and Mann's encouragement) broke all the precepts of stated AID policy. First, he took on an area where everyone assumed that population control was contrary to national culture, conscience, and habit. Second, he took the initiative himself in finding individuals and organizations who would use help rather than waiting for requests to come to him. Third, he emphasized the private sector and international agencies and paid little attention to the presence or absence of an official government population policy. Finally, he did what very few other AID and State Department officials have done even yet: he sought out the very highest-ranking officials who would see him and brought the issue directly and candidly to their attention. With great charm and a gallant air, he carried off what many thought impossible.

Berman had a separate population unit in January 1964 five months before the HRSD unit. He had a larger population budget in fiscal years 1964 and 1965 than the rest of the agency combined, and he insisted on having a population officer in every Latin American mission nearly a full year before the other missions were asked to appoint them. Although many ambassadors and U.S. missions in Latin America did very little to implement Berman's appeal, a clear start had been made.

Admittedly, the Alliance for Progress enjoyed a privileged place in the State Department and AID and a much more generous appropriation. Admittedly, too, Edgar Berman had less official standing than Leona Baumgartner, an assistant administrator with worldwide responsibility. He was less likely to call his own free-wheeling activities the position of the U.S. government. Therefore he could say more. But the two critical variables in the population program seem to have been the strong support from the top—Moscoso, Mann, Rogers, Jack Vaughn, Lincoln Gordon—and Berman's own enterprise. After the support from above disappeared and Berman, Duffy, and their immediate successor, George Coleman, left, the program declined appreciably.[21] But in the mid-1960s when the issue was still controversial the Latin American region had led the agency in suggesting that population be considered "a priority area" in U.S. foreign aid.

Thus by late 1964 the U.S. government had moved a considerable distance from President Eisenhower's assertion that birth control was "not our business." The Kennedy administration came into office publicly committed to the view that population was a legitimate policy issue even though most of the top officials were privately determined not to raise it. Below the top level, however, a handful of activists were convinced that population growth was important, so important that the government had to find a way to do something about it.

The first steps were assigning personnel and semiopenly discussing the issue. Well-supplied with advice and encouragement from private groups, fortified by the first signs of a religious accommodation, and pressured by the United Nations and foreign governments, the U.S. government advocates moved cautiously ahead to define the problem and identify program possibilities. Sometimes they exceeded their authority and found themselves rebuffed. Sometimes they rebuffed the increasingly insistent activists outside government who were willing to take much greater risks to achieve a decisive result. But generally the policy shift proceeded without major setback. Within three years the State Department and then AID were officially on record, first, that population policy was relevant to economic development, and second, that a population program concentrating on research and information was politically feasible and technically useful.

10

PRESIDENT JOHNSON
SPEAKS OUT,
1965

The year 1965 was in the words of one journalist "the year in which the politicians, at home and abroad, awoke to the population explosion."[1] As before, the progress publicly recorded was, on the one hand, a continuation of accelerating behind the scenes activity and, on the other, a reflection of new people in key positions and new problems rising to national attention. As before, the arguments of relevance were repeated, refined, and reenforced but the major policy debates of the middle 1960s centered on questions of feasibility and priority. To what extent was it feasible to provide help beyond information and research? And then, to what extent did birth control deserve priority over other programs in order to achieve the basic objectives of the Johnson administration?

Immediately after the 1964 election activists both inside and outside of government were ready and waiting to raise the issues to the highest levels of government. On November 9 Draper announced that former Presidents Eisenhower and Truman would serve as honorary chairmen of Planned Parenthood.[2] Each had agreed separately to Draper's invitation—on condition that the other also accept. Thus, both were enlisted in the cause they had once deplored. Thomas Mann, then assistant secretary of State and U.S. coordinator for the Alliance for Progress, became the highest U.S. official yet to address a Planned Parenthood gathering. Contrary to the official line that still emphasized government requests and avoided all reference to Planned Parenthood, Mann candidly admitted that the alliance was already working with private organizations here and in Latin America.[3]

Shortly after the election both William H. Draper, Jr., and John D. Rockefeller 3rd, sought appointments with President Johnson. To their disappointment the president did not want to see them. After several attempts AID officials were emphatically advised not to send any more birth control advocates to the White House.

In mid-November Rockefeller was invited instead for lunch with Secretary Rusk and other officials at the State Department. Rockefeller strongly urged creation of a presidential commission to study the whole population problem. Rusk and most of the others were equally strongly opposed. They were afraid that any such commission, acting under White House sponsorship, might provoke a premature and unnecessary confrontation with the Catholic Church that could only embarrass the president. Out of the impasse came an alternative suggestion: that the president include some reference to population in the State of the Union Message. Rusk agreed to try to arrange it.

The same suggestions reached the White House through several other channels. Rockefeller also spoke to McGeorge Bundy, then Johnson's top White House adviser on foreign policy. Bundy was equally negative about the commission but agreed that the president might make some public statement about the problem. Cass Canfield was in touch with several personal friends of President and Mrs. Johnson, including Horace Busby in the White House, about the possibility of a statement. Hugh Moore ran an advertisement in Texas papers to catch the president's eye after he had been talked out of his first plan to organize a birth control march on the White House. Leona Baumgartner was in touch with Donald Hornig, President Johnson's science adviser, who was also developing a possible policy statement for Johnson.[4]

Most important, Secretary Rusk as he had promised sent a memorandum directly to the president in late November noting that:

> .... President Kennedy made the subject of population a matter proper for urgent and responsible public consideration, and did so without having to lend explicit support to particular programs— except research. By moving a little further along this line, it is possible, I believe, for our government to avoid becoming a target for attack, and still encourage responsible research and program activity on many fronts, both governmental and private.[5]

He advised against a commission but recommended that Johnson express concern in the State of the Union Message. Rusk also suggested that the president assign someone on the White House staff responsibility for population matters, that he "direct the NIH to explore" ways to respond "to the increasing demand for more knowledge about human fertility," and that he "direct other agencies to expand research, training, and health services related to the population problem." Rusk's memorandum to the president of December 1, 1964, was reminiscent of McGhee's 1961 suggestions that Rusk had rejected but even more specifically designed to activate domestic agencies.

The various imputs converged on the desk of Richard Goodwin, Johnson's speech writer. The outcome was a single sentence in the State of the Union Message, delivered January 4, 1965:

> I will seek new ways to use our knowledge to help deal with the explosion in world population and the growing scarcity in world resources.[6]

Only 25 words out of several thousand, yet in those words President Johnson gave greater encouragement to the birth control movement than any of his predecessors had done. Although reflecting the traditional concept of over-population and static resources rather than the newer formulation of economic growth and development, the president's statement set a new and deliberate priority upon the issue. The sentence was an open invitation to federal agencies to move forward more freely. It was undoubtedly the most-quoted sentence in the message.

Despite Johnson's desire to remain somewhat aloof from the birth control activists and to spring his own surprises upon them, he fully accepted the economic and health arguments for birth control and questioned only how fast and how far he could move without provoking resistance, either from Catholics or later from black militants. He did not want to alarm the pope, just to prod him gently and steadily in the direction of change. He also wanted to be sure that everything was checked out first with the Catholic Church. "You can do a lot if you observe the amenities," he would insist.

During 1965 President Johnson volunteered four specific references to the population problem. They represented a "calculated escalation" designed partly to test the public reaction but increasingly to encourage federal government officials to act. At the twentieth-anniversary celebration of the United Nations in San Francisco (June 25, 1965), Johnson urged:

> Let us in all our lands—including this land—face forthrightly the mutiplying problems of our multiplying populations and seek the answers to this most profound challenge to the future of all the world. Let us act on the fact that less than five dollars invested in population control is worth a hundred dollars invested in economic growth.[7]

When John Gardner was being sworn in as secretary of Health, Education, and Welfare, Johnson declared:

> This Administration is seeking new ideas and it is certainly not going to discourage any new solutions to the problems of population growth and distribution.[8]

Upon the opening of the Second World Population Conference in Belgrade, August 30, 1965, President Johnson sent a special message to United Nations Secretary-General U Thant, which Ben Duffy wrote and routed through the State Department in record time:

> . . . it is my fervent hope that your great assemblage of population experts will contribute significantly to the knowledge necessary to solve this transcendent problem. Second only to the search for peace, it is humanity's greatest challenge.[9]

Of these four statements—which were widely acclaimed and circulated by the population activists—only the San Francisco comment aroused any criticism. The purely economic formulation that assigned a quantitative value to population control 20 times higher than to other economic development programs annoyed Latin Americans, who suspected that Johnson only wanted to reduce foreign aid; it annoyed some health professionals who saw their own values ignored; it annoyed many Catholics, like Ralph Dungan, then ambassador to Chile, who feared that what communists called the "Johnson genocide" approach to economic development would put economic efficiency above common humanity; and it annoyed economists of different theoretical schools who doubted that any precise formulations of economic benefit could be derived entirely from measures of demographic change. The reactions were an example of the pitfalls that lurked along any but the broadest, most unspecific pathways of population policy.

Johnson's first population statements were directed toward the foreign problem. But within the United States birth control was becoming increasingly relevant to domestic goals. Willard Wirtz, secretary of Labor, and Stewart Udall, secretary of the Interior, whose department provided health care to impoverished American Indians and the Pacific territorial islands, were the first cabinet members to endorse birth control in trial balloon statements preceding Johnson's comment. They saw it as a domestic economic benefit.[10]

At the heart of Johnson's Great Society program was the war on poverty, formally initiated by Congress in 1964 and directed by Sargent Shriver, President Kennedy's brother-in-law. Just as during the Kennedy administration a stronger government commitment to the strategy of economic development overseas inevitably focussed more attention on the population factor, so the commitment of the Johnson administration to a U.S. war on poverty focused attention on the big families and the lack of adequate birth control facilities characteristic of the American poor. Television scenes of large impoverished families became in effect the best advertisement for Planned Parenthood. Shriver agreed that a "local option" policy would permit communities to support birth control if they wished.[11] The first birth control project in Corpus Christi, Texas, was actually underway before Johnson's State of the Union Message.

By late 1965 more than a dozen projects—developed largely by Planned Parenthood affiliates—were under way in which the Office of Economic Opportunity was financing medical personnel, clinics, and even contraceptive supplies for indigent women. Although Shriver and particularly his wife Eunice Kennedy Shriver insisted on restrictions against public propaganda, against sterilizations, against unmarried women, and even on dollar limits on contraceptives—all of which were strongly opposed by Planned Parenthood and some officials in HEW—his program was in fact publicly subsidizing birth control services at a time when other agencies were still talking about research and information.[12] A policy that Kennedy might not have relished made genuine good sense to Congress and to President Johnson. In fact, Johnson once commented to a group of visitors at the White House, "Why should a woman with money be able to control her family size while a poor woman has got nowhere to go? We're going to quit that." As far as foreign aid was concerned Johnson was equally down to earth—if there were not enough doctors to provide family services in a country like India, the sensible approach for the United States was to help them out by sending jeeps.[13]

Johnson's wholehearted support for family planning services to under-developed nations overseas and to poor families at home pushed the research strategy of the early 1960s into the background. Planned Parenthood had at first greeted the State of the Union Message with a plea for a new $100 million research effort,[14] but attention quickly shifted toward federal support of service programs. A significant goal-directed research program at the National Institutes of Health was still opposed by Dr. Shannon, the NIH director, and by Congressman Fogarty (D.-R.I.), a Catholic, who was chairman of the Labor-HEW Appropriations Subcommittee and NIH's most generous advocate.[15]

Other benefits of birth control were highlighted in the spring of 1965 by several major developments that had been long in the making. In May, the National Academy of Sciences issued a second report on *The Growth of U.S. Population* that called family planning "a basic human right."[16] Even more significant, in June 1965 the Supreme Court finally ruled on an issue Planned Parenthood had been litigating for nearly 10 years. By a 7 to 2 vote the Court overturned the "uncommonly silly" Connecticut law that prohibited the use of contraceptives and proclaimed a new marital "right to privacy."[17]

The timing of President Johnson's 1965 statements also coincided with a quantum jump in birth control technology—from condoms, diaphragms, and douches to the pill and intrauterine device (IUD). Even the *Saturday Evening Post*, the voice of small-town America, approvingly called these two new methods "implements of . . . one of the most dramatic socio-medical revolutions the world has ever known."[18] Certainly until medical science had devised means of fertility control that could work in the city slums and the illiterate rural areas of the underdeveloped world no large-scale government program was possible. By 1965 the pill was proving itself a remarkably popular and effective method in the United States, regularly used by about 4 million women.[19] Also by 1965 intrauterine devices had been widely tested overseas. Following the successful second International Conference on Intra-Uterine Contraception, sponsored by the Population Council in October 1964, IUDs were just about to be incorporated in the new nationwide programs of Taiwan, Korea, Hong Kong, Singapore, India, and Pakistan.[20] President Johnson's political endorsement of birth control came just as medical and popular endorsement of the new techniques opened the way for the very programs that could use substantial government support. To put it another way, the research of U.S. scientists had made technically feasible what President Johnson in 1965 declared to be both politically feasible and nationally important.

AID MOVES—SLOWLY

What was the effect in AID of a presidential commitment obviously intended for the foreign aid field? How much difference did four presidential statements make in 1965 for a policy that was ambiguously articulated and a program that was just beginning to move?

In retrospect the president's words seem to have made a tremendous difference. Virtually all official AID accounts of population programs from

1965 through 1968 cite Johnson's statement as the beginning of the AID population program. Earlier expenditures were not even recorded. The State of the Union Message was followed two months later by a new AID airgram announcing that technical assistance (although not contraceptives) would be available for family planning and, by the first funding, just over $2 million, for population. After January 1965 AID officials began making public speeches in the United States about AID support for population.

But actually there is considerable evidence that within AID the president's statement did not turn night into day or alter policy radically at all. In fact all of the actions taken in the next six months had been decided upon in principle in December 1964 and were not substantially changed as a result of Johnson's initiative. The reconstructed accounts, the repetition of Johnson's statements, the protection afforded by the president's support eventually clouded the fact that AID policy was in the short run much less influenced by the president's words than by its own internal momentum—and its own internal constraints.

Informal requests for help had by late 1964 come to AID from the governments of India, Pakistan, South Korea, Turkey, and the United Arab Republic. Further guidelines were due to be sent to the field. In December 1964 two executive staff meetings were held on population policy. The immediate need, Leona Baumgartner felt, was to persuade AID economists to look beyond five-year projections, to recognize the new birth control technology, and to overcome their repugnance toward some of the publicity tactics of the birth control activists. A memorandum prepared by Bruce Jessup with help from Dr. Leslie Corsa of the University of Michigan argued for U.S. government support of research, training, and technical assistance, including grants to expand maternal and child health services, loans for jeeps and other transport for family planning workers, a release of local currencies held by the United States, and more attention to demographic factors throughout the economic planning process. Most convincing to Assistant Administrator Hollis Chenery at the December meeting and to other critical AID economists, who tended to look on population as an independent variable not subject to deliberate alteration, was a very simple graph based on Pakistani statistics that showed how per capita income would be affected by 1970 both with and without a comprehensive family planning program.[21]

At the AID executive staff meeting held on December 1, 1964, a definite decision was made to go beyond the information policy defined by Gardner and the research policy authorized in the 1963 Fulbright amendment:

> It is proposed that the full complement of assistance tools available to AID be brought to bear on the population problem. This would involve: . . . provision of commodity inputs (with the exception of contraceptives); . . . authorizing releases of counterpart and PL-480 Loans and Grants . . . provision of technical assistance . . . it is clear that private resources in the U.S. cannot alone cope with the demand . . . . We therefore propose to provide on request, technical assistance for less developed country family planning programs. To the extent possible, such assistance will be given in the context of maternal and child health projects.[22]

That decision, proceeding to Rusk in draft form for approval, then back to Baumgartner's office and the program office for drafting, led directly to the airgram that subsequent history attributed to President Johnson's intervention. The first draft of the airgram, by Philip Lee, was written before Johnson spoke (December 29, 1964); the next draft, by Robert Smith in the program office, included the president's sentence in the third paragraph (January 1, 1965). During most of January the airgram was cleared through all the AID bureaus. Characteristically, Berman wanted to go faster to make grants to Planned Parenthood openly; the Near East-South Asia Bureau with the biggest populations as well as the biggest government programs was most negative, questioning the need for either special population officers or additional resources. The AID information officer complained that there was not much specific news in the message, but David Bell wanted to keep the airgram deliberately low-key. Various Catholic advisers quietly reviewed and approved it.

Horace Busby in the White House complained that the AID draft included too much "strained review of U.S. policy positions" which contributed "nothing except a false and unneeded image of continuity."[2][3] As with Richard Gardner's United Nations speech in 1961 the first internal formulations sought to play down the extent of the policy shift. Only later was the policy significance upgraded and even exaggerated. It was Busby who put President Johnson's statement first. AID officials agreed with some of Busby's editing that made the first page "more dramatic" but they insisted on including their review of policy positions. Except for the opening statement by President Johnson the final text reflected prior AID policy decided upon and drafted within AID.

Therefore, despite President Johnson's support and White House clearance, AIDTO Circular Airgram 280 sounded cautious and negative. Although the message actually authorized AID missions to support a broader range of activities than before, it conveyed less sense of priority and urgency than Edgar Berman's Latin American directive of May 1964. Basically, the guidelines asked that each AID mission assign one officer to become familiar with population dynamics and related programs (not a high official, as in the 1964 Latin American message); and indicated that:

> . . . Requests for technical assistance will be considered as in any other field, on a case by case basis. We are prepared to . . . consider requests for commodity assistance . . . such as vehicles and education equipment . . . also . . . requests to assist in local currency financing.

But for each positive statement there seemed to be at least two negatives or qualifications, for example,

> Requests for assistance in this field, as in others, will continue to be considered only if made or approved by appropriate host government authorities. Such assistance would, in any case, be merely additive to the host country's own efforts and assistance from other sources . . . .
>   AID will not consider requests for contraceptive devices or equipment for manufacture of contraceptives. Experience has made

it clear that the cost of these latter items is not a stumbling block in countries that are developing effective programs.

... Finally, AID does not advocate any particular method of family regulation .... Freedom of choice should be available.[24]

Nowhere did the airgram identify population as a "priority program." Nowhere did it suggest, as the 1964 Latin American message did, that the time had come "to convert the broad principles of AID policy into meaningful programs."

Clearly, Johnson's—and Rusk's—recognition that the time was politically right was not fully shared in AID. David Bell told his staff he would rather be criticized for going too slowly than for going too fast. He was most insistent that the program be an inconspicuous, relatively minor part of AID's activity. Bell's decision to proceed was minimal; it was not, like President Johnson's, an attempt to influence or lead others; it was rather what Bell himself called "catching up with the L.A. program." It reflected not only Bell's reluctance to jeopardize any of the rest of the AID program but also his continuing doubt that birth control could be an effective part of economic development or that the United States could promote it without a political backlash from developing countries.

Following the airgram, by the end of fiscal 1965 some 15 different grants totalling $2,134,000 (of which $1,197,000 was in the Latin American Bureau) were made and publicly acknowledged, a funding level that had been agreed upon in December before the president's statement. The largest went to the Universities of California (Berkeley), Notre Dame, Johns Hopkins, and North Carolina to provide a variety of long-term professional training and consultative services. Some of these extended programs that the Population Council and the Ford Foundation had originally supported. Agreements that had been made in the past with government agencies like the Census Bureau and National Center for Health Statistics were now more explicitly oriented toward the problems of population change.[25]

The newest elements of the program in 1965 were, on the Latin American side, support for private organizations such as the Latin American Center for Studies of Population and Family (CELAP) headed by a controversial Jesuit priest in Chile; the Colombian Institute for Social Development (ICODES) to prepare audio-visual materials; the International Planned Parenthood Federation (Western Hemisphere Region) for family planning conferences and education; the American Assembly of Columbia University for a population conference of Latin America leaders in Cali, Colombia; and the Population Council for various research and analysis projects. From Baumgartner's office there were innovations in the support of a Children's Bureau (HEW) training program for foreign midwives and of a Johns Hopkins orientation course for AID personnel.

What difference did President Johnson's statement really make if the basic policy shift had been decided upon in December and the specific program and budgetary actions were already under way?

First, the president had changed the whole atmosphere and environment in which the issue would be handled. Originally a daring step quietly taken by a nervous agency, support for population was after January a legitimate government policy supported by the president.

Second, although the language of the airgram and the grants did not fully reflect this new atmosphere of approval, the very fact that the airgram was sent was significant. Many plans, projections, and airgrams had been prepared by the Population Branch in the past and would be prepared for several years to come without necessarily being dispatched or implemented. Had President Johnson not spoken, the December decisions would probably not have become the March-June actions. Had plans not already been under way for a presidential statement, the December decisions might not have been made.

The effect of the president's interest was, moreover, cumulative. When the first reference was followed by three more statements in 1965, when the Gruening hearings both publicized and pushed the president ahead, all the AID initiatives were reinforced. The momentum was forward. Although in the next few years many opportunities in AID were lost through inertia or nonaction, few were deliberately vetoed as they had been before.

Certainly for the agency as a whole the president's support was a powerful moral stimulus. In late 1964 Leona Baumgartner had concluded that "what we need is less talk and more action." After President Johnson's statement in January 1965, just as after President Kennedy's statement in April 1963, it was easier for AID both to talk and to act. In many cases talk began to lead more directly toward action. The gist of the March 3 airgram, for instance, was made immediately available to the public in a question-and-answer format. Dr. Lee repeated the language in a March speech at Michigan State University. Each of the regional bureaus in Washington followed the Latin American example by assigning someone to handle population. The Far East and the Near East-South Asia Bureaus dispatched additional messages of encouragement to their overseas mission.[26] In Taiwan and Korea where local currency had already been used to support family planning, this practice was at last publicly acknowledged and encouraged by Washington.

OBSTACLES WITHIN AID

President Johnson affirmed in terms that no federal official could dispute that the population problem was relevant to government policies and that government programs to deal with it were politically feasible. But, as many presidents have noted, even the president's orders do not always get carried out. It was quite obvious in 1965, for example, that very few AID officials really believed, as Johnson had said, that "less than five dollars invested in population control is worth a hundred dollars invested in economic growth."

From the top of the agency right down to the lowest levels the priority of the issue was evaluated and the possibilities for action were weighed by existing institutional and personal standards rather than by the president's words. Thus David Bell told the House Foreign Affairs Committee,

The population field, as distinct from the food field, is not a field in
which AID has any major activities. While I expect our activities will
gradually grow, I foresee no big change in the immediate future.[27]

Despite President Johnson's interest in jeeps for India, most of the vehicles
were negotiated as part of a complex AID loan agreement and not actually
available until mid-1969.

Symbolic of the agency's "Yes-I-will; no-I-won't" attitude toward birth
control was the refusal to provide any kind of funding for contraceptives. It
was the first and most obvious target for activist criticism. "Pretty timid," was
the verdict of the *New York Times*. "This plan to provide propaganda in ways
without supplying the means is an obvious attempt to appease foreign and
domestic critics of birth control."[28] In part, of course, this was true. Catholic
opposition centered around contraceptives, since these were the "artificial
methods" specifically condemned by Rome. Bell called contraceptives "the
reddest red flag of all." Liberal Catholic support for the March airgram
depended, Dr. Duffy emphasized, on four points: no coercion, freedom of
choice, only responding to requests, and no contraceptives.[29] The principle of
family planning was permissible, but the contraceptives were not.

To some extent AID's ban on contraceptives—particularly after 1965—
reflected still another ambiguity in AID policy. How was it logically possible to
affirm in one sentence that "freedom of choice" as to method "should be
available" and in almost the next sentence that "the cost of contraceptives is
not a stumbling block?" These statements were actually made in the year 1965
when nearly 5 million U.S. women were regularly taking oral contraceptives at
a monthly cost of $1 to $2 and when any casual newspaper reader knew that
"the pill" was an important element in the agonizing reappraisal by the
Catholic Church.

These apparent contradictions were reconciled by the assumption most of
the population professionals made in 1965 regardless of U.S. or Puerto Rican
experience, that the pill at any price was unsuitable for the developing countries. If, as they believed, the little plastic IUD, which could be produced
cheaply anywhere, was the new solution to the world's population problem,
then it was true that the cost of contraceptives was not an important stumbling
block to an effective national program.

The controversy of pill versus IUD, as it developed in the AID program,
can be seen in some ways as a continuation of the old activist-scientist rivalries.
The activists, usually associated with the various Planned Parenthood associations, had to supply whatever methods their patients demanded or else close
their clinics. Increasingly Planned Parenthood clinics in the U.S. and overseas
relied on the pill because that was what the women seemed to prefer.[30]

The professionals, however, following the public health strategy for birth
control developed in the 1940s and 1950s, looked at the experience of
successful public health programs like smallpox eradication and malaria control
and concluded that a one-time, no-variation method not requiring daily cooperation of the patient and which could be administered on an assembly-line
basis by an extended public health bureaucracy would be best. The IUD
seemed to fit that pattern.[31] Just as many physicians of the 1920s and 1930s

found it difficult to embrace a medical solution to a nonpathological problem, so many public health administrators and statisticians of the 1960s found it difficult to support the concept of a genuine patient's choice of contraceptive method. The medical norm that the doctor knows best was translated in government policy terms into the concept that for the developing countries the program administrator knows which contraceptive is best.

The principle of free choice was duly repeated in AID policy statements to protect the rhythm system even though funding prohibitions made it impossible to apply the principle to any AID-assisted programs until 1968. The final irony was that the method most readily acceptable to individual Catholics, after the rhythm method, was the oral contraceptive which, because of cost, was most effectively barred by the 1965 guidelines. For Catholics as for non-Catholics, protecting institutional doctrines was given a higher political priority than protecting the free choice of individuals. In 1965, however, these conflicts over method were barely visible below the surface of an AID policy that was still trying to define what technical assistance in population really was and how the United States could provide it.

Top AID and State Department officials were also inhibited in 1965 by the view that the United States, which had a high postwar birth rate and no government family-planning programs of its own, should not try to impose a policy on other nations. In one sense, it was the old "coercion" and "psychological mistake" argument that Kennedy had once used, but with new stress on the notion that the U.S. government should not subsidize overseas what it was reluctant to provide for citizens at home.

There was renewed pressure upon the Department of Health, Education, and Welfare after 1965 to support family planning services. The antipoverty program continued to set the pace with family planning projects developed by Lizabeth Bamberger Schorr and then Dr. Gary London. But gradually in HEW the replacement of Secretary Celebrezze by John Gardner, the public statements of Katherine Oettinger, director of the Children's Bureau,[32] and early in 1966 the release of guidelines for domestic family planning programs by Secretary Gardner helped to bring domestic and foreign aid policies into better alignment.[33]

AID was also handicapped institutionally by its difficulties either in recruiting high-calibre medical or demographic personnel on a permanent basis or in removing less competent people from the agency. AID was widely known as a "dumping ground for the least enterprising and the least capable Public Health Service officers." Unable to develop a satisfactory relationship with the Public Health Service, which was itself involved in a permanent feud over medical programs with the Children's Bureau, and continually susceptible to the theft of its best people by the foundations, AID was hardly in a position to provide the professional advice and consultation that it seemed to be offering instead of contraceptives. Efforts to borrow or fund experts from other U.S. government agencies worked reasonably well in a noncontroversial field like census taking but did not work at all in family planning where no one wanted to be out in front.

Efforts to finance the specialized agencies of the United Nations in a technical assistance role ran aground on the reluctance of the World Health

Organization either to take the lead itself or to allow UNICEF (the UN Children's Emergency Fund) or the Food and Agriculture Organization to enter a field of medical competence. AID was therefore compelled to turn to the private organizations including a few universities willing to undertake overseas projects, the Ford Foundation, the Population Council, and even the International Planned Parenthood Federation (which in 1965 was still not mentioned by name in any public statements) to provide the know-how that was needed for government programs.

From an administrative point of view population work was further handicapped by its location in the agency. The Population Reference and Research Branch of the Office of Technical Cooperation and Research (TCR) possessed little leverage and a very small budget. "Action programs" had to be funded by the geographic bureaus or country missions; in the mid-1960s, these could only be advised of persuaded, never commanded.

For the agency as a whole, a complex funding pattern that required loans for all commodities, U.S. purchases and shipping wherever possible, local currency expenditures for nonforeign exchange costs, and innumerable time-consuming program reviews that made it almost as difficult to supply commodities as it was to hire people. To these routine bureaucratic difficulties were added the extra challenges of a politically sensitive subject and a declining economic assistance appropriation.

The final impediment to action in 1965 and 1966 was personnel. At the very point when Johnson offered his presidential blessing and encouragement to the program, most of the individuals associated with it left the agency.

Their replacements came gradually from other activities and learned slowly how to work in AID. With concern increasing over world food shortages, Dr. Baumgartner's successor was Albert Moseman, an agricultural specialist from the Rockefeller Foundation. Dr. Malcolm Merrill from the Health Department of the State of California replaced Lee and recruited Dr. Reimert Ravenholt, an epidemiologist who took Jessup's job in February 1966. George Coleman, an information specialist, replaced both Drs. Berman and Duffy in the Latin American Population Office in the spring of 1966. Just as the new men were beginning to find their way about in 1966, David Bell left AID for the Ford Foundation to be succeeded by his former deputy, William Gaud. Although many of the new people were eager to push ahead in population work, the time lag was considerable. As in 1961 and 1962 there was no clear focus of experienced leadership for AID population programs for nearly two years.

How great a loss this was may be measured by the final recommendations that Baumgartner made on leaving the agency—recommendations that clearly called for a reordering of priorities within the agency that only continuous determined leadership could provide. In a memorandum for Bell dated August 11, 1965, she urged more attention to ambassadors and mission directors whose "personal interest and knowledge" makes more difference than the actual population problem of the country; more qualified and high-level staff in the field and in Washington; more vehicles and support for medical personnel in rural areas; more analysis of economic and social aspects; and above all "a flexible attitude . . . without endless review in Washington and the field."

"Ideally," she observed, "the Missions probably ought to earmark funds for population programs. . . . [Freedom] from many of AID's usual bureaucratic practices is important if we want to move programs along. We now are likely to be criticized for not doing enough."[34]

In a final comment to David Bell in November 1965 she reiterated:

> AID's ability to be useful to the LDCs [less-developed countries] in family planning operations will be directly related to the imagination, flexibility and realism with which problems are attacked. I have a real concern over handling affairs in a routine way—waiting for "a project" to be completely outlined before some immediately useful activities are undertaken, second guessing all along the line without further information, being afraid to work with Population Council, Ford, et cetera, having program officers massage proposals endlessly, being maladroit in working for or handling requests, having inadequate AID staff. These are some of the worst pitfalls.[35]

Unfortunately, she was accurate in her prediction but unsuccessful in her persuasion. All the obstacles she mentioned continued to plague the program. To the extent that they *were* surmounted, that funds *were* earmarked, that more adequate personnel *were* assigned, and that AID *did* finally develop a more flexible program, it was done over the objections of many of the agency and bureau chiefs. The first initiatives came from outside the agency, from the activists, and from Congress, with increasingly effective internal support from a forthright and determined program director.

In sum, the president's words made some difference. In the short run the difference was minimal; in the long run it was far greater. The willingness of a chief executive at last to involve his own prestige and influence by talking about population did reinforce the population activists in AID. The president's words did help to bring the issue out from the bureaucratic bowels of a nervous and insecure agency into the open where programming could be measured against policy, where political pressures could be measured against economic benefits, and where, in continuing sequence, the level and timing of the population program could be measured against the level and timing of comparable programs. But until the president—or Congress—was willing to provide more than just verbal support, this impact could all too easily be diluted simply through the normal procedures, personal predispositions, and personnel changes of a complex operating organization.

11

THE GRUENING
HEARINGS,
1965-68

The most enthusiastic response to President Johnson's statement came not from the executive agencies of government directly under his jurisdiction but rather from the supposedly reluctant Congress. During 1965, 1966, and 1967 Congress—both individual legislators and specific committees—set the agenda for public discussion of the population problem, defined the issue in ever more acceptable terms, reiterated the relevance and feasibility of action, drew up specific proposals to establish priority in funds as well as in words, and enacted these proposals into binding legislation, largely against the opposition of the executive agencies. (See Chart 11.1.) To the political scientists' charge that Congress has lost its powers of initiative and innovation,[1] the history of birth control legislation offers direct refutation.[2]

There were five major channels of congressional initiative in the mid-1960s leading toward legislation on population and birth control: first, Senator Ernest Gruening (D.-Alaska) whose personal interest and subcommittee hearings swept away the underbrush and debris of past taboos; second, the House of Representatives Committee on Agriculture and a freshman congressman, Paul Todd (D.-Mich.), who turned routine renewal of the Food for Peace Act into a full-scale Malthusian review; third, Senator J. William Fulbright (D.-Ark.) whose chairmanship of the Committee on Foreign Relations enabled him to introduce and enact significant amendments to the Foreign Assistance Act; fourth, the House Committee on Foreign Affairs which included the first earmarking of population funds in the foreign aid bill; and fifth, the various senators and congressmen like Joseph S. Clark (D.-Pa.), Joseph D. Tydings (D.-Md.), Robert Packwood (R.-Ore.), Alan Cranston (D.-Cal.), Robert Taft (R.-Ohio), Morris Udall (D.-Ariz.), James Scheuer (D.-N.Y.), and George R. Bush (R.-Tex.), who sponsored legislation to promote family planning in the United States as well as overseas.

No single government undertaking had greater impact in publicizing birth control as a legitimate public policy issue in the mid-1960s than the Senate subcommittee hearings chaired by Senator Gruening. Through 31 days of

CHART 11.1

Congressional Record Coverage of Birth Control and Population, 1950-69
(number of inches in Index)

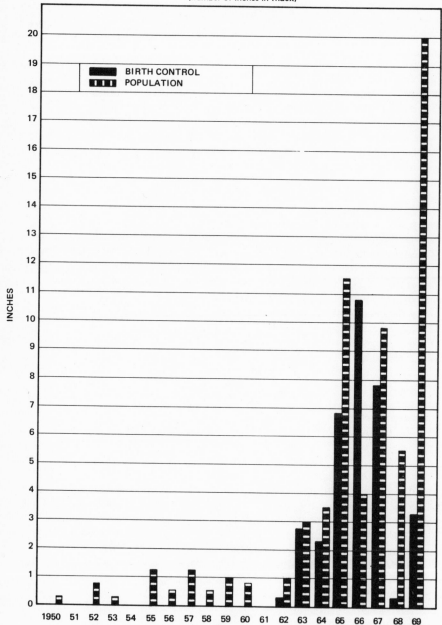

testimony from 120 witnesses extending for nearly three years, the problems of birth control and population growth were explored from every possible angle by every kind of expert. (See Table ll.l.) Gruening's own interest in birth control did not originate with the president's words. As a medical student at Harvard in 1909 he had wanted to offer birth control to the poor Irish families in the slums of South Boston—but found both law and medicine opposed. As a crusading young journalist in Boston he had tried to write about Margaret Sanger's work—but found both publishers and advertisers hostile. As a federal administrator in Puerto Rico in the 1930s he had tried to support birth control within the public health clinics—but found Cardinal Spellman and James Farley against him. As a co-sponsor of the Clark-Gruening resolution he had hoped to start a congressional dialogue in 1963—but found no one else yet willing to talk. In President Johnson's words, he saw a new opportunity.

On April 1, 1965, Gruening with six Senate and two House co-sponsors introduced a measure innocuously entitled "A bill to provide for certain reorganizations in the Department of State and the Department of Health, Education and Welfare." The bill, S.1676, was deliberately drafted to come under the jurisdiction of the Committee on Government Operations, where Gruening was chairman of the Subcommittee on Foreign Aid Expenditures. It would have established an Office of Population Problems, under an assistant secretary, in both the State Department and the Department of Health, Education, and Welfare and called for a White House Conference on Population in January 1967.[3] By prior arrangement with the chairman, the bill was referred to Gruening's subcommittee, where, without waiting for agency comments, the senator commenced hearings in June 1965.

TABLE 11.1

The Gruening Hearings on the Population Crisis, 1965-68

	1965	1966	1967	1968	Totals
Duration	June- Sept.	Jan.- June	Nov.	Jan.- Feb.	
Number of days	15	13	1	2	31
Total witnesses	56	42	8	14	120
Congressional	13	1a	3	0	17
Executive branch	3	5	5	8b	21
Not U.S. government	40	36	0	6	82

aOne statement not made in person but read by another witness.

bSeveral of the congressional and executive branch witnesses testified twice.

Source: U.S. Congress, Senate Committee on Government Operations, Subcommittee on Foreign Aid Expenditures, Population Crisis, Hearings on S. 1676, 90th Cong., 2nd Sess., 1968, pt. 4, pp. 1-5.

Passage of the bill itself was not Gruening's immediate objective. Rather he hoped to open a dialogue in which the whole community could participate and perhaps finally agree on measures to be taken. The first year of hearings, from June 1965 to June 1966, was mainly designed to banish the old taboos and reassure the federal bureaucracy. His objective was to bring the whole subject out into the open. "We should proceed boldly and openly and frankly, and let the world know why we think this is an important issue, and to get help for it."[4] During the first 12 months of hearings, 28 of the 31 sessions were held and all but 6 of the 82 nongovernment witnesses testified.

The first testimony in the record was an eloquent letter from former President Eisenhower. Responding to an invitation from Gruening, Eisenhower again admitted his error as president and wrote, in words that Gruening was to repeat again and again:

If we now ignore the plight of those unborn generations which, because of our unreadiness to take corrective action in controlling population growth, will be denied any expectations beyond abject poverty and suffering, then history will rightly condemn us.[5]

The galaxy of witnesses who appeared during 1965 and 1966 included 13 members of Congress who were willing to stand up and be counted on the issue; 3 Cabinet members; the American ambassador to India; a former president of Colombia; the director of the Swedish foreign aid agency; President Eisenhower's science adviser; John D. Rockefeller 3rd; William H. Draper, Jr.; Dr. John Rock; leaders of most of the population organizations; former Senator Kenneth B. Keating of New York, who had just become national chairman of the Population Crisis Committee, a newly formed Washington group established by Hugh Moore to educate Washington policy makers about population problems; Dr. Jack Lippes of Buffalo, who described his intrauterine contraceptive device for the subcommittee; Nobel prizewinners, who had dispatched a personal appeal to the pope; a dozen Catholics, including members of the papal study commission, a Jesuit lawyer, a couple who explained how badly the rhythm system worked, and a spokesman for the National Catholic Welfare Conference who opposed the bill; blacks and whites; men and women; welfare administrators and welfare recipients; lawyers, demographers, educators, clergymen, economists, conservationists, public health administrators, and agriculturalists. The witness list was a veritable *Who's Who* of the population movement, plus a significant number of scientific, professional, and government notables not previously associated with birth control.[6]

Many witnesses not only testified to their own experience and concern but also followed the gnome-like Senator from Alaska down a trail of leading commentary deliberately designed to locate the issue in a new political environment. Again and again Gruening observed,

This is entirely a matter of freedom of information and freedom of choice, without compulsion, with complete respect for the views of the individual, his religious inhibitions, and it is merely a matter of making knowledge available, it is mainly an exercise in freedom of speech, freedom of thoughts, freedom of information.[7]

Altogether, Gruening explored and affirmed every conceivable argument in favor of contraception and responsible parenthood—including the economic gains related to the new antipoverty program—the resource and conservation benefits that were just beginning to take on a broader environmental cloak, the personal health and welfare approach, the antiabortion pitch that more family planning would result in fewer abortions, and finally, the increasingly urgent food and nutrition imbalance that was challenging the underdeveloped countries. But in terms of government policy it was the freedom-of-information, civil libertarian, personal-freedom-of-choice argument that received the greatest emphasis.

The cumulative impact of Gruening's approach was to redefine the basic public policy issue. Before 1965 the question birth control advocates and policy makers usually had to face was, "How can you justify using taxpayers' money for a cause that many taxpayers consider immoral?" It was a hard question to answer, even for such an experienced advocate as Margaret Sanger.* The Gruening hearings seized the initiative and asked instead, "How can you justify withholding such important and useful information as birth control from the poor and disadvantaged who want to have it?" Gruening would contrast the case of the affluent woman who could easily get advice from her private physician with the poor welfare mother who had to rely on public clinics that were prohibited from offering birth control.

Using that formulation in a changed climate of opinion, even California Governor Edmund (Pat) Brown, who had hardly dared comment in 1959, could in 1966 deliver a whole speech enthusiastically endorsing state support of family planning. "For the poor Californian," Brown declared, "the lack of freedom of choice . . . in the planning of his family forges social and economic chains."[9] Gruening was only too happy to fill the hearing record with evidence that nonsupport of family planning meant discrimination against the poor and restriction on freedom of information.

Significantly, the Catholic opposition was expressed in August 1965 by a lawyer, not a theologian. It emphasized the "right of privacy," first enunciated in June 1965 by the Supreme Court in overturning the Connecticut law that Catholics had long defended. The attorney William Ball of Pennsylvania, speaking for the National Catholic Welfare Conference, argued that government support of birth control violated a citizen's "right to privacy." He did not object to additional research or activity by private organizations but he did urge "with respect to birth control, that the Government neither penalize it nor promote it, but pursue a policy of strict neutrality."[10] Ball raised very sharply the questions that were to face birth control supporters in the United States for the next few years: What about economic and racial pressures on the poor and the blacks? What about the dangers of coercion when the power and prestige of government are placed behind birth control services?

---

*For example, during a Mike Wallace interview in 1957 Margaret Sanger was asked, "Do you feel that Catholics should not have a right to have a say when the City Administration contemplates spending their tax dollars on the dissemination of birth control information? To which she replied, "I have no objection to their having a right, but I think we should have the same rights.[8]

Gruening responded politely but firmly that the federal government was engaged in supplying birth control, adding,

[It will be] engaged in it increasingly in response to public demand. And this is really a demonstration of the democratic process ... I believe in this case the important thing is to work together with openmindedness, and with a hope that a better society and more human happiness will be created as a result of exploring these different avenues.[11]

Gruening's approach was hard to oppose. Moreover, as Gruening very well knew, the Catholic Church was deeply involved after 1964 (and until the papal encyclical of July 1968) in reconsidering its traditional position. Pope Paul VI had reconstituted, enlarged, and placed considerable responsibility upon the study group originally gathered by Pope John XXIII. In May 1964 he announced to an obviously divided church that the question was "being subjected to study, as wide and profound as possible, as grave and honest as it must be on a subject of such importance."[12] In 1966 he assumed personal cognizance of the problem. The lively dialogue in Washington owed much to the uncertain silence in Rome.

National publicity attended Gruening's procession of distinguished witnesses, all of whom were seriously recommending birth control and contraception in a public Senate hearing with, for the first time, only mild legalistic remonstrances from the Catholic Church. The lesson was certainly not lost on official Washington, since Senator Gruening carefully inserted a list of each day's witnesses in the *Congressional Record* for every member to read and sent copies of all the testimony directly to the White House. Nor did Gruening forget that his biggest asset in Washington in 1965 and 1966 was the personal interest of President Johnson. "A part of the motivation for these hearings, which are probably long overdue," he announced at the opening session, "is found in President Lyndon Johnson's State of the Union pledge."[13] For many months Gruening opened nearly every hearing with a new quotation from President Johnson and a word of praise for the president's foresight. For a time the senator seemed to be holding a dialogue not only with the witnesses before the committee but also over their heads and over the heads of the executive agencies with the president himself. Gruening and Johnson both seemed to be urging the federal agencies to get on with the job. Through 1966 the Gruening arsenal of quotations included 26 separate statements by President Johnson about population and family planning. By late 1967 as the hearings were drawing to a close the total was 41 presidential statements, carefully tabulated and widely distributed.[14]

As long as Gruening's goal was to open the subject for dialogue and to prove that birth control no longer meant political suicide, he was tremendously effective. In persuading the executive agencies of the U.S. government, however, to endorse his legislation or indeed to take any other major steps toward a high-priority population program, Gruening was not so successful. As the hearings progressed, Gruening became increasingly convinced that the best way to assure a higher government priority was to pass the specific legislation he had introduced. To that end he cajolled, disputed, and ultimately attacked those federal officials who kept on raising objections.

The first government witness to testify directly on federal programs was the Secretary of HEW John Gardner, who appeared before the subcommittee in April 1966.[15] Much to Gruening's chagrin, Gardner would not support bill S.1676, insisted that HEW had all the legislative authority it needed, and considered an Office of Assistant Secretary for Population "undesirable."[16] The session turned into an angry confrontation. Gruening like an old-fashioned schoolmaster lectured the secretary sternly and read aloud to him one by one some 20 statements by President Johnson on the population problem. Gardner in turn called Gruening's proposals "formalistic and superficial."[17] He made no new suggestions, other than to release publicly family planning guidelines that had been approved in January and to indicate plans for regional family planning conferences throughout the United States. "We have been so occupied in doing adequately what we should have been doing," Gardner concluded, "that we have not addressed ourselves to the next steps."[18] Gruening and Senator Metcalf, both infuriated by Gardner's attitude, told him to take a second look and come back when he had changed his mind.*

The confrontation with AID and David Bell was almost equally negative, if not quite so dramatic. Bell did not want any new legislative authority either. He took the opportunity to oppose strongly several other bills that had been introduced to earmark for family planning activities foreign currencies held by the United States. Bell repeated the basic AID policy as set forth in the March 1965 airgram. Gruening in turn catechized Bell about population activities in every corner of the globe and found him less than fully informed. Bell promised to supply additional information, which Gruening afterwards complained arrived six months late. But one clear pronouncement, like the words of President Johnson, became an important part of the record. In his prepared statement, Bell announced:

> AID's dollar obligations for population activities are estimated at $2 million for fiscal year 1965; about $5½ million in fiscal year 1966; and about $10 million in fiscal year 1967. We would anticipate further increases in subsequent years.[19]

A month earlier AID had provided the same figures to the House Appropriations Committee, suggesting a redoubling to $20 million for fiscal 1968.[20] This ambitious estimate made it difficult to criticize AID for inaction in 1966, but for several years thereafter the 1966 estimates provided a handy and sometimes embarrassing yardstick to measure the program against.

Only Thomas Mann, testifying for the Department of State, was publicly responsive to Senator Gruening's overtures. Mann observed that "the world is not moving fast enough—especially the developing part of the world." He

---

*A month later Dr. Milo D. Leavitt was appointed deputy assistant secretary for science and population, a nonstatutory title—but he did not remain long in the job, which lacked any program authority.

agreed "completely" with Gruening's assessment that since late 1964 "there has been a real breakthrough in public thinking—the subject is now freely discussable."[21] Furthermore, Mann announced that he was appointing a senior Foreign Service officer, Robert Adams, to serve as special assistant for population in the office of the under-secretary to carry out many of the functions outlined in the Gruening bill.[22] Although Gruening grumbled that the new position was "an adventure in anonymity,"[23] he praised Mann for past and present efforts. Most of his criticism was still reserved for Gardner—"I think the Department of HEW should have taken the lead in this respect."[24]

In June 1966 the first and most important phase of the hearings ended. Birth control, or family planning as the federal agencies preferred to call it, was a public concern but the bureaucrats were still "skittish." Gruening allowed them more than a year, until November 1967, to take another look and, he hoped, to revise their opinion of his bill.

The final phase of the hearings in November 1967 and in January and February 1968 consisted mainly of government witnesses. On the domestic side, Gardner had finally been goaded into appointing an outside consultant in the summer of 1967 to assess the HEW efforts. Oscar Harkavy from the Ford Foundation, with the help of Fred Jaffe from Planned Parenthood and Samuel Wishik from Columbia University, looked at Gardner's programs and pronounced them lacking—in personnel, in funding, and, above all, in priority. "A clear signal from the Secretary" was missing, they concluded in a report that might never have seen the light of day had Gruening not scheduled a public hearing upon it.[25] Secretary Gardner stayed away from that session so that Dr. Philip Lee, who had moved from AID to become HEW assistant secretary for health, received the full crescendo of well-orchestrated criticism from Senators Gruening and Tydings, Congressmen Scheuer and Bush. Even the appointment of Katherine Oettinger, director of the Children's Bureau, as a new deputy assistant secretary for population and family planning did not remove from HEW's programs the stigma of a leaderless effort without much encouragement at the top or very much enterprise in the ranks.

AID and the State Department came up for their second round of criticism in February 1968 when both agencies continued to object to the appointment of an assistant secretary and the earmarking of family planning funds. But by that time a new special assistant for population matters had already been appointed in the Department of State. Even more important, Congress had just earmarked $35 million of foreign aid funds exclusively for population activities. AID administrator Gaud spoke to deaf ears as he argued against further earmarking.[26]

By February 1968 the real issues of financial priority had already been settled elsewhere. Ernest Gruening versus the federal bureaucracy was a contest without victors. Using President Johnson's public pronouncements like well-aimed bullets, the senator could win an open battle. But Gruening and his adversaries both knew that he could not win the war or get his legislation enacted without President Johnson's private backing as well. Forty firm public statements from the President made for an exciting exchange, but without equally firm legislative and budgetary commitments they did not persuade federal officials to venture forward boldly on what was still perceived as a political minefield.

Actually, by 1966 Johnson was increasingly preoccupied by the war in Southeast Asia and urban race riots in the United States. Black militants were beginning to look askance at birth control for the poor. Gruening was more and more active as one of Johnson's principal Vietnam critics. Both the budgetary margin and the presidential effort that would have been needed to satisfy Johnson's original hopes and Gruening's persistent demands were applied elsewhere. In place of the assistant secretaries Gruening had recommended, special assistants or deputy assistant secretaries were eventually appointed without the power or staff to make any major changes—a step in the direction Gruening wanted but only a small and cautious one. Except for these appointments, the principal impact of the Gruening hearings was to create a new climate of Washington opinion about birth control, to define a new issue for government responsibility, and to set the stage for other action in committees that had more direct jurisdiction, where the promises that Gruening had extracted could be measured against the performance of the reluctant bureaucracies.

CHAPTER

12

**FAMINE
TRIGGERS
ACTIONS,
1966**

While Gruening proceeded patiently to define the issues and impatiently to prod the executive agencies, events in the rest of the world overtook the slow progress of Washington policy making. As Samuel Huntington points out:

> Innovation ... involves the balancing of two incommensurables: time and resources. The decision-maker weighs the potential consumption of resources in innovating .... As long as time appears to be in reasonable supply, the balance is tilted against innovation. The function of a trigger event is to clarify and dramatize the shortage of time. Its message is: "There is no time."[1]

The triggering event that moved Washington and raised the population problem to higher priority and new urgency in the mid-1960s was a world food shortage. Caused in part by bad weather, in part by inattention to agriculture in the developing countries, and certainly aggravated by population increase, the food deficit reached public notice by the summer of 1965. Then in the autumn of 1965 the monsoon rains failed in India; again, in unprecedented repetition, the monsoon failed in 1966. Floods and drought plagued other food-producing areas. For the first time in two centuries statisticians could document what birth control supporters described as a genuine Malthusian crisis.

In their reactions to this challenge the professionals and the activists tended once again to divide along discernible lines. The scientifically oriented professionals—in population, health, economics, or foreign aid—tended to see the immediate problem as a complex agricultural dilemma, to be resolved by better seeds, more fertilizer, more irrigation, new marketing systems, and more fortunate weather. They did not want to link the food crisis exclusively to the population crisis.[2] The activists, on the other hand, glimpsed world starvation around the corner and argued with new force that as long as 35 million additional mouths had to be fed every year world food production would never suffice.[3]

112

Famine-1975! an alarming book by William and Paul Paddock documented what the population crisis had hitherto lacked—a precise and appalling threat close enough to require action but not so close that effective action would be hopeless.[4] The activists seized upon the book and the argument with eager and genuine conviction. The professionals, on the other hand, deplored it. Moore and Draper distributed the book widely; Frank Notestein, president of the Population Council, considered it a misleading simplification.

The professionals looked with considerable suspicion on the campaign for immediate massive government activity because they doubted that the government or anyone else knew what to do. The very idea of a "crash program" in response to a "crisis" or outside trigger event was unprofessional; education, training, and experience had to be a gradual process. From 1965 on the activists, and particularly Draper, were increasingly in favor of specific large sums allocated in advance for an immediate period. The more professional approach, on the other hand, was to wait and see what could be usefully spent and what requests were made before deciding on budgetary commitments. The activists thought that money could solve most problems; the professionals were sure that only time and training could really provide a solution. As the policy-making process developed, the impatience of the activists out of government was increasingly shared by Congress, whereas the academic inhibitions of the professionals continued to be reflected in the gradualist approach of many of the established federal agencies.

THE FOOD FOR PEACE ACT

The first official hint that the food-population imbalance was reaching crisis proportions came indirectly from the work of an Agriculture Department, State Department, and AID task force that began meeting in January 1965. The immediate goal of the task force was to develop new guidelines for extension of Public Law 480, commonly called the Food for Peace Act, which expired in 1966. But by spring of 1965 Lester Brown, an Agriculture Department economist, began to point out publicly from the task force data that food production per capita had been declining in Asia, Africa, and Latin America since 1961 and that unless yields per acre on their existing croplands were increased adequate food would simply not be available for their rapidly increasing populations. (See Chart 12.1.)

As the Food and Agriculture Organization of the United Nations announced in October 1965, "The population explosion in the developing countries is undoubtedly the most important single factor dominating the world food and agriculture situation during the whole of the postwar period."[5]

Private and semiprivate organizations began to mobilize, with the encouragement of both Congress and the administration. On the food side, the farm lobbyists plus the private voluntary agencies like CARE that received surplus U.S. foods under the Food for Peace Program organized a Washington Conference on the World Food Crisis in early December to promote renewal of the Food for Peace legislation on terms favorable for

Per Capita Food Production

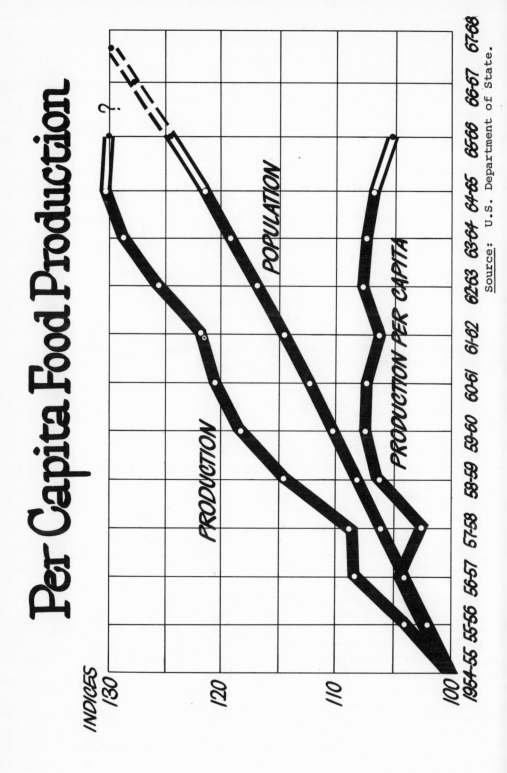

Source: U.S. Department of state.

114

them. For the first time among agricultural lobbyists, population spokesmen were also heard.

On the health side, the White House Conference on Health, meeting in November 1965, also included a panel on family planning. Despite protests from the National Catholic Welfare Conference, both Planned Parenthood and Catholics played prominent roles. The panel endorsed federal support of family planning, especially to provide services for the medically indigent.[6]

On the foreign aid side, the White House Conference on the International Cooperation Year also included a panel on population. Richard Gardner, then at Columbia University, was chairman; Rockefeller, Draper, Canfield, and Mary Lasker were among the members. Along with the usual recommendations based on the Draper Committee report—for technical assistance on request, more research, and a more conspicuous domestic commitment—was a new and startling figure. The panel recommended U.S. foreign aid expenditures of $100 million a year for the next three years to help other nations, on request, with family planning and population work.[7] The figure was incredible. Gardner had wanted to set some target. He thought $50 million was as high as anyone could justify; but Mary Lasker insisted, "That's not enough. Let's double it." So $100 million became the goal, established at a time (fiscal year 1966) when AID was actually spending barely $5 million.

By the end of 1965, in addition to being represented at two White House conferences the population activists were following government policy far more closely. Hugh Moore, with Edgar Berman's encouragement, had organized the Population Crisis Committee in Washington, first under former Senator Kenneth B. Keating of New York, then with William H. Draper, Jr., as national chairman. Moving to Washington a year later, Draper began to devote his full time, in a voluntary capacity, to altering government attitudes in general and AID policy in particular. Planned Parenthood also opened a Washington office and for a time the Population Council had a Washington representative. This concentration of open and avowed interest was a new experience for the federal agencies. Although not directly related to the food crisis, these moves put key people in accessible places early in 1966 when the full dimensions of the Indian food shortage became apparent.

Public Law 480, officially the Agricultural Trade and Development Act of 1954 but unofficially known as Food for Peace, provided legal authority for the sale or donation of U.S. surplus agricultural commodities overseas, with government assistance, at subsidized prices, and for "soft" foreign currencies. These "local currencies" could be employed in turn by U.S. or host governments for development programs. Ordinarily, as in 1961, 1964, and later in 1968, that legislation was renewed by Congress without much fanfare. But in 1966 the routine extension of the Food for Peace Act became a much-publicized vehicle in which farm groups, population groups, senators, congressmen, the Department of Agriculture, AID, and President Johnson pursued their various objectives against the darkening background of a world food deficit and disappearing U.S. surpluses. Population and birth control were among the least of the controversies involved, yet the progress of population policy as a result of this legislative and executive activity was great.

President Johnson's goals were put forward in a special message of February 10, 1966 which called on the United States to lead a worldwide war against hunger. Besides expanding food shipments, Johnson particularly stressed the concept of self-help as "an integral part of our food aid effort." "Exploding" populations were cited as the president declared, "A balance between agricultural productivity and population is necessary to prevent the shadow of hunger from becoming a nightmare of famine."[8] "Self-help" implied at least an awareness of population problems although President Johnson never explicitly said that birth control should be a condition of U.S. aid.

Reflecting this new direction, President Johnson made 19 different references to population or family planning, by Gruening's count, during the first six months of 1966.[9] In the International Educational and Health Acts Message of February 2, 1966, for example, as in the Foreign Aid Message of February 1, 1966, he pledged increased family planning research, training, and technical assistance overseas to meet "the increasing number of requests."[10]

Yet despite the worldwide need to "face the population problem squarely and realistically,"[11] which the president emphasized again and again in discussing food problems, the draft Food for Peace (renamed Food for Freedom) bill prepared by the executive agencies contained no mention of population, birth control, or family planning. The task force had discussed the possibility of including a reference; Agriculture Secretary Freeman was willing but David Bell did not want to publicize the issue.

Meanwhile, several senators and congressmen, stimulated by the Gruening hearings and by their own personal interest, were looking carefully at the population issue. Congressman Paul Todd of Michigan, a Democrat elected from a Republican district during the Goldwater defeat in 1964, asked Draper to come and talk to him about the population situation. Todd wanted to know, "What can I do that would be useful?" Draper suggested an amendment to the Food for Peace legislation, explicitly earmarking a certain percentage of the local currencies generated by food sales overseas to support family planning programs.

Technically, such an amendment was not necessary. The authority did already exist in the statutes and had quietly been used in Korea and Taiwan. Moreover, the usefulness of "local currency holdings" was increasingly in doubt, since they represented no real addition to a country's resources. But the amendment would be valuable in other ways: it would put Congress on record in support of technical assistance for family planning; it would link population control and the food crisis in a way that few could contest; it would make funds available in the very countries where population growth had created the heaviest dependence on U.S. food surpluses; it would raise the population issue first in the Agriculture Committees of both houses, which had few Catholic members or constituents. Finally, too, it would coincide with the strategy of the chairman of the House Committee on Agriculture, Harold Cooley (D.-N.C.), who was planning very broad hearings, including economists and demographers, to stress the need for a new approach to food and farm legislation, not just an extension of the old bill.[12]

Tood was not on the House Committee on Agriculture, but he saw the possibilities at once. He first raised the possibility on the House floor on February 10,[13] developed several drafts with some help but not much encouragement from AID, attended many of the well-publicized agriculture committee hearings himself, enlisted the support of committee member Spark Matsunaga (D.-Hawaii), testified before the committee, and spoke personally with many of the members. AID strongly opposed any hint that help might be conditioned on population control programs and insisted that no additional authority was needed.[14]

Much to the surprise of all concerned, the bill that was reported by the House Committee on Agriculture and passed by the House of Representatives in June 1966 contained not one but *four* different references to "family planning" or population problems. The concept of self-help or self-reliance included not only growing more food but also "resolving . . . problems relative to population growth."[15] The committee report underlined the point:

This new legislation, amending Public Law 480 . . . recognizes for the first time, as a matter of U.S. policy, the world population explosion relationship to the world food crisis, providing that the new food-for-freedom program * shall make available resources to promote voluntary activities in other countries dealing with the problem of population growth and family planning.[16]

Paul Todd announced his initial success at a big Washington conference organized by Planned Parenthood in May 1966, a conference that recorded many firsts. The first Cabinet member to speak at a Planned Parenthood function was, significantly, the Secretary of Agriculture Orville Freeman. His audience included other government officials, members of Congress, and for the first time a handful of nuns and priests. At the same session Wilbur Cohen, under-secretary of HEW, announced appointment of the first deputy assistant secretary of HEW for science and population.[17] The conference itself was the first activity of the new Washington office of Planned Parenthood, headed by Jeannie Rosoff.

Despite a mild protest from the National Catholic Welfare Conference, the population and food amendments went through the Senate with little change. Senator Jack Miller (R.-Iowa) tried to eliminate the word "promote" in front of family planning but it was restored in conference. Signing the bill on November 12, 1966, President Johnson commented:

The sound population programs, encouraged in this measure, freely and voluntarily undertaken, are vital to meeting the food crisis, and to the broader efforts of the developing nations to attain higher standards of living for their people.[18]

Once again something like a dialogue was taking place between the president and Congress. The innovators and initiaters in Congress were taking up the president's suggestions faster than the executive agencies. The private organizations served more and more as brokers of information, providing legislators with data, knowledge, and suggestions that would not have been available to them directly from the executive agencies. Precisely as Lester Milbrath suggests, the existence of these organizations and individuals enhanced the independence of Congress by providing alternative information and ideas.[19] In the case of birth control policies, Congress and the president both were more like activists, looking for a solution. The executive agencies were more like professionals, hesitant to tackle a new problem because it did not easily coincide with jurisdictional lines and professional disciplines and because it might arouse public controversy.

SENATORS PRESS AID

The House of Representatives, and particularly Todd, Cooley, and Matsunaga, took the initiative in writing the population problem firmly into the Food for Peace Act. The Senate, and particularly Fulbright and Tydings, took the lead in writing new language into the foreign aid bill in 1966.

Joseph D. Tydings (D.-Md.) offered an amendment, which became Section 201(c), to reinforce the Food for Peace language by giving AID specific authority to use foreign currencies for family planning. Tydings, like Gruening, took a special interest in the issue and had received an informal *nihil obstat* from Catholic leaders in Maryland. His amendment, also developed in consultation with Draper, included two further contributions: it made local currencies available to "private nonprofit United States organizations" as well as to governments "in countries which request such assistance"; and, even more important, it provided the first statutory definition of "voluntary family planning program" in such a way as to cover "the manufacture of medical supplies, and the dissemination of family planning information, medical assistance, and supplies to individuals who desire such assistance."[20] As a result of this outflanking maneuver, the AID ban on funding contraceptives, which had once been intended to placate Congress, stood almost in contradiction to later congressional intent.

Senator Fulbright also offered an amendment in the Senate Foreign Relations Committee to end the dispute with Zablocki by specifically authorizing technical assistance for population.[21] Fulbright's amendment was deleted in conference when Zablocki insisted Catholics would not support the bill with that provision. The conference report, however, made it clear that AID possessed legal authority to support family planning programs. The Tydings amendment was accepted by both Houses.[22] By 1966 it was increasingly clear, as the Senate committee report emphasized, that:

> ... AID officials have taken too conservative an attitude toward use of this authority.... The Committee is deeply concerned about the impact of population growth on the developing countries. Many of the benefits from aid are offset by population growth.... The Committee will follow closely the work of the Agency for International Development in implementing these sections and will expect to see a significant increase in activity by the time of the next Congressional presentation.[23]

FAMILY PLANNING FOR THE UNITED STATES

Many members of Congress were just as impatient to see birth control activity within the United States as overseas. Actually, the first federally supported family planning program was approved in 1962 for Washington, D.C. The appropriation for the District Health Department included $1,000 for family planning information in fiscal 1963 and $24,000 for family planning services in fiscal 1964 and again in 1965.[24] Up to $200,000 for a full-fledged program was appropriated for fiscal 1966 and from that time forward family planning became a continuing component of D.C. public health.

Although the executive agencies proposed no new legislation directly linked to family planning, several bills were introduced in the 89th Congress (1965-66). Congressman James Scheuer (D.-N.Y.) introduced two bills in 1965 to repeal the nineteenth-century Comstock laws that classified contraceptives as obscene materials and prohibited their mailing or importation.[25] These laws remained an awkward relic of government distrust even though their impact had been nullified by the courts. (See Chapter 2.) Scheuer's bills, later combined into a single measure, were among the very few legislative initiatives that were supported by the agencies affected. Yet because of objections or anticipated objections by other congressmen the measures, H.R. 8440 and H.R. 8451, were not finally combined into one and enacted until January 8, 1971 (Public Law 91-662). Even then the Post Office Department insisted on barring unsolicited advertising or mailing.[26]

In addition to this largely symbolic measure Senator Joseph S. Clark (D.-Pa.) and Congressman Scheuer consistently tried to expand family planning programs in the Office of Economic Opportunity and the Department of Health, Education, and Welfare. OEO was both more sympathetic and more susceptible to such pressures than HEW. In 1965 Clark added "family planning" as one of the specific health programs to be supported by the war on poverty. Although the words were deleted in conference, the conference report confirmed that "these programs are now being carried on and are to be encouraged."[27] In 1966, responding to increased criticism of federal restrictions, especially the ban on services for unmarried women, Clark and Scheuer were successful in adding a new section to allow community action agencies to determine locally who was eligible for assistance.[28]

The amending of OEO legislation in 1965 and 1966 was somewhat comparable to making foreign aid amendments. Both changes were made by the authorizing committees that had substantive jurisdiction and were ignored (though not countermanded) by the appropriating committees. Both consisted, first, of a statement in a conference report affirming legal authority for family planning programs because House conferees opposed specific legislation, and second, of an indirect congressional relaxation of restrictions that had been applied administratively. In both cases, the agencies involved, AID and OEO, took a negative or neutral stance.

The Department of Health, Education, and Welfare was the most difficult agency for birth control supporters to influence. It was such a large and complex organization that members of Congress had difficulty even locating an effective lever to move it. In 1966 Senator Tydings introduced the first of several bills to authorize funds for specific family planning projects to public agencies and private, nonprofit organizations. Senator Clark held a day of hearings before his Subcommittee on Employment, Manpower, and Poverty, but the bill was never reported by the full committee.[29] HEW as usual supported "the basic objectives of the bill" but opposed any specific allocations for family planning because that approach would contradict the department's new emphasis on comprehensive, noncategorical programs. Family planning must be a part of the other health programs, Dr. Lee argued, not a separate item.[30] Wilbur Cohen, HEW under-secretary, went so far as to assure Senator Tydings that $20 million was "contemplated" for family planning under the comprehensive administration bill, S.3008, passed in 1966.[31] But, as the financial and inflationary pressures of the Vietnam War increased, the possibility of finding additional money for new health programs in any framework diminished.

Since HEW, unlike both OEO and AID, did not require annual authorizations for its research or service programs, it depended for program expansion on increasing appropriations. Unfortunately for birth control, the chairman of the House Appropriations Subcommittee for the Departments of Labor and HEW (until early 1967) was John Fogarty, a Democrat and Catholic from Rhode Island who disapproved of birth control. The chairman of the Senate HEW Appropriations Subcommittee until 1969 was Lister Hill (D.-Ala.), a Southern gentleman who also veered away from the issue. Those few HEW officials like Forrest Linder, director of the National Center for Health Statistics, who tried to promote fertility research were rebuffed. With the legislative route that seemed to work for AID and OEO impeded by the size, complexity, and continual reorganization of HEW health activities and with the appropriations route blocked by several key congressional opponents, the birth control advocates were less able to influence HEW.

But as 1966 ended, birth control supporters were optimistic. Legislative action had made it clear that birth control could be legally included with minimal opposition in appropriate programs. Such support was both relevant and feasible, politically and technically. In 1966 AID and HEW officials publicly spoke of doubling their programs each year or reaching $20 million by fiscal year 1968.* If that projected level of priority and timing could actually be maintained, the advocates of birth control would in two short years of public discussion have achieved a real breakthrough. Senator Tydings observed in October 1966 that "The 89th Congress . . . has done more to expand U.S. support for voluntary family planning programs than in all other previous years combined . . . . It now remains for the administration to provide the initiative, the energy and the staff to implement these programs effectively."[33]

---

*The $20 million figure projected by HEW in 1966 was for family planning services. The research program at the National Institute of Child Health and Human Development was increasing from about $4.2 million in 1965 to $8.9 million in 1968.[32] (See Table 17.1.)

13

THE BUREAUCRACY: SHIFTING INTO SECOND GEAR, 1966-67

"We were only in first gear in 1965. During 1966 and 1967 we moved slowly into second gear, trying to mobilize more people in the State Department and AID to take more initiatives instead of just waiting for proposals to come in from the field."[1]

"Shifting into second gear" was the term Philander P. Claxton, Jr., the Special Assistant to the Secretary of State for Population Matters used to describe the change from a passive policy of "responding to requests" to an active program of "stimulating organizations and governments to move." But, as Leona Baumgartner had warned in 1965, even though "a complete change of policy was made between 1959 and 1965 . . . a two year lag may ensue" while old bureaucratic attitudes are changed, money provided, personnel recruited, an organization set up, and tactics developed.[2]

The two-year lag in transforming the new policy into an actual program began in 1965 as the first generation of population advocates moved to other jobs and the second generation assumed new responsibilities. The guidelines AID sent to the field in August 1965 reflected greater urgency and asked missions "to give top priority to sensible Technical Cooperation proposals in this area." Nevertheless, from mid-1965 to mid-1966 AID in Washington was still primarily reacting to outside pressures rather than generating any of its own. AID representatives participated in two major conferences in the summer of 1965, the United Nations World Population Conference in Belgrade (to which President Johnson sent his encouraging message) and a conference on family planning action programs in Geneva sponsored by the Population Council. By early 1966, AID had received inquiries from at least 15 countries, 7 of them in Latin America where Berman's early spadework had prepared the ground. Ernst Michanek, director of the Swedish International Development Agency (which emphasized population assistance) told David Bell that the Swedish government had more requests than they could handle. Yet the response of AID was still cautious. For instance, in 1966 when the enterprising Yugoslav demographer Dr. Milos Macura, who headed the United Nations

Population Division, asked whether the United States would support regional demographic research centers in Asia and Africa (as the Alliance for Progress had supported CELADE in Chile since 1964), he was told only that the possibilities would have to be fully explored. A UN request for training fellowships for Africa and the Middle East remained pending in the Technical Cooperation and Research office for nearly a year. When the White House Conference panel recommended in December 1965 that AID spend $100 million a year on population assistance, one of the most sympathetic AID program officials commented that in the long run $10 million "would appear to be about the maximum under our current policies."

One reason for agency caution was the campaign Congressman Clement Zablocki was waging. The Milwaukee Democrat insisted that the elimination of the words "technical assistance" in Fulbright's 1963 amendment signified congressional intent to prohibit any technical assistance in the population field.[3] Although AID officials had no doubt of their legal authority they did doubt the political wisdom of defying an influential, internationalist Catholic congressman. "Don't put Zablocki and his colleagues in a position where they will be forced to object publicly," was the advice from the White House.[4] To a considerable degree, AID's reluctance to endorse some of the first legislative initiatives in the population field was based on fear of how a single congressman might react.

But apart from growing criticism of foreign aid itself and even larger cuts in funding, the biggest problems of the infant AID population program were not in Congress at all but inside the agency. The function of the Office of Technical Cooperation and Research was to provide professional expertise and technical advisers in a staff capacity. But in the population field in the mid-1960s there were very few experts indeed, none in AID, and no one anywhere in the world who could yet speak from the experience of a successful national family planning program. When Draper went to call on Baumgartner's successor, Albert Moseman, in January 1966 to urge more attention to food and population problems, he found to his dismay that AID genuinely did not know what to do. In India, for example, was birth control even included in the existing government clinics? What would be necessary to include it? Did mobile units work in rural areas? What about the 75 people reportedly requested by the Indian government as advisers? Where were these experts, government or private, to come from? What were they to do? Moseman and his staff did not have the answers.

"Good night!" exclaimed Draper afterward, "Haven't they thought about these things at all?"

With the hope of stimulating more interest at the top, Draper proposed directly to David Bell that AID might help the International Planned Parenthood Federation expand its activities. Bell, who had turned down a similar suggestion from Berman in 1965, was more sympathetic to Draper's proposal in 1966. He also wanted to increase U.S. help to India where the food crisis was steadily worsening. Several experts from the Public Health Service had just joined the AID mission in New Delhi and Washington was waiting for their recommendations, but Bell agreed with Draper that it might be useful for Dr. Jack Lippes, who had developed the intrauterine device, to visit India and encourage Indian physicians not only to go ahead with the IUD but also to include pills.

Bell's testimony to congressional committees in March and April 1966, although far from satisfactory to Gruening, did reflect the fact that AID was slowly beginning to translate population assistance requests into the terms that AID knew and could handle—local currencies for health programs to provide an infrastructure for family planning, loans for purchase of vehicles and audio-visual supplies, and grants for fellowships, training, and attendance at international conferences.

CLAXTON AND RAVENHOLT

Three days after Bell's confrontation with Gruening, the new head of the Population Branch Dr. Reimert T. Ravenholt, an epidemologist from the University of Washington in Seattle, arrived to head the Population Branch. His first few months on the job were occupied in answering Gruening's questions to Bell about family planning programs around the world. Thanks to the senator's interest, an elaborate swearing-in ceremony was held for Ravenholt, to which all those in Washington even remotely connected with population were invited.

Less than a month later, Gruening was allowed to announce the appointment of Philander P. Claxton, Jr., a high-ranking Foreign Service Reserve officer, as special assistant to the secretary of state for population matters. Claxton was (after Adams) the first State Department official to be assigned that responsibility since 1963 when Barnett had transferred to the East Asia Bureau. He was the first ever to have such a clear and public title and no other responsibilities.

Claxton and Ravenholt had completely opposite and often complementary approaches to their new and undefined jobs. Claxton, a lawyer and a diplomat, brought to his new position 20 years of experience in the State Department. His main challenge, as he saw it, was policy, the publicly articulated position of the United States government on population problems. His approach was comprehensive and encyclopedic. Claxton's long-term strategy was to involve as many different people as possible throughout the department, at every level and from every angle, helping to formulate and then to implement " a more positive policy." He wanted to "institutionalize the activity so that not just one person, but the whole Department, was involved."[5] Like a missionary, he never gave up trying to convert as many souls as he could.

Ravenholt, on the other hand, a public health physician by profession, brought to his job no experience with the federal bureaucracy, little patience with its failings, and few inhibitions about saying so. His main work, as he saw it, was to build a program, "to get the action moving" as fast as possible. His approach was to identify the priorities and to concentrate on one or two key issues or bottlenecks at a time. He wanted to disentangle extraneous people from the programming process, to clear away the innumerable offices and advisory opinions that seemed to hover around every AID action. Ravenholt wanted to organize and direct the program himself. Those whom he could not easily convert he was perfectly ready to damn.

Both Claxton and Ravenholt established quick rapport with Draper. Claxton had known Draper from Marshall Plan days. He and Ravenholt both saw in Draper a potent ally who could tell agency heads as well as members of Congress that population programs needed money and staff as well as eloquent speeches. For a bureaucrat bucking the bureaucracy, as Richard Gardner observed, that kind of outside support has a psychological as well as a practical and political value.[6]

The first assignment that Claxton set for himself was an exercise in education and persuasion: first, to update the earlier State and AID airgrams; second, in the process to inform Washington agencies and officials more fully; and third, to raise the priority of the issue. To this end, Claxton prepared an extensive but classified paper, relating population growth to everything from food to civil war, from cost-benefit analysis to basic human rights, and from presidential and congressional pronouncements to executive branch "short-falls." Above all, he emphasized that two thirds of U.S. foreign aid was being absorbed by the population growth. Adopting completely the Coale-Hoover thesis that population growth rates, not population density, were critical to economic development, Claxton argued that the U.S. government must move from reaction and response to initiation and persuasion.

By the time the paper reached the secretary of state's desk, it had already achieved part of its purpose. All the appropriate State Department and AID bureaus had reviewed, revised, commented, added to, and finally cleared the document. The rest of its purpose was accomplished when Rusk agreed to every single one of Claxton's ten recommendations.

"Rusk never held me back in any way," Claxton later commented.[7] "He approved whatever I suggested. When I asked him, 'Should I ride or push the issue?' Rusk said, 'Push as hard as you can within the limits of the policy statement.' "

The statement recommended minimal but important advances including: a new airgram to the field; AID "encouragement of national public and private population control programs . . . as a matter of priority"; State and AID regional bureau guidelines for country assistance, as well as long-range guide-lines from the Policy Planning Council; support for the Peace Corps, the U.S. Information Agency (USIA), and the United Nations to increase their popula-tion work; an official population briefing by outside experts for the secretary and other high officials; and also separate intradepartmental, interagency, and outside advisory and coordinating groups.[8]

In one way or another, most of Claxton's recommendations, like most of George McGhee's in 1961, led to some action. A classified airgram that Rusk approved was dispatched at once to all State, AID, USIA, and Peace Corps representatives; it included much of the data in Claxton's paper. All ambassadors were urged once again to appoint a senior official as population officer, to discuss the population problem with host country officials (unless they saw a special reason not to do so), and to report back to Washington "their plans for carrying out the President's policy." The proposed briefings were held in November and again in January for the whole department.[9] Claxton distributed a folio of population charts, graphs, and papers throughout the government.* Various government committees were established.

AID officials, however, remained somewhat suspicious of a State Department officer who tried to tell them their business. The AID administrator, for example, commented on Claxton's paper. "I agree with all the recommendations but not all the prefatory discussion and commentary." Claxton usually deferred to their pressure. His recommended budget and personnel levels for AID were deliberately buried in the middle of the paper and not presented as recommendations. Claxton could only suggest ambiguously that AID funding "might be in the order of $50 million per year or two or three times that amount, mostly in local currencies." He compared the 1,100 professional AID employees in agriculture with barely 13 in population, but did not propose a specific increase.

Claxton's missionary activities within the executive branch could not provide the money and staff that AID needed, but the various meetings and briefings, like the Gruening hearings, helped to soothe the still-uneasy feeling many officials had about population. Anything that could help remove the stigma of "a sensitive subject" from the population field would increase support in the diplomatic community. In the long run Claxton's presence plus his conscientious pursuit of every possible opportunity demonstrated, as in Barnett's day, that one way to make things happen in a large organization is to appoint a person whose only job is to see that they do happen.

Ravenholt's presence in AID also made a difference but in a different way. After being sworn in with the pomp of an assistant secretary, Ravenholt found it impossible to hire additional staff or even to replace his own secretary when she left the Population Branch. "It's not a Branch; it's a twig," Ravenholt complained, "We have no secretary, no staff, no money, and no program."

After finally acquiring a secretary, reviewing the situation, and visiting India, Ravenholt concluded that the greatest gap in AID's barely existent program was the ban on contraceptives.[10] This was the most sensitive area of the whole program, what top officials feared would be their political Achilles heel. At a time when most of the country missions had just reached the point of being willing to provide the conventional forms of assistance, Ravenholt began to argue that what the United States really should do was to supply large quantities of oral contraceptives, at U.S. expense, to all the developing countries.

Arguing that Congress had defined family planning to include "medical supplies," that IUD removal rates in India were high, that the Indian government wanted condoms, and that a free choice of method was impossible without U.S. support, Ravenholt called the contraceptive ban "an important obstacle to effective engagement of U.S. resources." While Claxton begged him not to rock the boat he noted bluntly in a memorandum to the administrator, "At best this agency operates under many constraints; and it can ill afford

---

*Three of these are reproduced in this volume as Charts 1.1, 1.2, and 12.1.

additional unnecessary encumbrances . . . the present policy prevents AID from providing forthright leadership for evaluation of contraceptive materials."[11]

To many AID officials "forthright leadership" in this new, sensitive, and potentially expensive field at a time of declining appropriations was the last thing they wanted. The new Administrator of AID William Gaud, Bell's deputy, did not approve Ravenholt's recommendation, commenting, "I am not convinced that it really matters."[12]

Ravenholt spent the next three months in a frustrating—and frustrated— effort to get an appointment with Gaud so that he could argue the case for contraceptives in person. Just as his fourth appointment was cancelled and he was about to pack up his bag and return to Seattle in disgust, a major shift took place, completely transforming the position and priority of the population program.

FAMINE TRIGGERS THE WAR ON HUNGER

While Claxton fussed and Ravenholt fumed the darkening shadows of the world food crisis were making an impression on the executive branch of government as well as Congress. Not so much at the specific level of population programming as at the top levels of priority and organization, the food crisis demanded attention.

The joint Agriculture, State, and AID reviews increasingly linked food production possibilities with population growth probabilities. A graph that showed food and population intersecting in 1984 was widely circulated. Moreover, under Freeman's vigorous leadership the Agriculture Department seemed to be moving toward a larger role as purveyor of technical assistance overseas including nutrition and health as well as agriculture productivity.

Meanwhile AID's appropriations grew smaller every year. Bell's leadership, while it had upgraded AID considerably, attracted new talent, and introduced the concept of long-range development planning, was called by one observer "the golden age of economists." Bell had made AID and country programming "more professional" but at the same time considerably less humanitarian and appealing to Congress. Bell had not discouraged Freeman's expanding programs. By mid-1966 AID was in some danger that its most popular activities, voluntary food relief and people-to-people technical assistance, might be stolen away by the Agriculture Department, leaving AID with nothing but economic growth charts, program loans, and the political perils of negotiating with ungrateful foreign governments.

Bell's successor at AID, William Gaud, was a lawyer less interested in economic theory and more determined not to let his agency be disemboweled. Like Freeman, he was stubborn and ready to fight for his programs. As administrator, Gaud had two main objectives for AID: first, to promote private enterprise in the development field; and second, to put more stress on the broad problems of food and population.[13] Long before coming to AID he had been active with Planned Parenthood in Connecticut. He thought the population issue was important but he was aware of the potential dangers.

At the same time, within AID Herbert Waters, a politically attuned former administrative assistant to Vice President Hubert Humphrey, saw a multiple opportunity—to expand his own work with the voluntary agencies that distributed surplus PL-480 food, to give foreign aid a new image of direct humanitarian concern, and to develop more effective political support. Gaud was congenial to Waters's approach, if not to Waters's personally. Just as the domestic program was a "War on Poverty," so the foreign aid program should become a "War on Hunger," with all the different components of food, health, and population included under a comprehensive and politically potent slogan.

Thus in November 1966 Gaud announced that the "War on Hunger" would be "accorded the highest functional priority in AID's total range of program operations."[14] It "transcends agriculture alone" and should include "all forms of assistance," collaboration with private and international organizations, and broader strategies such as population control. The concept of self-help, which President Johnson personally dramatized by his tight control over food shipments, called for new initiatives from AID "to exert the maximum leverage and influence . . . to assure that the host country has fulfilled its obligations to help itself increase food production and, where necessary, control population increases."[15]

Yet Gaud's November statement proposed no institutional changes, only a new name and a new priority. The extramural contest between Agriculture, AID, and State waxed even hotter after passage of the Food for Peace Act. Finally, the Bureau of the Budget, through Waters, the Vice President and the White House staff, brought Gaud and Freeman together. Freeman had to agree that the War on Hunger program really belonged in AID rather than in the Agriculture Department.

To protect his title to the program from the internal autonomy of the AID regional bureaus as well as the external initiatives of Secretary Freeman, Gaud soon recognized he would have to change the organization of the agency. By establishing a specific new War on Hunger office, Gaud hoped to develop the administrative machinery, or the internal gadfly, to carry out more effective food and population programs. The War on Hunger office was designed both "to emphasize the human, social problems of development" and "to keep the heat on" the regional bureaus.[16]

To give the new operation even more emphasis and priority, Gaud, Waters, and Humphrey persuaded President Johnson to announce the change. The President too was sympathetic to the grass roots, project-type, Point IV approach that could help starving people. He and Gaud agreed that the more the AID program was related to hunger the better it would fare in Congress.

President Johnson's Foreign Aid Message of February 9, 1967, announced the establishment of "An Office of the War on Hunger to consolidate all AID activities relating to hunger, population problems and nutrition."[17] The announcement came as a surprise to both Claxton and Ravenholt, who had played no part in the high-level intramural conflict and intrigue. Herbert Waters, it was later revealed, would become the first assistant administrator of the war on hunger, which replaced the Office of Technical Cooperation and Research.

What the change meant for population programs was quickly apparent and all to the good. Population moved out from underneath health and gained equal footing with health, agriculture, nutrition, voluntary agency programs, and the like. The Population Branch with 3 professionals and a secretary was transformed by March 23 into the Population Service with 24 authorized positions, a sevenfold increase.[18] In the new organizational structure, the Population Service became "the principal staff element in the Agency responsible for providing leadership, initiative, coordination, and assistance in and technical guidance on the conduct of population family planning program activities"[19] The new Population Service was given authority to initiate "pilot programs" overseas (with the concurrence of the regional bureaus) and to develop and administer research programs.[20]

From a political point of view the Population Service was safer than ever before, wrapped tightly around the hunger issue and close beside the voluntary agencies like Catholic Relief Services that recognized the population problem and wanted AID help for their own work. Pope Paul VI privately assured Waters that as long as the War on Hunger was just as much concerned with those already born as it was with preventing births, then the Catholic Church could live with it.

From the point of view of all involved, the creation of the Office of the War on Hunger was a critical innovation. It emphasized the president's interest in the food and population crisis. It met Gaud's personal and institutional needs, both in fighting off other agencies and in regaining greater control over his own regional and country programs. It moved population up one notch in the organizational structure and up several notches in personnel strength—all in a way that no one could contest. And it brought together under one roof the voluntary organizations, which were AID's only real constituency; the universities, which were receiving larger support grants; and the professional groups, which would ultimately expand their stake in the program. Professionals and activists both were closely linked in the war on hunger effort which was, in a very few years, to become the real heart of the foreign aid program.

FAMILY PLANNING IN THE WAR ON HUNGER

Yet even as the focus and staff of the population program moved upward in the war on hunger, the tools, techniques, and presuppositions of AID programming remained much the same through fiscal 1966 and 1967. Even the new positions, however welcome, took more time to fill in fiscal 1967 than the amount of work they produced. Bell had estimated in April 1966 that AID would be spending $2.5 million in 1965, $5 million in 1966, and $10 million in 1967.[21] But by December 1967 it was clear that despite the War on Hunger population obligations were lower in 1967 ($4,700,988) than they had been in 1966 ($5,263,828).[22] The most conspicuous feature of the AID population program seemed to be the high ratio of talk to action.

Many of the old hands in AID looked upon the War on Hunger as nothing but window dressing. Even among its supporters skepticism prevailed, especially about population programs. As one official observed:

There is a notable gap between what the President has demanded of us and what can be delivered on the working level. . . . We have plenty of agricultural agents to send to India to train a county agent. We have absolutely no backlog of experience in government family planning programs.[23]

The first highly publicized action did indeed turn out to be a great disappointment. A $3.6 million loan was announced in late 1966 to enable the government of Turkey to purchase 1,400 jeeps plus audio-visual equipment for rural family planning work.[24] The Turkish loan was the first major government-to-government support for family planning. Yet whether the commitment was premature, whether the U.S. mission was too eager to stimulate the Turkish government, whether U.S. terms were not sufficiently attractive, or whether the shifting personnel in the Turkish ministries really changed their minds about the loan, after two years of negotiation $1.5 million of the $3.6 million loan was deobligated—an unhappy monument to the difficulties of government-to-government population assistance.

The Turkish loan had been arranged by the Near East-South Asia Bureau. The Population Service, on the other hand, concentrated on grants. In 1967 the Population Council received a $300,000 grant to evaluate the international effectiveness of postpartum family planning programs in large maternity hospitals.[25] The Pathfinder Fund, a smaller pioneering organization set up in the 1930s by Dr. Clarence Gamble of Boston, received $194,000 for testing and evaluation of different shapes of IUDs by physicians throughout the world.[26] Also, the International Planned Parenthood Federation, under Draper's, Moore's, and Canfield's encouragement, had begun to expand its horizons and applied in 1967 for major U.S. government support. The grant of $3 million to the International Planned Parenthood Federation arranged in October 1967 was in Gaud's judgment a major innovation.[27] By far the largest population grant to date (none had previously been over $500,000), it reflected not only the increasing pressure of Congress on AID but also the increasing recognition by Ravenholt and Gaud that private organizations had a major role to play in the population field as well as in other areas of economic development.

Although most of the policy pronouncements on population referred to assistance on request to governments that were providing a choice of method and determining their own national population policies,[28] the figures clearly showed that from the very beginning government-to-government aid, i.e., that negotiated by the country missions (like the Turkish loan), was a relatively small part of the AID program. (See Tables 13.1 and 13.2.) In speaking continually of government-to-government aid, in asserting that free choice of method must prevail while refusing to finance contraceptives, and in emphasizing country requests when some of the most useful projects were those initiated by Washington staff, AID officials were describing a program that did not exist. To some extent, of course, these formulations reflected political or economic judgments. Presumably AID officials thought it would be more

TABLE 13.1

AID Dollar Obligations by Region for Population and Family-Planning Projects, Fiscal Years 1965-67

	1965	1966	1967	Total 1965-67
(thousands of dollars)				
Nonregional	892	872	971	2,735
Latin America	1,197	834	2,369	4,400
Near East-South Asia	0	2,100	337	2,437
Africa	10	9	34	53
East Asia (including Vietnam)	35	77	734	846
Total	2,134	3,892	4,445	10,471
(percentages)				
Nonregional	42	23	22	27
Latin America	56	21	53	42
Near East-South Africa	0	54	8	23
Africa	*	*	*	*
East Asia (including Vietnam)	2	2	17	8
Total	100	100	100	100

*Less than 1 percent.

Source: U.S. Agency for International Development, Population Program Assistance (Washington, D.C., October 1969), p. 28.

palatable in the United States to help the government of India than to subsidize Planned Parenthood. They thought is would be more effective overseas to finance a foreign government program than a private enterprise. But as far as the population program was concerned these preconceptions blinded some AID officials to the opportunities that did exist and prevented them from thinking in terms of a larger program.

Almost the only voice within AID during 1967 that was raised in continual protest against some of these preconceptions and many of the normal agency procedures was that of Ravenholt.[29] Having taken up the most sensitive issue—contraceptives—first, Ravenholt proceeded to attack all the other bottlenecks he saw. The use of local currencies, for instance, he called "a complete hoax" that could not possibly provide useful assistance to a new and uncertain program like family planning. U.S. grants of local currency were no different, he maintained, from the government itself printing more money. Impoverished, underdeveloped countries constantly warned by U.S. economists against "inflationary pressures" did not benefit at all from the use of these "local currencies."

Ravenholt also objected to loans for family planning programs. "If the federal government offered a poor state like West Virginia a loan for family planning clinics or supplies, do you think the West Virginians would start a program?" he kept asking. Unless vehicles, contraceptives, or whatever else was needed could be supplied promptly, on a grant basis, AID would not be much help. Many of the same criticisms that Leona Baumgartner had quietly passed on to David Bell in 1965 Ravenholt was proclaiming loudly to anyone who would listen in 1966 and 1967.

Finally, as Gaud and much of the agency furiously opposed congressional efforts in 1967 to earmark funds for population, Ravenholt frequently pointed out that unless funds *were* earmarked the program would not work.[30] As long as every ongoing project had to be financed first out of a reduced appropriation, even the largest population staff, supported by the most eloquent speeches of President Johnson, would not be able to get a new program going. Therefore, while Ravenholt recruited a bigger staff in the Office of the War on Hunger he made no secret of the fact that his real hopes for action were based not on the agency's estimates but on Draper's influence and the Congress. In that expectation, to the consternation of officials inside the agency and the surprise of professionals outside, he proved to be correct.

TABLE 13.2

AID Dollar Obligations by Source of Funding for Population and Family-Planning Projects, Fiscal Years 1965-67

	1965	1966	1967	Total 1965-67
(thousands of dollars)				
Nonregional	892	872	971	2,735
Country missions	137	2,455	1,903	4,495
Regional projects	1,105	565	1,571	3,241
Total	2,134	3,892	4,445	10,471
(percentages)				
Nonregional	42	23	22	27
Country missions	6	63	43	43
Regional projects	52	14	35	30
Total	100	100	100	100

Source: U.S. Agency for International Development, *Population Program Assistance* (Washington, D.C., October 1969), p. 28.

Next to the pursuit of peace, the really great challenge to the human family is the race between food supply and population increase. That race tonight is being lost. The time for rhetoric has clearly passed. The time for concerted action is here, and we must get on with the job.[1]

With this rhetoric in his 1967 State of the Union Message, President Johnson called for action. Congress was ready to act, at least in the population field. Uninhibited by the budgetary, programmatic, and personnel problems that delayed AID, Congress needed only some specific suggestions and a little outside encouragement to move forward independently of the executive agencies. The president's own words would often be turned, as he may have intended, against his own subordinates in the executive branch of the government.

TITLE X, PROGRAMS RELATING TO POPULATION GROWTH

If, as James March and Herbert Simon suggest, innovation is most likely to arise from that part of an organization which is most dissatisfied with the existing effort and least programmed into routine administrative tasks, then by 1967 Congress had become a very likely source for innovation in foreign aid.[2] The authorizing committees especially were increasingly dissatisfied with foreign aid activities and very loosely programmed in their evaluations of AID and of foreign policy in general.

Even before President Johnson's call for action the population activists were planning a major approach to Congress. On January 18 Elmo Roper the public opinion analyst invited a dozen senators to lunch with him in the Capitol. Roper served in an advisory capacity to several action-oriented population groups. At the same time he was on close terms with a number of senators for whom he had often raised campaign funds. Roper was impatient at federal inaction. He asked Draper, who was already in Washington, to join them. Draper, having made preliminary contact with Senators Clark, Gruening, and Fulbright, arrived at the luncheon with a rough draft of the legislation in his pocket to authorize an additional $50 million for AID population assistance. The luncheon discussion generated a "critical mass" of Senate support. Most of those present agreed to co-sponsor the bill if Fulbright would take the lead. Draper agreed to revise his proposal as a specific amendment to the foreign aid bill and try to persuade the administration to support it.

On March 14, 1967, Senator Fulbright introduced S. 1264 with a total (eventually) of 18 co-sponsors. The bill added a new Title X to the Foreign Assistance Act authorizing an additional $50 million a year for three years to support voluntary family planning programs overseas.[3] Among the 12 Democratic and 6 Republican co-sponsors were the ranking Republican on the Foreign Relations Committee and 4 other members.* As he introduced the measure, Fulbright contrasted President Johnson's statements, the several mandates from Congress, and the $100 million program recommended by the White House Conference panel with AID's current plans to spend only $10 million on population problems in fiscal 1967. He observed:

> Congress has shown increasing concern over the world population crisis beginning with the approval in 1963 of my amendment . . . to conduct research . . . AID officials have not given the problem the high priority it deserves.[4]

Fortified by Senate support, Draper called on Congressman Thomas Morgan (D.-Pa.), chairman of the House Committee on Foreign Affairs. Morgan did not want to introduce Fulbright's measure as a separate bill but promised to see that it was brought up for consideration during the committee mark-up. Morgan also invited Draper to present the issue before the full committee during the foreign aid hearings.

The hearing was unexpectedly successful. Altogether more than a dozen members attended the sessions—unusual for public witnesses—and were obviously fascinated by a subject that had never before been seriously discussed.[5] To testify with him before the committee, Draper had invited Richard Gardner the former State Department Deputy Assistant Secretary and Chairman of the White House Conference panel that recommended the $100 million program; Dr. Louis Dupre, a Catholic professor of philosophy at Georgetown University; Dr. Raymond Ewell, an agricultural specialist and vice-president of the State

---

*The original co-sponsors were Clifford P. Case (R.-N.J.), Joseph S. Clark (D.-Pa.), Peter H. Dominick (R.-Colo.), Ernest S. Gruening (D.-Alaska), Phillip A. Hart (D.-Mich.), Mark O. Hatfield (R.-Ore.), Bourke B. Hickenlooper (R.-Iowa), Gale W. McGee (D.-Wyo.), Lee Metcalf (D.-Mont.), Wayne Morse (D.-Ore.), Frank E. Moss (D.-Utah), Charles H. Percy (R.-Ill.), Joseph Tydings (D.-Md.), Ralph Yarborough (D-Tex.), and Stephen M. Young (D.-Ohio). Subsequently, Frank Church (D.-Idaho), Thruston Morton (R.-Ky.), and Thomas Kuchel (R.-Calif.) joined.

University of New York at Buffalo; and Dr. Sheldon Segal, director of the Bio-Medical Division of the Population Council. Because Gardner's testimony was unusually long—including a review of previous government policy, an estimate of the costs of providing worldwide family planning services, a proposal for a U.N. World Population Program, and a projected $100 million population budget for AID—the group was invited to return again May 13 for further questioning.[6]

Draper's own appeal to the committee was direct and straight-forward. From his own 20 years of experience in foreign aid he had "gradually become convinced that unless and until the population explosion now erupting in Asia, Africa, and Latin America is brought under control, our entire aid program is doomed to failure. . . . We must start now. I plead for priority—the highest priority—for this program."[7]

With Gardner to emphasize the international concern, Dupre to indicate the expanding scope of Catholic thinking, Ewell to stress the urgency of the food problem, and Segal to help assure committee members that contraceptives were safe, the two days of testimony made a strong case. Against the background of a second year of drought in India, even Zablocki was constrained to start his questioning from a neutral position:

> Let me begin by saying that I am not opposed to family planning . . .
> I am concerned, however, about the political effects these under-takings may have in certain countries. I am very pleased, therefore, that the emphasis in your presentations this morning was on voluntary programs.[8]

Congressman Paul Findley, a dynamic and persistent Republican, introduced an amendment requiring not less than $75 million to be earmarked in the foreign aid authorization for population control projects and research.[9] The strongest opposition also came from a Republican, a Presbyterian bachelor, Congressman James Fulton (R.-Pa.), who suggested that "the United States needs to increase its population promptly to 500 million or 750 million" to compete with the communist giants.[10]

During the committee mark-up Findley offered his population amendment, which was defeated. Then with the support of Chairman Morgan and Congressman Wayne Hays (D.-Ohio) a substitute was developed that earmarked $50 million of total AID funds as a floor, not a ceiling, for population assistance. The committee retained the broad definition that included contraceptives but added a further provision offered by Zablocki to prevent expenditure of U.S. funds "in connection with any family planning program involving the use of abortion, sterilization, or euthanasia as a method of population control."[11]

Citing the "impressive evidence" that "population growth is outpacing food production," the House committee report, which in the past had toned down all Fulbright's proposals, was unequivocal:

> In order to counteract any possible tendency for the Agency for International Development to continue business as usual and to

regard family planning as a fringe operation, $50 million of economic assistance funds have been set aside to be used only for this purpose. This amendment will enable them to reorganize their operations in order to deal more effectively with the food-population problem.[12]

When the Foreign Assistance Act of 1967 finally reached the House floor so many other political controversies surrounded the measure that birth control, on request, for voluntary programs was hardly a major issue. Although a bill had been introduced, public hearings held, testimony distributed, and no thought given to avoiding publicity, the passage of Title X actually attracted very little attention. As Sagar Jain and Steven Sindig suggest in considering the passage of abortion reform in North Carolina, the less publicity, the less controversy, the less the perceived impact and importance of the measure, and the more deadlocked the legislative body is with other more "emotionally charged issues," the more likely a given measure is to pass. By chance rather than by design that was the case with Title X.[13]

Nevertheless, on the House floor Congressman Barratt O'Hara (D.-Ill.) offered an amendment to ensure that family planning would not "be made a condition for the granting of any aid or benefit under this Act."[14] But supporters argued that language already in the bill required the president to "establish reasonable procedures to insure ... that no individual will be coerced to practice methods of family planning."[15] With considerable force, Congressman Dent (D.-Pa.) declared:

> I happen to belong to that faith that has never believed in family control other than by some method best known to Catholics—which fails pretty often—but I say to you no matter what your religion is or the faith of the peoples of the world, especially those people who have not, until this time through the centuries been able to take care of themselves with respect to this problem, who have not been able to feed themselves—if they up until this time have failed to meet these problems, then someone had better do something.[16]

O'Hara's amendment was defeated by voice vote.[17]

A second amendment, offered by Fulton the next day, did succeed in cutting back the earmarked funds for population from $50 million to $20 million.[18] Fulton prevailed because he had a letter written by AID Administrator Gaud to Fulbright insisting that $20 million was all that AID could usefully spend on population. Fulton implied, from Gaud's letter, that the extra $30 million would be wasted at a time when U.S. domestic programs were being cut back for lack of money. Morgan the committee chairman accepted Fulton's amendment.

During the debate Congressman Donald Fraser (D.-Minn.) established for the record the fact that the bill permitted general budgetary grants to private and international bodies. Carey objected that the bill was deliberately worded to include the International Planned Parenthood Federation:

> This language is broad enough to include any conceivable agency for any purpose in this field that could ever be contrived in the time and

tenor of this bill. We have never given such a blank check to anyone before.[19]

O'Hara complained that "it includes the whole world. It is all a mess."[20] Yet the committee language was not changed.

On the Senate side Fulbright's amendment progressed in parallel fashion. Draper and Gardner testified before the Senate Committee on Foreign Relations in July.[21] Gardner stressed the proposal for a UN World Population Program, perhaps administered through the UN Development Program, based on voluntary contributions, with U.S. support of $20 million. It was one of the first moves toward what Draper and Rockefeller later persuaded U Thant and Paul Hoffman to establish as the UN Fund for Population Activities.[22]

While Congress was moving toward specific legislation, AID officials became increasingly apprehensive. From the moment Fulbright had introduced his bill with 18 co-sponsors Gaud began moving—almost in step with the congressional process—to demonstrate his own concern. The War on Hunger, with its elevated and expanded Population Service, had been announced by the president in February but it was not until the end of March, after Fulbright's bill was introduced, that the internal allocation of $20 million for population work in fiscal 1968 was finally settled and publicly announced.

Early in April Gaud took another big step. During hearings before the House Committee on Foreign Affairs Zablocki asked whether Gaud foresaw any policy changes during fiscal 1968. On the spur of the moment, though he had been mulling over the issue for months, Gaud seized the opportunity:

Gaud: I see no change in the policy. Yes, I will take that back. I
             see one possible change in our policy in this area, Mr.
             Zablocki. To date we in AID have not financed any
             contraceptives or the materials to manufacture contra-
             ceptives. My guess is, and it is only a guess, it won't be
             too long before we will be faced with the issue of
             whether we should use our resources for that purpose.

             My inclination would be to change our policy in that
             respect and use our funds for that purpose.

Zablocki: There will be no coercion?

Gaud: None; no, sir.[23]

Zablocki immediately changed the subject.

In the publicity that followed, Gaud's trial balloon stayed aloft. There was editorial praise and no criticism. In May 1967, after nearly 20 years, contraceptives were officially removed from the prohibited list.[24] But this initiative, although welcomed by birth control supporters, did not reduce the pressure to earmark more money. In fact, the possibility of providing oral contraceptives to the developing countries increased the need for money.

By late July, when it was widely known that the House committee had reserved $50 million from the authorized funds for population, Gaud announced a further increase in the agency's internal allocations, from $20 million to $25 million.[25]

While AID uncompromisingly opposed the concept of earmarking, Philander P. Claxton, Jr., the State Department Special Assistant on Population Matters recognized both Gaud's objections and Congress's determination. He proposed, at first through official State-AID legislative channels, that a special provision be added, allowing loan funds to be used as grants to support population activities. This unusual feature was the only significant proposal to come from the executive branch during the entire consideration of the measure. AID officials did not object so Claxton took the proposed language and personally explained and recommended it to the Foreign Relations Committee staff.

The Senate bill, as reported from the committee, authorized up to $50 million and provided that "funds used for such purposes may be used on a loan or grant basis."[26] Citing the still-limited personnel and funding in AID, the report praised the "new attention and emphasis" yet insisted on adding "broader and more specific authority." Reflecting Draper's promptings about the International Planned Parenthood Federation and Fulbright's support for the United Nations, the report urged AID "to develop and support programs making maximum possible use of multilateral channels for population assistance."[27] The bill passed the Senate with Catholic opposition confined to a pro forma letter in the hearings record.

When the House and Senate conferees met to resolve their considerable differences, Gaud was still trying to prove that no earmarking was necessary. In mid-September AID issued new guidelines to all the missions, setting forth "what are now higher levels of priority in U.S. policies"[28] and new emphasis on "action programs." At the same time, Gaud made a deliberately publicized speech to the General Federation of Women's Clubs announcing to the ladies that pills and condoms would be sent to India and that substantial grants would be made to the International Planned Parenthood Federation and the Population Council.[29]

Nevertheless, despite Gaud's efforts the birth control supporters emerged from conference with the best of both worlds. The House language on mandatory earmarking was accepted but the references to sterilization, abortion, and euthanasia were not. The Senate language turning loan funds into grants was accepted. The dollar amounts were split at $35 million.[30]

The final language of Title X, Programs Relating to Population Growth, was short, simple and, as House opponents observed, extremely broad. The president could provide voluntary assistance to governments, UN agencies, U.S. and international private nonprofit organizations, universities, hospitals, and "voluntary health or other qualified organizations," for programs relating to population growth, including research, information, services, and manufacture and "provision of medical assistance and supplies." Sec. 292 established, in a single sentence, the priority and timing:

Of the funds provided to carry out the provisions of Part I of this
Act for the fiscal year 1968, $35,000,000 shall be available only to
carry out the purposes of this title and, notwithstanding any other
Provisions of this Act, funds used for such purposes may be used on
a loan or grant basis.[31]

In other words, AID had from November 14, 1967, when the authorization was
signed, until midnight on June 30, 1968, to obligate $35 million on population
work or the remainder would revert to the Treasury.

One more hurdle remained—the appropriation process. Resenting the fact
that Draper's word seemed to carry more weight with Congress than his own,
Gaud urged the Senate Appropriations Committee to reduce the population
money:

In a year in which our funds are going to be as restricted as they are
this year, does it make any sense to earmark $35 million and say we
can only spend it on family planning? We will not spend it. I am
convinced of that. . . . This is the first time I can remember when we
have in our bill a provision that we must spend so many dollars for a
specific purpose. . . . I think it is wrong. We should not force this on
any country.[32]

The House and Senate appropriations committees sympathized with
Gaud, who offered to help in drafting the necessary language.[33] The Senate
appropriation bill, like the House version, limited to $20 million the amount of
technical cooperation and development grant funds that could be spent on
family planning.[34]

But, in fact, the appropriations committees had not achieved their
purpose. The $20 million restriction applied only to one category of funds.
Population projects could still be supported from a half dozen other loan or
grant categories that were not restricted. To clinch the matter, in January after
nine months of conflict Fulbright asked Gaud's confirmation of the earmarking. Gaud had to admit that "the earmarking of $35 million for popula-
tion programs is unaffected by the appropriation act."[35] Furious at Draper—
and not too pleased with Ravenholt, who in February 1968 told Senator
Gruening that the principal impediment was lack of funds and personnel—Gaud
nevertheless set out to implement the congressional mandate promptly and in
good faith.

WHY AID RESISTED

The evolution of Title X was a clear and undisputed case of legislative
initiative. The concept was originally developed and prompted by Roper and
Draper—like many other government programs it originated with private individuals or organizations; it gained status and authority from Fulbright and
the Senate co-sponsors; it was publicly discussed at the House hearings; it was

modified and strengthened by the interaction between House and Senate; and
it was enacted over the continuing protests of the agency involved. This
congressional action was possible in 1967 for many reasons, but most directly
it was triggered by the pervading concern over the world food crisis and the
growing credibility gap between AID and Congress.

Actually, at the very point when Title X was introduced AID had begun
to move faster than ever before. The Office of the War on Hunger was
announced just before the bill was introduced and more staff was being
recruited. Yet Gaud continued to resist the earmarking. In part, Gaud's objections were based, as he said, on a genuine fear that $35 million was more
money than could be usefully spent in 1968 on population assistance. Under
the officially articulated policy help could be provided only to and at the
request of governments. That would entail long, tedious negotiations with
foreign agencies that were often even more bureaucratic and hesitant than AID.
Ravenholt's brash assurances that he could spend the money were taken to
reflect only his own inexperience. All the advice coming to Gaud from the AID
missions overseas and the regional bureaus in Washington, which were responsible for bilateral assistance, stressed the difficulty of negotiating government-
to-government aid programs on a short time schedule.

David Bell, who had left AID to become vice-president of the Ford
Foundation, warned Gaud that a vigorous AID population program would
boomerang. Bell declared in October 1967 (in a speech that was reprinted in
the AID magazine in February 1968):

> Members of Congress who recently pressed for $50 million a year for
> assistance to family planning programs in developing countries would
> do more good at present by pressing half that much upon the
> National Institutes of Health for research in reproductive biology and
> contraceptive technology.[36]

Most of the population professionals, foundations, and universities tended to
agree.

In part, too, AID opposition to earmarking reflected the serious funding
and personnel pressures on the whole agency caused by declining appropriations. Technical cooperation and development grants, from which everyone
originally expected most of the population money to come, had been reduced
through the authorizing and appropriations process from $243 million re-
quested by the administration to $180 million appropriated—and of which $35
million was earmarked for the new population program. Although the loan-
to-grant language in effect added nearly 20 percent to technical cooperation
and development grants, which were the heart of the program, Gaud always
depicted Title X as a subtraction from AID resources rather than an addition to
grant funds.

Samuel Huntington in discussing Defense Department funding suggests a
further reason for such bureaucratic resistance—the fact that in a basically
hierarchical situation the power to allocate scarce resources may seem more
important than the resources themselves. Thus AID Administrator Gaud, confronted with the possibility of congressional earmarking, conformed to the

pattern Huntington predicted, namely, that an official, "if forced to choose, normally prefers fewer resources and greater freedom to allocate them as he sees fit than more resources less subject to his control."[37] With both resources and the freedom to allocate them substantially reduced, Gaud resisted strongly.

Moreover, Gaud, and in fact many executive agency officials, shared a basic sense of rivalry with the legislative branch. Although Senator Gruening preceded and outlasted HEW Secretary John Gardner in office and Senator Fulbright long preceded and still outlasts Administrator Gaud, neither Gardner nor Gaud would admit the senators to genuine partnership in setting policy or priority. Even where there was no disagreement over objectives, even where Congress and the president were of the same party, even where the issue was one of relatively little national concern with low political payoff, still the reflex of the executive branch was to oppose any suggestion that originated in Congress. At best, the legislators' population initiatives were accepted in principle but rejected in practice by the federal agencies. Over the long run, however, in the population field as in other more conspicuous areas of policy, one of the results of the determination of the executive branch to control all innovation in government was actually to stimulate congressional resistance and innovation.

From an administrator's point of view almost any proposal offered by Congress—aside from providing additional unlimited funds or personnel—represents some restriction of authority or flexibility. The very same proposal originating within the executive branch, however, is not seen as a limitation of power but rather as a normal exercise or even an expansion of control. Thus Gardner opposed Gruening's bill to appoint an assistant secretary for population, yet Gaud enthusiastically initiated a War on Hunger under an assistant administrator, a move he viewed as adding not only to AID's public image but also to his personal control over the agency. One can only surmise what the respective reactions would have been if Gaud had proposed substantial internal earmarking of population funds in 1966 and Fulbright had introduced legislation to create an Office of the War on Hunger under an assistant administrator before President Johnson's message.

The determination of priorities in U.S. government policy is in the final analysis a political question. The crucial decisions are not made by the experts who know their own professions or institutions inside out. They are made by the generalists or activists from the president down who must balance dozens of conflicting claims and values to find the best solution possible. Whe Gaud refused to make the decisions Congress wanted on program priority, Congress used its ultimate fiscal or political control to set those priorities directly. Moreover, the power was exercised by the substantive authorizing committees whose proper concern is policy and priority in such a way that it could not easily be overturned by the appropriations committees whose usual concern was efficiency and good management.[38] The resulting legislation established a program and a pattern of operation that in the long run has had an impact beyond population activities alone.

CONGRESS PUSHES DOMESTIC PROGRAMS

During the same year that saw the legislative earmarking for foreign aid, Congress also earmarked funds for two domestic family planning efforts—the antipoverty program and HEW's maternal and child health activities. Fulbright was not alone in his impatience; Senator Clark, whose committee handled the authorizing legislation for the Office of Economic Opportunity (OEO), and the House Committee on Ways and Means, which handled the maternal and child health programs, were also somewhat ahead of OEO and far ahead of HEW in raising the priority of family planning work.

Prodding OEO, Clark in the Senate and Scheuer in the House succeeded in designating family planning one of eight "National Emphasis programs."[39] OEO spent over $4 million on family planning projects in fiscal 1967. Despite appropriations cuts by the end of fiscal 1968, OEO had obligated $9.6 million for family planning services by June 1968, in most cases supporting Planned Parenthood, community, or demonstration clinics.[40] Thus OEO, like AID, more than doubled family planning expenditures between 1967 and 1968.

The major breakthrough in domestic legislation in 1967 seemed to come, however, via the Social Security Amendments of 1967, on initiatives undertaken by Congressmen George Bush (R.-Tex.) and Herman Schneebeli (R.-Pa.) of the Ways and Means Committee. Bush and the rest of the Ways and Means Committee had been impressed by the testimony of Planned Parenthood's persuasive president, Dr. Alan Guttmacher, and by the increasing number of women with dependent children on welfare. When the Social Security bill emerged from committee with a detailed revision of old age, welfare, and health insurance programs, it contained seven direct references to family planning and a number of indirect ones. Specifically, not less than 6 percent of appropriated funds for Maternal and Child Health Services and for Maternal and Infant Care projects were to be "available for family planning services."[41] State departments of health were required to include family planning services in their comprehensive planning.[42] On the welfare side, states were required to make family planning available to all appropriate individuals.[43] Coercion was specifically prohibited; nevertheless, the House version of the bill required even mothers of young children to seek employment, if possible, and barred increases in federal aid to states where the proportion of dependent children on welfare increased after January 1968. Planned Parenthood and the Catholic church could join forces in opposing these restrictions, which were modified by the Senate.[44]

Yet, while the economically oriented antipoverty bill and welfare-oriented Social Security bill stressed family planning, the broader HEW health programs deliberately downgraded the issue. The Johnson administration's main "Partnership for Health" bill was designed to eliminate categorical grants for specific health problems. Lee again opposed a separate birth control bill. On these grounds, Tydings's second attempt to add specific family planning money in a new authorization died without consideration.[45]

The attitude of the HEW appropriations subcommittees was similarly ambivalent toward family planning. As the Senate committee report on NIH all too clearly revealed, the primary emphasis on health actually inhibited an energetic search for new solutions to the population problem:

> The Institue [National Institute of Child Health and Human Development] not only has a responsibility for improving family planning methods, as a partial solution to the population problem, but also—and more importantly—to investigate the health aspects of various family planning techniques.[46]

As a result funds for new contraceptive development came very slowly. Even appropriations for family planning services clearly authorized in the Social Security bill were nearly eliminated in fiscal 1969 when the House appropriations subcommittee tried, despite the earmarking, to cut out all new programs.

As in the case of the foreign aid funding the appropriations committees were basically opposed to sudden large increases. Even though, during the 1950s and early 1960s the Labor-HEW appropriations subcommittees had—uncharacteristically—forced extra money into NIH research,[47] they did not feel the same enthusiasm for birth control as for cancer control. Moreover, without an interested authorizing committee looking at the program every year it was difficult for anyone outside of these small appropriations subcommittees to influence HEW priorities.[48] Although agencies do not like the double congressional review, the attention of authorizing committees to broader policy issues was essential for the development of population programs.[49]

By 1967 the greatest enemy of federal birth control programs appeared to be not the Catholic Church nor the black militants but rather the ponderous workings of the federal agencies themselves. The older, the bigger, the more complex, the more professional the agency, and the more insulated from substantive committees in Congress, the longer it took to institute new programs related to population or family planning. On the other hand, AID and OEO, both relative newcomers, small, insecure, unprofessional, and completely at the mercy of Congress, were pushed by two sets of Congressional committees into vigorous family planning programs.

15

**A NEW PROGRAM
IS BORN,
1968-69**

When Lyndon Johnson affixed his signature to the Foreign Aid Appropriation Bill for 1968, all the rudiments of a substantial AID population program were finally at hand. Birth control was accepted as relevant to the more-or-less-established U.S. objective of economic development overseas. Birth control was known to be scientifically and politically feasible because of the new technology and the diminshed Catholic opposition. Finally, by 1968 birth control seemed urgent, a program that could no longer be postponed because the costs of inaction were becoming drastically higher than the costs of action. In AID, birth control had gained a higher priority than programs like health and education because it was more closely related to the war on hunger; in other words, it was doubly relevant—not only to the abstract concept of economic development but also to the more vivid appeal of worldwide famine prevention.

The biggest question that still remained was whether AID could do the job that Congress and the president wanted done. Could an agency condemned on every side as a moribund bureaucracy on the verge of dismemberment with little hope of attracting professional talent develop a viable program in a new field on short notice? In the 1950s when the foreign aid program was merely an ad hoc amalgam of military assistance, defense subsidies, and Point IV technical assistance projects the task would have been unthinkable even if the subject had not been. Even in the early 1960s when AID was carefully linking grants and loans and other resources into coherent country programs the governments would surely have required years to draw up the kind of family planning actions that could use $35 million of foreign exchange. But by the late 1960s development was increasingly interpreted not only as an economic process but also as a social and cultural transformation. AID was becoming an institution-builder, supporting the kind of institutions—like universities and international organizations—that could adapt and disseminate new technology into traditional cultures.[1]

In that overall pattern of AID transformation the development of the agency's population program may itself be seen as an example of institution

building. The process of building a new program in AID, like the process of
building a new university in Nigeria, would require resources, strategy, and
leadership.[2] The activist aim of solving the population problem would conflict
not only with the aim of each profession to pursue its own independent skills
but also with the aim of every bureaucrat to maintain his own official fiefdom.
In the years after 1967 the AID population program moved rapidly ahead to
acquire the resources, design the strategy, exert the leadership, and develop the
institutional structure to deal with the population problems in the developing
nations.

RESOURCES, 1968-69

The most important resource of the population program after 1967 was
the money earmarked by Congress. In an unorthodox, self-imposed, and
entirely informal division of labor Draper had assumed responsibility for
persuading Congress to provide the resources. Thus no sooner were the funds
available for fiscal 1968 than Draper began arguing for a larger sum to be
earmarked for 1969. Even before the 1968 funds were fully obligated Draper
told the House Committee on Foreign Affairs, "AID has now established a
pattern of assistance that may well be a model for future AID programs. Mr.
Gaud, his War on Hunger, and the entire Agency are to be congratulated."[3]

He assured the congressmen, "At least $50 million could be wisely
expended in 1969 to continue the expansion and effectiveness of family
planning programs."[4] Quick to perceive the importance of the world food crisis
for population policy, Draper suggested in 1968 that the long-term, goal-
oriented approach of the Ford and Rockefeller Foundations that were creating
the Green Revolution in agriculture was also relevant for population.

At Draper's initiative the vice-president of the Rockefeller Foundation
testified before the House committee on the foundation's commitment to
research and development in agriculture. Congressman Fulton still objected, "If
there are too many people and not enough straw hats, the answer is, don't kill
off the people, but make more straw hats."[5] Nevertheless the committee,
encouraged by Congressman Robert Taft, Jr., (R.-Ohio), increased the earmarking to $50 million for fiscal 1969.

AID Administrator Gaud remained just as vigorously opposed, but
Fulton's second attempt to cut the amount with an amendment on the House
floor was unsuccessful. Committee Chairman Morgan argued against any cutbacks in the population program for 1969. "This program is now moving very
well in the developing countries. I would hate to see any limitation of funds
put on it by cutting it back."[6] The Senate adopted the same figure and
language as the House. Thus $50 million was earmarked for population in 1969
out of a final appropriation of $1.9 million, the lowest in AID history.

As a result of Draper's efforts the overworked population staff was partly
relieved of the time-consuming chore of justifying their programs, item by
item, against the competition of the rest of the agency. As long as the
allocation that really counted was made by Congress, the Bureau for Policy and

Program Coordination lost its veto over funding. The Population Service could devote its attention and staff to the basic issues of population programming rather than the procedural tasks of budget review. Within AID, as in Congress, earmarking meant that units with substantive rather than housekeeping responsibilities asserted control over the program.

To be sure, the other offices in AID did not easily give up their ambitions to be quarterback. Technically, the central management offices retained the right to allocate funds among the country missions, regional bureaus, and the nonregional programs. The population unit always had to go through the motions of an annual review—if only to help the rest of the agency save face—for a budget that was as a rule considerably lower than Congress would provide. But at the end of each fiscal year the real power of the earmarking would surface above procedural quagmires; missions and bureaus would begin to report that they could not meet their allocated funding; the population staff would produce a backlog of unfunded projects and stand ready to absorb the difference right up to and over the earmarked total. Because the floor established by Congress was a generous one the real power to allocate the funds gravitated toward the individuals and offices that took the greatest initiative and worked the hardest.

In the three years before 1968 the Population Branch allocated an average of 27 percent of AID population funds and its share was declining. In the four years after 1968 the Central Population Office allocated an average of 46 percent of the funds and its share was increasing. The 50-some overseas missions of AID, each of which by 1968 had one full- or part-time population officer and some of which, like India, had five to ten full-time, accounted for only 39 percent of the dollar funding between 1968 and 1971 (see Tables 15.1 and 15.2). (This figure reflected a grant of $20 million to India, which was technically a country mission obligation but was in fact largely the result of Ravenholt's intervention.) The regional bureaus in Washington, each with one to ten professional staff members, averaged only 15 percent of the total funding between 1968 and 1971.

Gradually the Population Service, which in 1969 became the Office of Population, extended its jurisdiction to include nearly all university grants, assistance to private organizations working overseas, and support for United Nations agencies. The UN program, growing rapidly after 1969, received a steadily increasing share of funds and attention from the central population unit: $500,000 in fiscal 1968; $2.5 million in 1969; $4 million in 1970; $14 million in 1971; and $24 million in 1972. (See Chapter 19).

In making use of the agency's resources after 1967, therefore, the central Population Office played a larger role than all the country missions combined and three times as large a role as all the geographic bureaus in Washington combined. Apart from the substantial increase in the nonregional and United Nations funding the other major change in resource allocation was the decline in the Latin American program and the increase in the various Asian and African efforts as government programs took hold in Asia and Africa but lagged in Latin America.

Title X conveyed other resources besides money. It provided a legislative mandate to ignore some of the legal and administrative restrictions that delayed

TABLE 15.1

AID Dollar Obligations by Source of Funding for Population and
Family-Planning Projects, Fiscal Years 1968-71

	1968	1969	1970	1971	Total 1968-71
	(thousands of dollars)				
Nonregional	11,596	21,369	28,291	53,330	114,586
Country missions, including Vietnam	18,447	13,779	39,682	25,327	97,235
Regional projects	4,707	10,296	6,599	17,211	38,813
Total	34,750	45,444	74,572	95,868	250,634
	(percentages)				
Nonregional	33	47	38	56	46
Country missions, including Vietnam	53	30	53	26	39
Regional projects	14	23	8	18	15
Total	100	100	99	100	100

Source: U.S. Agency for International Development, *Population Program Assistance* (Washington, D.C., October 1969 and December 1971).

other AID activities. Congress had called for maximum flexibility. Although the Bureau for Program and Policy Coordination, the general counsel, some contracting officers, and even the program office in the War on Hunger tried to apply the usual rules, they did not always succeed. Thus, for example, use of the "clasped hands" symbol of U.S. assistance, required for food and other aid, was waived for condoms, contraceptives, and family planning equipment; International Planned Parenthood Federation officials were spared the need to exchange all funds at a U.S. disbursing office or travel exclusively on U.S. airlines; private foreign hospitals and family planning associations were not required to open their books directly to U.S. government auditors. But each of these exceptions required a considerable struggle and often an appeal to higher levels. During these struggles the bureaucratic skills and persistence of "old AID hands" like Irene Walker and Burt Johnson in the Population Service were indispensable.

The population program also benefited from another congressional innovation in the foreign aid program. In 1966 Senator George McGovern (D.-S.D.) succeeded in adding a new section, 211(d), to the Foreign Assistance Act that authorized general programmatic support "to research and educational institutions in the United States, for the purpose of strengthening their capacity to develop and carry out programs concerned with the economic and social development of less developed countries."[7] McGovern was thinking of agricultural training, but in fiscal 1968 the Population Service negotiated the first two "Section 211(d) grants" with the Johns Hopkins University and the University of North Carolina "to develop specialized competency in the family planning and population field."[8]

The major resource not specifically allocated by Title X but left within AID's discretion was personnel. Both the number and grade-level of the population staff were determined internally under overall AID personnel ceilings set by Congress. Despite annual and substantial increases in funding there were only two major increases in personnel for the central population unit—in spring 1967 when the Population Service was established in the new Office of the War on Hunger and in early 1970 when the Population Office was expanded in the new Bureau for Technical Assistance. Because of the agency-wide cutbacks, only three new professional positions were assigned to the

TABLE 15.2

AID Dollar Obligations by Region for Population and
Family-Planning Projects, Fiscal Years 1968-71

	1968	1969	1970	1971	Total 1968-71
(thousands of dollars)					
Nonregional	11,596	21,369	28,291	53,330	114,586
Latin America	7,925	10,327	10,957	15,246	44,455
Near East-South Asia	9,716	4,312	23,185	6,590	43,803
Africa	663	1,440	2,663	7,783	12,549
East Asia, including Vietnam	4,850	7,996	9,476	12,919	35,241
Total	34,750	45,444	74,572	95,868	250,634
(percentages)					
Nonregional	33	47	38	56	46
Latin America	23	23	15	16	18
Near East-South Asia	28	9	31	7	17
Africa	2	3	4	8	5
East Asia, including Vietnam	14	18	13	13	14
Total	100	100	101	100	100

Source: U.S. Agency for International Development, Population Program Assistance (Washington, D.C., October 1969 and December 1971).

central population unit between June 1967 and December 1969—an indication of how funding levels might have fared in the absence of congressional earmarking.

The main personnel expansion according to AID records occurred in the overseas AID missions, where population staff increased from 18 in June 1967 to 80 by June 1970 (see Table 15.3), but this increase reflected not so much new or qualified population officers coming in as the increased work load in population forced upon the existing personnel by the congressional earmarking. In other words, although AID administrators complained that they could not expand their population staffs because of a shortage of available experts,[9] actually the expansion in funding forced their unqualified staff to spend time on population anyway and to get some training on the job. As Ravenholt once observed with more candor than tact:

> This population program reminds me of one summer I spent as a farm worker trying to get a harvest in with an untrained, unmatched team. We just had to hitch up anyway and get started. If it didn't go one way, we tried another. By the time the harvest was gathered we were all working together just fine.[10]

It was the same point Berelson often made: "The best way to begin is to begin."

STRATEGIES

The first and foremost strategy of the population program in 1968 and 1969 was to prove that AID could, despite everyone's doubts, spend the earmarked funds "sensibly." Overcoming his initial annoyance, AID Administrator Gaud took a broad view of his responsibilities. "It is my purpose," Gaud cabled all the AID missions on January 13, 1968, "to see that the Congressional intent is carried out to the fullest while avoiding any form of coercion."

> Unusually rapid project and program formulation and action will be necessary. All practicable steps will be taken ... to facilitate development and approval of projects and programs. ... Assistance can take many forms and be programmed through a variety of non-government as well as government institutions and organizations. Consideration will be given to all proposals for useful action including large-scale activities involving substantial commodity assistance. ... Adequacy of all key program components, such as demographic data, technical facilities, trained personnel, contraceptive supplies, communication services, and transportation should be ensured.[11]

The verbal barriers and inhibitions were gone at last. "Family planning," the message concluded, "will be a continuing major preoccupation of AID."

TABLE 15.3

**Professional AID Staff Assigned to Population, Fiscal Years 1965-72
(Full- or major-time, authorized positions)**

Fiscal Year	Obligations (millions of dollars)	Professional Personnel — Washington			Missions Total	Agency Total
		Population Office	Other Washington Offices	Washington Total		
June 1965	1.2	1	1	2	1	3
Dec. 1965		1	1	2	1	3
June 1966	3.0	2	2	4	7	11
Dec. 1966		3	2	5	9	14
June 1967	3.4	20	7	27	18	45
June 1968		20	8	28	22	50
Dec. 1968	34.8	20	8	28	33	61
June 1969		23	11	34	50	84
Dec. 1969	45.4	23	11	34	50	84a
June 1970		38	26	64	80	144
Dec. 1970	74.6	38b	30	68	82	150
June 1971		38	31	69	82	151
Dec. 1971	95.9	38	33	71	82	153
Mar. 1972	125.0c	38	32	70	79d	149

aOn November 7, 1969, AID, in response to President Nixon's Message on Population indicated that authorized population positions would be increased to 160.

bThe December 1970 tally lists 42 authorized positions but four of those positions, expected to be approved, were turned down later within AID.

cEstimated.

dIn March 1972 AID distinguished between clerical and professional Mission staff for the first time. The apparent decline represents overseas clerical staff previously counted as professional.

Source: Personnel figures from mimeographed AID reports, *Positions in Population as of dates indicated*; funding figures from AID *Population Program Assistance* (Washington, D.C., December 1971); p. 23.

Ravenholt who had drafted much of the cable was even more determined than Gaud to meet or exceed the congressional targets of $35 million in 1968 and $50 million in 1969. Under his leadership the Population Service became more than just a staff office and moved deliberately to fill the gaps left by country missions and regional bureaus. For him, the first challenge in 1968 was to make sure that the earmarked money was in fact going to population programs. "The bees are coming to the honey pot," Ravenholt would say as he fought off other offices that suddenly wanted to redefine their ongoing projects as "population control." The Alliance for Progress, for instance, wanted to finance maternal and child care programs that included no contraceptives and to call them family planning. The Ford Foundation wanted AID to turn $10 million directly over to the National Institutes of Health where Congress had cut back population research. Every bureau, every discipline had tentative plans for using the money that Gaud had called excessive. But Ravenholt insisted that it was all needed for population programs with direct impact. In most cases, Gaud backed him up.

In order to meet the short fiscal-year deadlines, Ravenholt's strategy also required other channels of funding in addition to government-to-government agreements negotiated by the overseas missions. In practice, the only way that a small central staff could obligate large sums of money in a short time was through private intermediaries, either universities, professional institutions like the Population Council, or other organizations already active in the field like the International Planned Parenthood Federation or the Pathfinder Fund in Boston. Because of the time pressure and the limited number of qualified organizations in the field, a strategy emerged of relatively large grants to those who could perform in a variety of places and programs. Thus the trend of funding by the central population unit was consistently toward larger, less specific, more programmatic grants. The average size of individual Population Service grants increased steadily, a trend not evident in regional or country grants. (See Table 15.4.)

Furthermore, in a field where few experts existed at a time when financial stringency prevented AID from hiring any of them anyway (and skepticism about AID prevented any of them from wanting to be hired) the use of intermediaries became a virtue dictated by necessity. Within the framework of the War on Hunger, support for nongovernmental organizations also made considerable sense to Gaud because he wanted to promote private enterprise generally; it made sense to Waters because he appreciated the political support that private agencies could bring to hear; it made sense to Ravenholt because he found the private groups more willing than governments to undertake the specific contraceptive distribution, evaluation, and demonstration projects that he wanted to encourage. Finally, as Draper constantly reiterated, the history of the birth control movement, from private voluntary groups to family planning associations to government programs, suggested that vigorous private sector activity was necessary to persuade governments to take action. In birth control programs, too, even governments are basically intermediaries in reaching the individual decision maker—and often intermediaries with less experience and conviction than many private organizations.

TABLE 15.4

Average Size of AID Population Grants, Fiscal Years 1965-72[a]
(amount and average size in thousands of dollars)

	1965	1966	1967	1968	1969	1970	1971[c]	1972[c] (est.)
Nonregional								
Number	8	5	5	23	30	37	54	42
Amount	892	872	971	11,596	21,369	28,225	36,248	52.5
Average size	112	174	194	504	712	763	671	1,226
Latin America								
Number	7	4	8	9	10	10	9	
Amount	1,105	565	1,191	2,468	7,255	5,518	8,161	
Average size	158	141	149	274	726	552	907	
Near East-South Asia[b]								
Number	0	0	0	4	6	2	5	
Amount				655	976	324	1,449	
Average size				164	163	162	290	
Africa								
Number	0	0	0	2	4	2	8	
Amount	0	0	0	259	457	181	5,699	
Average size				130	114	91	712	
East Asia								
Number	0	0	2	2	2	2	5	
Amount	0	0	350	1,325	1,608	623	1,942	
Average size			175	663	804	208	388	
Regional Average								
Number	7	4	10	17	22	16	27	20
Amount	1,105	565	1,541	4,707	10,296	6,646	17,251	12,400
Average size	158	141	154	277	468	415	635	620

[a]Regional does not include country mission programs.

[b]Including CENTO project.

[c]Excluding UN contributions of $14 million and $24 million in 1971 and 1972 respectively.

Source: U.S. Agency for International Development, *Population Program Assistance* (Washington, D.C., December 1971), pp. 215-31; for 1965, 1966, and 1967 figures see *ibid.*, October 1969, pp. 29-41.

In general, Ravenholt wanted to simplify AID programming, to concentrate on the easiest, most direct methods and ignore or denounce the others. In AID, that meant direct dollar grants with as few strings as possible. It also meant a long feud with the Near East-South Asia Bureau of AID where personnel had been thoroughly imbued with the need to use up the millions of dollars of local currencies for local costs and to negotiate program loans on tough terms for any U.S. commodities. The fact that Title X allowed grants instead of loans did not prevent the NESA Bureau from negotiating a $2.7 million loan for vehicle parts with India in fiscal 1968. Only the NESA Bureau continued to advocate loans in spite of the disappointing results in Turkey and later problems with the Indian loan.

Beyond the pressures of time and money, Ravenholt also developed a basic program strategy that went beyond the still-repeated but more and more meaningless principles of assistance on request to governments for voluntary programs, offering free choice of method, with no AID advocacy of policy or method.[12] In a 1968 article in *Demography* he listed six major and continuing areas of AID program emphasis: project and program grants to qualified organizations like the Population Council, the International Planned Parenthood Federation, and the Pathfinder Fund; basic support to university population centers; grant assistance to government family planning programs; purchase of commodities, especially contraceptives; contributions to the United Nations Population Fund, and research funds for evaluation of specific methods and delivery systems.[13]

The goals that Ravenholt outlined for the program were very simple: "To make family planning information and services fully available to and used by all elements of these developing societies."[14] Family planning programs were thus broadly defined to include information, education, clinics, general availability of contraceptives, and elimination of restrictive laws.

The strategy sounded elementary but the underlying issues were complex. In November 1967 the sociologist Kingsley Davis rocked the family planning world with a forceful article in *Science* magazine insisting that family planning could not solve the population problem.[15] Motivation, not birth control, was the critical factor, he argued. Motivation depended not on contraceptives or on family planning as he narrowly defined it, but rather on laws, customs, and social policies that in most countries still encouraged childbearing.

Many of the population activists were horrified. Planned Parenthood came down firmly on the side of family planning. As Fred Jaffe put it, the sociologists' stress on motivation or in the United States on "the culture of poverty" was a "cop-out" to excuse the fact that family planning was still not easily accessible for poor disadvantaged women and that social services were still inhibited in making it available.[16] One irate businessman suggested, "Why don't we lock all these academics up in a room somewhere and not let them out until they can agree on something?"

Nevertheless many professionals, especially those with a social science background, began to move in the direction that Kingsley Davis was beckoning. When his wife Judith Blake, also a professor of sociology, later raised the demand for alternative, non-child-bearing careers for women, the feminists also were attracted.[17] "Motivation" became the newest word in the population jargon. The Kingsley Davis article, Bernard Berelson observed, marked "the end of the honeymoon period, when we still thought that the answers were simple and that we were all on the right track."[18] Berelson's formal response was a judicious synthesis entitled, "Beyond Family Planning," in which he pointed out that many of the other proposals were still not politically or technically feasible while family planning was.[19]

Ravenholt, like Jaffe, considered the whole approach a "cop-out." Family planning administrators who were supposed to be delivering the services were falling down on the job, he declared. Ravenholt, in Washington, trying to push family planning support out into the field despite the resistance of regional bureaus and country missions, handicapped at every point by the organizational weakness of the War on Hunger office, was determined not to dissipate AID resources in a will-of-the-wisp pursuit of "motivation." Women with full access to family planning would not overreproduce, he declared. Furthermore, he insisted it was a waste of time even to talk about motivation until a full range of methods was available.

Another conspicuous and even more controversial feature of the AID program was Ravenholt's predilection for pills. Draper and Ravenholt were both impressed by the 1965 Westoff and Ryder study that revealed unexpectedly rapid U.S. acceptance of orals.[20] Both believed that it made no sense at all deliberately to keep oral contraceptives out of national programs in Taiwan, Korea, India, and Pakistan. Some experts, on the other hand, feared that making pills easily available would reduce the overall effectiveness of family planning programs because IUDs stayed in place longer than pill users continued with their daily pills. The Population Council, which had officially sponsored and promoted the intrauterine contraceptive device, and many others considered the pill at first too expensive. When AID bulk procurement reduced the price to less than $0.20 a month, opponents argued that a once-a-day medication required too much motivation. When Ravenholt began to suggest that pills could be dispensed by paramedical personnel or even freely sold over the counter,[21] the Population Council began to circulate warnings to its overseas representatives about newly suspected health hazards. Thereafter, opponents of the pill emphasized old and new evidence of medical dangers, including the perennial threat that had been raised against all forms of contraceptive, namely that they caused cancer.[22] Pill proponents, on the other hand, and the AID program officially took the position that the data on thromboembolism, establishing a real but small risk, was quite irrelevant in most of the developing countries where pregnancy was often a life-threatening experience and thromboembolism almost nonexistent.[23]

The controversy over pills may be seen in different lights but as a matter of government policy and programming it followed the characteristic patterns that Huntington noted of weapons development rivalry.[24] Although such debates take the form of technical reviews, susceptible to prolonged research and objective evaluation, they are as much issues of power as issues of science. The real question is not only whether this army missile actually performs better than that air force missile but also whether the army or the air force will dominate the program.

The pill-IUD debate (in the absence of any more conclusive medical evidence than that produced to date) can be seen in terms of a power struggle. Before 1968 the professional organizations like the Population Council that were associated with the IUD and the activist organizations like Planned Parenthood that received help from the drug companies were fairly evenly balanced. Governments and administrators seemed to favor the IUD while most women chose the pill.

The advent of the population program in AID, however, which by June 1969 had become the largest single supporter of population and family planning programs in the world, upset the prevailing balance of power. By aligning himself strongly with the pill supporters, Ravenholt brought the issue out into the open at a time when some drug companies had quietly spread rumors against the IUD and some professional organizations were using their channels of communication to tell only the IUD side of the story.

The final results are still in doubt, although IUD programs have run into increasing difficulty while the newer pill programs still seem to be gaining. Whichever method may ultimately be a better weapon in the birth control armory it will, because of AID involvement, be much more widely available, both to individual seekers and within national programs. It will also be more thoroughly tested and evaluated by its proponents—in self-defense—because of the increased professional concern.

LEADERSHIP

Besides resources and strategy, the other element in the revitalized population program was leadership. In addition to Dr. Ravenholt—who served as chief of the Population Branch, then director of the Population Service, and, after 1969, director of the Population Office—Draper, Claxton, and Gaud were leaders in the early development of the population assistance program.

Draper's obvious role, as noted, was in raising money—first, for the International Planned Parenthood Federation to help bring its budgets from less than $1 million in 1965 to $25 million in 1972; second, for the AID population program by encouraging and persuading Congress to earmark funds; and third, for the UN Fund for Population Activities by encouraging and persuading governments to make voluntary contributions. Draper took no pay for his 20-hour days and even refused to invest in any financial interest connected with population, but his concern went beyond raising the money and included defining the ways in which it should be spent. Even if he did not know the details of a special programming situation, as he advised one government official:

I do know from many years experience in both government and business that a truly important objective can be achieved far more rapidly if the necessary priorities are established both in personnel and in available funds.[25]

Over the long run, Draper's greatest contribution was in establishing priorities—usually at a level of financial resources that would cause everyone else first to gasp, then to argue, gradually to acquiesce, and ultimately to applaud. Even before his targets were accepted Draper himself would go after the money, often to the consternation of those who would have to take on the new responsibilities that a higher budget might entail. With no administrative duties himself Draper was free to concentrate on what he thought should be happening three to five years ahead. Each official within an organization, as J. G. March and H. A. Simon point out, tends to see "elements of structure and existing programs that are one or two steps removed from him in the formal structure as 'given' and unchangeable."[26] Draper, essentially outside of all the organizations he influenced, saw almost nothing as "given and unchangeable."

He was just as ready to work with the chairman of the board, the president of the United States, or the secretary-general of the United Nations as he was with the program officers to change any institution that seemed to need changing. This did not always endear him to those who were trying to administer the organizations that he was trying to change. For instance, he shocked NIH officials by proposing that for development of specific contraceptives NIH should make contracts like those of the Defense Department instead of relying on independent peer group evaluation to fund the individual projects of academic colleagues.

Draper's attention was fixed on the particular problem to be solved rather than on the normal procedures of institutions or on the personal predilections of individuals. He always took it for granted that if a genuinely good proposal were offered, reasonable people would support it. Thus in the very middle of the 1967 fight for earmarking, knowing that Gaud resented his intervention with Congress, Draper still did not hesitate to ask Gaud directly for a large grant for the International Planned Parenthood Federation. Acting on the assumption that a common purpose rather than a personal or institutional rivalry would prevail, Draper often succeeded in turning the assumptions into actualities—although not without occasional conflicts with those who took personal or institutional considerations more seriously than he ever did.

If Draper was a sharp and constant spur, many other forces operating from within the government were constantly chipping away, smoothing down the sharp edges of Draper's proposals, trying to accommodate at least a part of his larger visions to the smaller possibilities of bureaucratic behavior. Secretary Rusk, for example, almost never directly agreed to any of Draper's suggestions—for a major reevaluation of the Indian family planning program, for a task force on population, for a new "world plan" of food and population, for a systems-analysis of the whole population problem, for a half dozen ambassadors-at-large on population, and several others—but he never directly vetoed any of Claxton's many efforts to translate them on a lower level. Claxton was a steadying influence, struggling to steer both Draper and Ravenholt away from unnecessary conflict and controversy. If compromise was possible—or even if it was not—Claxton would try to do the leg work as well as the brain work to achieve it.

Despite the supposed hierarchy that placed Secretary Rusk and Claxton above AID and Ravenholt, Rusk rarely intervened in AID operational issues. As in the early 1960s the gradual accumulation in AID of personnel with funds to disperse tended to shift real power from the policy-oriented State Department to the program-oriented AID. Claxton would argue cogently, for example, on the need to develop an injectable contraceptive or the importance of research on motivation, but he could not provide the funds. He could not break the ever-stronger link between operations and policy. Thus Claxton's role remained essentially persuasion and accommodation although after 1968 AID funds were often more persuasive to outside organizations than was State Department diplomacy.

William Gaud served as Administrator of AID from 1966 to 1969, but he had many other problems besides population. Even as he fought against earmarking in any form, opposed further personnel increases, and refused to intervene against reluctant bureaus and missions, he approved without hesitation the major population grants to private organizations. Far more ready than his predecessor to go along with the activist line in the agency, Gaud was still not willing to jeopardize other parts of the agency to advance or concentrate more specifically on population work.

Under Gaud, Herbert Waters served as assistant administrator for the war on hunger until February 1968. Both in stimulating and administering the War on Hunger, Waters did not hesitate to overrule his program officers, but as a "political type" in an agency filled with those who considered themselves "foreign aid professionals" his influence outside his own office was low. After his departure, although his deputy and later acting administrator, Irwin Hedges, was consistently sympathetic, there was no permanent, experienced assistant administrator from February 1968 until the middle of 1969.

The real leadership for the new program was supplied with increasing effectiveness by Reimert T. Ravenholt, the director. Starting at what was easily the very bottom of the least influential office in an unpopular agency, Ravenholt spent his first year trying to line up one secretary and make one appointment with the administrator. Then Draper and the War on Hunger came along. In a year and a half, Ravenholt was running an office of 28 people, trying to spend $35 million in an unknown field in less than six months. The enfant terrible of the agency, who had seriously proposed that AID should distribute oral contraceptives around the world, was placed through no evident action of his own in a position of real power.

Under these peculiar circumstances the first and most important element of Ravenholt's leadership was his own unshakable conviction that he did indeed know what needed to be done and that he was personally well able to do it. His certainty and determination communicated itself to the rest of the Population Service. Working long hours under great pressure in an agency that still privately disapproved of the subject and resented its sudden affluence, Ravenholt drove the program forward partly by personal force.

Moreover, Ravenholt not only believed in his own judgment, he also believed that the population problem itself was susceptible of solution by the methods that he emphasized and with the means at AID's disposal. His optimistic outlook stood out in sharp relief in an agency where most of the employees looked upon economic development as a lifetime career and certainly not an immediate goal. "I want to hurry up and get this population problem settled," he would say, "so that I can get back to cancer research." Like Draper he was much more interested in solving the problem than in maintaining the existing institutional patterns of AID, but unlike Draper he genuinely expected to see the problem solved or at least well along the way in just a few years.

Ravenholt's convictions were a source of strength within the program. They generated a strong loyalty and sense of direction among his own staff even when he was not completely correct as, for instance, when he expected to distribute $10 million of contraceptives in the first year (but actually would dispense only $5 million and that with difficulty). He expected that governments would welcome U.S. aid for family planning programs but many did not. However, on the major issue of 1967-69, namely, whether $35 to $50 million could be "sensibly" utilized, he was clearly vindicated

On the other hand, Ravenholt's certainty that he knew best was a mixed blessing. He antagonized some of the outside experts who regarded Uncle Sam as a nouveau riche competitor in the population field. As Harkavy had warned in 1965:

> We must resist assuming the attitude of the "old settler" toward a newcomer which, human nature being what it is, has undoubtedly manifested itself as each new agency has entered the population business. Underlying this attitude is the notion that these parvenues may have a lot of money but we old settlers have the brains and experience.[27]

Ravenholt had the money but he did not show the deference calculated to help win the "old settlers" over. They considered him a "wild man."

Ravenholt's confidence also made his own superiors, all technically less qualified in population work, exceedingly nervous. He was so insistent on setting clear priorities that as a matter of principle he did not want to buy off his critics by providing them any support at all. He was too ready to criticize his colleagues' programs instead of keeping quiet as a tactful bureaucrat should. One of his superiors remarked that he was "incredibly inept administratively" and "too full of enthusiasms to build a well-rounded program." But Ravenholt, on his part, regarded a lot of AID "administration" as a waste of time. "A well-rounded program," he thought, was often just an excuse for avoiding the very decisions that ought to direct the effort.

The development of a new program, Herbert Simon observes in his study of the beginnings of the Marshall Plan, is like a "series of pictures in the minds of different people."[28] The pictures are drawn from past training and experience and applied to the new situation until by mutual adjustment a composite picture emerges. In the initial process of "arriving at a single picture held more or less in common," the view with the cleanest outlines is likely to dominate the pattern. Right or wrong, Ravenholt's mental picture of what needed to be done was clear and highly visible as the AID program took shape.

DELAY IN DOMESTIC PROGRAMS

In the rest of the federal government, program followed policy more slowly. President Johnson, preoccupied by the Vietnam War and no longer a candidate for reelection, was reluctant to undertake any new initiatives. Nevertheless, at the urging of Douglass Cater in the White House and John D. Rockefeller, 3rd, he agreed to establish a Presidential Committee on Population and Family Planning. Primarily designed to activate the still-sluggish programs of HEW, Johnson's appointment of the committee, which was to report right after the election, proved that birth control was no longer regarded as a sensitive subject.

It was a surprise to many therefore that Pope Paul VI on July 29, 1968, announced the conclusion of his four-year reappraisal of birth control. The answer in the encyclical *Humanae Vitae* was an unequivocal "No." As popular posters put it, "The Pill is a 'No No.' "

> Excluded is every action which, either in anticipation of the conjugal act or its accomplishment, or in the development of its natural consequences, proposes, whether as an end or as a means, to render procreation impossible. . . . If the mission of generating life is not to be exposed to the arbitrary will of men, one must necessarily recognize the insurmountable limits to the possibility of man's domination of his own body and its functions.[29]

The uncompromising encyclical, which rejected the majority views of the papal study commission, shook the Catholic Church. For six months following, stories of doubting theologians, reluctant bishops, and rebellious priests dominated the press. A Gallup poll promptly revealed that 53 percent of American Catholics disagreed with the pope's decision and hoped that somehow it would be changed.[30]

But the anguished directive from Rome, which two or three years earlier might have silenced or postponed the development of government programs, came too late to make any visible impact on U.S. population policy. The politicians ignored it. Not a single senator or congressman discussed or included the encyclical during 1968 in the pages of the *Congressional Record*. On the very day *Humanae Vitae* was published President Johnson signed an extension of the Food for Peace Act with additional language—over and beyond the 1966 amendments—making "voluntary family planning programs" one of the criteria of self-help.[31] Questioned later on the papal pronouncement, President Johnson replied, "I do feel that our country and our government should be helpful and responsive to those who desire our assistance and counseling in connection with population matters."[32]

Both the Republican and Democratic party platforms, adopted in July and August respectively, urged "priority attention" for the population problem "to expand and strengthen international cooperation" (Republican), and "to launch effective programs on population control" (Democratic).[33] Draper had testified before both platform committees and been cordially received. Both candidates were fully on record in support of government-aided birth control as a necessary element of economic development programs. Despite Pope Paul VI, the issue that had rocked the 1960 campaign aroused no partisan debate whatever in 1968.

Through the summer of 1968 President Johnson's Committee on Population and Family Planning, jointly chaired by John D. Rockefeller, 3rd and Wilbur Cohen the secretary of HEW, deliberated. Gaud, a member of the committee, persuaded the others that no budget figures should be mentioned for population and family planning in AID. "It was just wasteful to keep naming bigger sums as if the problem could be solved by throwing money around,"[34] he explained later.

The committee's recommendations for the AID population program, lacking precise figures, tended to endorse ongoing policy: expansion of assistance "as rapidly as funds can be properly allocated by the U.S. and effectively utilized by recipient countries and agencies"; continuation of the Population Council's postpartum program; more attention to communications and administration; continued use of nongovernmental organizations and multilateral agencies; a two-year authorization; and an international advisory committee.[35] The only area in which the committee's recommendations might have influenced AID programs was research. Since the Center for Population Research in the National Institute of Child Health and Human Development (NICHD) was established in the summer of 1968, some HEW representatives wanted to exercise greater supervision over AID programs, but Ravenholt, who paid little attention to the rest of the exercise, insisted on retaining AID's research authority.

In other areas the committee's review and recommendations did have a long-range impact. Great emphasis was placed on the need for expansion of the Center for Population Research; $30 million was recommended for a program in 1970 and $100 million in 1971.[36] Also recommended was a Commission on Population to be appointed by the president "to highlight for the American people, the urgency and importance of the population problem."[37] First proposed by Dr. John Rock in 1963, rejected by Rusk in 1964, but still pursued by Rockefeller, such a commission was on the verge of becoming acceptable. But with the Democratic defeat in November, the national preoccupation over Vietnam, and the bitter conflicts raging within the Catholic Church, birth control dropped to still lower priority. Several attempts to schedule a meeting with President Johnson for formal presentation of the report failed. Finally, early in January, just before President Johnson's departure, the report was officially released with little fanfare.

Even more disappointing was the Johnson administration's refusal to support the recommended amounts in the fiscal 1970 budget.[38] Where the committee urged about $60 million for 1970 family planning services, the 1970 budget contained only $45-50 million; where the committee urged $30 million for research, the budget contained only $13.5 million. For the AID population program, just as the fiscal 1969 budget had recommended only $35 million, no increase over 1968, so the fiscal 1970 budget recommended $50 million—no increase over 1969.

President Johnson had opened his full term in 1965 with bold and well-timed leadership in population policy. He ended it in January 1969 unable or unwilling to provide the resources necessary to turn the new policy into a full-fledged domestic program. The transformation in government attitudes had been complete over the four-year period but the development of meaningful government programs had occurred first in the two agencies—OEO and AID— where Congress legislated the priorities and funding.

President Johnson had wanted programs up to the limit of Catholic opposition. He had called for new initiatives. Unlike President Kennedy he invested his own personal and political prestige in the issue. The presidential assistants in the White House also wanted to see programs initiated and expanded in the population field. Not being experts, however, they relied on the executive agencies. None of the agency heads after 1966 were opposed to family planning. In fact, Rusk, John Gardner, Cohen, Lee, and Gaud all considered themselves strong supporters. At first, they hesitated to act because they expected opposition from Congress. Soon, to their surprise, the opposition came from Congress because they were not acting. Without the pressure of Congress the federal agencies would have done much less than they did. After 1966 the veto power on population policy, which earlier had been exercised by the Catholic Church, was increasingly exercised by the federal agencies themselves and was primarily internal, jurisdictional, organizational, and budgetary.

16

PRESIDENT NIXON'S
MESSAGE ON
POPULATION,
1969

When Richard Nixon was inaugurated in January 1969 with some 30,000 jobs to fill, a war in Vietnam to manage, and a $100 billion budget to review, the population problem was no higher on his agenda than it had been on Lyndon Johnson's. Likewise within AID the inauguration of a new president made little immediate difference to ongoing population projects. In January 1969 the distance between the White House and a $50 million operating program seemed vast. Gradually, however, the gap was bridged. At first through the private initiatives of interested individuals and organizations and then through the public requirements of budgeting and personnel appointments, new links were forged between the White House and the population supporters that further heightened both the importance of population issues and the standing of the AID program.

Long before anyone in the State Department or AID raised a population question to the White House, the private birth control supporters were beating a path to the new president's door. By the end of December, for example, Draper had found occasion to discuss population briefly with the new Secretary of State William Rogers, the new Secretary of Health, Education, and Welfare Robert Finch, and Presidential Counselor Bryce Harlow. Even before the inauguration, Nixon and his staff were plied from several quarters with suggested statements to go in various messages and recommendations for jobs. Within a few weeks Rockefeller was personally calling on the White House to repeat the proposals made in the report of President Johnson's committee.

CONCERN FOR U.S. PROBLEMS

From the beginning the Nixon administration both reflected and encouraged a changing focus of attention in the population field—away from the receding food crisis in India toward social problems closer to home. In the foreign policy field, Henry Kissinger the president's top adviser was more interested in the balance of power than economic development or population problems. At the same time the chief domestic affairs adviser and "White House intellectual" was Daniel (Pat) Moynihan, a sociologist-urbanologist who wanted to focus attention on urban demography, population distribution, and family life in the United States. Widely criticized by blacks because he had blamed many of their problems on "the social disintegration of the black family," Moynihan remained a liberal Catholic intellectual who equated family and social stability. Draper and Rockefeller both urged Moynihan to support the domestic budget levels suggested by President Johnson's committee and also to appoint a U.S. Population Commission to review the whole population question and recommend a long-term policy for the United States. Moynihan saw in this approach a way to combine his own social concern with the no-longer sensitive and highly relevant family planning question. The principal impetus for what eventually was to be President Nixon's Message on Population and the U.S. Commission on Population Growth and the American Future came therefore through Moynihan's office with gentle but insistent pressure from Rockefeller and a variety of inputs from the rest of the government and the population organizations.

The first and most favorable response to the recommendations of the Rockefeller-Cohen committee had, as usual, come from Congress. Several of the committee's specific recommendations, for example, to establish a separate Population Institute in the National Institutes of Health, were seized upon by individual congressmen and introduced as separate bills. In a major coordinated effort, Senator Joseph D. Tydings (D.-Md.), Congressmen James Scheuer (D.-N.Y.), George Bush (R.-Tex.), and Tim Lee Carter, M.D. (R.-Ky.) introduced legislation with some 60 co-sponsors to create a National Center for Population and Family Planning in the Department of Health, Education, and Welfare with a five-year authorization for research, services, training, population study centers, project grants, and support to state programs.[1] Tydings, with the full agreement of the private population organizations, concluded that one central office under strong direction with ample funds would be the best way to develop leadership in an agency that was supposed to be leading U.S. policies. Eventually nearly 100 members of the House and Senate co-sponsored these or similar bills that authorized up to nearly $1 billion.

Other population bills also were offered in the first few months of 1969, pointing toward environment and resources as well as family planning. In the House of Representatives, Congressman Morris Udall (D.-Ariz.), who in 1964 had introduced "the first population bill ever sponsored in the House,"[2] introduced a bill to establish a Bureau of Population and the Environment and a two-year Commission on Population and Environment.[3] Several bills called for special congressional committees and even a Department of Resources, Environment, and Population. George Bush (R.-Texas) persuaded Congressman Taft (R.-Ohio) to let him chair a House Republican Task Force on Earth Resources and Population that would explore informally the whole population field.[4] With a perennial interest in new issues and no jurisdictional reasons to avoid wide-ranging, interdisciplinary problems, many members of Congress were beginning to take a greater interest. Particularly when the population problem was perceived as more than just birth control it seemed increasingly acceptable and important.

But the first decisions of the new administration were, by necessity, budgetary rather than organizational and the Bureau of the Budget was less easily persuaded about the priority of the population programs than were members of Congress. Private supporters argued vigorously that research funds should be increased above the fiscal year 1970 figure of $13.6 million proposed by the Johnson administration, but the Bureau of the Budget felt no great confidence in the directed research program just being established by the Center for Population Research at NIH. HEW Secretary Finch was more successful in winning extra money for family planning services. Planned Parenthood, working through its own new Center for Family Planning Program Development set up by Fred Jaffe, could convincingly document a gap in services that left some 5 million women without access to family planning. Bureau of the Budget officials could see the cost-effectiveness of preventing unwanted births among the poor but they were not convinced that NIH population research would have a comparable or immediate payoff. Throughout the 1960s, additional support for research was a policy issue that Rockefeller, the foundations, innumerable advisory committees, Moynihan, and the president himself would all publicly endorse, but against the pressures of a tight domestic budget it was usually the research funding that suffered. Not only among the critical budget examiners but also in Congress, among right-wing opponents of welfare as well as among liberal supporters of expanded health care, there was more enthusiasm for the activist line of family planning services than the professional plea for more population research.

TECHNICAL ASSISTANCE IN AID

The population program in AID, which had been launched successfully on the issues of food and famine at a time when birth control was a risky issue, seemed by 1969 to depend more on the fate of AID and foreign aid than it did on population. Only very indirectly and over a long time would the AID Population Service be affected by the 1968 report of President Johnson's committee, the activities in Moynihan's office, the new spate of legislation, and the other population initiatives, but it was immediately and directly affected by the thrust of Nixon's policies on foreign aid.

The first impact of the transition was felt in AID with the appointment of Dr. John Hannah to replace William Gaud as AID administrator. President of Michigan State University for 27 years, Hannah saw development in terms of social problems and institution building as well as government economic plans or long-term capital development. "The full development of a country," Hannah observed, "requires a multiplicity of institutions—political, economic, and social"; furthermore:

The building of enduring institutions is a long term proposition and is fundamental to success of our developmental assistance policy. . . .

The criteria for initiation and phase-out of institution building projects are considerably different from the criteria for capital assistance
projects.[5]

More grants to universities, research centers, and qualified intermediaries, fewer
specialists on the AID payroll, more attention to professional skills and expert
technology—that was the direction Hannah wanted to go.

The model for the revised programming was the university contract
relationship that Hannah had helped to establish and, increasingly, the International Wheat and Rice Institutes in Mexico and the Philippines, which,
supported by the Rockefeller and Ford Foundations, had developed the
miracle grains that produced the Green Revolution. But by 1969 no program in
AID conformed more closely to Hannah's design than did the Population
Service. Not precisely by design but rather by the combination of sufficient
funds with insufficient time and insufficient personnel the population program
was moving toward the strategies that Hannah recommended from his own
experience.

The first Presidential Message on Foreign Aid, sent to Congress on May
29, bore signs of Hannah's influence:

We must emphasize innovative technical assistance. . . . We must
build on recent successes in furthering food production and family
planning.

"The main emphases of technical assistance," Nixon declared, "must be in
agriculture, education, and in family planning." A Technical Assistance Bureau
headed by an assistant administrator would replace the Office of the War on
Hunger. In that bureau:

Our assistance to voluntary family planning programs and support
for the United Nations and other international organizations in this
field must continue to have high priority.[6]

During the 1969 reorganization of the agency the population program
progressed once more, as the Office of the War on Hunger was promoted to a
Bureau for Technical Assistance and the Population Service was upgraded to a
Population Office with more personnel.[7] The President's message included a
subtle protest from the unhappy programming, budgeting, and auditing side in
the form of a paragraph in the population section calling for "better means of
continuous management inspection" but the thrust of the message was clearly
in exactly the direction that the population program had been going.

Before any further changes were made, however, the president and
Hannah both deferred to congressional demands for a full-scale review of
foreign aid. After considerable delay, during which the international Pearson
Commission reviewed the whole subject of economic development and
assistance, President Nixon appointed Rudolph Peterson, president of the Bank
of America, to head a Presidential Task Force on AID that did not finally make
its report until March 1970.

During the interim, long-term foreign aid strategy was in abeyance and the major problem for the AID population program, as in the past, was not the president's forthcoming Message on Population but rather the annual struggle for earmarked funds and particularly in 1969 for additional staff. In 1969 as in 1967 and 1968, Draper played a critical role. Draper had deliberately advised AID officials in May 1969 that Congress should double the $50 million earmarked for population to $100 million for 1970. In a five-page letter to Deputy Administrator Rutherford Poats, Draper observed that only 3 percent of AID funds were spent on population compared to about 30 percent on food production. Since, according to Hannah, population programs had "highest priority second only to food production," Draper proposed that the 60 professional staff members in population (compared to 720 in agriculture) be increased to at least 400.[8]

Nevertheless, from mid-1968 until late 1969 AID kept a freeze on all new positions in the agency. Reflecting the new administration's lower profile and lower priority for foreign economic development, AID was cutting back across the board and not even adding new personnel in the one program where funds had increased. The continuing short-falls in population staffing, however, reflected not deliberate malice toward the new program but rather the continued normal reaction of a large bureaucratic organization that lacked the high degree of internal control necessary to accord high priority to some programs while simultaneously cutting back very hard on others. An evenly balanced state of agencywide discontent and deprivation could be tolerated—in fact, in AID it seemed normal—but to give priority and new staff to one program while enforcing penury on others was difficult.

Nevertheless, choices had to be made. Because the financial priority was set by Congress, it had to be implemented. Because the personnel priority was not set by Congress, it lagged several years behind the program emphasis. Both Gaud and Hannah cursed the earmarking of funds at the time. Both have subsequently indicated that it was useful for the population program and for the agency. In retrospect, Gaud commented:

> When Congress put that burr under our saddle, we did move faster than we otherwise would have. Far from being a brake, as we expected, Congress acted as a spur, leading and driving us on. It was really very useful.[9]

Nevertheless, in 1969 with AID appropriations still declining Hannah felt constrained to resist the earmarking. He like Gaud certainly did not disapprove of family planning, but like his predecessor he wanted the agency to have the flexibility to determine how much money and how many people should be assigned to the program. As in previous years, therefore, AID proposed amendments in 1969 which would have eliminated the Title X earmarking.

During the Senate authorization hearings on foreign aid, Senator Fulbright questioned Secretary Rogers and Administrator Hannah severely on the proposed shift. "General Draper and his associates," Fulbright charged, "are very disturbed by the fact that although you give lip service . . . you have actually changed the provision. . . . They would like to have the same language restored." Finally, Rogers and Hannah both conceded, "No objection."*

On the House side, after hearing testimony again from Draper, Dr. Alan Guttmacher, and Ambassador James Riddleberger,[11] Congressman Taft won support for a committee amendment to earmark $100 million for fiscal 1970. Later the House Foreign Affairs Committee voted for a two-year authorization. The Senate committee also earmarked $100 million but approved only a one-year authorization. When the two committees finally met in conference they compromised and approved for the first time a two-year earmarking of $75 million for population in 1970 and $100 million for 1971. A congressional move to upgrade the staffing and appoint an assistant administrator for population was dropped, however. It was on all sides an acceptable compromise that increased and protected AID population funds for two more years.

THE MESSAGE ON POPULATION, JULY 18, 1969

The final stages of the foreign aid struggle coincided with Moynihan's last-minute preparations for the President's Message on Population. Originally designed by Moynihan to concentrate on metropolitan growth, the message underwent several major transformations before receiving final approval. Claxton was not satisfied at the early emphasis on U.S. domestic issues; the population organizations resisted Moynihan's efforts to concentrate on urban and distribution problems; the president himself did not want to link the message directly with the first successful moon landing, as one draft would have done. There was fear in some quarters, in fact, that President Nixon might change his mind and not approve the message after all.

Finally, in mid-July, the message was cleared for release. Moynihan, after briefing congressional leaders, noted to Secretary of State Rogers:

Having had occasion to observe those gentlemen restraining their enthusiasm with regard to some of the programs we've sent up, I must say they seemed very genuinely interested in this one. Any number asked me for materials they might use in supporting the program. . . .

Representative Taft raised specifically the matter of earmarking of AID funds for family planning. He indicated that the State

---

*Secretary Rogers was more amenable to earmarking than was Hannah, as the exchange revealed:

The Chairman. General Draper is very interested in it, as you should know.

Secretary Rogers. I think there is some advantage in having it mandatory. I suppose it will make us try to work harder to use the money for this purpose.

The Chairman. Well the trouble is in this enormous bureaucracy as you have observed, the bureaucracy does not always agree with the Secretary once the bill has passed. Unless there is an inducement to implement the program, even the Secretary of State does not always get his way within the Department, I dare say. If you do, you will be unique, I think.[10]

Department had, even until very recently, opposed this practice, but that more recently you had indicated you supported it. The President thereupon said, 'As far as I am concerned, I am for earmarking.'

Throughout the briefing the President indicated that this subject has his strongest support. In repeated comments and interventions, he made clear that he sees little progress for the world if we do not seriously attend to this issue, and that, of course, he looks to the Department of State to take the lead. He was not less emphatic in his statements that HEW must move forward with a strong research program if our foreign activities are to be effective.[12]

The first presidential Message on Population was formally transmitted to Congress July 18, 1969.[13] The statement dealt primarily with population growth in America and suggested that:

Many of our social problems may be related to the fact that we have had only fifty years in which to accommodate the second hundred million Americans.

The principal recommendation was for a Commission on Population Growth and the American Future to be established by Congress to study population changes and the role of government.

After the commission, the first specific proposal was for "increased research on birth control methods of all types and the sociology of population growth." The Department of Health, Education, and Welfare was also exhorted to develop an action program that would achieve "as a national goal the provision of adequate family planning services within the next five years to all those who want them but cannot afford them." Legislation was promised from the secretary of HEW in the near future to "help the Department implement this important program by providing broader and more precise legislative authority and a clearer source of financial support."

Completing the full policy reversal since President Eisenhower's ban on birth control in December 1959, Richard Nixon, Eisenhower's vice president, officially declared in July 1969:

It would be unrealistic for the Federal Government alone to shoulder the entire burden, but this administration does accept a clear responsibility to provide essential leadership.

With reference to foreign policy and programs, the message was brief and direct. Citing the problems of economic development and world food sufficiency (but not mentioning President Johnson's War on Hunger), Nixon called population growth "a world problem no one can ignore." There was strong emphasis on the newly developing role of the United Nations (see Chapter 19).

It is our belief that the United Nations, its specialized agencies, and other international bodies should take the leadership in responding

to world population growth. The United States will cooperate fully
with their programs.

Yet Nixon also gave full credit to the ongoing AID program: "Already we are
doing a great deal in this field. . . . For example, we provide assistance to
countries which seek our help in reducing birth rates." Referring to the earlier
Foreign Aid Message, the president repeated Hannah's insistence "that our
programs should give further recognition to the important resources of private
organizations and university research centers." The key sentence for the AID
population program was,

> "I have asked the Secretary of State and the Administrator of the
> Agency for International Development to give population and family
> planning high priority for attention, personnel, research and funding
> among our several aid programs."

In fact, in funding and in formal priority the population assistance program was
a recognized government responsibility.

Following up on the message, White House staff specifically asked each of
the federal agencies to examine its population programs and to report on plans
and progress by the fall of 1969. For HEW, still without strong or coordinated
leadership in the field, the renewed White House interest spurred the establishment of a new National Center for Family Planning Services, a search for
family planning staff, and a recognition at last that new legislation would be
necessary. For domestic population programs President Nixon's public support
marked a watershed, fully legitimizing past initiatives and stimulating new ones.
For AID, with generous funds already being earmarked by Congress and a
helpful reorganization well under way, White House support made it possible to
solve internal gaps. The Office of Population in the new Bureau for Technical
Assistance under a shrewd and capable administrator, Joel Bernstein, and his
deputy, Samuel Butterfield, at last won the additional staff it needed as well as
additional influence throughout the agency. With Dr. Willard Boynton and
Randall Backlund as deputies, Ravenholt was by mid-1970 well-staffed with
experienced AID personnel.

As in 1965, a word from the White House could dissolve many bureaucratic problems within the agency, like clearance on airgrams or more personnel. But also as in 1967 and 1968, the real force of the AID population
program derived from congressional earmarking, carried out with tacit support
from the president but against the opposition of the agency. In 1969 both
congressional and White House support plus Hannah's interest, Bernstein's
steadying hand, and Ravenholt's continued leadership—at a level too low
bureaucratically for political replacement but too energetic to be ignored—
guaranteed that the program would proceed with new force along the channels
that its own momentum was providing.

17

TECHNOLOGY
AND BUREAUCRACY
IN AID,
1969-71

Not only in its leadership, with Draper gathering resources from Congress and Ravenholt forcing the pace within the agency, but also in its timing the AID population effort had an important head start over domestic activities. During the two-year period of 1968-69 when HEW programs were still marking time, waiting for the White House, looking for new leaders, and planning reorganizations that always seemed exceptionally difficult in HEW, the AID program was actively defining strategy and developing specific tactics.

The AID effort had been initiated in the heat of a world food crisis. But the notable success of the Green Revolution, far from discrediting population control, could be used by Draper, Ravenholt, and others to argue that a well-directed program of technical assistance and research backed by adequate long-term funding could actually solve problems that had once seemed insoluble. Where experts had previously warned that it would be harder to increase the harvests of millions of illiterate peasants than it would be to send a man to the moon, the rapidity of the Green Revolution led many to believe that directed research and better technology could provide a check on population growth faster than any other approach.

THE NEW RESEARCH STRATEGY

From the first suggestion of earmarked money in 1967 there had been growing pressure on AID to use some of these funds to finance a systematic search for better family planning methods. On the one hand, many of the scientists and foundations who had eagerly supported Planned Parenthood's "research strategy" in the early 1960s still wanted research, not as a political tactic but for its own sake to expand knowledge on reproduction. At the same time in India the intrauterine devices, which had looked like a perfect solution in 1965 and 1966, were by 1968 being removed almost as fast as they were being inserted. Even in Korea and Taiwan the life expectancy of an IUD in utero was about two years.[1] Continuation rates with pills and other methods were even lower.[2]

Furthermore, the Ford and Rockefeller Foundations, the Population Council, and the National Institutes of Health, all of which had insisted earlier that money was not the main obstacle, were by 1968 and 1969 financing the training of about 600 researchers every year.[3] These freshly educated and qualified scientists wanted government support at the very time that the Vietnam War was forcing such expenditures down. NIH, like AID, was moving into a period of fiscal stringency.[4] McGeorge Bundy, then president of the Ford Foundation, urged the federal government to expand its research support, even as he announced new Ford grants in November of 1967 of over $15 million specifically for contraceptive development.[5] David Bell suggested that Congress should provide additional funds for NIH, not AID.[6]

The population research program at the National Institute of Child Health and Human Development did not enjoy the congressional support that AID did. In fact, population research, which had increased from $5.1 million in fiscal 1966 to $8.1 million in fiscal 1967, hardly increased at all in 1968. The contract program, which was specifically directed toward the study of contraceptive side effects and the development of new methods, was cut back by 50 percent in fiscal 1968 in favor of the program of nondirected, peer-selected grants.[7] This was the traditional NIH pattern that Frank Notestein once described as "a system providing established investigators with an opportunity to scratch each others' back."[8] Despite the 1967 Harkavy report that urged worldwide contraceptive research of about $150 million per year,[9] in NIH basic research usually prevailed over all pressures to develop a new product. (See Table 17.1.) When his recommendations for NIH were not fully implemented Harkavy became a vigorous advocate for expanded research support by AID.

On January 26, 1968, the State Department and AID, responding to the strong foundation interest, held a joint Conference on Direction and Support of Research in Technical Methods for Control of Human Reproduction. Sheldon Segal, director of the Bio-Medical Division of the Population Council, argued that just at the threshold of development there were a number of possible new methods that might flourish with adequate funding.[10] It was clear that the scientists and the foundations wanted the government to pay the cost of crossing those thresholds.

Suddenly in the spring of 1968 an even greater demand for research sounded forth from India. After reviewing the minutes of the January meeting in Washington, the Ford Foundation Advisory Group and the AID Mission in New Delhi concluded that not enough was being done. John Lewis the AID Mission director started the campaign with letters to Gaud and Dr. Philip Lee, then assistant secretary of Health, Education, and Welfare, who had titular authority over NIH.[11] Ambassador Chester Bowles wrote to Phillip Claxton; the message was clear: despite recent progress "thanks in part certainly to the earmarking of AID funds for family planning"[12] the India program could not succeed without a "technological breakthrough."

TABLE 17.1

**National Institute of Child Health and Human Development Grants and
Contracts in Population Research, Fiscal Years 1964-73[a]**

(millions of dollars)

	1964	1965	1966	1967	1968	1969[b]	1970	1971	1972	1973 (budget request)
Reproductive biology and contraceptive development										
Fundamental biomedical research (grants)	2.5	3.0	3.7	4.7	5.6	4.8	7.3	7.8	12.5	13.7
Directed biomedical research (contracts)						1.4	3.9	3.8	4.0	4.0
Product development								2.2	3.5	4.2
Medical effects of available contraceptives			0.1	1.2	0.7	1.3	1.6	3.2	6.0	6.5
Social sciences		0.5			0.2	1.0	2.1	6.1	5.5	6.7
Manpower development	0.2	0.7	1.2	2.0	2.1	2.4	2.7	3.0	2.6	2.6
Population research centers								0.3	1.5	2.5
Staff support			0.1	0.2	0.3	0.3	0.7	0.8	1.0	1.2
Total	2.7	4.2	5.1	8.1	8.9	11.2	18.3	27.2	36.6	41.4

aIntramural research not included.
bCenter for Population Research established.

Source: National Institute of Child Health and Human Development, January 14, 1972, briefing and 1973 congressional presentation.

A paper by Frances Gulick, combining data on the Indian program with Ford Foundation material on contraceptive research, concluded on a note reminiscent of Dr. Rock's 1963 appeal for a "Manhattan Project"—that an effort similar in urgency and method to the "intensive and coordinated research and development effort which solved the critical problem of controlled nuclear explosion" could produce better birth control methods.[13]

With that memorandum of May 1968, the second resea :h campaign was well under way. Bell then suggested to Gaud "a possible transfer to NIH of $10 million or so of the AID funds earmarked for family planning for support of research in fertility control."[14] But at Ravenholt's insistence and because of his own concern over congressional reactions Gaud turned down his former chief, saying that AID could only finance projects that "are demonstrably relevant to LDC [less-developed country] needs" such as a once-a-month pill that "would eliminate much of the costly training and programming now needed."[15]

Furthermore, during fiscal 1968 AID had neither time nor personnel to consider any systematic research program. Ravenholt was extremely skeptical of the new initiatives that seemed to be coming out of India. He suspected at first that they were just an excuse to explain visible short-falls in the Indian program. Somewhat sarcastically, Ravenholt commented, "Given the difficulties of the Indian situation, it is natural that John Lewis should give thought to the possibility of an easy solution to the problem by means of a remarkable new contraceptive."[16] The proponents of more research, he observed, were often the same people who refused to introduce oral contraceptives.

In fiscal 1969, with $50 million earmarked and more time for programming, the pressures for contraceptive research were harder to resist. Harkavy and Dr. Anna Southam of the Ford Foundation persisted. They talked with many officials in AID, State, and HEW, trying to find some way to cover the $3.5 million of projects approved by the NIH study sections but beyond NIH's ability to fund. Rutherford Poats the deputy administrator of AID found himself drawn into the campaign but he was in a dilemma. Poats "didn't know beans" about biological research and assumed that NIH should take the lead. But "looking at long lists of unfunded projects and slapping money on them" did not seem to be the best way to proceed either.[17] A consortium of funding agencies under NIH leadership was one possible solution. Poats tried to persuade Bureau of the Budget officials to push the National Institute of Child Health and Human Development ahead as a lead agency. The Center for Population Research in NICHD under Dr. Philip Corfman was given additional responsibility and a higher budget for fiscal 1969. But top NIH officials really did not want to do product-oriented research; the congressional appropriations subcommittees really did not want to develop more contraceptives; and in this situation Corfman really was not quite sure what he could do.

Again, the only person who was sure what he wanted to do—and even surer of what he did not want to do—was Ravenholt. He did not want to follow NIH leadership or simply pick up the bill for left-over NIH projects. As early as March 1968 while listening impatiently to an NIH discussion of male contraceptive possibilities he began to decide where he wanted to put priority:

We can now define rather precisely the *ideal* additional means of birth control needed and we should do what we can to focus research with maximum intensity on that goal. The methods of birth control now available are quite effective when used with adequate *foresight*. Naturally, however, many people are unable to exercise sufficient foresight and many unwanted pregnancies occur. It appears that only slight improvement in birth control can be expected from perfection of 'foresight' methods of birth control. Research should be directed toward perfection of *hindsight* methods of birth control: What is needed is a pill which women could take whenever needed at the end of a monthly cycle to ensure menstruation, and which, because of its ease of use, could be made generally available to women throughout the world.[18]

The first AID research grant to develop this once-a-month pill went, over the objections of NIH and foundation advisers, to the Worcester Foundation for Experimental Biology in Massachusetts, which had done the basic research on oral contraceptives in the 1950s. The grant was only $109,000 but it was a step that led directly toward the contraceptive threshold that Ravenholt was seeking. It was an effort to find an elusive uteolytic substance in the uterus of sheep that might be useful to terminate pregnancy.

Ravenholt's decisiveness was much more alarming to his superiors than indecision would have been. Because he wanted to make the key judgments of priority and determine the program direction himself, his recommendations were usually suspect. Gaud assured Bell that "Any decisions we make will follow wide consultation."[19] Under pressures of too little time and staff a compromise was reached. Looking over the various categories of unfunded NIH projects Ravenholt finally agreed to provide $1.5 million for NIH projects, all involving corpus luteum functions, as well as some $3 million to the Population Council over a four-year period to develop a once-a-month pill.

The Center for Population Research was understandably annoyed at being dependent on AID to rescue unfunded projects. *Science* carried a story in May 1970 about HEW population research that revealed the continuing behind-the-scenes rivalry between NIH and AID, between basic and directed research:

One question likely to generate controversy will be concerned with the size of certain contracts awarded by the AID Office of Population Research [sic]. Several of these are larger than some scientists at HEW think can be justified. In their view, not enough is known yet about the matters under investigation to warrant large-scale programs of directed research.[20]

Actually Ravenholt did not see any immediate prospects for a contraceptive breakthrough until December 1969 when he discovered that Dr. Sune Bergstrom at the Karolinska Institute in Sweden had used a natural hormone, prostaglandin, as a chemical abortifacient to evacuate the uterus in the early stages of pregnancy. Prostaglandins, which had been increasingly used to induce

TABLE 17.2

AID Centrally and Regionally Funded Population Research,
Fiscal Years 1967-71
(in thousands of dollars)

Subject	1967	1968	1969	1970	1971
Corpus luteum studies					
Worcester Foundation	–	109	–	–	99
NICHD-CPR	–	–	1,510	53	–
Antiprogestins, Population Council	–	–	3,000	–	–
Prostaglandins					
Worcester Foundation	–	–	–	2,980	–
University of Wisconsin	–	–	–	–	227
Washington University	–	–	–	–	293
Makerere University	–	–	–	–	821
Other	–	–	–	–	217
Gonadotropin releasing factor inhibitors,					
Salk Institute	–	–	–	2,255	–
Intrauterine devices					
Battelle Memorial Institute	–	–	–	150	475
Other	–	–	–	–	12
Contraceptive safety, Southwest Foundation	–	–	–	913	–
Contraceptive and disease prophylaxis agent,					
University of Pittsburgh	–	–	–	581	–
Devices and sterilization					
Battelle Memorial Institute	–	–	–	–	830
University of North Carolina	–	–	79	–	135
Field trials					
International IUD Program–Pathfinder Fund	194	–	1,289	–	–
International Fertility Research Program–					
University of North Carolina	–	–	–	–	3,106
Other studies	–	–	–	–	120
Total	194	109	5,878	6,932	6,355

Source: U.S. AID, Population Program ASSISTANCE (Washington, D.C., December 1971), p. 37.

labor at term, were included among the 28 NIH-approved, AID-funded research projects involving the corpus luteum. The new stress on innovation and technology in AID strengthened Ravenholt's hand. To the amusement of some and the dismay of others, AID research funds were promptly mobilized for testing and evaluation of the new drug. Three million dollars went to the Worcester Foundation, developers of "the pill," in 1970 to develop prostaglandin. A Japanese firm, not restricted by the U.S. Food and Drug Administration, tooled up independently for rapid production.

At the suggestion of Dr. Joseph Speidel the new Research Division chief and Ravenholt, prostaglandin was tested by Dr. S. M. M. Karim at Makere University Hospital in Uganda in the form of a vaginal suppository that could be self-administered to induce menstruation. Speidel and Ravenholt rapidly moved to support and enlarge a conference on prostaglandins at the prestigious New York Academy of Sciences in September 1970 to explore the chemical, biological, medicinal, and production problems and to accelerate international research.[21] When Karim reported on his success in vaginal administration Ravenholt was convinced that prostaglandins were the breakthrough to meet his 1968 definition of "a nontoxic and completely effective substance or method which, when self-administered on a single occasion, would ensure the non-pregnant state at the completion of the monthly cycle."[22]

Prostaglandins filled the crucial need for a postconceptive, self-administerable method. With characteristic affinity for the most controversial element of the program Ravenholt supported prostaglandin research wholeheartedly. While some officials and experts smiled at another one of Ravenholt's "enthusiasms" and refused to become involved in the new research effort, the tone of the comment from NIH changed perceptibly between 1970 and 1971. Where NIH officials had once criticised AID grants as too big,[23] they began to blame AID successes for the reluctance of the Bureau of the Budget to increase NIH population funds substantially in fiscal 1972 and 1973. *Science* magazine reported:

> Dismayed HEW officials attribute this to budget planners in OMB, who are apparently not satisfied with the progress the CPR had made toward "product-orienting" its contract research program. . . .
> Another, though lesser, factor said to have influenced budget planners is described by one HEW official as a "public relations coup" by the Agency for International Development (AID) which spends about $10 million a year on population research and which plunged nearly $3 million two years ago into projects to examine the birth control potential of prostaglandin compounds. HEW subsequently followed suit with its own program of prostaglandin research but found itself in a "me-too position with pie on its face" that did nothing to establish an image of imagination and aggressiveness.[24]

By early 1972 prostaglandins, already hailed by Ravenholt as the "penicillin of reproduction" were being compared in importance to the steroids.[25] A *New York Times Magazine* article called prostaglandins "one of the most promising fields in the biological sciences."[26]

Actually, as the program chronology reveals, the greatly enlarged research program that developed in AID was not originally conceived or promoted by Ravenholt. Like the earmarking it was largely stimulated from outside as a result of perceived slack or excess funding, then directed by Ravenholt and restrained by his superiors into carefully defined channels. It was ironic that the generous research money that AID officials had begged Congress in vain to provide in other fields for nearly a decade became available to the agency only through an earmarking procedure that the agency opposed, in an area where the heads of the agency had no special competence.

Ironically, too, the research strategy in birth control, which was first proposed by a clergyman and carefully promoted as a tactic to blunt Catholic opposition, achieved one of its greatest successes in an agency where research itself was a liability, not an asset. In other words, population research as a substitute for action never won support. However, research to produce specific results that would have been valued even without the research did win support even in a most unlikely place. Moreover, the results of the research to date—a postconceptive chemical method that may one day be self-administered—did not offer the easy political or medical solution that many hoped for. In some ways, it would be an embarrassment rather than a blessing.

TABLE 17.3

Population as Percentage of AID Personnel and Obligations, Fiscal Years 1965-72

	1965	1966	1967	1968	1969	1970	1971	1972 (est.)
AID direct-hire full-time U.S. personnel (Washington and overseas)	6,469	6,886	8,225	8,306	7,352	6,939	6,513	6,277
AID professional population personnel	3	11	45	50	84	144	151	149
Professional population personnel as a percentage of AID personnel	.04	.2	.5	.6	1.1	2.1	2.3	2.3
AID obligations (millions of dollars)	2,187	2,677	2,419	2,176	1,690	1,877	1,861	2,053
Population obligations	2.134	3.892	4.445	34.750	45.444	74.572	95.868	125.000
Population obligations as a percentage of AID obligations	.1	.1	.2	1.1	2.7	4.0	5.2	6.2

Source: U.S. AID, calculated from congressional presentation, Fiscal Year 1973, and from *Population Program Study*, July 1972, pp. 25-26.

HELPING THE GOVERNMENT OF INDIA

If research, and especially prostaglandins, became an unexpected AID success, the continuing effort to assist the government of India with its family planning program remained a great frustration. Although India represented the most populous noncommunist nation with the oldest official birth control program in the world, U.S. help and Indian programs never quite seemed to mesh. Neither the Planned Parenthood effort to teach the rhythm system in the 1950s nor the U.S. foundation-supported campaign for IUDs in the mid-1960s achieved the hoped-for results. Ravenholt wanted to provide the government of India with substantial dollar grants, thousands of jeeps, and as many oral contraceptives as could be used. But in AID the Near East-South Asia Bureau insisted on loans, local manufacture of vehicles, and main reliance on the billions of Indian rupees generated by PL-480 food sales. In India doctors mistrusted U.S. drugs with their commercial overtones and emphasized the danger of unknown side effects and officials procrastinated in using PL-480 rupees.

In the fall of 1969 Ravenholt decided to bring the conflict to a head. He dispatched a memorandum to the administrator attacking the whole population strategy of the Near East-South Asia Bureau and the New Delhi Mission, which he considered the biggest short-fall of the program to date. Ravenholt recommended direct assistance to the government of India up to $50 million to provide commodities, vehicles, and, above all, supporting financial resources.[27] Ravenholt's open challenge forced a reassessment. Maurice Williams the experienced and skeptical assistant administrator of the NESA Bureau warned against pouring AID funds into an Indian sieve. Nonetheless, Williams worked his way carefully from a general commitment of up to $50 million at the World Bank Consortium meeting in Stockholm in November 1969 to a specific obligation in June 1970 of "twenty million dollars for U.S. imports in order for the Indian Government to spend an equivalent amount for rupee local currency."[28]

Before the grant could be made, the agency had to translate Ravenholt's attack on the NESA Bureau into an optimistic evaluation of the Indian government's own readiness and organizational ability to proceed. Williams had to follow up with months of negotiation to win from the Indians a commitment to increase their own activities so that the U.S. grant could support about half of the increase.

Yet nearly a year of concentrated U.S. effort produced mixed results. On the one hand, the $20 million additional funding did encourage building of new primary health centers during 1971; it allowed for a doubling of the number of auxiliary nurse-midwives, always in short supply, and it unclogged some of the administrative channels between central and provincial programs. Most important, it created a precedent for broad budgetary support to government programs rather than specific project funding. On the other hand, regardless of U.S. help the Indian government did not make oral contraceptives available. Many of the U.S. population advisers sent by the Ford Foundation and other private groups were not asked to renew their contracts. By 1972, regardless of prior commitments the political and budgetary strains of the war with Pakistan and Bangladesh relief forced the Indian government to cut back on family planning as well as many other programs.

Furthermore, during 1971 and 1972 the Indians, generally infuriated by official U.S. "tilting toward Pakistan," were also considering new family planning activities that raised more problems on the U.S. side. In 1971 the Indian Parliament legalized abortion, which became openly available in April 1972. Although most of the population experts welcomed the move the U.S. government was uneasy about providing assistance for abortion programs in India or in the United States. At the same time an enterprising Kerala official, S. P. Krishnakumar, organized several highly successful vasectomy camps. In the carnival atmosphere of these camps several hundred thousand men in Kerala and Gujurat volunteered for sterilization and each received as an incentive not only the usual $6 cash payment but also a bag of supplies and a new sari for his wife.[29] Indian officials hailed the vasectomy camps as a successful, uniquely Indian approach to population control and applied for international assistance. Many U.S. officials, however, doubted that sterilizing thousands of men, many in their late 30s or 40s, would greatly reduce the fertility of 90 million Indian couples. Ravenholt disapproved of adopter incentive programs in general. Like Williams in 1969 and 1970, Ravenholt in 1971 and 1972 began to suspect that dollar aid to the Indian program for the payment of incentives would be more "water through a sieve." Finally, in Washington the large grant of dollars to India, where the United States government held millions of rupees, brought some of the first congressional criticism of AID population programs from the Senate Appropriations Committee.[30]

After nearly a decade of trying, therefore, the most visible sign of U.S. help to India was a project originally developed by a young Ford Foundation adviser to encourage the subsidized distribution of condoms. The many differences between Indians and Americans—over specific methods as well as on broader administrative, financial, and political issues—usually managed to obscure the overall effect of U.S. assistance. Whether the generally unsatisfying results were caused by the "shrill voices" of U.S. population activists, or the basic program model of an extended public health delivery system, or the political liabilities of family planning generally—as AID Mission Director John Lewis later suggested[31]—or whether they were inherent in any complex bilateral assistance program for a large country like India would be difficult to prove.

Certainly the American-Indian relationship was the most conspicuous example of the hazards of bilateral aid, even when U.S. rules were bent. It was also apparent in other parts of the world that governments were often not the best vehicles for U.S. family planning assistance. Even where the relationship on the program level was good, as in Pakistan, the political liabilities of other government policies could be damaging to family planning. In large or ambitious nations like Brazil, Mexico, the United Arab Republic, and Nigeria direct U.S. government aid for population programs was simply not welcome. In the nations with the greatest food deficits where family planning seemed most urgent, as in India, a massive supply of U.S.-held local currencies often blocked meaningful assistance. Even in smaller countries like Korea, Taiwan, and the Philippines where AID gladly supported government requests the work of private organizations often provided a driving force that government bureaucracies lacked.

Despite the original expectation that only government programs could solve national population problems it became increasingly evident that the U.S. Agency for International Development could provide its assistance most rapidly and most easily to private organizations or to international bodies. Although tacit government approval was necessary, the work of the International Planned Parenthood Federation with its national family planning associations, the hospital-based postpartum programs of the Population Council, the organizational initiatives of the Pathfinder Fund, and even crash programs like the 1972 IPPF-Bangladesh relief that offered free abortion to women raped by West Pakistani soldiers—all these produced results faster than the diffuse and difficult government agreements.

Thus, despite the early pressure to aid governments like India, in fact AID assistance for population work tended to follow the paths of lesser resistance and more immediate impact. With AID support the private organizations, including several U.S. universities, were substantially strengthened in their capacity to help overseas. Training programs in the private sector expanded. Under the pressure of AID funds the professionally oriented Population Council moved toward greater activism while the activist IPPF became increasingly professional. The International Planned Parenthood Federation recruited from the United Nations as secretary-general first David Owen and then Julia Henderson. The latter brought to IPPF not only a positive outlook, personal charm, and administrative ability but also continuing links to the UN system.

Although the Bureau for Program and Policy Coordination, the Legal counsel, and various auditors would still try from time to time to bring the private organizations more closely under AID control, both Ravenholt and Hannah defended the use of qualified independent intermediaries to do the jobs AID wanted done. In early 1971, AID actually relaxed some of its program and project controls, giving broader budgetary support to both IPPF and the Population Council.

Ravenholt's long-term strategy continued to emphasize pills. AID funds supported a tremendous increase in the worldwide availability of contraceptives, especially orals. Even when several epidemiological studies implicated the pill as a factor in thromboembolism[31] and two months of hearings chaired by Senator Gaylord Nelson (D.-Wisc.) publicized researchers' fears about the pill,[32] Ravenholt held his ground. When in fact little new or conclusive evidence was produced and the drug companies were able to shift to lower estrogen formulations, oral contraceptives continued to gain, spurred by the increasing number of young women just entering their fertile years. Oral contraceptives, as Ravenholt had predicted, appealed to younger women more than IUDs. Between 1968 and 1972 AID financed over $17 million of contraceptives, including $9.5 million of orals, $4 million of condoms, $2 million of aerosol foam, and over $1 million of IUDs and inserters.[33] (See Tables 17.4

TABLE 17.4

Contraceptive Units Financed by AID, Fiscal Years 1968-72
(purchase orders placed, by units)

	1968 and 1969	1970	1971	1972	Total 1968-72
Orals (million cycles)	6.9	12.0	11.1	21.9	569
Condoms (thousand gross)	1,197	52	146	81	1,476
IUDs (thousands)	334	547	941	1,156	2,978

Source: U.S. AID, Office of Population, Purchase Order Report Computer Print-Out, July 15, 1972.

and 17.5.) Ironically, by 1972 the major threat to wider use of orals was their own increasing popularity and AID's success in reducing the bulk order price. Drug firms that had at first supplied pills to AID for $.19 to $.14 per cycle under competitive bidding no longer wanted to diminish their growing commerical sales at $1 to $2 per cycle by supplying pills at bargain rates for free distribution through AID. The danger loomed that the United States, which could develop and produce a technology the world badly needed, could not make that technology available at a price the rest of the world could afford. Oral contraceptives produced in Europe, on the other hand, were available for about one half the U.S. price, through the Swedish government program and the United Nations, but AID regulations required U.S. procurement.

Besides stressing technology the AID population program moved into another new area in 1970 and 1971. Information, education, and communication support, which had originally been included only as a part of IPPF and Population Council work, increased from about $250,000 in 1968 and in 1969 to $700,000 in 1970 and $4.3 million in 1971.[34] Although Ravenholt still rejected the concept of motivation he freely admitted that women in the less-developed countries needed not only pills and family planning services but also knowledge and information in order to recognize the new opportunity to fill their existing family planning need. "Need, opportunity, and knowledge" rather than motivation and attitudinal change were the concepts that justified AID communication support. More than just a semantic difference to counter the political pitfalls of propagandizing by AID, the "need, opportunity, and knowledge" formulation reflected above all Ravenholt's confidence that the population problem could be solved when governments finally provided the services that people understood and needed.

Originally Ravenholt had navigated his precarious program more by intuition—and a competitive impulse to outdistance other organizations—than by explicit or formal strategizing. During 1970 and 1971, however, largely as a result of Joel Bernstein's insistence, the objectives and directions of the program were more deliberately articulated in terms of specific goals, or categories of assistance, namely, the development of adequate

- demographic and social data (including censuses and program evaluation)
- population policy and understanding of population dynamics
- means of fertility control
- systems for delivery of family planning services
- systems for the delivery of information and knowledge
- multipurpose institutions and trained manpower.[35]

Just as population control itself had first to be justified as a tactic in the strategy of economic development, so each of these specific goals was in fact justified as a tactic in a strategy of population control—one of a number of tactics that were, each to some degree, relevant, feasible, important, and urgent.

OPPOSITION AND REORGANIZATION FOR AID

While the population program was strengthening its own tactics within the agency, however, AID itself was increasingly threatened by congressional opposition to the basic strategy of economic development and overseas involvement. The respite provided to AID by the two-year authorization ended in the spring of 1971. The report of the President's Task Force on International Development, headed by Rudolph Peterson and released in 1970, although not

TABLE 17.5

Contraceptive Costs Financed by AID, Fiscal Years 1968-72
(purchase orders placed, by thousands of dollars)

	1968-69	1970	1971	1972	1968-72
Orals	1,436	2,170	2,035	3,886	9,527
Condoms	3,035	177	567	269	4,048
IUDS and Inserters	95	239	403	475	1,212
Aerosol Foam	214	998	271	546	2,029
Other	240	24	58	131	453
Total	5,020	3,608	3,334	5,307	17,269

Source: U.S. Agency for International Development, Office of Population, Purchase Order Report, Computer Print-Out, July 15, 1972.

sent to Congress for action until 1971, went even further than Hannah in separating the economically justified loan program from the socially oriented technical assistance program. The Peterson report called for five separate organizations: one for all military- and security-related assistance; one for long-term capital loans; one to encourage overseas private investment; one to function as a council on the multilateral and policy level; and—most important for population—an International Development Institute to continue technical assistance under its own board of trustees with much reduced staffing to support mainly private intermediaries, concentrating on a few fields and emphasizing new technology and professional skills.[36] The Green Revolution and foundation programs were cited as the model for the proposed institute but the methods and strategies recommended were in many ways those already adopted by the Population Office.

The "Special Problem of Population" received special attention in the Peterson report with a call for international leadership, a world-wide study, and greater expenditure on population programs. The report gave little recognition, however, to the initiative of Congress in developing Title X or the effectiveness of the Population Office in implementing it.[37] In fact, the overall report seemed all too obviously to jeopardize continuing congressional oversight.

Deep in battle with Senator Fulbright and other influential Democrats over the continuing Vietnam war, the White House was not eager to consult or share credit with the legislative branch of government on foreign aid policies. AID was not eager to be subdivided and diminished, as Peterson proposed. The legislation based upon the Peterson report reached Congress at the last minute in fiscal 1971 and was basically stillborn—reviewed in part by the House Committee on Foreign Affairs but largely ignored by the Senate Committee on Foreign Relations.

Instead, in 1971 the course of previous years seemed at first to be somewhat repeating itself. AID, seeing loan funds sharply reduced by the House Foreign Affairs Committee, again tried to eliminate the mandatory earmarking language and asked for $100 million for population, no increase over 1971 funds. Freshman Congressman Pierre (Pete) DuPont IV (R.-Del.), replacing Taft as an advocate within the committee, succeeded in raising the sum to $125 million for fiscal 1974. In the Senate, AID officials also persuaded Republican committee members to eliminate earmarking, but Robert Taft (R.-Ohio), elected to the Senate in 1970, restored the original Title X language and earmarked $125 million in a floor amendment, explaining that the record of previous earmarking showed the value of such language.[38]

Then, just as population funds seemed secure again, the Senate, led by liberals angry over military assistance and President Nixon's Vietnam policy, rejected the entire foreign aid bill. A month of politics ensued during which many Republican senators joined the liberal Democrats in insisting that the House of Representatives vote yes or no on a Vietnam deadline amendment already passed by the Senate. AID barely hung on, through one continuing resolution after another, often without power to obligate funds, until the House and Senate—the former generally following presidential wishes, the latter opposing them—settled their jurisdictional disputes and compromised on AID funds. The second Senate foreign aid bill firmly earmarked $125 million for population. When, as a last-ditch effort, AID officials persuaded Senator Robert Packwood (R.-Ore.), a population supporter, to try to replace the earmarking requirement by a regular authorization, Packwood's amendment was defeated on the floor.[39] After a brief debate during which Senators Fulbright, Edward Kennedy (D.-Mass.) and a number of others spoke eloquently of the world population crisis, the Senate, clearly in no mood to add extra money, decisively approved earmarking of $125 million for population.[40] Supported by a record vote of 50 to 33 on the Senate floor, the 1967 earmarking language prevailed in conference, an unquestionable mandate from Congress.

But another hurdle had been erected. After the House had replaced the earmarking by usual authorization language the House Appropriations subcommittee, headed by Otto Passman, proceeded to cut the program, which the subcommittee had not been able to reach before, down to $50 million.[41] The Senate Appropriations Subcommittee was headed by William Proxmire (D.-Wisc.), an early and independent-minded supporter of conservation and environmental protection. He had heard and been impressed by Ravenholt and was inclined to agree with former Senator Tydings and Draper that rapid population growth posed a world-wide threat. His Senate subcommittee appropriated $125 million[42] and, to the surprise of many, the House Subcommittee agreed in conference to the Senate figure.[43] Actually, $125 million had been earmarked securely in the authorization, for both 1972 and 1973, but the separate appropriation guaranteed for the first time that population funds would not need to come out of moneys authorized for other loans or grants.

For AID as a whole the process was a near-disaster, beginning with the divisive Peterson report and ending with the bare survival of the agency, its funds, personnel, and morale sharply depleted. For the population program, however, the outcome brought unsought and unexpected triumph. Where once a birth control program had seemed to threaten the life of the agency, by 1972 that very program seemed the only popular activity in the agency, untinged by partisan conflict and unrelated to controversial military and economic problems.

One final hurdle remained. Congress had clearly ordered AID to cut back programs and personnel and streamline its organization. The first reorganization plan devised by Ernest Stern, head of the Bureau for Program and Policy Coordination, would have fragmented the Population Office into two planning and action units and demolished the geographic bureaus while claiming from the State Department authority over all multilateral assistance.[44] Strongly opposed by the regional bureaus and the State Department, the Stern proposal metamorphosed into a plan that accorded new status to population. A separate Bureau of Population and Humanitarian Assistance was established in which the Office of Population obtained greater control over the regional population staff.[45]

The Assistant Administrator of the new bureau Jarold Kieffer, an active Republican, experienced in public administration, was prepared to work easily and sympathetically with the once-again upgraded population program. In May 1972 the Office of Population was awarded a meritorious unit citation. The unit, under Ravenholt's leadership, was praised for vigorous, effective, positive, sustained performance combining "broad professional involvement in high policy" with "narrowly focussed technical problem-solving." The citation was:

> For conceiving and executing, during the period 1969-1971, a wide, innovative, interregional technical assistance and research program that is a major support of family planning efforts of developing nations around the world.[46]

In spite of itself, the Agency for International Development had initiated a significant program, setting a new world priority under leadership that still searched for a genuine solution, not merely a continuing bureaucracy.

18

ECOLOGY,
EQUALITY,
ETHICS,
AND ABORTION

Between 1969 and 1972, while the Agency for International Development and other organizations were adjusting their operating programs toward a new technology and bureaucracy, the public policy debate on population also took on new dimensions. Before 1969 U.S. government support of birth control was justified primarily by its economic impact and to a lesser degree by the impact on individual health. Individuals and nations both, it was thought, could accelerate their economic transition to affluence if they would also accelerate their demographic transition to lower fertility.

In 1969, however, the issues of environmental protection and women's rights burst into public attention even more abruptly than had the population explosion. Ecologists, biologists, feminists, and students demanded zero population growth, more contraceptives, and abortion. For these ardent new advocates, both professional and activist, birth control was more than just an economic asset, a way to get rich faster. It was a natural and social imperative to stave off ecological disaster and guarantee equal rights to women and the younger generation. At first these ideologies had little impact on government population programs but gradually they provided strong reinforcement for existing programs and increased urgency for new ones.

ENVIRONMENT AND ECOLOGY

The environmental argument was hardly new. It dated back at least to the conservation movement at the turn of the century and such continued warnings as Fairfield Osborn's 1948 book *Our Plundered Planet*. For decades conservationists and scientists both had lamented diminishing resources but, like that of Malthusian economists, their doom-saying was always rebutted by new discoveries, new technology. In the later 1960s, however, such warnings took on new relevance. Increasing and well-publicized pollution—in water, air, and land, by oil spills, electric power failures, traffic jams—gave the issue special urgency. Evidence came through all the senses that even though resources might be expanded the very expansion would damage other parts of the environment.

Dr. Durward Allen, a wildlife ecologist, put population and conservation together with a powerful new twist in March 1969. Addressing the National American Wildlife and Natural Resources Conference he bluntly observed that at the American standard of living the entire world could support only half a billion people. Not only was economic development on the American model impossible for the rest of the world, he warned, but also increasing environmental pollution was the price America would have to pay for its own "growth obsession." Population control was necessary, not for economic progress but for ecological survival. "The problems of human welfare," Allen insisted "are biological, behavioral, and economic—in that order."[1]

For the population movement, which was still debating the merits of family planning services versus motivation and calculating cost-benefit ratios, the advent of ecology coincided with President Nixon's message and the triumphant moon-landing. Like Johnson's comment in July 1965, the July 1969 message had a ratchet-like effect on public debate. No sooner did the president promise family planning services for all Americans and priority for population research than the policy debate moved on to more radical formulations. Even the spectacular Apollo flight, hailed in the message, instead of bolstering confidence in science portrayed instead on worldwide television a hostile and uninviting universe. The whole country could see what the pessimistic population-controllers had predicted. There were no alternatives in outer space to "our precious little planet, this blue-green cradle of life."[2]

While the president stressed better planning and help for the indigent, the new breed of advocates began to criticize the behavior of the affluent. Dr. Jean Mayer of Harvard took direct aim at the notion that rich countries or rich families could afford to keep on growing. Even with no population growth at all, he pointed out, the developed nations used more nonrenewable resources and produced more pollution than the developing ones.[3]

Speaking with the prestige of the scientific community the National Academy of Sciences issued a report in 1969 on *Resources and Man* in which it observed,

> Although it is true that man has repeatedly succeeded in increasing both the space he occupies and its carrying capacity, and that he will continue to do so, it is also clear that both the occupiable space and its carrying capacity have finite limits which he can approach only at great peril.[4]

Minimizing the power of science to produce new technological miracles, the scientists urged as their first policy recommendation,

> ... that efforts to limit population increase in the nation and the world be intensified by whatever means are practicable, working toward a goal of zero rate of growth by the end of the century. ...

> Ultimately this implies that the community and society as a whole, and not only the parents, must have a say about the number of children a couple may have.[5]

The academy's report was publicized in two days of congressional hearings chaired by Henry Reuss (D.-Wisc.) during which several witnesses criticized President Nixon's message for not specifically recommending a two-child family, a stabilized population, and legalized abortion.[6]

To the studies of the ecologists and biologists in the late 1960s were added the unexpectedly vociferous voices of an active younger generation. During the 1950s and 1960s Planned Parenthood and the other population organizations represented mainly an older generation. Past child bearing themselves, they looked with some suspicion at the coming youthful cohorts whose very numbers made population growth inevitable. In 1968 Hugh Moore again helped to light the new fuse and arouse the new generation by subsidizing nationwide distribution of Paul Ehrlich's book *The Population Bomb*, which was an immediate success on college campuses.[7] Moore also persuaded one of his protégé organizations, the Association for Voluntary Sterilization, to cooperate with the National Conference on Conservation in October 1969 for what was billed as the first joint meeting of conservation and birth control groups. At that session the AVS became the first of the population groups to adopt a resolution favoring the two-child family.[8] Also at that session Paul Ehrlich, a professor of biology at Stanford University, who had had a vasectomy himself, was a featured speaker. Shortly thereafter he became president of a small organization founded by a Connecticut lawyer with the provocative title "Zero Population Growth."

Under Ehrlich's charismatic leadership Zero Population Growth (ZPG) grew from a technical demographic term to a popular slogan to a national organization that by the spring of 1970 rated a cover story in *Life*.[9] Earth Day, April 22, 1970, marked a new highwater mark of student and teenage concern over the deteriorating environment. It was followed by a National Congress on Optimum Population and Environment (COPE) in Chicago in June 1970 that tried with mixed success to explore the broad policy issues that might unite birth controllers and conservationists, youths, blacks, and women. Compared with controversial ideas like stopping economic growth, support for voluntary birth control was taken almost for granted. Even militant black pronatalists, who often equated birth control with genocide, refocussed their protests against the new possibility that environmental protection for the future might jeopardize their opportunities for the present.

The reaction of the professionals in the population field, to the environmental approach was at first ambivalent. Paul Ehrlich's *Population Bomb*, like Hugh Moore's bomb 20 years earlier, was considered too polemical, not sufficiently objective. Ehrlich was described somewhat sarcastically in a Planned Parenthood publication as the "new high priest of ecocatastrophe,"[10] The pollution problem, like the earlier food problem, had complex causes of which population growth was not the major one, family planners argued. Crisis rhetoric was dangerous because it could weaken the commitment to long-term programs. As Frank Notestein put it at the 1970 session of the Population

Association of America, "In political terms, relating pollution to population may have done harm to a serious attack on both pollution and on population growth."[11]

The demographers' answer to ZPG, a term that suddenly dropped out of technical use, was NRR—Net Reproduction Rates. A net reproduction rate of one meant that each mother would have one daughter and thus each generation would exactly replace itself. A 1968 analysis by Tomas Frejka of the Population Council, however, demonstrated that even if a net reproduction rate of one were established in the United States immediately, a zero rate of natural growth, with births equalling deaths, would not be achieved for 70 years, after an overall population increase of nearly 40 percent.[12]

The intricacies of net reproduction rates, however, had far less public impact than did ZPG, which by January 1971 had nearly 30,000 members, increasing by 1,000 each month.[13] Far from discouraging the younger generation, the call to ZPG on a polluted planet seemed entirely congenial to the baby-boom generation that had felt the pressures of overpopulation since it first entered kindergarten. Whether from conviction, or economic pressures, or social change, the younger generation already seemed to appreciate the lessons of demography better than did its parents. U.S. birth rates, which in the late 1960s had risen much less than demographers predicted, dropped in 1971 to 17.3, the lowest level since 1820, even as the number of potential parents rose.[14] The Washington Center for Metropolitan Study in a well-publicized report called the phenomenon a "baby bust" instead of a "baby boom."[15] Young people were staying single longer, having children later or not at all.

Even the older generation was demonstrating new concern about population growth in the United States as well as overseas. In the fall of 1965 and 1967, 54 percent of the population considered U.S. population growth a serious problem.[16] By 1971, 65 percent considered it serious.[17] Despite rebuttals by some experts, 57 percent agreed in 1971 that population growth was "causing the country to use up its natural resources too fast."[18] It was agreed by 48 percent that "population growth is the main reason for air and water pollution."[19] That "population growth is producing a lot of social unrest and dissatisfaction" was agreed to by 64 percent.[20] Not surprisingly, therefore, 56 percent of those polled in the spring of 1971 thought that the government should "try to slow down population growth in the United States."[21] Interest, if not yet support, was clearly developing for a broad range of population and environmental measures that might challenge not only motherhood but also the economic, political, and sexual status quo in America.

ETHICS, EQUALITY AND ABORTION

The economic justification for birth control emphasized enlightened self-interest as the stimulus that would in time bring families and nations to lower fertility. The ecological justification almost demanded individual birth control for the good of society. Garrett Hardin in a provocative article entitled "The Tragedy of the Commons" put the case for government control of repro-

duction on the common need to protect a limited environment from ex-
ploitation by a few.[22] To the older generation—the activists and the professionals, the doctors and demographers—as to most Americans—such arguments
remained impractical, even repugnant. Individual rights were more important
than social restructing. Economic growth to benefit all was a more attractive
goal than the redistribution of finite resources. Among the general public, even
though in 1971 57 percent thought people should "limit the size of their
families even though they can afford a larger number of children,"[23] nevertheless 68 percent opposed even the largely symbolic pressure of antinatalist
tax laws.[24]

Within the population field the logic that rebutted, at least temporarily,
the ethics of coercion was developed in large part by Charles Westoff, professor
of sociology at Princeton, from the data of National Fertility Surveys and used
enthusiastically by family planning activists to support ongoing programs.
Coercion was not needed, Westoff argued, because surveys showed that some
20 percent of American births were unwanted and therefore could be prevented by purely voluntary means such as better contraceptives and better
clinics.[25] Even talking about compulsory birth control is "unnecessary and
dangerous," Harriet Pilpel, counsel to Planned Parenthood, argued when most
states still placed innumerable and unnecessary restrictions on voluntary family
planning.[26]

Easier access to better birth control methods, including repeal of outmoded restrictions, offered a logical and seemingly acceptable alternative to
coercion. That tactic coincided with the developing strategies of another
movement. Women's liberationists also demanded greater freedom and an end
to all measures that forced women into second-class status. In the field of
reproduction, a woman's right to choose included not only pills and IUDs but
also abortion—legal, safe, and inexpensive. The "right of marital privacy"
proclaimed in the 1965 Supreme Court decision on birth control was translated
by a militant feminist movement and sympathetic physicians into the right of
women to control their own bodies, the right to avoid "compulsory pregnancy" by legal, medically protected abortion. The international publicity in
1969 and 1970 over the safety of oral contraceptives added fuel to feminist
fires. Why, the women wanted to know, should they be guinea pigs for unsafe
drugs? Why not more research for better male contraceptives?[27]

On the issue of abortion, the environmentalists, the younger generation,
the militant women, the family planners, and most of the doctors and
demographers could agree. To fulfill Margaret Sanger's demand that women
control their own bodies, to reduce the pressures of rapid population growth,
to rebut arguments for coercion by ensuring that no unwanted babies be
brought into the world, to increase the safety margin of other contraceptives by providing a backstop when they failed, and above all, to lower
the mortality and distress from continuing illegal abortions that took place
in any case—the logical solution was legal abortion. Abortion as a surgical
procedure had already become technically feasible and safer than childbirth
decades earlier. In the late 1960s the new technique of vaccum aspiration made
abortion possible on an outpatient basis, as a clinical service not very different
from inserting an IUD.

While the Catholic Church was absorbed, first waiting for the pope's decision on contraception in *Humanae Vitae* and, after July 1968, arguing about it, the women, the doctors, and the lawyers began to work on abortion laws. With strong professional legal reassurance through the model liberalized abortion law drafted by the American Law Institute, 4 state legislatures amended existing statutes in 1966 and 1967 (Mississippi, California, Colorado, and North Carolina). By mid-1971, 17 states had removed legal restrictions to some degree, 3 by judicial interpretation of existing statutes. Even more significant, in 1970 New York, Alaska, and Hawaii enacted bolder laws allowing abortion on request without a health justification. In April 1970 Senator Packwood introduced federal legislation to make abortion available on request regardless of state law. In abortion policy the transition from stress on professional, medical, or legal judgment to greater individual choice seemed to have taken barely five years.

Suddenly Catholic leaders perceived that their internal debate over a cause already lost had given the abortion advocates a powerful head start. Within the Catholic Church abortion in 1969 occupied approximately the same place as birth control in 1959. Militants organized Right to Life groups which, beginning in 1970, effectively blocked further liberalization of the Maryland law and threatened new restrictions in New York. The issue that abortion advocates defined as a woman's right to privacy and a doctor's right to professional judgment, the Catholic opposition defined as murder. Opponents spoke of abortion "on demand," instead of "by request." As a decade earlier in the birth control struggle, political leaders caught between militant proabortionists and organized religious opposition faced an unhappy choice. When, in 1971 the Defense Department relaxed restrictions on abortion in military installations the White House was deluged with letters of protest. President Nixon responded that laws regulating abortion were a state matter not to be overruled by the Defense Department. But he went still further to give his own personal comment. Abortion was "an unacceptable form of population control," he said. "Unrestricted abortion policies, or abortion on demand, I cannot square with my personal belief in the sanctity of human life—including the life of the yet unborn."[28] Again in May 1972 when Right to Life groups were trying to repeal New York's liberal abortion law the president wrote directly to Cardinal Cooke applauding as "truly a noble endeavor . . . your decision to act in the public forum as defenders of the right to life of the unborn."[29]

Unlike President Eisenhower who had suppressed his personal views to avoid a religious confrontation, President Nixon intervened directly to make his personal views known even on a question of state jurisdiction. Although the New York State Assembly and Senate passed the repeal bill, Governor Nelson Rockefeller vetoed it—as he had earlier pledged to do— with a strong statement.

> I can see no justification now for . . . condemning hundreds of thousands of women to the dark ages once again. . . . Every woman has the right to make her own choice. . . .
>   I do not believe it right for one group to impose its vision of morality on an entire society. Neither is it just or practical

for the state to attempt to dictate the innermost personal beliefs and conduct of its citizens.[30]

But it was clear that Catholic opposition, stressing the rights of the unborn, would not only contest any further liberalization of abortion laws but also would seek whenever possible to reinstate restrictive laws or conditions.

Actually, public support for unrestricted abortion was nowhere near the level of public support for birth control even a decade earlier. Throughout the 1960s, as Judith Blake has documented, a majority of men and women approved of abortion only for health reasons, that is, only where the mother's health might be jeopardized or where the child might be deformed.[31] Throughout the 1960s a majority of men and women disapproved of abortion for economic or social reasons, that is, where the family could not afford or simply did not wish to have another child. Despite the active role of women's liberation groups, among the public at large, males, the well-educated, and non-Catholics were most favorable to abortion reform.[32]

But between 1969 and 1971 a substantial change took place both in the formulation of the issue and in the public and political response. While advocates, especially female, stressed freedom of choice and legislators struggled with the various alternatives such as length of pregnancy, place for termination, and residency, the moral question was supplanted by a jurisdictional one. As reflected precisely in public opinion polls, the issue in the 1969 was, "Would you favor, approve or legalize abortion under various circumstances?" To that formulation, a majority throughout the 1960s answered "No. Not unless the mother's life or health are endangered." The issue in 1971 and 1972 was, "Do you think that the decision to have an abortion in the early months of pregnancy should be made solely by the couple—or the woman—and her doctor?"[33] To that version, in May 1971, 50 percent of the total population and 39 percent of the Catholic population said "Yes." In January 1972, 57 percent of the total population and 54 percent of the Catholic population said "Yes."[34] In other words, at the policy level abortion could be permitted— even by those who did not approve of it—as a lesser evil than government interference in private behavior. By redirecting attention from the pros and cons of abortion itself to the level at which the decision should and in fact would be made, advocates of abortion hoped ultimately to win the substance of their argument.

Thus political support for abortion, which five years earlier seemed impossible, developed not only as a tactic in an economic or even a health strategy but also as part of a struggle for equal rights. As Catholic opposition became more vocal, abortion advocates sought to substitute the jurisdictional question of "who should decide" for the moral question of approval or disapproval. In an atmosphere of greater concern over population and environment, abortion seemed to be gaining both relevance and urgency through the agitation of women's liberationists and the arguments of the professionals—on health, safety, and pragmatic grounds. Publicized more by opponents than by advocates, abortion reform in the 1970s, like birth control in 1960, was becoming an issue of public policy that could not easily be ignored or controlled by political leaders, whatever their views.

THE COMMISSION ON POPULATION GROWTH
AND THE AMERICAN FUTURE

Ecology, equality, ethics, and abortion had not yet burst into public attention in the spring of 1969 when President Nixon and his advisers decided that family planning and population growth were sufficiently important to warrant study by a Population Commission but not sufficiently controversial to embarrass the White House. Legislation to establish a national, not merely a presidential, commission was drafted through Moynihan's office and introduced without hesitation by Republican and Democratic members of the appropriate committees. Promptly approved in the Senate, the measure was amended in committee in the House of Representatives at the suggestion of Rodney Shaw, an enterprising Methodist minister. Besides population trends and government programs, Congress directed the commission to inquire into:

The impact of population growth on the environmental pollution, and on the depletion of natural resources; and
    The various means appropriate to the ethical values and principles of this society by which our nation can achieve a population level suited for its environmental, national resources and other needs.[35]

The House of Representatives delayed action, partly because of a personal rivalry between retiring Speaker John McCormack and Morris Udall, a population advocate, and partly because of the Speaker's traditional Boston Catholic dislike for the whole issue. But in March 1970, eight months after the president's message, the bill became law. John D. Rockefeller 3rd was named by President Nixon as chairman and by June 1970 the 24-member body was ready to start work.

The Rockefeller Population Commission, compared to the Draper Committee of 1959, was much more professional and academic in its membership, much more representative of the whole country, including men and women, young and old, public figures and private citizens. The population professionals included Bernard Berelson, president of the Population Council; Joseph D. Beasley, M.D., founder of the Louisiana family planning program and chairman of Planned Parenthood; Otis Dudley Duncan, professor of sociology at the University of Michigan and a noted demographer; Margaret Bright, professor of behavioral sciences at the Johns Hopkins University; and David Bell, executive vice-president of the Ford Foundation. Two economists, D. Gale Johnson and John R. Meyer, professors of economics at Chicago and Yale Universities, respectively, were included, as were a businessman R. V. Hansberger, chairman and president of the Boise Cascade Corporation, and a banker, George D. Woods, director and consultant, the First Boston Corporation (and former president of the World Bank). Howard D. Samuel, vice-president of the Amalgamated Clothing Workers of America, represented labor. Dr. Paul B. Cornely, M.D., former president of the American Public Health Association and professor at Howard University; Lawrence Davis, an Arkansas college president; and Arnita Young Boswell, a University of Chicago professor, represented blacks. Christian N. Ramsay, Jr., M.D., a young physician, James Rummonds, a law student, and Stephen Salyer, an undergraduate, were the youngest members. Marilyn Brant Chandler and Joan F. Flint were housewives, although exceptionally able, active, and well-connected ones; Grace Olivarez was a Mexican-American lawyer.

Six members of Congress served on the commission but the four remaining at the end were Senators Robert Packwood (R.-Ore.), Alan Cranston (D.-Cal.) and Congressman John Erlenborn (R.-Ill.) and James Scheuer (D.-N.Y.). Although three members were Catholic there was, deliberately, no specific representation of any religious denomination. Nor were there any biologists or ecologists. A major concern of the White House was to avoid people who might take uncompromising positions on any issue. The most conspicuous activists were the only members not chosen by the White House— Senators Tydings (later replaced by Cranston) and Packwood and Congressman Scheuer (who replaced Blatnik). Although their influence within the commission was minimal, except-for the more conservative Congressman Erlenborn, one or another of the congressional members had in fact proposed or supported all the major or controversial recommendations—although in different, less acceptable form—before they were reviewed, argued, modified, accepted, and to a further degree legitimized by the commission.

The commission started slowly, reviewing the whole field, commissioning outside research, avoiding publicity. However, the chairman and administration spokesmen emphasized that the commission studies were not intended to delay other actions. The Tydings-Scheuer-Bush Family Planning Services and Population Research bill, introduced in May 1969, passed the Senate in June 1970. At Senate hearings in December 1969 chaired by Senator Thomas Eagleton (D.-Mo.) the only serious opposition came from the Department of Health, Education, and Welfare which at the last minute proposed a different bill with less money that would keep services and research separate.[36]

In the House of Representatives, however, by the summer of 1970 hostile Catholic witnesses were attacking the bill as a back door route to federally subsidized abortion. Sympathetic Catholic spokesmen had to reassure Speaker McCormack that no such thing was intended. The final version, a three-year bill authorizing $382 million for services and research, passed the House of Representatives by a vote of 298 to 32.[37] It included the sentence, "None of the funds appropriated under this title shall be used in programs where abortion is a method of family planning."[38] Nevertheless it was a major victory for Planned Parenthood. Family planning was no longer controversial even if members of Congress, caught between birth control and the right to life, wanted as little as possible to do with abortion. Dr. Louis Hellman, who had helped to precipitate the 1959 birth control confrontation in New York City, became the new deputy assistant secretary for family planning and population.

Three months after passage of the first comprehensive bill providing separate federal support for family planning and population research, the Population Commission issued its interim report. Widely acclaimed for translating demographic expertise into language clear to the general public, the report moved a step beyond family planning to ask, "What kind of national population policy is desirable now for the long run?"[39] The single most salient point was made by a graph that showed how much faster U.S. population would grow if the three-child family—not the two-child family—remained the norm. Within 100 years, a difference of one child per family would mean the difference between 950 million or 350 million Americans.

For six months following the interim report the commission heard testimony around the country. Some members were impatient at the first year's pace. Senator Cranston introduced a sense of Congress resolution with eventually some 50 co-sponsors to declare zero population growth as a national goal.[40] After a series of hearings and finally in December 1971 after winning the endorsement of the commission the resolution was postponed when a flood of Catholic telegrams labelled it proabortion. It was a warning that the Catholic opposition was alert and on the offensive.

From December 1971 to March 1972 in a new environment of plummeting U.S. birthrates and mounting controversy over the role of women, youth, and abortion, the commission tackled the final recommendations and language of the report. As the first chapter suggests, the commission was divided into three major viewpoints:

1. The unwanted child view, put forth most cogently by Charles Westoff the executive director, Berelson, and Beasley, that emphasized the need to help individuals control reproduction through better birth control methods and services,

2. The social justice view, urged by Cornely, Olivarez, and Boswell, that gave first priority to equalizing the rights of women and racial minorities and minimized the importance of other population factors, and

3. The crisis or ecological view, presented strongly by Rummonds, Duncan, and Packwood, that called for basic changes in economic and other value systems to restore a sharply deteriorating environment.[41]

All three positions were reflected in various parts of the report. Of the 22 major recommendations, 9 dealt with improved education, information, services, and techniques for individual fertility control, reflecting primarily the voluntarist, wanted-child approach; 5 dealt with population distribution and statistics calling for more federal, state, and local planning, better data, and an end to discrimination in housing; 4 sought higher status or better care for women, children, and racial minorities; 2 proposed limits and studies on immigration; and 1 recommended governmental changes including a Department of Community Development, a National Institute of Population Sciences within NIH, and an Office of Population Growth and Distribution in the White House to consider the further need for national population policies.

Most of the commission members were reluctant to endorse any overall population policy that would be inconsistent with the general stress on avoiding coercion and enlarging individual freedoms. The phrase "zero population growth" was avoided; answers were given in "qualitative not quantitative terms."[42] Nevertheless, common sense concern over population growth rather than an ironclad logical proof of the link between individual choice and social goals dictated the commission's overall conclusion:

> Recognizing that our population cannot grow indefinitely and appreciating the advantages of moving now toward the stabilization of population, the Commission recommends that the nation welcome and plan for a stabilized population.[43]

There were no specific recommendations for economic, tax, or environmental policies although these had been included to some extent in the outside research. In part this gap reflected the untimely death of Ritchie Reed, who had directed the economic research; in part it reflected the Commission's own reluctance to spell out the implications and options of nongrowth. The economic message of the report was simply, "We have looked for and we have not found any convincing economic argument for continued national population growth."[44]

The two specific points on which major political controversy loomed were abortion and contraceptives for teenagers. Yet despite dissents on varying grounds the report declared that "no woman should be forced to bear a child" and recommended that the New York law, most liberal in the country, be the model for other state laws.[45] Moreover, federal, state, local, and insurance funds should be available, the commission recommended, to finance abortion services. The commission also urged that contraceptive services and sex education be fully available to minors and that legal impediments to such services be eliminated by the states.[46]

The report was released in three parts in March and April 1972 with publicity and Catholic opposition centering on the abortion issue. For several weeks President Nixon remained silent. Then on May 5 he commented, singling out for attention two points.

> . . . I consider abortion an unacceptable form of population control. In my judgment, unrestricted abortion policies would demean human life. I also want to make it clear that I do not support the unrestricted distribution of family planning services to minors. Such measures would do nothing to preserve and strengthen close family relationships. . . . I believe in the right of married couples to make these judgments for themselves.[47]

Like President Eisenhower on the eve of a critical election, President Nixon rejected the most controversial findings of the group he had appointed. But unlike Eisenhower he deliberately stimulated "an emerging debate of great significance." Whether and which political figures will benefit from the debate is not clear but, if history is any guide, for the thousands of women seeking abortion and the millions of minors using contraceptives a national debate on the issues seems more likely to promote than retard the commission's objectives.

In a literate society like the United States with active communications media the very selection and definition of issues through the policy-making process becomes itself a means to the resolution of the problem. More particularly in a field like population, unlike, for example, space exploration, the ultimate success or failure of the policy will depend in the final instance not on the government program but on the individual response. As Samuel Huntington concludes:

> The continuing debate and discussion over the adequacy of the programs, however, and the conflict over what did constitute desirable criteria tended to insure that at least the minimum programs would be innovated in time and maintained sufficiently. Prophecies of disaster when credited by the right people are self-non-fulfilling.[48]

For American population policy in the field of reproduction the right people are not the president and his advisors, but rather the millions of young women and men who will reproduce in this and future generations. During the late 1960s and early 1970s they were already deciding for more contraceptives, legal abortion, and lower fertility. Within the United States the history of birth control policy may well be a series of self-non-fulfilling prophecies in which the informed public response to the crisis obviates the need for a more drastic policy.

19

POPULATION
AND DEVELOPMENT
IN THE UNITED NATIONS

No account of U.S. policy toward world population growth would be complete without recognition of the increasingly important role played by the UN system. On the one hand, the initiatives of Rockefeller, Notestein, Gardner, Baumgartner, Draper, Claxton, Ravenholt, and other Americans, the policy directions of the State Department, and eventually, the resources of AID strongly influenced and accelerated UN programs. On the other hand, the development of a major UN role in the population field will increasingly affect the nature of AID programs. How the population mandates and activities of the UN system were formally established has been told by others.[1] The purpose of this chapter is to identify some of the crucial initiatives and to compare very briefly the process of institution-building in the UN system between 1965 and 1972 with that which took place in AID during the same period. Necessarily and regrettably, very little attention is given to specific programs of the specialized agencies like the World Health Organization (WHO), UNESCO, the International Labour Organization (ILO), the Food and Agriculture Organization (FAO), or to regional programs of the UN Economic Commissions and demographic centers, or to the World Bank, each of which would in itself represent a separate case of institution-building. The focus of this overview is on the UN itself, operating primarily from its New York headquarters, and on the inception and growth of the Population Fund as a coordinating unit for international population programs.

In the UN, population policymaking can be traced through the same arguments of relevance, feasibility, priority, and urgency that marked U.S. policymaking. Although the UN process remained throughout the 1960s about two years behind U.S. moves, significant parallels exist in the events and some of the institutional changes that characterized the growth of both programs. The first full-fledged General Assembly debate in 1962, like the first U.S. public discussion following the Draper Committee report in 1959, revolved around the question of relevance: was population control relevant to economic development and should it therefore be included as an integral part of systematic technical assistance programs? In both cases, the official answer was "No" as President Eisenhower rejected his committee's proposals and the General Assembly in 1962 deleted the words "technical assistance" from the proposed resolution. But the interest and publicity aroused by these discussions led in both cases to a growing recognition by policymakers that the problem was indeed relevant and that some public action might well be feasible.

The legitimizing of the issue represented in U.S. politics by President Johnson's statement of January 1965 occurred in the UN in December 1966 when Secretary-General U Thant first accepted a Declaration on Population from twelve world leaders. At the same time the General Assembly approved a resolution linking population and economic development, thereby putting the stamp of relevance and political feasibility on some form of technical assistance in population.

From 1967 to 1970 in the UN, as in AID from 1965 to 1968, priority on the program level lagged behind the announced feasibility on the policy level. Recruiting staff and meeting national needs under the constraints of a tight central budget and in attempted coordination with stronger, independently funded bodies proved difficult. In both cases, a somewhat separate unit was then designated to mobilize a larger effort. The transfer of the Secretary-General's Trust Fund to the UN Development Program in 1969 for worldwide administration corresponded roughly with the establishment of the AID Population Service in the War on Hunger in 1967.

Higher priority for both programs came largely from new and generous funding mechanisms promoted by nonbureaucratic outsiders and activists who controlled the purse strings—that is, for AID by the U.S. Congress and for the UN by contributing governments—and rather reluctantly accepted by high administrative officials. Thus, the first substantial AID funding—$35 million —came from earmarked Title X funds in 1968 over Gaud's objections, whereas the first major UN commitments for population work—about $32 million— were made through the Fund for Population Activities (UNFPA) in 1971 against a background of UN rivalries.

For both programs, the urgency or timing factor has depended primarily upon external events such as crop failures, shortfalls in meeting development targets, environmental concerns, and in the UN system the necessity, stimulated by governments, of planning for the World Population Conference and Year in 1974. A key element in the timing of the UN program has also undoubtedly been the timing of U.S. efforts. Each advance in U.S. policy or resources was followed, after a period of U.S. reorientation and consolidation, by U.S. pressures on the UN for similar advances. These pressures were applied in the official positions that the U.S. took on policy resolutions and funding commitments as well as through the nonofficial influence of population activists like Rockefeller and Draper.

The Scandinavian governments, especially Sweden, were often ahead of the U.S. in promoting UN population programs. Not only by precipitating the first General Assembly debate in 1962 and making an initial contribution to the Population Fund in 1967, but also more recently during the May 1972 sessions of the Economic and Social Council (ECOSOC) by calling for a Global Strategy on Population Sweden set the pace. But without support from the

U.S., Swedish initiatives could not prevail against the combined hostility or indifference of Catholic and communist governments.

From the first General Assembly debate in 1962 it was clear that in the UN there were consistently two opponents to Malthusian thinking, rather than one. Not only did the Catholic countries oppose birth control—on similar grounds as American Catholics—but also the Communist countries contested the Malthusian formulation, even as refined by Coale and Hoover, that rapid population growth could retard economic development. For Marxists, population control was a capitalist strategem to postpone the real solutions—a reorganization of society and redistribution of wealth. Therefore the relevance of population policy throughout the UN could not be as strongly identified in economic terms as it was in the U.S. UN population policy also had to include, in the words of the 1966 General Assembly resolution, "consideration of economic, social, cultural, psychological, and health factors in their proper perspective."[2]

Human rights were repeatedly stressed in the mid 1960s as a justification for population programs. The World Leaders' statement, a broad declaration of support which was circulated by John D. Rockefeller 3rd and signed by thirty heads of state by December 1967, emphasized that "the opportunity to decide the number and spacing of children is a basic human right."[3] U Thant first received and officially welcomed the statement with twelve signatures on Human Rights Day, December 1966, commenting "We must accord the right of parents to determine the number of their children a place of importance at this moment in man's history."[4] The economic implications in the Declaration were muted: "We believe that the population problem must be recognized as a principal element in long-range national planning if governments are to achieve their economic goals. . . ."[5] Yet even so, compared with three leaders of Catholic countries, only one Communist leader, Tito of Yugoslavia, signed. In language considered "noncontroversial," the 1968 International Conference on Human Rights at Teheran reaffirmed for couples the "basic human right to decide freely and responsibly on the number and spacing of their children."[6] Within the UN Secretariat, Julia Henderson, Director of the Office of Technical Cooperation and an early birth control supporter, was influential in helping to define the need for birth control in social and cultural terms rather than exclusively economic ones.

For enunciating policy and drafting resolutions, human rights provided an eloquent and acceptable framework. But for allocating funds and initiating programs, human rights and social concerns were much less persuasive. In the UN, even more than in the U.S., both the relevance and the feasibility of family planning programs as a social benefit were weakened by lack of wholehearted support from the professional health organizations. Just as the U.S. Department of Health, Education, and Welfare (HEW) did not have a family planning policy until more than a year after President Johnson's statement and continued until 1969 to oppose any specific authorization of funds for family planning, so also WHO was slow in assigning priority to family planning work. At the 1966 session of the World Health Assembly, Director General M. G. Candau argued that overly vigorous promotion of family planning would divert funds from malaria and cholera control and that public health services had to precede family planning programs.[7] Rejecting a U.S.-sponsored resolution, the World Health Assembly restricted WHO's role to giving "technical advice upon request, in the development of activities in family planning, as part of an organized health service, without impairing its normal preventive and curative functions."[8] Although the 1966 resolution represented a considerable advance over a 1965 resolution which had specifically precluded WHO even from advising operational activities, family planning in WHO, as in several U.S. health programs, was long considered a "special interest" rather than a "normal function" of health programs. WHO was not authorized to help "integrate family planning within basic health services"[9] until 1968 and, despite the efforts of the U.S., Scandinavian, and some Asian governments, did not actively seek funds to do so until 1971.

TECHNICAL ASSISTANCE FOR FAMILY PLANNING

As long as the health professionals denied that birth control was relevant to health and the communists denied that it was relevant to economic development, the UN system could not easily move beyond demographic research and training into full-fledged technical assistance for national family planning programs. The birth control advocates had to work through the existing, mainly demographic institutions of the UN secretariat to try to build a case against Catholic and Communist opposition in the intergovernmental bodies. Through the mid 1960s the Population Commission, and its staff in the Population Branch, later Division, continued to provide the major internal impetus. The General Assembly resolution of 1962 had deleted the words "technical assistance" but on French initiative called for a Demographic Inquiry from the secretary-general to governments on the relationships between population growth and economic development.[10] Analysis of the replies and preparation for the 1965 World Population Conference kept population issues alive within the UN structure.

Yet in spite of Communist objections, as economic development became a major UN objective, population growth was increasingly and publicly linked to it. Statements by U.S. and UN leaders in 1965 and 1966 signalled the policy shift. At the 1965 summer session of ECOSOC, after President Johnson's first statement, Secretary-General U Thant called special attention to the "preoccupying" problem of population. Despite the efforts of the first UN Development Decade, he observed, the gap between per capita incomes in the rich and poor nations was widening. At the same session ECOSOC for the first time specifically authorized technical assistance for family planning.[11] Although the World Population Conference of August 1965 barely mentioned the words birth control, much of the discussion emphasized the relevance of demography to development. The widely distributed nontechnical summary of the Conference was entitled *World Population: Challenge to Development.*[12]

In 1966 the Population Commission was enlarged from 18 to 27 members to accommodate more of the developing nations. The new members from Asia, Africa, and Latin America were more interested in finding out what the real impact of population growth on development might be than in rehashing theoretical Malthusian or Marxist arguments. Again in 1967, with even greater emphasis and strong U.S. support, the Commission approved expanded research, training, and assistance to governments on request for action programs in population.

For the UN as for AID, the critical world food shortages of 1966 and 1967 hastened a policy change that was already emerging from the preliminary evaluations of the first Development Decade. B. R. Sen, Director-General of FAO, blamed high rates of population growth for declining per capita food production.[13] Through FAO's Indicative World Plan, projecting future food needs and production, he sought to document for agriculture what the Coale-Hoover thesis proved for other areas of economic development. In this climate of international concern, just as the routine reenactment of the Food for Peace Act by the U.S. Congress in 1966 became a vehicle for additional amendments on population, so also the routine adoption by the General Assembly of the biennial resolution approving the expanded two and five year work programs of the Population Division became in 1966 a clear mandate to expand UN population activities. The 1966 General Assembly resolution referred specifically to the secretary-general's concern, the World Population Conference, and "the growing food shortage in the developing countries which is due in many cases to a decline in the production of food-stuffs relative to population growth"; it called on the entire UN system "to assist when requested in further developing and strengthening national facilities for training, research, information, and advisory services in the field of population."[14]

The real thrust of the resolution was to focus further attention on the Population Division within the Department of Economic and Social Affairs. Milos Macura, an energetic Yugoslav, had been appointed director of the enlarged Population Division in 1966. But as in AID the new title and personnel did not immediately mean extra money for technical assistance. Thus Macura, instead of continuing the traditional demographic studies for which the division was known, found most of his time occupied trying to develop a technical assistance program in a new and controversial field with restricted resources from a position of limited bureaucratic leverage. Although the United Nations post was more prestigious than AID's Population Branch, the two units faced similar problems in 1966. Like Ravenholt, Macura soon became discouraged by the prospects before him. In December 1967 he observed:

> I am less optimistic than I was eight months ago about the pace of developments because we will be faced soon not with lack of money but of personnel. Before the momentum comes, staff should be trained, the organization should be prepared, people should be more thoroughly informed.[15]

Funding and personnel were both serious obstacles for the UN population effort in the late 1960s because many governments refused to pay assessments for the Congo peace-keeping operation. The UN resources allocated to population in 1966 and 1967 were $1.6 and $1.7 million respectively, compared with $1.2 million in 1955, a decade earlier.[16] For the United Nations, as for AID, at the very moment that birth control was becoming politically acceptable as a tactic in the organizations' larger strategies those larger strategies lost some of their own political acceptability. Tight budgets made it impossible to start any new program without external pressures or resources. During the period 1966-69 Macura struggled to line up the resources and develop the strategy for an expanded UN population program.

On the resource side, Draper tried to play the same role for the United Nations that he had played for AID and the International Planned Parenthood Federation. He had concluded in 1966 that three men held the key to world action in population—President Johnson, Pope Paul VI, and U Thant.[17] President Johnson was already moving; Pope Paul's study commission was reviewing the subject; and in mid 1966 Draper approached U Thant. The secretary-general was fully sympathetic. At his invitation an important luncheon was held June 14, 1967. When, at the last minute, U Thant was detained, the meeting was chaired by Under Secretary Philippe de Seynes. It included Draper, Rockefeller, Richard Gardner, senior officials of the International Planned Parenthood Federation and the Population Council, Julia Henderson, and Milos Macura. The real issue, it was agreed, was no longer research, statistics, or even training but rather how to put together and finance under UN auspices a major technical assistance program that could encourage and co-ordinate the resources of the entire UN system to help national population and family planning needs.

The first solution—agreed upon in principle, outlined, and announced by the secretary-general within a month—was to establish a trust fund, comparable to those used by WHO to promote international health campaigns, and open to voluntary contributions from governments and private sources. U Thant acted boldly and promptly without waiting for further mandates. The fund was intended to support not only the five-year program of activities approved in the December 1966 General Assembly resolution but also "experimental field projects." Macura estimated the cost between 1967 and 1971 as only $5.5 million, of which $4 million would provide increased staff resources at UN headquarters, in the regional economic commissions, and elsewhere overseas.[18]

The secretary-general's fund, initially called the United Nations Fund for Population, was never the massive international program of technical assistance envisaged by Draper and Gardner. Rather it was "seed money" that, as Julia Henderson pointed out, could build the UN infrastructure for "careful planning and imaginative programming" that would enable the United Nations to help government family planning programs.[19] In other words, to answer the recurring question that also troubled AID in 1967, of how generous funding could sensibly be used to support population programs when no one knew what needed to be done, the United Nations proposed to train staff and build up technical competence. Since UN aid funds that could actually be turned over to governments for their own use were considerably less than U.S. AID funds, the natural tendency of UN officials, even more than of AID officials, was to give priority to training.

With the announcement of the Trust Fund by U Thant and the contribution of $500,000 from the United States, the UN seemed ready to move forward. Two obstacles—both essentially the product of bureaucratic constraints within the UN system—held the Population Division back between 1967 and 1969. One was the long time-lag required by UN procedures for recruiting staff. The first Population Program officers, whose mission was to help governments prepare projects for UN or United Nations Development Program (UNDP) funding, did not complete their training and go to their posts until February 1969. That was nearly two years after the time proposed in the original aide-memoire, which had emphasized that

> elaboration of detailed regional programs and the working out of regional and country projects, should be carried out in 1967 and 1968. This is the most critical element of the whole program, on which future expansion of the United Nations activities in the field of population will largely depend.[20]

That two-year delay in hiring and training what were essentially middle level demographic program officers seriously undermined support for the Population Division's program.

The other major roadblock was coordination, especially between the UN and the specialized agencies. Most of the UN bodies were divided along professional and disciplinary lines; their headquarters and regional offices were, for political reasons, located in many different countries. The function of coordination was undertaken by UN headquarters and exercised through an interagency working group which in 1968 became a subcommittee of the Administrative Committee on Co-ordination. But, as an outside consultant's report pointed out, "much time is spent on what might be called negative coordination, of a jurisdictional character. There is, however, a need for 'positive coordination' by which the resources of all relevant disciplines can be rapidly and harmoniously brought to bear at the planning, programming, operational and evaluation stage in population activities."[21]

Relations between the United Nations and the World Health Organization were particularly difficult. "The restrictive mandates" of the World Health Organization barred WHO from providing assistance to family planning services, where, as in Pakistan, they were not integrated within the health services.[22] Inter-disciplinary assistance projects, which were an increasingly important part of Ford Foundation, Population Council, and AID programs, were supposed to be a major UN contribution, but they were increasingly handicapped by independent initiatives from WHO, UNESCO, and the Population Division, by duplication of experts, or by "very lengthy negotiations between agencies" that took place "before assistance is given which requires cooperation between disciplines."[23] Governments wanting help were impatient. As one recipient observed:

> Multilateral agencies . . . have very little funds, very little experience and very little expertise . . . I think it is unfair for a country that is embarking on a program also to have to subject itself to getting assistance from an agency that is learning to administer assistance.[24]

In short, the coordination of equals proved difficult. No one agency could seriously influence the policies or funding levels of the others. Lacking an ample funding mechanism like the earmarked AID population money, Macura and the Population Division had no leverage either with UN agencies or with governments seeking aid. Awkward jurisdictional disputes often surfaced during the interagency missions dispatched to governments, such as to India in 1965, to Africa, to Pakistan, and to Colombia in 1968, and to India again in 1969. These missions constituted a major UN activity. Their purpose was to evaluate existing programs and lay the groundwork for comprehensive UN technical assistance in the future. Their voluminous reports usually pointed to a broad range of needs or program deficiencies in every field which the developing countries could not easily repair—certainly not without more sustained programming assistance and more resources.

Apart from the UN missions and the Population Program officers, however, the Population Division interpreted the Trust Fund mainly as a means for augmenting the demographic research and training programs of the secretariat rather than an operational arm for technical assistance from the entire UN system. Paradoxically, although the need for resources seemed limitless, contributions to the Fund and expenditures from it lagged. Of the $1.1 million contributed mainly by the United States, the United Kingdom, and the Scandinavian countries during 1967 and 1968, very little was allocated until 1969.

During 1968 it became increasingly clear that the limited functions of the fund, the negative coordination of the UN system, and the training and advisory emphasis could not generate the level of technical assistance requests or resources anticipated. Not only individuals like Draper and Rockefeller but also donor governments like the United States and Sweden grew restive. Furthermore, by July 1968, the successful earmarking and then obligation of $35 million by AID strengthened the arguments of activists like Draper that much more money was needed and could be well spent. Declining birth rates in Korea and Taiwan strengthened the influence of the professionals, like the Population Council, who for the first time could point to a pay-off in these programs.

Draper's strategy had always been to persuade Paul Hoffman that birth control was an integral part of economic development and should be supported as such. Hoffman was in many ways the father of intergovernmental development assistance, first through the Marshall Plan for Europe and then through various UN funds and activities which eventually became the United Nations Development Program. Draper, a close friend, had helped to recruit him for both jobs and kept reminding him that population growth in many areas was thwarting economic gains. At first skeptical about birth control, by the late 1960s Hoffman was ready to agree that rapid population did retard economic development, that national family planning programs could help reduce fertility, and that the issue was no longer so controversial as to undermine the fragile base of development assistance. In December 1967, at a panel discussion Draper arranged, Hoffman declared:

We have had conferences and conferences, all perhaps very useful . . . But the time now is for action. As far as the United Nations Development Program is concerned, we act only on the request of governments. But we are very willing to give quick consideration to any request from any government for an action program in the population field.[25]

Only the UNDP had a worldwide network of resident representatives with experience in framing, processing, and monitoring technical assistance projects. Hoffman, at Draper's suggestion, agreed to ask the resident representatives what kind of population requests might be made if funds were available. In April 1968, almost a year after the first meeting, another luncheon took place including Draper, Hoffman, and U Thant. To Hoffman's complaint that it was not lack of money but lack of requests for aid that deterred UNDP, Draper responded:

> The situation is very similar to what has transpired in AID in our own government program. During the past two fiscal years, less than one-quarter of one per cent was obligated for family planning. . . . These small programs resulted from the fact that family planning is comparatively new as a source of projects, just as it is with the UN, and all such projects have to compete with those already under way. However, last December $35 million were earmarked by Congress for family planning and could not be used for anything else. More than $50 million of project requests came in from the field.[26]

Draper proposed to Paul Hoffman and U Thant that a new fund should be set up, consisting of voluntary contributions specifically for population, and administered through UNDP. Working closely with Phil Claxton as Special Assistant to the Secretary of State for Population Matters, with Leighton Van Nort and John McDonald in the International Organization Bureau, and counting on earmarked funds available from AID, Draper unofficially conveyed to Hoffman, U Thant, and other high UN officials the message that the U.S. and other governments would support a UNDP population assistance program based on separate voluntary contributions. While the various policymaking organs of the UN system continued under U.S. and Swedish pressure to approve increasingly favorable resolutions, the wheels began to turn in the secretariat. In May 1968 Richard Symonds, a British expert in development policy, was appointed as a consultant, first to the Population Division and then to the secretary-general, to study how the Population Fund could best be developed into a flexible UN technical assistance program. Finally in July 1968, ECOSOC, upon U.S. initiative, provided an official green light and recommended by a vote of 12 to 7 that UNDP give technical assistance to population programs.[27] Shortly thereafter negotiations began between the secretary-general and Paul Hoffman on the management of the fund.

Symonds's report, presented to the secretary-general in September 1968 although not released until June 1969, emphasized the problems of coordination and responsibility in a still sensitive field. Ideally, he suggested, an international population agency should be created, but if that proved impossible, Symonds recommended that a commissioner for population be appointed to give visible priority to population. His role would be defined by agreement between the secretary-general and the administrator of UNDP. He also suggested an interagency division, to foster a "positive coordination," an International Interdisciplinary Training Institute, joint arrangements at the regional level, and a brochure explaining what assistance the United Nations could provide. Whatever institutional arrangements were devised, Symonds emphasized the need for "an identifiable point of responsibility for the mobilization of resources. . . ."[28] Symonds's report echoed the same arguments that Leona Baumgartner had made to David Bell in 1965—flexibility was needed above all to react quickly to national needs, to solve interdisciplinary problems, and to take advantage of new technologies.

Nevertheless, even as the climate of support for population programs grew warmer throughout the UN system, that "identifiable point of responsibility" remained missing through 1968 and much of 1969 since Macura lacked means or authority to influence programs in other UN agencies. During that period, the specialized agencies received encouraging new mandates to expand their professional involvement in the population field, always with due respect for the sovereign rights of governments. Voluntary family planning was thoroughly accepted as "a basic human right." An important convert to the population cause was Robert S. McNamara, president of the World Bank, who in 1968 announced that the Bank would devote new attention to population growth as a major obstacle to economic development. At the same time, the debate over the Second United Nations Development Decade focused the attention of all governments again and again on the relationship between population growth and per capita income. Although U.S. officials had hoped for even stronger language, in fact the International Development Strategy for the 1970s included for the first time a per capita annual economic growth target of 3.5 percent based on an

> average annual increase of 2.5 percent in the population of developing countries, which is less than the average rate at present forecast for the 1970s.[29]

Reducing population growth was undeniably a relevant policy for many developing countries.

Outside the United Nations system, other strong pressures for institutional change were building up. A Population Policy Panel of the private United Nations Association of the United States was established with Ford Foundation funding under the chairmanship of John D. Rockefeller 3rd and including Richard Gardner, David Bell, George Woods, Frank Notestein, Oscar Harkavy, John Hannah, William Rogers, and other notables. The study, prepared after Symonds's review by Stanley Johnson, a young British economist, came to much the same conclusions about UN bureaucracy but in bolder, more picturesque language:

> Although the population cake has been sliced this way and that in an endless series of co-ordinating meetings, very few crumbs have as yet fallen into the lap of a hungry world.[30]

The major recommendations were for a Commissioner for Population to be appointed within the UNDP with a high-calibre staff to be responsible for planning, coordinating, implementing, and expediting UN population projects through the Population Trust Fund. The fund would allocate money to UN agencies, governments, or other bodies with the approval of donor and recipient governments. Under this system of "strong central coordination and direction," with the commissioner for population serving as principal United Nations representative at intergovernmental population forums, it was proposed that the fund be increased to $100 million in three years.

The plan in effect called for what critical UN Secretariat officials privately described as a population czar in the UNDP in effect downgrading the Population Division and restricting new WHO plans to finance reproductive biology research and family planning services through its own voluntary health fund. This public appeal by a private U.S. organization was warmly endorsed in President Nixon's Message on Population where he urged that the United Nations assume world leadership in the population field under the proposed plan. In 1969 President Nixon was urging the United Nations to do much the same thing that Congress had pressed upon AID in 1967. The U.S. State Department was also pressing for a major UNDP role.

Meanwhile, within the United Nations, de Seynes, Henderson, Macura, and others were looking for a compromise that would preserve an important role for the Secretariat and not alienate the specialized agencies. A memorandum of May 6, 1969, outlined major changes to be made by the secretary-general, including:

1. Considerable expansion of the fund, requesting contributions of $5 million in 1969, $10 million in 1970, and $20 million in 1971 (the same sums Symonds had proposed)

2. Management of the fund "for direct assistance purposes" to be vested in the Administrator of the UN Development Program (that is, Paul Hoffman)

3. The Population Program and Projects Office of the Population Division to "be responsible for co-ordination and presentation of the substantive analysis and appraisal of requests in collaboration with the agencies" and to "recommend action to the Administrator of the UNDP"

4. Execution of projects in full or part "by the various agencies according to their competence and with appropriate consultation."[31]

In other words, Paul Hoffman would manage the money but the Population Division would handle programming and the specialized agencies would do the implementation.

By the end of 1969, the fund had been effectively transferred to Hoffman's management. Rafael Salas, senior Cabinet member and executive secretary of the Philippine government, had been appointed by Paul Hoffman as director of the fund and $1.5 million of projects formally approved for financing.[32] Although Salas later became executive director at the level of assistant secretary-general, the title of commissioner was deliberately avoided.

The events of 1968-69 in the UN system provided an almost exact parallel to the course of the AID program in 1966 and 1967. During this period, officials in the UN Secretariat were considering internal measures to justify additional funding, to make funds more readily available to the specialized agencies and to develop programs more flexibly, just as AID had done in organizing the War on Hunger, but other pressures overtook them. Despite resistance from UN officials (comparable to the objections of the Bureau for Program and Policy Coordination in AID) another mechanism was established to ensure higher priority. The new arrangements in both cases centered around generous funds to be administered by a technical assistance office but clearly earmarked only for population. In both cases the health agencies that had originally been expected to take the lead hesitated in tackling interdisciplinary problems and thus lost control of programs which were finally accorded priority on economic grounds. But even though yielding to the power of the purse as exercised by legislatures and governments respectively, program officials in both AID and the United Nations successfully resisted providing the full authority, the appropriate title, or the necessary staff to facilitate the new program.

UNFPA: RESOURCES, STRATEGY, LEADERSHIP

Nevertheless, Salas and the United Nations Fund for Population Activities (UNFPA) in 1969 were in a far better position than Ravenholt had been in 1966 or Macura in 1967. UNFPA benefited from two years more of international support for the concept of family planning; UNFPA benefited from two years more of confidence that government programs really could make a difference in fertility rates. Despite an uneasy relationship with the Population Division and specialized agencies, UNFPA also benefited from fairly clear control over the final allocation of funds. Relevance in terms of economic development and feasibility in terms of program administration were thus established.

Priority and urgency for UNFPA programs as for AID would depend on resources and events stimulated by outside action. Draper once again set out in 1970 at Paul Hoffman's request to raise the additional funds necessary for a major program. The AID program demonstrated more vividly each year that generous funds could overcome many organizational bottlenecks. In January 1970, on Draper's recommendation, the U.S. readily agreed to provide $7.5 million to UNFPA on a matching basis, that is, if other nations would contribute an equal amount and announced the pledge in fulfillment of President Nixon's message. The Swedish government contributed $1.5 million as did the German government, never before involved. Despite pleas from Salas and the U.S. Department of State to maintain a low profile, Draper approached either in person or by letter, every potential large contributor, including especially Germany, Japan, Great Britain, Canada, and the Scandinavian countries. Largely as a result of his insistent and uninhibited fund-raising, more than $15 million was pledged in 1970 from 24 countries and nearly $30 million in 1971 from 46 countries. Once again an ambitious target that was clearly based on judgments of priority rather than immediate program requests had generated substantial support.

Therefore the first challenge for Salas, as for Ravenholt, was not raising money but rather allocating sensibly the money Draper raised. Laboring, as AID had, with insufficient staff for program development, but equally unable in the face of UN and agency opposition to build up its own personnel immediately, the fund initially had to support any UN agencies or governments on whatever terms the recipients named. Still, as Table 19.1 shows, most of the agencies held back with their requests and even more so with their programming. WHO, which originally hoped for direct U.S. aid, turned to the fund in 1970 in hopes that there would be fewer strings attached. When in 1971 UNFPA began to ask for detailed program submissions, WHO began to look for direct contributions from governments again. Yet, with UNFPA aid, WHO programs in research and services gradually expanded. UNESCO remained unwilling to alter its own internal structure so that population education or mass communications could expand as interdisciplinary programs. The United Nations, including both the Population Division and the Office of Technical Cooperation, received the major share of UNFPA funds, most of which went to provide additional staff for regional Economic Commissions in Asia, Africa and Latin America, regional demographic centers, and to support training, conferences, and advisory missions. Of all the agencies, UNICEF by the end of 1971 still maintained one of the best records in putting to work promptly the substantial funds allocated to it. Much of UNICEF money went into midwifery training, vehicles, and contraceptive supplies.

Besides allocating money, there was at first little room for strategy. The fund was deliberately defined by the secretariat and the specialized agencies as a bank account rather than a programming or implementing agency. Its purposes as first drafted were

    1. To provide systematic and sustained assistance to countries desiring such assistance

    2. To enable the UN and agencies related to it to respond better to the needs of member countries

    3. To help to coordinate the population programs among the various elements of the UN system, and

    4. To assist governments and agencies in the execution of population policies by helping the United Nations system to serve as a clearing house for information.[33]

But even the clearing house role was questioned by other UN bodies and dropped from later statements. During 1970 Salas and Hoffman both took pains to insist that UNFPA was not an operating agency but rather a managerial group without expert knowledge in the specialized field of population. At first, the fund moved slowly, allocations going primarily to the UN specialized agencies. Only two agreements were negotiated directly with national governments—Pakistan and Mauritius—totalling $1.8 million. By the end of 1971, however, agreements were signed or well under way for short or long term

TABLE 19.1

International Agency Allocations, Remittances, and Expenditures from UNFPA Funds, 1969-71

Agency	Allocations			Remittances			Expenditures			Cumulative Expenditures as a Percentage of Cumulative Allocations
	1969	1970	1971	1969	1970	1971	1969	1970 (Combined)	1971	
FAO	–	137,625	446,134	–	–	412,823	–	823	177,382	31
IBRD	–	–	440,000	–	–	–	–	–	–	0
ILO	63,000	261,730	285,300	–	63,000	170,000	–	65,742	265,811	54
IPPF	–	450,000	750,000	–	450,000	–	–	450,000	750,000	100
UN	67,000	977,636	846,827	352,670	286,219	408,311	–	529,926	736,926	67
UNOTC	483,840	2,360,794	4,318,882	171,155	2,001,289	1,282,371	–	729,347	1,628,169	33
UNDP	–	84,995	133,010	–	57,523	15,943	–	84,995	133,010	100
UNESCO	–	423,860	852,350	58,000	110,000	342,000	–	158,330	349,911	40
UNICEF	–	665,400	3,124,861	–	285,000	1,905,000	–	59,500	2,096,880	57
UNIDO	–	–	42,500	–	–	–	–	–	16,448	39
WHO	500,000	1,312,590	4,116,030	–	800,000	1,800,000	–	786,534	1,945,396	46
Total	1,114,578	6,674,630	15,315,894	581,825	4,053,031	6,336,448	–	2,865,197	8,099,933	

Source: UNFPA, March 1972.

assistance to six governments totalling nearly $24 million.[34] A major and increasing emphasis of the UNFPA program was to encourage medium and large scale government programs, supported and coordinated through multilateral channels.

In order to help governments directly, however, UNFPA had to move beyond normal UN emphasis on training, advisory missions, and foreign exchange. What many developing countries wanted and needed was general budgetary support for local costs. The issue which Ravenholt had bitterly fought and won in AID over India was easier for UNFPA. By 1971 aid recipients openly advocated and donors acknowledged the need for broader forms of assistance. Unlike AID, the UNFPA was not hamstrung by local currency holdings that had to be liquidated first. Although UNFPA insisted that its funds be additive, not a substitute, and that governments pay a major share of local costs, unlike AID, it agreed from the start to provide "counterpart services and related costs normally paid in local currencies" especially "in countries with serious budgetary problems."[35]

Private organizations like the International Planned Parenthood Federation, the Population Council, professional associations of physicians, demographers, statisticians, midwives, home economists, and the like were from the start recognized as useful channels for support. Although UNFPA, like AID, at first proposed to clear nongovernmental requests through the Resident Representatives, Population Program officers, and government, the attempt was soon dropped. By 1972, the UNFPA was ready not only to make grants to private organizations but also to consider the International Planned Parenthood Federation (IPPF) or others as executing agencies for assistance projects. UNFPA was also ready to admit openly, as AID rarely could, that it would take the initiative in promoting new programs to fill any important gaps.[36]

Even as the resources expanded, Salas, like Ravenholt, tried to keep the procedures simple and, above all, flexible.[37] The priorities were not research or demography but "operational programs and projects assisting efforts to moderate high rates of fertility where these constitute an obstacle to economic and social progress."[38] During 1971 approximately 54 percent of UNFPA funds were allocated to family planning, 23 percent to demography, 8 percent to population education and communications, 8 percent to multisector activities, and 7 percent to infrastructure. (See Table 19.2.) The programming breakdown was remarkably similar to that of AID, although somewhat more stress was placed on demographic research.

For Salas, however, the programming was less important than jurisdictional and managerial issues. Leaving many of the program specifics to his capable, hardworking deputy Halvor Gille and Operations Officer John Keppel, Salas focused on the threats to basic UNFPA authority. As long as Macura, who had seen the fund removed from his own control, remained director of the Population Division, that is, through 1971, personal as well as institutional rivalry prevailed between the division and the fund. Some of it centered around the Population Program officers in the field, reporting to the Population Division, but submitting projects for funding through the UNDP resident representatives. For a time, governments seeking aid, like Indonesia, still found

TABLE 19.2

UNFPA and AID Sector Programming, 1971-1972
(percentages)

	1971		1972 (est.)	
	UNFPA	AID	UNFPA	AID
Basic population data[c]	–	8	15.7	10
Population dynamics[d]	–	–	11.4	–
Population policy[e]	–	10	2.9	9
Subtotal	23.3	18	30.0	19
Family planning[b]				
(including new techniques)	53.9	46	30.3	39
Communication and education[g]	8.0	11	8.9	8
Multisector activities[h]	8.3	7	21.5	8
Program development[i]	6.5	3	9.3	3
(contribution to UNFPA)[j]	–	15	–	23
Total (percentages)	100	100	100	100
Total (millions of dollars)	32.1	95.9	43.5	125

[a]Estimated February 1972.

[b]Estimated April 1972.

[c]Headings given are UNFPA terminology. AID terms in parenthesis: adequate demographic and social data.

[d]Adequate population policies and understanding of population dynamics.

[e]Included for AID in (c), above.

[f]Adequate family planning delivery systems and adequate means of fertility control.

[g]Adequate delivery systems for information and education.

[h]Multipurpose institutional development and use.

[i]AID/W support. For UNFPA in 1971 Infrastructure.

[j]AID budget only. Includes also 1972 AID unprogrammed.

Sources: UNFPA, Tentative Work Plan, February 20, 1972; UNFPA/PCC/IV/4; AID, Population Program Study, July 1972, p. 10.

that reaching agreement with WHO, the World Bank, and UNFPA took longer than formulating their own government program. Coordination remained the most controversial of the fund's attempted roles. Another source of friction was the proposal for a World Population Training Institute (WPTI), endorsed by Symonds, but later interpreted by many as a possible rival to UNFPA that would be controlled by the Population Division, WHO, and UNESCO.[39]

In fact, during 1970 and 1971 jurisdictional questions complicated every major population activity. In 1969 the secretary-general recommended that a third World Population Conference be held in 1974 and that 1974 be designated World Population Year. When the Population Commission, ECOSOC, and the General Assembly approved, it was assumed that the Population Division, acting for the secretary-general, would be in charge. Yet the Division was short of staff even to manage the Conference. The special activities for the

World Population Year as well as the Conference would clearly require UNFPA resources. To disentangle the Conference and the year, to secure prominent public leadership, and to finance these additional activities still disputed between two rival units, would require diplomacy on all sides and take nearly as long as the preparations themselves. Outside government pressures (mainly from the U.S. and Sweden), rather than internal UN initiatives, stressed the importance and imminence of these events.

The controversies of programming, implementing, and coordinating technical assistance, of staffing the Population Fund itself, of maneuvering around earmarked support for WHO, and of managing the Conference and the year were aired continuously by the UN agencies in meetings of the subcommittee on population of the Administrative Committee on Coordination and of the UNFPA's own Inter-Agency Consultative Committee. In addition to these somewhat acrimonious sessions, the Fund itself established a Program Consultative Committee of donors, foundations, and population organizations which increasingly focussed on substantive issues and technical problems. Also significant was the Advisory Board appointed by Paul Hoffman, consisting of international leaders and spokesmen such as Alberto Lleras Camargo, former President of Colombia; John D. Rockefeller 3rd; B. R. Sen, former FAO Director General; Ernst Michanek, Director of the Swedish International Development Agency; directors of Regional Economic Commissions, and others.[40] Draper had long urged the secretary-general to appoint an advisory council, but U Thant, after consulting with the agency heads, was reluctant to set up such an unprecedented, ad hoc group. At first a somewhat anomalous body within the UN system, the panel served increasingly to guide the Population Fund in its major resource development and allocation policies and to counterbalance UN and agency pressures.

After its transfer to UNDP in 1969, the Fund was at first heavily dependent upon outside support—upon Draper and the U.S. government for major financial resources and upon other UN legislative bodies for legitimacy in the UN system. For example, at the Fifteenth Session of the Population Commission in November 1969 it was crucial that the commission, although not referring to the Fund for Population Activities by name, in the final draft resolution endorsed the concept that the fund be "truly international," "work closely together as a team" with specialized agencies, "be administered efficiently," and above all "provide assistance in all forms required to meet the needs of developing countries, including the financing of action programs."[41] Draper, who was appointed by President Nixon as the U.S. representative on the commission, not only guided the technical assistance language through the commission but also won approval for the World Population Year (which he had initially promoted as a member of the secretary-general's advisory committee).

Yet the very success of the UNFPA in obtaining generous resources and high level advisors made it a more conspicuous target for charges by suspicious Catholic or Communist nations that it had never been formally authorized by the General Assembly or provided with an official governing body or council of governments. By the fall of 1971 continuing problems of coordination could be blamed more directly on the fund. Criticism at the Sixteenth Session of the

Population Commission about delays in the Indonesian program led to a request in the draft resolution that the secretary-general "develop in cooperation with the United Nations agencies concerned, appropriate measures needed to accelerate the review of requests for technical cooperation and implementation of technical assistance projects."[42]

Thoroughly exasperated at this criticism and determined to strengthen the mandates of the fund directly, in December 1971, Rafael Salas moved behind the scenes to encourage an immediate General Assembly resolution that would provide full recognition and support for the fund. Bypassing the Population Commission resolution that required approval first from the Economic and Social Council, the General Assembly by a vote of 94-0 (with 20 abstentions) approved a resolution "noting with satisfaction the progress" of the fund and inviting governments to contribute. The General Assembly was "convinced that the United Nations Fund for Population Activities should play a leading role in the United Nations system in promoting population programs. . . ." With regard to administration, the resolution was:

> Requests the Secretary-General, in consultation with the Administrator of the United Nations Development Program and the Executive Director of the United Nations Fund for Population Activities, to take the necessary steps to achieve the desired improvements in the administrative machinery of the Fund aimed at the efficient and expeditious delivery of population programmes, including measures to quicken the pace of recruiting the experts and personnel required to cope with the increasing volume of requests, as well as to consider the training of experts and personnel in the developing countries. . . .[43]

Accordingly, early in 1972 Ernst Michanek was designated, by the new Secretary-General Kurt Waldheim, by the new UNDP Administrator, Rudolph Peterson, and by Salas to undertake a wide-ranging study of the operations and capacity of the fund, a study that would meet the needs of the secretary-general under the General Assembly resolution. At the same time in a parallel action Michanek was elected chairman of a subcommittee of the UNFPA Advisory Board to consider how the fund might "more effectively discharge its responsibilities for leadership within the UN system and provide a focus for coordinated international efforts to deal with population problems."[44]

Following the General Assembly resolution, the UNFPA staff was also reorganized and expanded. An important addition to the staff in 1971 was Dr. Nafis Sadik, an unusually able, experienced, and outspoken Pakistani family-planning program administrator. Designated program coordinator early in February 1972, her role in UNFPA effectively challenged WHO's monopoly on health competence.

The UNFPA gained further ground in June 1972 when the Economic and Social Council (ECOSOC) gave Salas responsibility for preparations for the World Population Year in 1974.[45] Additional staff was authorized. Furthermore, the Stockholm Conference on the Human Environment, held in June 1972 under the direction of Maurice Strong, convinced not only the U.S. and

Swedish governments but also UN Undersecretary Philippe de Seynes that the World Population Conference should be equally significant. Population policy was becoming a serious political concern of governments. ECOSOC therefore also called for a special secretary-general to organize the 1974 conference, with his own secretariat.[46] Thus ECOSOC simultaneously enlarged the jurisdiction of the fund and diminished that of the Population Division while leaving unresolved the long-term relationship between the UNFPA and the UN secretariat, between operational technical assistance and agreed-upon population policy.

Nevertheless, by mid-1972 Salas had been remarkably successful in transforming a unit that started without programming authority, implementing power, or even a staff of its own into a major UN body with General Assembly support. He had started with many of the same difficulties as Ravenholt plus the extra complications of intercultural differences as well as the extra prestige of an international base. Yet he approached them very differently. Where Ravenholt focussed with greatest interest on the substantive elements—oral contraceptives, new technologies, new evaluation methods—and only rather reluctantly on organizational factors, Salas concentrated on political and administrative problems. Where Ravenholt pressed forward, spoke his mind, and confronted his opponents directly, Salas proceeded cautiously, kept his own counsel, and tried to give his rivals as little opportunity to criticize as possible. Nevertheless, on the organizational issues that concerned him, he was just as determined to have his own way in the end. He moved, step by step, to consolidate his own position, not only against the Population Division and the agencies, but also against the insistent pressures of Draper, the U.S. government, and other donors. Benefitting tremendously from their support, he nevertheless retained his independence and guided the fund to a position of increasing international stature and influence.

Despite contrasting leadership the programs of UNFPA and AID retained much in common besides their goal of reducing population growth. Both grew rapidly, generated by an international recognition of population problems that was rapidly translated into necessary resources. Financial priority, constantly pursued and provided by Draper, gave both programs the momentum necessary to overcome many professional inhibitions, jurisdictional rivalries, and bureaucratic bottlenecks. Furthermore, strategies aimed at modernizing not only birth rates but also the channels of development assistance played a large part in both programs. Both were new and flexible enough to abandon initial approaches that did not work for ones that did. Just as the AID program had originally intended to support government-to-government assistance but shifted by necessity toward private intermediaries and multilateral agencies so the UNFPA objective originally was to support UN agencies but shifted by necessity toward governments and private international organizations. Both programs became, more by coincidence than design, prototypes for new concepts of development assistance. The AID population program fitted almost perfectly the model of a professional innovative International Development Institute described in 1970 by the Peterson Committee Report, whereas the UNFPA increasingly showed the potential of becoming the "head piece" for UN population programs, "that central coordinating organization which could exercise effective control" recommended by the Jackson Report in its study of the entire UN Development effort.[47]

Yet in their common search for effective population and development strategies, the two men and programs were also going in opposite directions. Ravenholt was looking for a technological solution with better contraceptives and delivery systems; Salas was reaching for a political-economic solution by making resources broadly available under comprehensive country programming. As Ravenholt pointed out in 1969 when asked about President Nixon's call for UN leadership, "I see AID and the UN playing essentially complementary roles in the development of family planning programs. The Agency is ahead of the UN which will follow trails blazed by AID."[48]

The struggles that Ravenholt fought and generally won in AID—for example, on aid to private organizations, general budgetary support, and directed contraceptive research—usually strengthened Salas' hand in similar struggles on the international level. But with all the advantages of a nonpolitical UN agency to deal with developing countries, the UNFPA was increasingly in a position to assist in large scale, sensitive, government actions, while AID, although often ahead in program analysis and substantive measures, still had to fend off political criticism at home and overseas.

After the winter of 1971-72, when the AID population program won its first Congressional appropriation to match earlier ear-markings and the UNFPA won its first General Assembly endorsement, both programs moved up a notch in the organization structure. In fact by 1972 UNFPA had nearly caught up with the AID program on the institutional side, if not in funding. Both had additional staff and authority, but at the same time both faced the possibility that more authority could also bring more specific guidelines, less flexibility, and less capacity to innovate in the future.

The first challenge both programs still faced and had not yet fully resolved was how to enhance the efficiency and effectiveness of the assisting organizations themselves. In 1969 the complaint had been voiced that "public multilateral agencies tend to be too bureaucratic and inexpert, bilateral tend to be too energetic, and the private are too poor."[49] By 1972 UNFPA and AID, together with other donor governments, possessed the necessary funds, experience, and skill to improve all three if they could cooperate sufficiently to do so.

By 1972 both UNFPA and AID faced the prospect also that their programs would in future be judged less by the ability to obligate money, often for intermediate organizations, and win bureaucratic battles than by their power to influence fertility rates and reduce world population growth. The spotlight of outside publicity and evaluation would be increasingly focussed on the specific accomplishments of both agencies. Despite their rapid growth, AID and UNFPA programs have benefitted from relatively low salience in the political and international arena. The opportunity to achieve higher priority and greater urgency through the World Population Conference and year carries also the danger of increased hostility from Catholic opponents of abortion on the one hand and from advocates of greater redistribution of wealth on the other. Sweden, again in the lead, has called for a World Population Plan of Action.[50] Can the UN—with AID and other public or private agencies—develop a population policy that stimulates the resources and leadership needed from the developed countries and at the same time satisfies the pressing political needs of the developing countries? A policy that is equally relevant, feasible, important, and urgent to the haves and the have-nots, to governments, and to individual men and women? The continuing progress of both AID and UN programs to and beyond 1974 will depend on those questions and answers.

The development of substantial government programs to meet the challenge of population growth in the developing countries has been unexpectedly rapid, especially in the Agency for International Development. Less than a decade after President Eisenhower's blunt prohibition, a much-criticized agency that was frowned upon by Congress, government employees, and many professionals had become the largest source of family planning assistance in the world, the lead government agency in the search for improved methods of fertility control, a conspicuous example of the practices recommended for other U.S. aid programs, and the major support of a growing UN effort.

Whether these programs will succeed in their substantive goal—whether birth rates in AID or UN-assisted countries will decline; whether AID or UN support would play any role in such declines; whether different kinds of strategies or support might cause greater declines; even, in the long run, whether declining birth rates will make a genuine impact on standards of living and economic development—these questions cannot yet be fully answered. But the change in policy and the growth of programs are now undeniable.

These innovations resulted primarily from the external environment—from the established facts of world population growth, the knowledge that impoverished populations were multiplying rapidly to live in still greater poverty, the recognition that another billion people would be added between 1963 and 1975, and finally, the awareness that even in the United States population growth could threaten the highest living standard in the world. But the impact of natural population increase is necessarily long-term and highly interdependent with economic, social, and technological change. Dealing with the problem directly requires massive, flexible, long-range, interdisciplinary and interagency programs. For any organization to initiate and operate such programs in a political context where leaders want perceptible short-term results with minimal opposition is a peculiarly difficult task. The policy-making process in the population field at the governmental or the international level is therefore not a smooth and easy road even where private acceptance of fertility control methods has been high. The main purpose of this study has been to identify chronologically some of the different variables that seemed to influence the development of U.S. population policy. These relationships can be tested more systematically in different countries, states, and policies under different circumstances.

The principal hypotheses and conclusions that emerge can be summarized under the following headings: the background of public opinion and media attention; the individuals and organizations who undertake deliberately to change government policy; the functioning of judicial, executive, and legislative bodies; the development of technology; and the dynamics of population policy itself.

PUBLIC OPINION AND MEDIA ATTENTION

Public opinion is a perverse guide to the development of government birth control policy. Long before polls were devised and in fact even before governments were established, control of fertility seems to have been practiced by many individuals. Yet until the twentieth century the private practice of birth control was publicly opposed by church and state. The more publicly that opposition was proclaimed, the more widely birth control was practiced. Two decades ago Kingsley Davis pointed out:

> As the birth control movement gains strength and vociferousness, the opposition will doubtless crystallize and gain strength as well. The capacity of a movement to evoke opposition is inevitable. It does not mean that the movement itself will fail. The very controversy itself will tend to spread contraceptive knowledge. In no country in the world has religious opposition been able to stop the diffusion of birth control any more than it has been able to stop the use of tobacco or alcohol.[1]

Certainly that statement has proved true in the United States. Since the 1950s controversy and publicity have spotlighted the population problem. Public opinion since it was first measured in the 1930s has favored the availability of birth control information. The practice of birth control is virtually universal in the United States. The method most widely publicized became within five years the method most widely used. Ever since the population growth problem of the developing countries was identified, nearly two thirds of the U.S. population have favored birth control assistance as one solution to the problem.

Yet the perception of Washington policy makers has been very different from the quantitative measure of public opinion. Even in 1962 a congressman could assert that "the great majority of our Americans would be against birth control."[2] The organized opposition of the Catholic Church, based on theological teaching but strongly reinforced by ethnic politics, carried more weight than public opinion or private practice. Until the mid-1960s "the intense minority" opposing government tolerance of birth control was able to "frustrate the ambitions" of the intense minority favoring birth control "with the passive acquiescence or indifference of a majority of adults or voters."[3]

The poll data suggest that in the United States as elsewhere whenever birth control advocates were able to confront the opposition publicly, their popular support even among Catholics increased; when they or government leaders remained quiet, Catholic popular disapproval seemed to gain strength. Ironically, government policy makers tended at first to react in an opposite way, avoiding the issue when it was controversial and taking it up only when controversy seemed to have died. But by the mid-1960s even Catholic opinion no longer showed any semblance of following its ecclesiastical leaders.

In this as in other fields not public opinion itself but the political leaders' perception of it and especially of its intensity was decisive. Only on two occasions did survey data on public opinion—Catholic opinion, in both cases—have immediate impact on the policy process. When President Johnson's first public reference to "the explosion in world population" was followed four days later by a Gallup poll indicating that over three fourths of American Catholics (a 50 percent increase since 1963) favored making birth control available, that specific information at that specific moment heartened supporters and discouraged the opposition. Again, when the papal encyclical of 1968 was immediately followed by surveys showing that most Catholics disagreed, the political impact of church spokesmen was undermined.

Basically the leaders on both sides of the issue became mediators of public opinion to one another. They were more influenced by one another's statements and interpretations than by public opinion directly. When Catholic organizations seemed to represent "millions of taxpaying Catholic voters" they carried weight in the political arena. When ethnic loyalties prevailed they also carried weight. When Catholic officials began publicly feuding with their constituency, however, their influence as political spokesmen diminished. Recognizing this, they became less vocal, thereby permitting proponents like Senator Gruening to redefine and shift the issue.

The influence of the news media, promptly publicizing polls like these and making the subject familiar, was critical. As long as threats of Catholic boycott, feelings of impropriety, or doubts that the issue was relevant could impose a "conspiracy of silence on the media," government policy did not develop. The "publicity explosion" that began in 1959 survived the political controversy of the 1960 election and promoted the policy shift.

After 1960, James Reston's critical columns, if they did not influence the country at large, did circulate widely through Catholic officialdom as well as through the "ever-nervous State Department" and the politically sensitive White House. Kennedy, according to Sorenson, read the newspapers not to learn the facts but to learn what the press thought was important enough to write about.[4] After 1960 the opinion-setting media seemed to take a special delight in emphasizing this "once taboo subject" and chiding government officials for neglect or "timidity." Once again, it was a case of elites influencing elites as the media deliberately challenged government leaders to catch up with the people they were supposed to be leading.

During the policy process the broad purpose of birth control and population legislation was publicized in relation to world hunger and poverty to such an extent that other, potentially more controversial aspects were smothered. The major legislation Congress passed on population in the 1960s was not widely covered by the media. Washington officials, including Catholic organizations, were aware of the proposed family planning amendments to AID, OEO, and Social Security legislation but the absence of wider publicity on those provisions and the considerable controversy over other provisions, may, as the study of abortion repeal in North Carolina suggests, have contributed to final passage. There was no time for opposition to mobilize. When publicity was deliberately sought, for example, by advocates of the Family Planning Services and Population Research Act in 1970, to bypass individual congressional leaders, or by abortion advocates in 1972 when Catholics tried to repeal the liberal New York law, such publicity often emphasized jurisdictional and procedural rather than substantive issues.

INDIVIDUALS

Policy studies "uniquely combine the role of the individual and the role of the system." The policy process, in fact, takes place at the boundary of interaction between the two.[5] How individuals shape institutions to meet their goals and then in turn find those goals modified by the needs of the institution is a classic dilemma of leadership. Max Weber's formulation of the "routinization of charisma" describes the growth of the population movement in and out of government. Organizations that proved influential were founded by women and men who possessed to some degree the charismatic qualities of personal self-confidence, unshakable conviction in the rightness of their cause, and ability to perform enough "miracles" to maintain the faith of their followers.[6] Some also possessed the charismatic liabilities of antagonizing nonbelievers, insisting on personal control and credit, and thereby to a degree weakening the very institutions that they had built. For the charismatic leader, the problem *will* be solved, the honeymoon will never end, and the task of institution-building will always seem secondary to the cultural revolution that is just around the corner.

In their extreme forms, charismatic leadership and institutional competence are contradictory qualities. Over time, the building of any institution creates pressures for institutional maintenance that challenge and often displace the original goals. For this very reason many professionals, for instance the physicians, already organized into their profession, found it hard to concede that birth control might help to achieve their goals. Yet, in the short run the rapid turn-about of government policy must in part be attributed to the considerable number of interested individuals who combined some of the qualities of charisma with the more prosaic ability to build, finance, and maintain lasting institutions. Many of these individuals could be classified as political elites. Their success in influencing foreign policy more than HEW domestic programs might be predicted from previous studies of the influence that elites and "attentive publics" exert in foreign affairs.[7]

Yet not only do elites create policy but also the policy process itself helps to create new elites. Those who were once looked down upon because of their active or professional involvement with "an immoral issue like birth control" rose in personal status as they won the moral support of government policy and the financial support of government programs. Initially or in the short run, elite status, based on income, professional background, and family contacts enhances a person's ability to gain access to high officials and an initial hearing, but the long-term influence of individuals and organizations depends both on the status of the policy area and on their ability to provide the kind of information and assistance that policy makers in government want at a particular time.

Even in a bureaucracy "the likelihood of personal impact increases to the degree that the environment admits of restructuring."[8] Like an idea whose time has come, birth control was ready to emerge as a public policy issue. Those who took the lead in promoting the new policy found not only that the time was propitious but also that in many instances the opposition was a deterrent only to those who perceived it as such.

ORGANIZATIONS

In the United States the birth control and population movement was from its inception uneasily divided between the activists, around Margaret Sanger, and the social scientists and physicians. Characteristically forming separate groups, they moved slowly into an uneasy alliance. Influencing public policy was a long-range goal for each, for the activists by rousing public demand and mobilizing a direct appeal and for the professionals by defining the problem and documenting the facts.

The activists like Margaret Sanger were the first to aim at government. In the typology of interest groups they started as an "attitude group."[9] Like the proponents of Prohibition in the United States or abolition of capital punishment in Great Britain, "They are pressure groups based on shared attitudes and the advocacy of changes in public policy rather than interest groups held together by the desire to obtain benefits for their section of the community."[10] Such ad hoc groups often look weak, poorly financed, and unstable in comparison with sectional or economic interest groups. In their single-issue approach they seem to lack the prerequisites for political bargaining and influence. But as the history of British birth control movement suggests, "If the ideological commitment implied a certain rigidity—always a weakness in a pressure group—it also entailed an emotional attachment of a peculiarly tough and lasting nature."[11]

As social reformers the birth control activists proceeded at first by "upsetting the balance" and "polarizing the issue."[12] Then they faced the triple task of recruiting a coalition of power (which was increasingly done by men like Hugh Moore and William H. Draper, Jr., through the business community);

respecting democratic traditions of participation (which was increasingly done by including the patient communities in the organization itself); and offering an objective scientific rationale for the program (which was increasingly done by closer cooperation with the professionals.)[13] This long term process gradually transformed some of the first activist groups into established or professional institutions, critized by the next generation of activists for their willingness to negotiate and compromise.

In the few areas where Catholic opposition was minimal, family planning could be quietly incorporated into policy without public or emotional confrontations, as Measham has described in North Carolina.[14] Yet in North Carolina counties as in U.S. government agencies or international UN bodies, family planning programs seemed to achieve highest priority and greatest impact when promoted by outside activists with extra-budgetary resources.

The professional organizations in the population field, closely linked to the foundations and university centers, were slower in trying to influence policy. They were first pushed in that direction by the activists, who stimulated a government demand for their services and a government support for their work that made some of the professionals nervous. In 1968 a leading public health physician wrote, "Professionals who have long been frustrated by public apathy as they warned about and worked on population problems, now find themselves in the anomalous position of having to urge reasonable caution and careful planning."[15] As with most policy problems, the issue became fashionable before the solutions were proven.

The foundations, too, did not seek directly to influence policy, only to educate the policy makers broadly toward certain problems. Congress they avoided completely but in the population field as in other areas of social policy the foundations and professionals discovered that "a national philanthrophy becomes a prestigeful and uniquely well placed broker of new ideas."[16] To the extent that ideas and information are the currency of government those who could deal with them moved closer into the policy-making process.

As government interest and policy developed in response to the problem itself but stimulated by outside organizations the role of some of those organizations shifted gradually, too. From the agitation of the outside pressure group, distributing pamphlets on street corners and engaging in publicized confrontations, the techniques of influence changed to more persuasive, rational, and personal contact. "The transition from a 'fringe' cause to a semi-consultative status does represent very considerable progress"[17] for any organization in its relations with government. Similarly, the power of government agencies to exclude population experts as "nonprofessional" or "special interests," which NIH did in 1962, is a sign that either the organization or the policy is still in its infancy. Unless purely personal rivalries are involved the progress of an organization from agitation to consultation to contractor or client relationship seems to be a natural part of the policy process, whether the policy is regulative like the Interstate Commerce Commission or distributive through grant-making procedures, whether the field is economic or more distinctly scientific or social. What Lowi condemns as "interest group liberalism"[18] and Bernstein attacks as agency degeneration[19] can from a different point of view represent the government acceptance of a social movement.

In discussing interest groups Eldersveld lists six different types, a typology that can also be applied to measure not only the status of the organization but also the progress of the policy. His categories of power and influence are, from the top down:

1. Penetration into formal policy roles
2. Maintenance of close political support and referral
3. Unchallengeable veto status
4. Attention, representative, and pressure relationship
5. Political reprisal relationship, and
6. Rejection by the power structure, agitation and resistance.[20]

During the 1930s birth control organizations were at the bottom of the ladder. By 1970 some professionals or representatives of professional organizations had reached the top. Thus Oscar Harkavy of the Ford Foundation was invited to review HEW policies and he in turn invited Frederick Jaffe of Planned Parenthood to help him. By the late 1960s many activists were just moving into the formal policy process, to perform the tasks that they and their organizations had persuaded the government were necessary.

THE JUDICIARY

In the development of government birth control policy to date, the judiciary began to play a significant role in the 1930s. At a time when religious opposition still deterred legislative and executive bodies, only the courts were sufficiently insulated from political processes to look at the policy issues.

The first major court action after World War II was the *Griswold* v. *Connecticut* (1956) decision of the Supreme Court, acknowledging the legitimacy of birth control beyond the confines of professional, medical consultation. Justice Douglas proclaimed a new marital "right of privacy" for all. In birth control decisions, as later in abortion decisions, the first generation of cases had recognized professional and institutional rights. Only later—in birth control 30 years later—were the rights of ordinary, nonprofessional women and men equally recognized.

The thrust of the *Griswold* decision, repudiating claims of church and state alike as sexual arbiters, was as much a warning as an encouragement to government policy makers. Catholic lawyers have already attempted to define those limits of privacy to exclude even government support for a voluntary service. Those very efforts, although not successful now, emphasize that the rights that the *Griswold* decision confirmed for individual citizens represent at the same time a basic limitation on the scope of any government policy.

Similarly in the abortion cases the first decisions emphasized the professional rights of physicians. Later decisions were based on the individual woman's right to privacy and choice. Restrictions on the distribution of contraceptives to minors and unmarried persons were also invalidated later on the same grounds of personal freedom. Thus just as some population control advocates were beginning to argue the social need for restraints on individual fertility the courts seemed to be setting new limits on government interference with reproduction for any social purpose.

THE PRESIDENCY

The power of the presidency in policy making on an issue of low priority that does not directly affect national security is checked by many restraints, not least of which is the president's own reluctance to use it. The four presidents of the United States who served between 1959 and 1969 all played a personal role in the development of population policy, using in different ways the presidential power to publicize, to persuade, to legitimize, or to condemn new programs. None of the four significantly utilized the budgetary, personnel, or command powers of the presidency even within the confines of government.

Eisenhower, for instance, interjected his own influence and prestige deliberately to keep birth control out of the partisan political arena. He succeeded in displacing the issue and perhaps strengthening national unity, at the cost of personal and perhaps party approval. He also proved Sorenson's point that "Presidential decision is usually the beginning, not the end of public debate."[21] Whether one agrees with Eisenhower's action or not, it was an effective public use of presidential power under the circumstances. There is no evidence to suggest that he or his immediate staff took any further steps to implement this near-command.

President Kennedy clearly did not want to invest his own time or his own influence in the issue except to the extent that was politically necessary. He used the birth control issue to prove other points—his own objectivity, his concern for the national interest, and later his support for research and the spread of scientific knowledge. He did not encourage the executive agencies, but neither did he or his aides oppose initiatives that others in government were ready to take. He hoped that government could avoid a major role.

President Johnson was the first American president to take a positive stand favoring birth control. He was prepared to utilize the publicity and prestige of major presidential statements to advance an issue he believed both relevant and important for the U.S. government. Through nearly 50 statements he assumed an educational and legitimizing role that helped to transform birth control from an uncomfortable taboo into a fully appropriate tactic in the wars on hunger and poverty.

But at the same time neither President Johnson nor his aides assumed a personal responsibility to implement those bold words at the program level. Seeing his role as a preacher not as a practitioner and increasingly absorbed by issues of higher priority, Johnson perforce allowed the agency heads to determine their own programs. Because the agency heads too saw birth control as less vital than other needs of their large, complex organizations they did not provide the "clear signal" from above that could have mobilized their staffs. As a result, during the Johnson administration a

government policy in support of birth control was fully developed and articulated but programs were implemented only where Congress insisted.

President Nixon took more important substantive steps than did any of
his predecessors. By issuing the first presidential Message on Population and
appointing a commission to study the problem, he gave to population an urgent
yet unmanageable status comparable to such issues as student unrest and drug
abuse. Immediately thereafter he encouraged budget increases for research and
domestic family planning programs. But at a time when zero population growth
was a popular slogan, protecting the environment a new national pastime, and
abortion an obvious solution to unwanted population growth, President Nixon
like his predecessors did not give the issue top priority. He allowed others to
promote it instead of doing so himself. On what seemed to be mainly personal
and political grounds he went out of his way to condemn abortion.

In each administration outside individuals, advisory groups, presidential
committees, White House conferences, task forces, and in one case a UN debate
raised the issue to government attention. By setting targets or proposing
organizational changes that executive agencies often would not suggest, these
groups became a source of innovation in each administration that led more
directly to the White House and Congress than to the specific agencies. The
statements of Kennedy, Johnson, and Nixon ultimately provided a cloak of
greater legitimacy under which congressional and outside supporters could
advance.

The strongest support for population policy initiatives was voiced by
Presidents Johnson and Nixon each at the beginning of a term in office, when it
was undoubtedly easier both to consider long-term problems and to disregard
short-term political repercussions. The greatest opposition or lack of interest
occurred at the end of a term or just prior to a new election—examples are
Eisenhower's repudiation of the Draper proposal in 1959, Johnson's waning
interest in the Cohen-Rockefeller report in 1968, and Nixon's criticism of the
Population Commission in 1972.

To stimulate favorable actions, Congress and the federal agencies joined
with the outside advocates in praising presidential leadership, even recon-
structing history to give credit for more than had actually been done. But while
publicly praising the president, the very same agencies were often privately
frustrating his intent in small ways and large. Even the Bureau of the Budget,
designed to strengthen the president's hand, could set its own management and
budgeting norms above the priorities of the president. With limited time,
limited information, and even more limited political resources, no president did
much more on the population issue than express his opinion with appropriate
pomp and circumstance and "wonder if the government will go along."

On the international level, the UN secretary-general, U Thant, even more
than Presidents Johnson and Nixon, moved beyond previous leaders and
official mandates to deal with the population problem. First in 1965, and
more emphatically in 1966, he called public attention to the issue.
Furthermore, by creating the first Population Trust Fund in 1967, and by
transferring it to the UN Development Program in 1969, he acted largely
on his own initiative to help the program expand. Yet, like Johnson and
Nixon, burdened with many more immediate crises, he, too, did not

prevent the imposition of bureaucratic constraints by his own subordinates upon the new program he had encouraged.

THE ADMINISTRATIVE BUREAUCRACIES

If the great anonymous bureaucracies appear to be the villians of this account, blocking at every turn the development of new policy, it is because such agencies offer built-in resistance to innovation of all kinds. The bureaucratic habits of both national and international agencies that first hindered population programs, then reluctantly incorporated them, and finally began to defend them, bear much resemblance to the propositions developed by Anthony Downs in *Inside Bureaucracy*. Certainly, growth of the population program within AID confirms the basic outline Downs suggests of a new activity bitterly opposed by the programming and budgeting offices of the agency, established under zealous leadership with more concern for content than organization, gradually establishing greater internal autonomy, wider external support, and a more precise strategy.[22]

AID innovation in the population field did not originate at the top of the agency or even in the agency at all but rather from outside or from what in AID was the bottom, the technical professional level. In part this was the result of a declining budget. With no slack, with every decision on priority a verdict against other programs, the power to allocate resources became more important than the resources themselves or the uses to which they were put.

In part too AID reluctance to move into any new field was a function of sunk costs, the unwillingness to cut back on started but unfinished projects. It was also a function of lack of confidence in the ability of the agency to develop a new program and lack of confidence to judge the substantive merits of a proposal. In an attempt to measure program efficiency against the annual yardstick of a hostile appropriations committee, the concept of program adequacy, difficult at best in foreign aid, was most readily sacrificed.

It is significant that the one innovation that developed strictly within the bureaucratic structure, with the typical secrecy of executive agency processes, was clearly related to what Edward Banfield describes as "the maintenance and survival needs of large complex organizations."[23] The establishment of the Office of the War on Hunger strengthened the administrator of AID by providing new leverage, both internally and externally. From Gaud's point of view it was justified by the same arguments of relevance, feasibility, priority, and urgency that marked outside initiatives. But, under increasing outside pressures Gaud's principal goal was to maintain and preserve rather than carve out new territory.

A most conspicuous feature of the AID population program was rapid expansion on a crash basis with a very small staff. Not since the European Recovery Program, often cited as the most successful modern foreign assistance effort, had an economic assistance program—although on a very much lower level—grown so rapidly. By 1969 the virtues born of necessity in the population program were being extended to other activities. In both AID and the UNFPA, initial emphasis was on gathering and deploying substantial resources rather than building up internal staff or training new experts. Both programs emphasized interdisciplinary problem solving rather than professional skills per se. In both cases, the need to allocate funds in a limited time forced policy to become more flexible. For both, coordination was achieved not by organizational structure or hierarchy, but by control over funds. The activist, resource-oriented growth of AID and UNFPA contrasts with the more professional but less effective efforts of the UN Population Division and U.S. HEW program to expand in an slow and orderly manner, emphasizing first training and infrastructure. It remains to be seen whether slow-moving, professionally oriented agencies like the U.S. Department of HEW and the World Health Organization will be able, in the long run, to support or maintain family-planning programs more effectively than problem-oriented but politically insecure agencies like OEO, AID, and the UNFPA.

THE LEGISLATURE

Deeply involved in the population policy process in the U.S., Congress moved ahead of parties, agencies, and often the White House to develop this new issue. In a sense, the role of Congress was residual because others failed to move, but in the overall progress Congress was a critical factor.

"The informing function of Congress should be preferred even to its legislative function,"[24] Woodrow Wilson observed. Certainly, with respect to population policy "the informing function" of Congress was fully exercised. Senator Gruening's deliberate and organized hearings educated official Washington to a remarkable degree, in the process defining the birth control issue and giving it public legitimacy. Hearings on the world food crisis and family planning as part of the poverty program suggested a new framework in which the issue could be treated by government policy makers. Later, environmental problems and the implications of zero population growth were explored also and publicized by hearings.

At first through committee exhortations and reports Congress set broad policy direction, treating birth control as a necessary ingredient for economic development and for adequate world nutrition. Then through the broad authority of Title X of the Foreign Assistance Act Congress made it clear that population programs should have greater flexibility, variety, and discretion. None of the domestic legislation and none of Title X (except the loan-to-grant provision), provided any new statutory power, but all served to direct emphasis toward a specific policy. In addition to such guidelines, through Title X Congress established fixed funding. Despite the reluctance of officials who believed that programming and budgeting were their responsibilities, Congress insisted on action. The separate amendments on domestic programs and the major policy thrust contained in the Family Planning Services and Population Research Act of 1970 were all to some degree enacted in spite of rather than because of executive agency concern.

Congress has so far used very little of its powers of personnel action, administrative oversight, or investigation in respect to the population program. Early efforts at administrative oversight by Senator Gruening and Congressman Moss were designed to reinforce rather than criticize the program, but being divorced from funding powers they carried little weight. More recently, Senator Cranston's and Congressman DuPont's hearings on research and family planning services are a start toward program review, but are still several steps removed from the purse strings.[25]

Within Congress the impetus came from single individuals like Fulbright, Clark, Gruening, Todd, Scheuer, Bush, Tydings, Cranston, and Packwood, who on this as on other issues have often assumed the role of innovators in government.[26] To the degree that by coincidence or seniority they were also committee or subcommittee chairmen, their power to achieve results was greatly enhanced. The frequent combination of high support for population policy and opposition to administration foreign policy, which would not hold true for the older generation of population advocates outside Congress, suggests that these legislators may have a different, more independent view of congressional roles in the policy process than do their colleagues. Although the majority of senators and representatives are lawyers, Fulbright, as a former university professor and president, and Gruening, as a former journalist, came from an educationally oriented background. With the exception of Robert Byrd, none of those who promoted birth control have sought or gained roles of political leadership except through specific policy issues.

The congressional impetus for birth control programs came from the substantive authorizing committees and was usually discouraged by appropriating committees. Partly because funding was involved on a crash program basis but partly also because birth control did not coincide precisely with established agency objectives, the appropriating committees often played a negative or neutral role. Where annual or frequent authorizations reduced the influence of appropriating committees' influence, birth control, as an innovation stemming from broad policy reassessments, seemed to proceed faster.

Is it the changing structure of Congress and the new roles assumed by different members that made an innovation like birth control policy depend largely on legislative action? Or is it the character of birth control itself as an issue that tends to emphasize the legislative route to policy?

The important role of Parliament in formulating British policies toward birth control (and also toward capital punishment)—even though party discipline and executive control are stronger in Britain than in the United States—suggests that "this type of controversy" may have a "greater likelihood of being played out in the legislative branch of government than is true of other types of public decision-making."[27] A British study on the abolition of capital punishment concludes: "Emotional issues that plumb deep-seated moral codes—for example, birth control, prostitution, homosexuality, and hanging—are 'hot potatoes' that party leaders find unpredictable and often diversionary in character."[28] Whether or not birth control really was a "hot potato" as an issue in the United States in the 1960s, the executive agencies thought that it was and left the initiative to Congress.

Similarly, in the UN system the legislative bodies of the various agencies were often ahead of the international civil servants. Ironically, U.S. bureaucracies like AID, the State Department, and even HEW, requiring pressure from Congress to step up their own programs, worked vigorously on the legislative, or policy and financial, level in the UN to step up UN programs. Administrative agencies, both national and international, needed the independent pressures of outside bodies controlling financial resources in order to undertake new population programs.

THE POLICY-MAKING PROCESS

The study of change apart from substantive content and social and economic environment may well prove to be the ultimate intellectual will of the wisp. Whether the process is called God's will, natural law, philosophy of history, evolution, thesis-antithesis-synthesis, challenge-and-response, incrementalism, or the policy process, generalizations prove all too often specific for one time, one place, one field—at best one very small part of a much larger whole.

Over the last generation the so-called policy sciences have become the "policy process." Change has become routine and stability unusual. There remains no control to measure change against. The specific changes documented in this study took place against a rapidly changing background that included:

1. The change in the world environment, that is, the population growth phenomenon itself, without which neither the policy nor the program would have developed at all

2. The change in the role of the U.S. government, which assumed new social and economic responsibilities both in the United States and overseas

3. The change in public attitudes toward, first, the practice, and then the public discussion of birth control and human reproduction

4. The change in the opposition to birth control from Catholic enforcement of prohibitions on all toward increased tolerance and Catholic practice of birth control

5. The change in the supporters of birth control from charismatic roles toward institution-building roles, including the activation of the professionals and the professionalization of the activists

6. The change in birth control technology that made government programs feasible yet sufficiently difficult to require massive effort.

Against that background the issue of birth control was first incorporated into U.S. government policy only as it appeared relevant, feasible, significant, and urgent in relation to national goals of economic development. Population and birth control policies at the government level were, like military weapons, means to another end, not an end in themselves.

Under the pressure of facts, theories, technology, argument, persuasion, and outside trigger events a population policy was defined in the public forum of Congress and to varying degrees implemented. The arguments progressed through various phases of relevance from optimum size to density to resources to rate of growth. Feasibility developed in relation to diminishing Catholic opposition and new improved technology. Priority was set from above in terms of financial resources by a dissatisfied Congress. Urgency was first the product of unexpected food gaps.

But even as population policy was being defined at the U.S. government level in relation to economic objectives other, noneconomic, goals were being articulated and defined for government policy making. These included better health care, elimination of pollution, concern for environment, liberation of women, and freedom from government interference in private sexual activities. In advancing each of these strategies, birth control and population policy could also be useful tactics. As improved health care was increasingly recognized in the United States to be a government responsibility, family planning could be increasingly incorporated within the health network. As concern for the total environment challenged arguments based on individual economic benefit, reduced fertility could be justified as a natural, ecological imperative. To the extent that equality for women and reduced government control over sexual behavior were acceptable, restrictions against birth control and abortion on social grounds could be removed. In each instance, as new national goals or strategies were developed by various groups, support for fertility control measuress could be strengthened to the extent that they were proven relevant, feasible, important, and urgent in achieving those goals.

The original government objective that justified birth control support, economic development, was based on an optimistic assessment of man's capacity for continued rapid economic and social improvement. To the extent that a basic strategy becomes less confident, less overreaching, less of a recognized panacea for many ills, a tactic based on limitation or control gains force. Population control, like arms control, is rooted in its supporters' perception of a finite world, with limited space, resources, and funds. Just as in the military field measures of arms control have become increasingly relevant as the cost of a full deterrent is no longer acceptable, so the tactics of population control may be more easily assimilated into government policy at a time when economic strategies are revised downward or limited.[29]

As long as the role of government remains primarily the enhancement of national power and the improvement of citizens' welfare, a government population policy will have to be related to the sources and objectives of that role. The more directly a population policy is related to the most valued government objectives, the more important it will become as a government policy.

On the international level, population control programs are increasingly viewed as a tactic in the strategy of economic development. But for some of the Communist and the developing nations other tactics, such as a greater redistribution of wealth, may be considered more relevant; for some of the developed nations environmental protection may become at least as important a strategy as economic development. Only when population control or arms control are seen by all nations as necessary tactics to achieve their other major strategies—whether they be prosperity, security, or survival—will they achieve higher priority on the policy level. Long before that day comes, individuals and couples in many countries may conclude for themselves, as they have already done in Europe and Japan and are now doing in the United States, that individual fertility must be controlled regardless of government policy.

CHAPTER 1

1. UN Department of Economic and Social Affairs, *The Determinants and Consequences of Population Trends* (New York, 1953), pp. 8, 11; *World Populatic . Prospects as Assessed* in 1963, ST/SOA/Series A41 (New York, 1966), pp. 23-24; and *Demographic Yearbook, 1968*, E/F .69.XIII.I (New York, 1969), p. 83.

2. UN Population Commission, "World Population Situation," E/CN.9/231 (Geneva, September 23, 1969), pp. 13, 116-20 (mimeo.).

3. For various views on declining mortality and population growth see Louis I. Dublin, Arnold J. Lotka, and Mortimer I. Spiegelman, *Length of Life* (rev. ed.; New York: Ronald Press, 1949), chap. 2; Sir A. M. Carr-Saunders, *World Population: Past Growth and Present Trends* (Oxford: Clarendon Press, 1930); Thomas McKeown and R. G. Brown, "Medical Evidence Related to English Population Changes in the Eighteenth Century," *Population Studies*, IX (1955), pp. 119-41; and *Determinants and Consequences*, chap. 3.

4. Frank W. Notestein, "Population—The Long View," in Theodore W. Schultz, ed., *Food for the World* (Chicago: University of Chicago Press, 1945), pp. 40-41.

5. Norman Himes, *Medical History of Contraception* (1963 ed.; New York: Gamut Press, 1936), pp. 333-35; also Regina Stix and Frank W. Notestein, *Controlled Fertility, An Evaluation of Clinic Service* (Baltimore: Williams & Wilkins, 1940), pp. 150-53. The foundation for the continuing debate over the primacy of technology and information versus the primacy of personal motivation as the key to lower fertility was laid in these studies by Himes, Stix, and Notestein. Ironically, Himes, the sociologist, stressed technology and information, while Stix and Notestein, the physician and demographer, respectively, stressed motivation.

6. Harrison Brown, *The Challenge of Man's Future* (New York: Viking Press, 1954), p. 237.

7. Interview with Leona Baumgartner, February 5, 1971.

8. Margaret Sanger, *The Pivot of Civilization* (New York: Brentano's, 1922), pp. 12-13; see also David Kennedy, *Birth Control in America, the Career of Margaret Sanger* (New Haven: Yale University Press, 1970).

9. Kennedy, *Birth Control*, p. 86.

10. Sanger, *Pivot of Civilization*, p. 26.

11. Margaret Sanger and Hannah Stone, eds., *The Practice of Contraception* (Baltimore: Williams & Wilkins, 1931), p. xv.

12. Kennedy, *Birth Control*, p. 103.

13. Frank Lorimer, "The Development of Demography," in Philip M. Hauser and Otis Dudley Duncan, eds., *The Study of Population* (Chicago: University of Chicago Press, 1959), p. 164.

14. Interview with Frank Notestein, April 14, 1970.

15. *United States* v. *One Package of Japanese Pessaries*, 86 F 2d 737 (1936). For an account of prewar judicial and legislative proceedings, see Kennedy, *Birth Control*, pp. 218-71, and Alvah Sulloway, "The Legal and Political Aspects of Birth Control in the United States," *Law and Contemporary Problems*, XV, 3 (Summer 1960), 600-12.

16. John T. Noonan, Jr., *Contraception* (Cambridge: Harvard University Press, Belknap Press, 1965), p. 37.

17. *Ibid.*, pp. 424, 437.

18. Cf. Norman St. John-Stevas, "An Ethical Appraisal," in Franklin T. Brayer, ed., *World Population and U.S. Government Policy and Programs* (Washington, D.C.: Georgetown University Press, 1968), p. 102.

19. U.S. Congress, House of Representatives, Committee on the Judiciary, *Birth Control, Hearings on H.R. 5978*, 73rd Cong., 2d sess. (Washington, D.C., 1934), p. 154.

20. Kennedy, *Birth Control*, p. 237 note.

21. Norman St. John-Stevas, "A Roman Catholic View of Population Control," *Law and Contemporary Problems*, XXV, 3 (Summer 1960), 460.

22. As quoted in Noonan, *Contraception*, p. 409.

23. *Ibid.*, p. 442.

CHAPTER 2

1. UN Department of Social and Economic Affairs, "The Past and Future Growth of World Population," *Population Bulletin*, No. 1 (New York, 1952).

2. UN Department of Social and Economic Affairs, "The Future Growth of World Population," *Population Studies*, No. 28 (New York, 1958).

3. For a brief review of UN activities in the population field see John W. Halderman, "Programs of the United Nations and Associated Organizations," in Luke T. Lee and Arthur Larsen, eds., *Population and Law* (Durham, N.C.: Rule of Law Press, 1971), pp. 389-436.

4. *Proceedings of the World Population Conference*, UN, Rome, 1954, *Summary Reports*, New York, pp. 131, 139. See also *New York Times*, September 1-5, 1954.

5. Marshall C. Balfour, Roger F. Evans, Frank W. Notestein, Irene B. Taueber, *Public Health and Demography in the Far East* (New York: The Rockefeller Foundation, 1950), p. 116.

6. *Ibid.*, p. 112.

7. *Population Council 1952-1964* (New York, July 1965), p. 19. Also, *New York Times*, June 4, 1953, p. 16 and *Editorial*, August 17, 1953, p. 14.

8. Population Council, *Annual Report, 1957* (New York, 1958), p. 7; Population Council *Annual Report, 1967*, (New York, 1968), pp. 25, 36.

9. *Population Council 1952-1964* (New York: July 1965), p. 57; see also Population Council, *Annual Reports*, 1952-64.

10. Frederick Osborn, *Population, An International Dilemma* (New York: Population Council, 1958), pp. 30-31, 54-64.

11. E.g., Joseph J. Spengler, "Economic Factors in the Development of Densely Populated Areas," *Proceedings of the American Philosophical Society*, XCV, 1 (February 1951), 20-53; Harvey Leibenstein, *A Theory of Economic Demographic Development* (Princeton: the University Press, 1954), and *Economic Backwardness and Economic Growth* (New York: John Wiley & Sons, 1957). For a summary of the relationships between demography and economic theory, see Joseph J. Spengler, "Economics and Demography," in Philip Hauser and Otis Dudley Duncan, eds., *The Study of Population* (Chicago: Chicago University Press, 1959), pp. 791-831.

12. Ansley J. Coale and Edgar M. Hoover, *Population Growth and Economic Development in Low-Income Countries: A Case Study of India's Prospects* (Princeton: the University Press, 1958).

13. Interviews with Bernard Berelson and Frank Notestein, June 30, 1970.

14. Peter Marris and Martin Rein, *The Dilemmas of Social Reform* (New York: Atherton Press, 1967), pp. 121-22. See also Oscar Harkavy, "American Foundations and the Population Problem," in Bernard Berelson, ed., *Family Planning Programs, An International Survey* (New York: Basic Books, 1959), pp. 242-48; speech by Oscar Harkavy, "The Role of Foundations in Population Research and Planning," the Johns Hopkins University School of Hygiene and Public Health, June 9, 1965 (mimeo.) pp. 3, 8; and Frederick Osborn, "American Foundations and Population Problems," in Warren Weaver, ed., *U.S. Philanthropic Foundations* (New York: Harper and Row Publishers, 1967), pp. 367-74.

15. Martin Rein, "An Organizational Analysis of a National Agency's Local Affiliates in Their Community Contexts: A Study of the Planned Parenthood Federation of America," (New York: Planned Parenthood, 1959), pp. 13-21 (mimeo.). See also Rilma Buckman, "Social Engineering: A Study of the Birth Control Movement," *Social Forces*, XXII, 4 (May 1944), 420-28.

16. Interview with Frederick Jaffe, June 30, 1970.

17. *Planned Parenthood News*, Winter 1958.

18. *New York Times*, January 15, 1953, p. 1, and May 30, 1953, p. 1, *passim*.

19. James Finn, "Controversy in New York," *Commonweal*, LXVIII (September 12, 1958), p. 586. For a full account of the incident, see Planned Parenthood, "Anatomy of a Victory," (New York, 1959) (mimeo.), which was prepared in part to encourage local affiliates to undertake similar confrontations.

20. Rein, "Organizational Analysis," pp. 109-10.

21. See comments of Dr. H. Parry Giles, professor of education, New York University, who referred to "a continuous, organized effort" (p. 33) and recommended, "use all the consultant help you can get . . . Mr. Jaffe's description . . . is the right kind of consultation" (p. 35). On the other hand, Jaffe, now a vice-president of Planned Parenthood, stated, "More important, I think, than professional public relations skill is determination and the skill that comes with determination" (p. 41). Excerpts from "Symposium," Planned Parenthood, "Anatomy of a Victory."

22. *New York Times*, June 21, 1948, p. 4. See also *Planned Parenthood News* throughout this period.

23. *New York Times*, May 20, 1952, p. 13; *Planned Parenthood News*, Fall 1953.

24. S. Agarwala, "Population Control in India: Progress and Prospects," *Law and Contemporary Problems*, LXXI, 3 (Summer 1960), 557-92. A summary of Indian family planning efforts is given in Gunnar Myrdal, *Asian Drama*, Vol. III (New York: Twentieth Century Fund, 1968), app. 12, pp. 2151-64.

25. *Planned Parenthood News*, Spring 1959.

26. *Planned Parenthood News*, Spring 1955.

27. Lawrence Lader, *Breeding Ourselves to Death* (New York: Ballantine Books, 1971), p. 59.

28. J. Mayone Stycos, "American Goals and Family Planning," in *World Population and U.S. Government Policy and Programs*, Franklin Brayer, ed., (Washington, D.C.: Georgetown University Press, 1968), p. 25.

CHAPTER 3

1. This statement is based on a search of index cards at the Roper Public Opinion Research Center at Williams College as well as on available articles and summaries.

2. Hazel Gaudet Erskine, "The Polls: The Population Explosion, Birth, and Sex Education," *Public Opinion Quarterly*, XXX, 3 (Fall 1966), 494.

3. Erskine, "Polls," p. 493. The question asked in December 1959 was phrased as follows: "In some places in the United States, it is not legal to supply birth control information. How do you feel about this—do you think birth control information should be available to anyone who wants it, or not?" (AIPO No. 621, question 30).

4. Ronald Freedman, Pascal K. Whelpton, and Arthur K. Campbell, *Family Planning, Sterility, and Population Growth* (New York: McGraw-Hill, 1959).

5. Arthur A. Campbell, John E. Patterson, and Pascal K. Whelpton, *Fertility and Family Planning in the United States* (Princeton: the University Press, 1966), pp. 358-59.

6. *Ibid.*, pp. 216-17.

7. *Ibid.*, pp. 284-85.

8. As quoted in Planned Parenthood, "Anatomy of a Victory" (New York, 1959), p. 23 (mimeo.).

9. Norman B. Ryder and Charles F. Westoff, "United States: Methods of Fertility Control, 1955, 1960, and 1965," *Studies in Family Planning*, No. 17 (February 1967), p. 4.

10. Norman B. Ryder and Charles F. Westoff, "Use of Oral Contraception in the United States, 1965," *Science*, CLIII (September 9, 1966), p. 1204.

11. *Ibid.*, pp. 1200, 1202.

12. Norman B. Ryder and Charles F. Westoff, "United States: The Papal Encyclical and Catholic Practice and Attitudes, 1969," *Studies in Family Planning*, No. 5 (February 1970), p. 4.

13. Norman B. Ryder and Charles F. Westoff, "Recent Trends in Attitudes Toward Fertility Control and in the Practice of Contraception in the United States," in *Fertility and Family Planning, A World View*, S. J. Behrman et al., (eds), (Ann Arbor: University of Michigan Press, 1969), pp. 388-412.

14. Gerhard Lenski, *The Religious Factor* (New York: Doubleday, 1961), p. 175.

15. Unpublished manuscript of Ernest Gruening's autobiography, chap. XXIX, pp. 716-20, gives an account of Gruening's birth control efforts in Puerto Rico.

16. Kurt W. Back, Reuben Hill, and J. Mayone Stycos, *The Family and Population Control* (Chapel Hill: University of North Carolina Press, 1959), pp. 116-18.

17. Reuben Hill *et al.*, "Population Control in Puerto Rico," *Law and Contemporary Problems*, XV, 3 (Summer 1960), 572.

18. Harriet Presser, "Puerto Rico: The Role of Sterilization in Controlling Fertility," *Studies in Family Planning*, No. 45 (September 1969), p. 8.

19. This account is largely summarized from Irene B. Taeuber, *The Population of Japan* (Princeton: the University Press, 1958), pp. 269-82, 369-79.

20. *New York Times*, February 13, 1950, p. 1. MacArthur had been under heavy Catholic criticism for allowing U.S. population experts—that is, Thompson and Whelpton—to "recommend a national birth control policy for Japan."

21. As quoted in Taeuber, *Population of Japan*, p. 370. The statement was issued on June 6, 1949.

22. Minoru Moramatsu, "Japan: Miracle in East Asia," in *Family Planning Programs*, Bernard Berelson, ed. (New York: Basic Books, 1968), p. 16.

23. Taeuber, *Population of Japan*, p. 373.

24. Chikao Honda, "Japan's Solution," in *Our Crowded Planet*, Fairfield Osborn, ed. (Garden City, N.Y.: Doubleday, 1962), p. 168.

25. *New York Times*, November 18, 1946, p. 11.

26. *New York Times*, June 14, 1953, p. 8. The members of the committee were Edwin G. Arnold, Ford Foundation; C. W. deKiewiet, president, University of Rochester; John W. Harriman, dean of the Graduate School, Syracuse University; Lester K. Little, former inspector general of Chinese Customs; Edward S. Mason, dean, School of Public Administration, Harvard; Stacy May, economist; and Whitney H. Shepardson, National Committee for Free Europe.

27. S. C. Hsuu, *From Taboo to National Policy* (Taiwan: Chinese Center for International Training in Family Planning, 1970), pp. 8-10.

28. *Ibid.*, p. 10.

29. *Ibid.*, pp. 10-11.

30. Interview with James Grant, September 15, 1970.

31. A summary of the Indian efforts is provided in Gunnar Myrdal, *Asian Drama*, Vol. III (New York and Toronto: Random House, 1968), pp. 2151-64.

32. Interview with C. Tyler Wood, fall 1969.

CHAPTER 4

1. U.S. President's Committee to Study the United States Military Assistance Program, *Composite Report* (hereinafter cited as *President's Committee Report*) Vol. I (Washington, D.C., August 17, 1959), pp. 185-87.

2. For background on the foreign aid program during this period see Field Haviland, "Foreign Aid and the Policy Process," *American Political Science Review*, LII (September 1958), pp. 689-724; John Montgomery, *The Politics of Foreign Aid* (New York: Praeger Publishers, 1962), chap. IV; Edward Mason, *Foreign Aid and Foreign Policy* (New York: Harper and Row Publishers, 1964).

3. Interview with Tracy Voorhees, January 30, 1970.

4. Theodore H. White, "No. 1 American in Europe," *New York Times Magazine*, December 21, 1952, p. 8.

5. *President's Committee Report*, Vol I, pp. vii, viii.

6. *New York Times*, November 27, 1958, p. 32.

7. Interviews with William H. Draper, Jr.

8. C. Tyler Wood Papers.

9. Speech by Marx Leva to Committee on Foreign Relations, Birmingham, Alabama, November 19, 1959, p. 1 (mimeo.).

10. U.S. Congress, Senate, Committee on Foreign Relations, *Mutual Security Act of 1959*, 86th Cong., 1st sess., 1959, Vol. II (Washington, D.C., 1959), p. 727.

11. Statement by John J. McCloy, personal interview, April 1970.

12. James Webb Papers; Millikan memorandum requested by Arthur Smithies, *President's Committee Report*, Task Group IV, February 20, 1959.

13. *President's Committee Report*, Task Group IV, *Revised Draft of Economic Section of Final Report*, May 8, 1959, p. 12 (mimeo., from Eisenhower Library, Abilene, Kansas).

14. *President's Committee Report*, Vol. I, pp. 94-97.

15. R. R. Adams, "The Population Explosion" (rev. ed., R. R. Adams, paper), *President's Committee Report*,Task Group IV, June 15, 1959, pp. 2, 14-19 (mimeo., from the Eisenhower Library, Abilene, Kansas).

16. *President's Committee Report*, Vol I, pp. 118-23. The committee's principal recommendations on the economic side were for an annual economic aid program of $1 billion beginning in fiscal year 1961; strong emphasis on self-help; more effective utilization of surplus agricultural products and resulting local currencies; maximum use of private companies, foundations, and universities; increased support of United Nations technical assistance programs (and multilateral aid); more effective field supervision under the ambassador in each country; and a more independent evaluation unit, as well as an independent aid agency with separate personnel.

17. *New York Times*, July 24, 1959, p. 1.

18. National Catholic Welfare Conference News Service, "Charges Made That U.S. Advisory Group 'Clearly' Implied Support of Birth Control to Curb Population," July 27, 1959, p. 2.

19. *New York Times*, December 6, 1959, sec. IV, p. 3.

20. *New York Times*, February 15, 1959, p. 19, and February 22, 1959, p. 31; *Planned Parenthood News*, Spring 1959, p. 8.

21. *New York Times*, October 7, 1959, pp. 1, 36.

22. John Noonan, Jr., *Contraception* (Cambridge, Mass.: The Belknap Press of Harvard University, 1965), p. 490; *Planned Parenthood News*, Spring, 1960, p. 5. The General Conference of the Methodist Church and the United Lutheran Church had already approved contraception in 1956.

23. U.S. Department of State, Bureau of Intelligence and Research, *World Population Trends and Problems* (Washington, D.C., July 23, 1959); *New York Times*, November 29, 1959, p. 1.

24. Stanford Research Institute, *Possible Non-military Scientific Developments and Their Potential Impact on Foreign Policy Problems of the United States*; U.S. Congress, Senate, Committee on Foreign Relations, *United States Foreign Policy*, 87th Cong., 1st sess. (Washington, D.C., 1961), p. 136.

25. *Ibid.*, p. 138.

CHAPTER 5

1. TRB, *New Republic*, December 2, 1959, p. 2.

2. Statement of the Catholic bishops of the United States, following their annual meeting, November 1959. Reprinted in the *New York Times* (p. 43) and the *Washington Post* (p. A-4), November 26, 1959. Statement was signed by the members of the Administrative Board, National Catholic Welfare Conference, including Cardinals Spellman, McIntyre, O'Hara, and Cushing as well as three cardinals-designate, four archbishops, and six bishops.

3. Arthur Krock, *New York Times*, December 1, 1959, p. 38.

4. *New York Times*, November 26, 1959, p. 1. Bishop Pike was serving at the time as chairman of the Clergymen's National Advisory Committee of Planned Parenthood.

5. *New York Times*, November 28, 1959, p. 1. An edited and approved text of Reston's questions and Kennedy's replies was reprinted in the *New York Times*, September 9, 1960, pp. 14-15.

6. *New York Times*, September 9, 1960, pp. 14-15.

7. Cf. "Meet the Press," January 3, 1960, as reprinted in *New York Times*, January 4, 1960, p. 33, and April 20, 1960, p. 28.

8. *New York Times*, April 22, 1960, pp. 16, 17.

9. Theodore White, *The Making of the President, 1960* (New York: Atheneum Press, 1961), app. C, p. 393.

10. *New York Times*, November 29, 1959, p. 43.

11. *New York Times*, December 1, 1959, p. 4.

12. *New York Times*, November 29, 1949, p. 43.

13. *New York Times*, April 9, 1960, p. 1.

14. *New York Times*, December 3, 1959, pp. 1, 18.

15. Interview with James Grant, September 15, 1970.

16. Interview with William H. Draper, Jr., December 1969.

17. Interview with James W. Riddleberger, April 29, 1970.

18. Dwight D. Eisenhower, "Let's Be Honest With Ourselves," *Saturday Evening Post*, October 26, 1963, p. 27.

19. V. O. Key, Jr., *Public Opinion and American Democracy* (New York: Alfred A. Knopf, 1964), p. 40.

20. Philip Converse, "Religion and Politics: 1960 Election," in *Elections and the Political Order*, Angus Campbell *et al.* (New York: John Wiley & Sons, 1966), p. 97.

21. Peter Bachrach and Morton Baratz, "Two Faces of Power," *American Political Science Review*, LVI (December 1962), p. 948.

22. The 1948 referendum is discussed in John H. Fenton, *The Catholic Vote* (New Orleans: Hauser Press, 1960), pp. 7-20. Paul Blanchard points out that Kennedy remained silent during this 1948 struggle, in *God and Man in Washington* (Boston: Beacon Press, 1960), p. 206.

23. Arthur Schlesinger, Jr., *A Thousand Days* (Boston: Houghton Mifflin, 1965), p. 603.

24. Theodore C. Sorenson, *Kennedy* (New York: Harper and Row Publishers, 1965), pp. 111-12.

25. *Ibid.*

26. *New York Times*, November 29, 1959, sec. IV, p. 10E.

27. Eleanor Roosevelt, syndicated column, *St. Louis Post Dispatch*, December 1, 1959: "This is a religious question and has always been so understood;" former President Truman: "A 'false issue' so far as the Presidency is concerned." Paul Butler, Democratic national chairman, "agreed with Eisenhower that birth control should not be in politics, The *New York Times*, December 6, 1959, p. 1.

28. Michael Lipsky, "Protest as a Political Resource," *American Political Science Review*, LXII (December 1968), pp. 1144-46.

29. *St. Louis Post Dispatch*, December 3, 1959.

30. Norman St John-Stevas, "A Roman Catholic View of Population Control," *Law and Contemporary Problems*, XXX, 3 (Summer 1960), 455-57; John Cogley, "The Bishops' Challenge," *Commonweal*, DCLXXI (December 18, 1959), p. 350; "Connecticut Birth Control Law," *Commonweal*, DCLXXII (April 22, 1960), pp. 48-49.

31. William J. Gibbons, S. J., "The Birth Control Issue—What Both Sides Say," *U.S. News and World Report*, December 21, 1959, pp. 58-59. He also suggested that U.S. Catholics might be "more rigid" than the church required.

32. "May a Catholic President Sign?" *America*, CII (December 12, 1959), pp. 353-54.

NOTES
NOTES

33. "CBS Reports The Population Explosion," November 11, 1959, p. 21 (mimeo. transcript).

34. Communication from CBS News, June 25, 1970.

35. *New York Times*, March 24, 1960, p. 12.

36. Richard F. Fagley, *The Population Explosion and Christian Responsibility* (New York: Oxford University Press, 1960).

37. *New York Times*, April 11, 1960, p. 1.

38. *New York Times*, December 6, 1959, p. 74.

39. *Planned Parenthood News*, Spring 1960, pp. 1-2. See also *New York Times*, May 20, 1960, p. 11.

40. As quoted by David Broder, *Washington Post*, August 6, 1970.

41. *New York Times*, October 21, 1960, p. 1.

42. Sorenson, *Kennedy*, p. 208.

43. *New York Times*, October 22, 1960, p. 12.

44. Sorenson, *Kennedy*, p. 209. See also Jerome Fischman, "The Church in Politics: The 1960 Election in Puerto Rico," *Western Political Quarterly*, XVIII (1965), pp. 821-39. In Puerto Rico, the party of Munoz Marin won 58 percent of the vote, the bishops' party won 6.5 percent.

45. Richard Scammon, *America Votes 4,1960*, (Pittsburgh: University of Pittsburgh Press for the Governmental Affairs Institute, 1962), p. 1.

46. V. O. Key, Jr., *The Responsible Electorate* (New York: Vintage Books, 1968), p. 120.

47. John Wicklein, "John Kennedy and the Catholic Issue," in *Religion and Contemporary Society*, Harold Stahmer, ed. (New York: MacMillan, 1963), p. 241. Also, Louis Harris, "A Pollster Defends the Polls," *New York Times Magazine*, November 5, 1961, p. 128.

48. Key, *Responsible Electorate* p. 138.

49. American Institute of Public Opinion, Poll No. 621, question 28, December 1962.

50. *New York Times*, November 10, 1960, p. 39.

51. Daniel Callahan, *The Mind of the Catholic Layman* (New York: Charles Scribners Sons, 1963), pp. 148-49.

52. White, *Making of the President*, p. 357.

53. *New York Times*, November 29, 1959, p. 43.

54. *Washington Star*, February 19, 1960; U.S. Congress, Senate Committee on Foreign Relations, *Hearings on United States Foreign Policy*, 86th Cong., 2d sess. (Washington, D.C., 1960), pt. I, pp. 17-19; U.S. Congress, House of Representatives Committee on Foreign Affairs, *Hearings on the Mutual Security Act of 1960*, 86th Cong., 2d sess., (Washington, D.C., 1960), pt. I, p. 66.

55. ICATO Circular Airgram X A-758, March 3, 1960. The statement by Schlesinger ("the ICA directive promptly banned birth control assistance or even consultation") is therefore not strictly accurate. Schlesinger, *Thousand Days*, p. 601.

56. American Institute of Public Opinion, Poll No. 621, question 27, December 1959.

57. Callahan, *Mind of the Catholic Layman*, pp. 148-70; William DuBay, *The Human Church* (New York: Doubleday, 1966), p. 53.

58. Sorenson, *Kennedy*, p. 148.

CHAPTER 6

1. Samuel P. Huntington, *The Common Defense* (New York: Columbia University Press, 1961), pp. 284-97. Cf. James G. March and Herbert A. Simon, *Organizations* (New York: John Wiley & Sons, 1958), chap. 7.

2. Leona Baumgartner, "Governmental Responsibility for Family Planning in the United States," in S. J. Behrman, Leslie Corsa, Jr., and Roland Freed, *Fertility and Family Planning in the U.S.* (Ann Arbor: University of Michigan Press, 1969), pp. 437-38. Leighton Van Nort, "The Development of U.S. Population Policy"; Malcolm Merrill, "Current Activities"; and J. Mayone Stycos, "American Goals and Family

Planning," in *World Population and U.S. Government Policy and Progress*, Franklin T. Brayer, ed. (Washington, D.C.: Georgetown University Press, 1968), pp. 1-48.

3. U.S. Department of State, Policy Planning Council, *Foreign Policy Implications of the World Population Explosion*, pub. no. PPC-61-3 (Washington, D.C., 1961).

4. *New York Times*, January 15, 1960, p. 7.

5. "Breakthrough, 1959," *Planned Parenthood News*, Spring 1960, p. 3.

6. As quoted in John T. Noonan, Jr., *Contraception* (Cambridge, Mass.: Harvard University Press, Belknap Press, 1965), pp. 445-46.

7. Carl G. Hartman, "Physiological Mechanisms Concerned with Conception—An Inventory of Unanswered Questions," *Planned Parenthood News*, Spring 1960, p. 1; *Perspectives in Biology and Medicine*, IV (Autumn 1960), sec. 1, pp. 70-90; *Journal of Reproduction and Fertility*, I (1960), pp. 283-93. Also, Solly Zuckerman, "Mechanisms Involved in Conception," *Science*, CXXX (December 6, 1959), pp. 1260-64. See also *Planned Parenthood News*, Spring 1960, p. 1.

8. David Broder, "Policy Planning Council Report," *Washington Evening Star*, April 25, 1962, September 6, 1962, and December 29, 1962; and *Washington Sunday Star*, December 30, 1962. Also, John Rock, *The Time Has Come* (New York: Alfred A. Knopf, 1963), pp. 193-200.

9. David Broder, *Washington Evening Star*, April 25, 1962; *Washington Sunday Star*, December 30, 1962.

10. "Shh! U.S. at Work," *Newsweek*, November 6, 1961, p. 93.

11. *New York Times*, April 27, 1962, p. 4.

12. *New York Times*, September 7, 1962, p. 25.

13. David Broder, *Washington Evening Star*, December 29, 1962.

14. U.S. Department of Health, Education, and Welfare, Public Health Service, *A Survey of Research on Reproduction Related to Birth and Population Control* (as of January 1, 1963) (Washington, D.C., 1963), pp. 27-28.

15. David Broder, *Washington Sunday Star*, December 30, 1962.

16. *New York Times*, September 20, 1961, p. 23.

17. Barnett's official title, however, was deputy director, Foreign Economic Advisory Staff.

18. *New York Times*, October 25, 1961, p. 48.

19. William Nunley, "To Be Born With a Begging Bowl," *AID Digest*, January 15, 1962, p. 4.

20. *New York Times*, August 27, 1961, sec. IV, p. 5.

21. U.S. Department of State, Office of Public Services, Bureau of Public Affairs, Form Letter, C.292, n.d.

22. U.S. Congress, Senate, Committee on Government Operations, Subcommittee on Foreign Aid Expenditures, *Population Crisis, Hearings on S. 1676*, 89th Cong., 2d sess. (Washington, D.C., 1967), pt. 4, p. 1000.

23. *New York Times*, October 11, 1961, p. 12.

24. U.S. Agency for International Development, *Manual Order* 1018, effective August 1, 1962.

25. Letter from Fowler Hamilton to Senator Thomas Dodd, November 10, 1962.

26. Nunley, "To Be Born."

CHAPTER 7

1. U.N. Document X/C. 2/L.657. Revised version printed in Richard N. Gardner, *Population Growth: A World Problem, Statement of U.S. Policy* (U.S. Department of State, January 1963), p. 13.

2. Interview with Richard N. Gardner, September 1970. Arthur Schlesinger Jr., *A Thousand Days* (Boston: Houghton Mifflin, 1965), p. 601.

3. *Population Growth*, pp. 8-9.

4. UN General Assembly, XVII Session, *Report of the Second Committee* (A/C.2/SR 875), A/5354 Annex 38, Summary Records.

5. *Population Growth*, p. 13.

6. Richard N. Gardner, "Toward a World Population Program," *International Organization*, XXII, 1 (1968), 350.

7. Richard N. Gardner, "The Politics of Population: A Blueprint for International Cooperation," *Department of State Bulletin*, June 10, 1963, p. 19.

CHAPTER 8

1. *New York Times*, November 18, 1960, p. 21.

2. *New York Times*, May 12, 1961, p. 12, and May 13, 1961, p. 12. This symposium was also the last public appearance for Margaret Sanger, who appeared to have more sympathy with Hugh Moore's boldness than with Planned Parenthood's caution.

3. *New York Times*, May 15, 1961, p. 30.

4. *New York Times*, September 17, 1961, p. 78. At the same meeting, John Durand suggested prophetically that "a spread of the idea of women's rights might generate a spontaneous birth control movement."

5. *New York Times*, November 7, 1961, p. 1.

6. Population Council, *Report for 1962 and 1963* (New York), pp. 13-14, 30.

7. John Rock, "We Can End the Battle Over Birth Control," *Good Housekeeping*, July 1961, pp. 44-45 (reprinted in the *Reader's Digest*, September 1961, pp. 103-7).

8. Letter from Senator J. William Fulbright to Cass Canfield, August 2, 1961.

9. John O'Brien, "Let's Take Birth Control Out of Politics," *Look* magazine, October 10, 1961, pp. 67-68. This was the first article on birth control to be inserted in the *Congressional Record* since the war.

10. Cf. Population Council, *Report for 1962 and 1963*, p. 11.

11. *New York Times*, July 14, 1961, p. 5. Also Lyndon B. Johnson, *The Vantage Point* (New York: Holt, Rinehart & Winston, 1971), pp. 339-40.

12. *New York Times*, November 6 and 10, 1961, p. 1.

13. Daniel S. Greenberg, "Birth Control: Swedish Government has Ambitious Program," *Science*, CXXXVII (September 28, 1962), pp. 1038-39. The National Council of Churches, comprising all the Protestant denominations in the United States, endorsed birth control in 1961. *New York Times*, February 24, 1961, pp. 1, 16.

14. *New York Herald Tribune*, October 28, 1962; *New York Times*, November 26, 1962, p. 1.

15. Population Council, *Report for 1962 and 1963*, pp. 7, 10.

16. This comment was made by one of Kennedy's political associates.

17. Lee Rainwater, *Family Design* (Chicago: Aldine Publishing, 1965), pp. 150-51.

18. Arthur Schlesinger, Jr., *A Thousand Days* (Boston: Houghton Mifflin, 1965), p. 603.

19. *New York Times*, March 22, 1961, pp. 1, 14.

20. *New York Times*, July 20, 1961, p. 10. The question had been raised by Mrs. May Craig, a deliberately provocative reporter, but the same theme was repeated a day later by James Reston, who warned that "there will be a decisive revolt against foreign aid one day if the population problem is not faced." *New York Times*, July 21, 1961, p. 22. Arthur Krock also referred to the "do-nothing, see-nothing attitude of the entire political community." *New York Times*, July 23, 1961, sec. IV, p. 9.

21. Kennedy responded in 1962: " . . . it goes to very basic national feelings, personal feelings. This is a matter which each individual, each family, each country must determine and cannot be determined by the actions of another country." *New York Times*, July 15, 1962, p. 10.

22. Interview with William H. Draper, Jr., February 6, 1961.

23. Ford Foundation, "Policy Paper: Population," presented at the meeting, March 28 and 29, 1963, pp. 3-9 (mimeo).

24. John Rock, *The Time Has Come, A Catholic Doctor's Proposals to End the Battle Over Birth Control* (New York: Alfred A. Knopf, 1963).

25. *The Pilot* (Boston) April 20, 1963, as quoted in the *New York Times*, April 20, 1963, p. 6.

26. National Academy of Sciences, Committee on Science and Public Policy, *The Growth of World Population* (Washington, D.C., 1963), p. 9.

27. *Ibid.*, pp. 27, 29, 37, 1-7.

28. *New York Times*, April 21, 1963, p. 62.

29. *New York Times*, April 25, 1963, pp. 15, 16.

30. *New York Times*, June 5, 1963, p. 3.

31. *New York Times*, October 16, 1963, p. 11.

32. Dwight D. Eisenhower, "Let's Be Honest With Ourselves," *Saturday Evening Post*, October 26, 1963, p. 27.

33. American Assembly, *The Population Dilemma* (Englewood Cliffs, N.J.: Prentice-Hall, 1963), pp. 178-87.

34. *New York Times*, May 8, 1963, p. 11; May 9, 1963, p. 9.

35. An exception, as usual, was Hugh Moore, who in 1962 persuaded Congressman Francis Walters (D.-Pa.), chairman, House Immigration Subcommittee, to conduct a hearing on population growth in connection with immigration.

36. *New York Times*, May 8, 1963, p. 11; *New York Herald Tribune*, May 8, 1963.

37. Letter from James A. Shannon, director of NIH, to Mary S. Calderone, medical director, Planned Parenthood, April 10, 1961; also letter from Boisfeuillet Jones, special assistant to the secretary of HEW, to William H. Draper, Jr., October 3, 1962.

38. William Vogt, memorandum of March 10, 1959, Planned Parenthood files.

39. U.S. Congress, Senate, Committee on Foreign Relations, *International Development and Security, Hearings on S. 1983*, 87th Cong., 1st sess. (Washington, D.C., 1961), pt. I, p. 166.

40. Letter from Senator J. William Fulbright to Cass Canfield, August 2, 1961.

41. Committee on Foreign Relations, *International Development and Security*, pt. I, pp. 472-73.

42. U.S. Congress, House of Representatives Committee on Foreign Affairs, *Mutual Security Act of 1960*, 86th Cong., 2d sess. (Washington, D.C., 1960), pt. I, p. 66.

43. U.S. Congress, House of Representatives Committee on Foreign Affairs, *Foreign Assistance Act of 1962*, 87th Cong., 2d sess. (Washington, D.C., April 18, 1962), p. 1108.

44. U.S. Congress, House of Representatives, Committee on Foreign Affairs, *Hearings on H.R.5490*, 88th Cong., 1st sess. (Washington, D.C., April 5, 1963), p. 27.

45. U.S. Congress, Senate, Committee on Foreign Relations, *Foreign Assistance Act of 1963*, 88th Cong., 1st sess., Report No. 588, H.R. 7855, filed October 22, 1963, p. 19.

46. *Ibid.*, p. 14.

47. Comments in speech by Congressman Zablocki, U.S. Congress, House of Representatives, 89th Cong., 2d sess., *Congressional Record*, March 31, 1966 (Washington, D.C., 1966), p. 6980.

48. U.S. Congress, Senate, Committee on Foreign Relations, *Legislation on Foreign Relations*, 90th Cong., 2d sess. (Washington, D.C., 1969), Sec. 24lb, p. 19.

49. Conversation between Dr. Leona Baumgartner and Senator Fulbright, February 6, 1964.

50. U.S. Congress, 88th Cong., 1st sess., *Congressional Record*, (Washington, D.C., 1963), pp. 15238-42, August 15, 1963.

CHAPTER 9

1. Memorandum to Dr. Leona Baumgartner from Harry J. Krould, "Briefing Memorandum on Population Meeting With Mr. Bell," June 10, 1963, and the documentation referred to therein; memorandum to Baumgartner from Leigh Miller,

PC/LCPS, June 21, 1963. The fact that most of the material is unclassified suggests a relaxation of the earlier tensions and anxiety over discussion of the issue. A less-detailed published account, with some conspicuous omissions, is *Chronological List of Developments in the Population Field, 1952-1964*, reprinted in U.S. Congress, Senate Committee on Government Operations, Subcommittee on Foreign Aid Expenditures, *Population Crisis, Hearings on S. 1676*, 89th Cong., 2d sess., (Washington, D.C., 1966), pt. 4, pp. 883-86.

2. AIDTO Circular Airgram 360, May 10, 1963.

3. Richard N. Gardner, "The Politics of Population: A Blueprint for International Cooperation, *Department of State Bulletin*, June 10, 1963.

4. U.S. Congress, Senate, Committee on Foreign Relations, *Foreign Assistance Act of 1963, Hearings on S. 1278*, 88th Cong., 1st sess. (Washington, D.C., 1963), p. 50.

5. Leona Baumgartner, "Asian Population Conference," press release, pp. 3-4 (typewritten), n.d.

6. Leona Baumgartner, "Population and Public Health Policy," in *Population Dynamics, International Action and Training Programs*, Minoro Maramatsu and Paul Harper, eds. (Baltimore: the Johns Hopkins University Press, 1965), pp. 235-37. Also Baumgartner, "Governmental Responsibility for Family Planning in the United States," in *Fertility and Family Planning: A World View*, S. J. Behrman *et al*, eds. (Ann Arbor: University of Michigan Press, 1969), pp. 435-48; Baumgartner, "Asian Population Problems and The United States," address at Planned Parenthood Conference, New York, January 23, 1964, AID-64-16.

7. Baumgartner, "Asian Population Conference," p. 5.

8. Conversation between Baumgartner and Senators Fulbright and Humphrey, February 7, 1964.

9. Conversation between Baumgartner and Congressman Passman, February 6, 1964.

10. Baumgartner, "Population and Public Health Policy," pp. 237-38.

11. Conversation between Baumgartner and Senators Fulbright and Humphrey, February 7, 1964.

12. Gardner, "Politics of Population."

13. Memorandum for William S. Gaud from Robert W. Barnett, "Population Policy," May 12, 1964; memorandum to Robert W. Barnett from William S. Gaud, "Population Policy," May 20, 1964.

14. Office of Population Affairs, "Action Program for AID/LA," memorandum, February 2, 1964, pp. 4-5.

15. Baumgartner, "Population and Public Health Policy," p. 237; statement by Edgar Berman, personal interview, January 25, 1971.

16. Ben Đuffy, "Report on the Alliance for Progress Population Program," in *Population Crisis, Hearings on S. 1676*, 89th Cong., 2d sess., 1966, pp. 961-67.

17. U.S. Congress, House of Representatives, Committee on Foreign Affairs, *Foreign Assistance Act of 1964*, 88th Cong., 2d sess. (Washington, D.C., 1964), pp. 301-03.

18. *New York Times*, April 21, 1964, p. 28.

19. AIDTO Circular Airgram LA-158, May 11, 1964, p. 1.

20. *Ibid.*, pp. 2-3.

21. See Tables 13.1 and 15.2.

CHAPTER 10

1. John Finney, "Birth Control Now a Major Part of U.S. Aid," *New York Times*, December 26, 1965, sec. IV, p. 4.

2. *New York Times*, November 10, 1964, p. 19.

3. U.S. Congress, Senate, Committee on Government Operations, *Population Crisis, Hearings on S. 1676*, before Subcommittee on Foreign Aid Expenditures, 89th Cong., 1st sess., August 30 to September 22, 1965 (Washington, D.C., 1966) pt. 4, p. 1060 (reprint of speech).

4. Leona Baumgartner, "Governmental Responsibility for Family Planning in the United States," in *Fertility and Planning in the U.S.*, S. J. Behrman *et al.* (Ann Arbor: University of Michigan Press, 1969), pp. 444-45; Information Memorandum for the Administrator, subject, discussion with Dr. Hornig regarding his conversation with the president on population, January 18, 1964 [sic].

5. U.S. Secretary of State, memorandum for the president, subject: "Population: Visit by Draper and Rockefeller Group," November 29, 1964, pp. 2-3.

6. *New York Times*, January 5, 1965, p. 16.

7. *Population Crisis, Hearings on S. 1676*, 89th Cong., 2d sess., 1966, pt. 1, "President Johnson's Statements on Population 1965-1968," pp. 3-4.

8. *Ibid.*

9. *Ibid.*

10. Wade Greene, "Federal Birth Control: Progress Without Policy," *Reporter*, November 18, 1965, pp. 35-37; *Population Crisis, Hearings on S. 1676*, 89th Cong., 1st sess., 1966, pt. 2-B, pp. 1129-30.

11. "Meet the Press," November 19, 1964.

12. *Population Crisis, Hearings on S. 1676*, 89th Cong., 1st sess., 1966, pt. 4, pp. 2238-40.

13. Lyndon B. Johnson, *The Vantage Point* (New York: Holt, Rinehart & Winston, 1971), pp. 339-40.

14. United Press International dispatch, *Washington Post*, January 8, 1965, p. 1.

15. Cf. Charles Bartlett, "The Government and Procreation," *Washington Evening Star*, April 22, 1965, p. A-21.

16. National Academy of Sciences, *The Growth of U.S. Population*, (Washington, D.C., May 1965), p. 23.

17. *Griswold* v. *Connecticut*, 381 U.S. 479, 1965.

18. Steven Spencer, "The Birth Control Revolution," *Saturday Evening Post*, January 15, 1960, p. 21.

19. Norman B. Ryder and Charles F. Westoff, "Use of Oral Contraception in the United States, 1965," *Science*, CXXXV (September 9, 1966), pp. 1199-205.

20. Population Council, *Annual Report, 1964* (New York), pp. 10-11, 17-18.

21. Baumgartner, "Governmental Responsibility," p. 444; action memorandum for the administrator, subject: "Executive Staff Discussion of Issues Presented by Population Growth Trends in Less Developed Countries," November 24, 1964. The most-complete published collection of materials relating to AID policy, 1965-66, may be found in *Population Crisis, Hearings on S. 1676*, 89th Cong., 2d sess., 1966, pt. 4, pp. 851-1071.

22. U.S. Agency for International Development, memorandum for the administrator, from Leona Baumgartner, AA/TCR, to Bartlett Harvey, AA/PC, subject: "AID and World Population," December 4, 1964.

23. Horace Busby, memorandum to Francis Bator, February 8, 1965.

24. The text of the airgram, although not identified as such, is given in *Population Crisis, Hearings on S. 1676*, 89th Cong., 2d sess., 1966, pt. 4, pp. 968-70.

25. U.S. Congress, *Congressional Record*, 89th Cong., 2d sess., March 31, 1966, pp. 6978-81 (daily edition).

26. AIDTO Circular FA49, March 6, 1965; AIDTO Circular NA23, March 17, 1965. See also "AID Activity in the Field of Population," in *Population Crisis, Hearings on S. 1676*, 1966, pt. 4, pp. 877-79.

27. U.S. Congress, House of Representatives, Committee on Foreign Affairs, *Foreign Assistance Act of 1965, Hearings on H.R.7750*, 89th Cong., 1st sess. (Washington, D.C., 1965) pp. 37-38.

28. *New York Times*, March 7, 1965, sec. IV, p. 8.

29. Information memorandum for the administrator, subject: "Population," March 2, 1965.

30. Reimert T. Ravenholt, *et al.*, "Oral Contraceptives, A Decade of Controversy," *International Journal of Gynecology and Obstetrics*, VIII, 6 (November 1970), 941-56.

31. Cf. Frederick Osborn, *Population, An International Dilemma* (New York: Population Council, 1958); Carl Taylor, "Health and Population," *Foreign Affairs*, April 1965, p. 486.

32. *Washington Post*, September 10, 1965, p. 1.

33. *New York Times*, April 2, 1966, p. 1, and April 8, 1966, p. 14.

34. Leona Baumgartner, information memorandum for the administrator, subject: "AID and Population Problems," August 11, 1965, pp. 1-5.

35. Leona Baumgartner to David Bell, subject: "Major International Conference on Family Planning Held in 1965—Summary and Implications for AID," October 1965, p. 6.

CHAPTER 11

1. Cf. Stephen K. Bailey, *Congress in the Seventies* (New York: St. Martin's Press, 1970), chap. 3; James A. Robinson, *Congress and Foreign Policy Making* (Homewood, Ill.: Dorsey Press, 1962); David A. Baldwin, "Congressional Initiative in Foreign Policy," *Journal of Politics*, November 1966, pp. 754-73.

2. For a more analytical proof of this statement see Phyllis T. Piotrow, "Congressional-Executive Relations in the Formation of Explicit Population Policy," prepared for the U.S. Commission on Population Growth and the American Future (Washington, D.C., forthcoming).

3. U.S. Congress, Senate, Committee on Government Operations, *Population Crisis, Hearings on S. 1676*, before Subcommittee on Foreign Aid Expenditures, 89th Cong., 1st sess., June 22-23, 1965 (Washington, D.C., 1966), pt. 1, pp. 1-5.

4. *Ibid.*, p. 94.

5. *Ibid.*, pp. 6-7.

6. A complete list of all witnesses and dates of their appearance is in *Population Crisis, Hearings on S. 1676*, 90th Cong., 2d sess., 1968, pt. 4, pp. 1-5.

7. *Population Crisis, Hearings on S. 1676*, 89th Cong., 1st sess., 1966, pt. 1, p. 361; pt. 2, p. 416; pt. 2-A, pp. 728, 799, 834, 844; pt. 2-B, p. 1266.

8. *Planned Parenthood News*, Fall 1957, p. 5.

9. *Population Crisis, Hearings on S. 1676*, 89th Cong., 1st sess., 1966, pt. 2, p. 418.

10. *Ibid.*, p. 1305.

11. *Ibid.*, pt. 2-B, p. 1308.

12. *New York Times*, June 24, 1964, pp. 1, 3; November 27, 1965, p. 1; March 3, 1966, p. 1; March 8, 1966, p. 16; October 3, 1966, p. 1. See also *Population Crisis, Hearings on S. 1676*, 89th Cong., 2d sess., 1966, pp. 385-415; 499-510.

13. *Population Crisis, Hearings on S. 1676*, 89th Cong., 1st sess., 1965, p. 5.

14. *Ibid.*, 90th Cong., 1st sess., 1967, pp. 3-9.

15. *Ibid.*, 89th Cong., 2d sess., 1966, pt. 4, pp. 775-834.

16. *Ibid.*, pp. 778-79.

17. *Ibid.* p. 789.

18. *Ibid.*, p. 811.

19. *Population Crisis, Hearings on S. 1676*, 89th Cong., 1st sess., 1965, p. 858.

20. *New York Times*, March 4, 1966, p. 1.

21. *Population Crisis, Hearings on S. 1676*, 89th Cong., 1st sess., 1965, p. 994.

22. *Ibid.*, p. 993.

23. *Ibid.*, p. 995.

24. *Ibid.*, p. 996.

25. *Population Crisis, Hearings on S. 1676*, 90th Cong., 1st sess., 1967, pp. 1-195. The text of the Harkavy report entitled *Implementing DHEW Policy on Family Planning and Population* is given on pp. 163-208.

26. *Population Crisis, Hearings on S. 1676*, 90th Cong., 2d sess., 1968, pp. 650-53.

248   WORLD POPULATION CRISIS

CHAPTER 12

1. Samuel P. Huntington, *The Common Defense* (Paperback ed., New York: Columbia University Press, 1966), pp. 291-92.

2. Cf. comment by Bernard Berelson at December 20, 1966, State Department briefing, "Arguments for population control should not be based on the food issue alone. The opportunity for a better quality of life is a more appropriate approach. We must not exclude the issue of personal freedom." Working Group on Population Matters, "Minutes of the Fourth Meeting," December 20, 1966, p. 6 (mimeo.). John P. Lewis, "Population Control in India," in Population Reference Bureau, *Population Bulletin*, XXVI, 5 (November 1970), 12-13.

3. Cf. Victor Fund for the International Planned Parenthood Federation, *Can Mass Starvation Be Prevented?* Report No. 7, Fall 1967, pp. 4-30.

4. William Paddock and Paul Paddock, *Famine—1975!* (New York: Little, Brown, 1967).

5. *New York Times*, May 20, 1967, p. 7; May 30, 1965, sec. IV, p. 7. See also U.S. Department of Agriculture, Lester Brown, *Increasing World Food Output: Problems and Prospects*, Report No. 25 (Wahington, D.C., 1965); *Man, Land, and Food*, Report No. 11, (Washington, D.C., 1963).

6. UN Food and Agriculture Organization, *The State of Food and Agriculture, 1965* (Rome, 1965), p. 5.

7. *New York Times*, November 5, 1965, p. 20.

8. *New York Times*, November 29, 1965, p. l.

9. As reprinted in U.S. Congress, House of Representatives, *A War On Hunger, Message from the President of the United States*, 89th Cong., 2d sess., Document No. 378 (Washington, 1966), pp. 3-4.

10. U.S. Congress, Senate, Committee on Government Operations, Subcommittee on Foreign Aid Expenditures, *Population Crisis, Hearings on S. 1676*, 90th Cong., 1st sess., 1967, pt. 1, pp. 3-9.

11. *Ibid.*, pp. 4-5.

12. U.S. Congress, House of Representatives, Committee on Agriculture, *World War on Hunger*, 89th Cong., 2d sess. (Washington, D.C., 1966), serial W, pt. 1.

13 U.S. Congress, *Congressional Record*, February 10, 1966, 89th Cong., 2d sess., (Washington, D.C., 1966), p. 2827.

14. *Population Crisis, Hearings, on S. 1676*, 89th Cong., 2d sess., 1966, pt. 4, pp. 858-59, 964-65.

15. The provisions are Sec. 103(a) and Sec. 405 dealing with self-help criteria; Sec. 104(b)(3) and Sec. 104(h) dealing with uses of local currencies in Public Law 89-808, 89th Cong., 2d sess., H.R. *14929*. Food for Peace Act of 1966, 80 Stat. 1526-1538 as reprinted in U.S. Congress, House of Representatives, *Agricultural Trade Development and Assistance Act of 1954 and Amendments*, compiled by Gilman G. Odell, Document Room (Washington, D.C., 1966), pp. 41, 45, 51.

16. U.S. Congress, House of Representatives, Committee on Agriculture, *The Food for Freedom Act of 1966*, Report No. 1558, 89th Cong., 2d sess. (Washington, D.C., 1966), p. 4.

17. *New York Times*, May 7, 1966, p. 1; May 8, 1966, p. 2.

18. U.S. President, *Statement by the President upon signing H.R. 14929—Food for Freedom Bill*, for release November 13, 1966, p. 2 (mimeo.).

19. Lester W. Milbrath, *The Washington Lobbyists* (Chicago: Rand McNally, 1963), p. 313, 356. Cf. Raymond Bauer, Lewis Dexter, and Ithiel de Sola Pool, *American Business and Public Policy* (New York: Atherton Press, 1968), pt. IV.

20. U.S. Congress, Senate Committee on Foreign Relations, *Foreign Economic Assistance*, Report No. 1359, 89th Cong., 2d sess. (Washington, D.C., 1966), pp. 19-20, 53.

21. *Ibid.*, p. 51.

22. U.S. Congress, House of Representatives, *Conference Report on Foreign Assistance Act of 1966*, H.R. *15750*, Report No. 1927, 89th Cong., 2d sess., (Washington, D.C., 1966), p. 26.

23. *Foreign Economic Assistance*, p. 18.

24. See testimony of Murray Grant, M.D., director of public health, District of Columbia Department of Health, in *Population Crisis, Hearings on S. 1676*, 89th Cong., 1st sess., 1966, pt. 2-B, pp. 1096-97.

25. *H.R. 8440*, 89th Cong., 1st sess. (referred to the Judiciary Committee); *H.R. 8451*, 89th Cong., 1st sess. (referred to the Committee on Ways and Means), U.S. Congress, *Congressional Record*, 89th Cong., 2d sess. (Washington, D.C., 1965), pp. 11186-87.

26. U.S. Congress, Public Law 91-662, January 8, 1971.

27. U.S. Congress, House of Representatives, *Conference Report on H.R. 8283*, Report No. 1061, 89th Cong., 1st sess. (Washington, D.C., 1965), p. 19.

28. U.S. Congress, Public Law 89-794, pp. 10-11.

29. U.S. Congress, Senate, Committee on Labor and Public Welfare, Subcommittee on Employment, Manpower and Poverty, *Family Planning Program, Hearings on S. 2993*, 89th Cong., 2d sess. (Washington, D.C., 1966).

30. *Ibid.*, p. 12.

31. U.S. Congress, *Congressional Record*, 89th Cong., 2d sess. (Washington, D.C., 1966), p. A5564 (October 25, 1966); see also *Ibid.*, p. 23789.

32. See *Population Crisis, Hearings on S. 1676*, 90th Cong., 1st sess., 1967, pt. 1, pp. 76-84.

33. U.S. Congress, *Congressional Record*, 89th Cong., 2d sess. (Washington, D.C., 1966), p. A5564 (October 25, 1966).

CHAPTER 13

1. Interview with Philander P. Claxton, Jr., spring 1970.

2. Leona Baumgartner, "Governmental Responsibility for Family Planning in the United States," in *Fertility and Family Planning in the U.S.*, S. J. Behrman, Leslie Corsa, Jr., and Ronald Freedman, eds., (Ann Arbor: University of Michigan Press, 1969), p. 445.

3. U.S. Congress, *Congressional Record*, 89th Cong., 2d sess., (Washington, D.C., 1966), pp. 6978-81 (March 31, 1966).

4. Interview with Harry McPherson, March 1971.

5. Interview with Philander P. Claxton, Jr., spring 1970.

6. Interview with Richard Gardner, September 17, 1970.

7. Interview with Philander P. Claxton, Jr., spring 1970.

8. U.S. Department of State, action memorandum from Philander P. Claxton, Jr., to the secretary "Statement of Policy on Population Matters," November 1966.

9. Population Crisis Committee, *Population Crisis, A Washington Newsletter*, January-February 1967, p. 5.

10. Luther Carter, "Population Control: U.S. AID Program Leaps Forward," *Science*, LIX, pp. 611-13.

11. Action memorandum for the administrator from A. H. Moseman, September 23, 1966, p. 3.

12. *Ibid.*

13. Interview with William S. Gaud, March 26, 1971.

14. U.S. Agency for International Development, *The War On Hunger, Policy Determination*, Manual Order 1018.4TL 9:86 (Washington, D.C., November 11, 1966), p. 35.

15. *Ibid.*, pp. 1-2.

16. Interview with William S. Gaud, March 26, 1971. Also quoted in David K. Willis, *The State Department* (Boston: Christian Science Publishing Society, 1967), p. 75.

17. *New York Times*, February 10, 1967, p. 16.

18. U.S. Agency for International Development, Office of the War on Hunger, Manual Order 204.3, March 23, 1967.

19. *Ibid.*, p. 4.

20. *Ibid.*

21. U.S. Congress, Senate, Committee on Government Operations, Subcommittee on Foreign Aid Expenditures, *Population Crisis, Hearings on S. 1676*, 89th Cong., 2d sess. (Washington, D.C., 1966), pt. 4, p. 29.

22. U.S. Agency for International Development, *Assistance for Family Planning Programs in Developing Countries* (Washington, D.C., October 1968), p. 17.

23. Carl T. Rowan, "The New U.S. Attitude Toward Birth Control," *Washington Evening Star*, May 22, 1966.

24. U.S. Agency for International Development, *Population Program Assistance* (Washington, D.C., October 1969), pp. 28-47.

25. U.S. Agency for International Development, "AID Loan for Turkey is First for Family Planning Effort," press release AID-GG-107, June 21, 1966.

26. *Population Program Assistance*, p. 31.

27. Interview with William S. Gaud, March 26, 1971.

28. *Population Crisis, Hearings on S. 1676*, 89th Cong., 2d sess., 1967, pp. 856-60; William S. Gaud, "Self Help and Need Given Priority in AID Family Planning Assistance," *War On Hunger, A Monthly News Report*, March 1967, pp. 4-5; *Population Crisis, Hearings on S. 1676*, 90th Cong., 2d sess., 1968, pp. 519-20.

29. Carter, "Population Control."

30. *Ibid.*

CHAPTER 14

1. *New York Times*, January 11, 1967, p. 16.

2. James G. March and Herbert A. Simon, *Organizations* (New York: John Wiley & Sons, 1958), p. 198.

3. U.S. Congress, *Congressional Record*, 90th Cong., 1st sess. (Washington, D.C., 1967), p. S3667 (March 14, 1967).

4. U.S. Congress, *Congressional Record*, 90th Cong., 1st sess. (Washington, D.C., 1967), p. S3666 (March 14, 1967).

5. John D. Rockefeller 3rd and Frank Notestein testified March 9, 1966, before the Far East subcommittee of the Foreign Affairs Committee of the House at an unpublicized session chaired by Clement Zablocki on population problems and programs in the Far East.

6. U.S. Congress, House of Representatives, Committee on Foreign Affairs, *Foreign Assistance Act of 1967, Hearings on ι.R. 7099 and H.R. 12048*, 90th Cong., 1st sess. (Washington, D.C., 1967), pp. 967-1013, 1127-58.

7. *Ibid.*, pp. 968-71.

8. *Ibid.*, p. 1005.

9. *Ibid.*, p. 1068.

10. *Ibid.*, p. 1154.

11. U.S. Congress, House of Representatives, Committee on Foreign Affairs, *Foreign Assistance Act of 1967*, 90th Cong., 1st sess., Report No. 551 (Washington, D.C., 1967), pp. 30-31, 73-74.

12. *Ibid.*, pp. 30-31.

13. Sagar Jain and Steven Sinding, *North Carolina Abortion Law 1967: A Study in Legislative Process*, Monograph 2, Carolina Population Center (Chapel Hill: University of North Carolina, 1968), pp. 52-53.

14. U.S. Congress, *Congressional Record*, 90th Cong., 1st sess. (Washington, D.C., 1967), pp. H11039-H11044 (August 23, 1967).

15. *Ibid.*, p. H11043.

16. *Ibid.*, p. H11042.

17. *Ibid.*, p. H11043. (Cf. *Washington Evening Star*, August 24, 1967, p. A-15).

18. *Ibid.* pp. H11137-11140 (August 24, 1967).

19. *Ibid.*, p. H11140.

20. *Ibid.*

21. U.S. Congress, Senate, Committee on Foreign Relations, *Foreign Assistance Act of 1967, Hearings on S. 1872*, 90th Cong., 1st sess. (Washington, D.C., 1967), pp. 47-74.

22. Cf. *Ibid.*, pp. 48-50, 66.

23. U.S. Congress, House of Representatives, Committee on Foreign Affairs, *Foreign Assistance Act of 1967, Hearings on H.R. 7099 and H.R. 12048*, 90th Cong., 1st sess. (Washington, D.C., 1967), p. 81.

24. *New York Times*, May 11, 1967, p. 36. Also U.S. Agency for International Development, *Removal of Contraceptives from Ineligible Commodity List*, Manual Circular 14543, May 11, 1967.

25. Memorandum for assistant administrators from the administrator, "AID FY 1968 Population Program," July 31, 1967 (typewritten).

26. U.S. Congress, Senate, Committee on Foreign Relations, *Foreign Assistance Act of 1967*, 90th Cong., 1st sess., Senate Report No. 499 (Washington, D.C., 1967), pp. 24, 61.

27. *Ibid.*, pp. 22-24.

28. U.S. Agency for International Development, *Guidelines for Assistance to Population Programs*, Manual Order 1612.57, September 15, 1967, p. 1.

29. Cf. AID press release, September 14, 1967; also *New York Times*, September 15, 1967, p. 1.

30. U.S. Congress, House of Representatives, *Conference Report on Foreign Assistance Act of 1967*, 90th Cong., 1st sess., Report No. 892 (Washington, D.C., 1967), pp. 8-9, 27-28.

31. U.S. Congress, Public Law 90-137, *The Foreign Assistance Act of 1967*, 81 Stat. 453, pp. 7-8.

32. U.S. Congress, Senate, Committee on Appropriations, *Foreign Assistance and Related Agencies Appropriations*, 90th Cong., 1st sess. (Washington, D.C., 1967), pp. 445-47.

33. *Ibid.*, p. 491.

34. U.S. Congress, Public Law 90-249, *Foreign Assistance and Related Agencies Appropriation Act*, 1968, 81 Stat. 936, p. 1.

35. Letter from J. William Fulbright to William S. Gaud, December 22, 1967; letter from William S. Gaud to J. William Fulbright, January 6, 1968.

36. David Bell, "U.S. Domestic and Foreign Policies and World Food Needs," *War on Hunger*, II, 2 (February 1968), 1 (paper presented in October 1967 at the University of Illinois Centennial Symposium).

37. Samuel T. Huntington, *The Common Defense* (New York: Columbia University Press, 1961), pp. 151-52.

38. Cf. Richard F. Fenno, Jr., *The Power of the Purse* (Boston: Little, Brown, 1966), pp. 7-20, pass.

39. U.S. Congress, House of Representatives, Committee on Education and Labor, *Economic Opportunity Amendments of 1967*, 90th Cong., 1st sess., Report No. 866 (Washington, D.C., 1966), pp. 25-26, 109.

40. U.S. Bureau of the Budget, *The Budget for Fiscal Year 1970, Special Analyses*, (Washington, D.C., 1969), p. 167.

41. U.S. Congress, Public Law 90-248, *Social Security Amendments of 1967*, 90th Cong., 1st sess. (Washington, D.C., 1967), p. 102.

42. *Ibid.*, p. 104.

43. *Ibid.*, p. 58.

44. *Ibid.*, p. 106.

45. U.S. Congress, House of Representatives, Committee on Interstate and Foreign Commerce, *Partnership for Health Amendments of 1957*, 90th Cong., 1st sess., Report No. 538 (Washington, D.C., 1967), p. 12-14.

46. U.S. Congress, Senate, Committee on Appropriations, *Report on Labor-Health, Education, and Welfare Appropriations*, 90th Cong., 1st sess. (Washington, D.C., 1967), p. 47.

47. Fenno, *Power of the Purse*, pp. 400-2, 586-89.

48. For an example in Defense Department funding, see R. H. Dawson, "Congressional Innovation and Intervention in Defense Policy: Legislative Authorization of Weapons Systems," *American Political Science Review*, LXVI (1962), pp. 42-57. Significantly, although the Family Planning Services and Population Research Act of

1970, Public Law 91-572, provides a three-year additional authorization and thus review procedure for population research at NIH, NIH has refused to request additional funds under that act in order to avoid both the perils and the possible innovations of an annual or frequent authorization.

49. Cf. Phyllis T. Piotrow, "Congressional-Executive Relations in the Formation of Explicit Population Policy," prepared for U.S. Commission on Population Growth and The American Future, *Research Papers*. (Washington, D.C., forthcoming).

CHAPTER 15

1. Cf. U.S. President, *The Foreign Assistance Program: Annual Report to the Congress, Fiscal Year 1968* (Washington, D.C., 1968), pp. 3-4; also U.S. President, *The Foreign Assistance Program: Annual Report to the Congress, Fiscal Year 1969* (Washington, D.C., 1969), pp. 4-7.

2. Milton Esman, "Institution-Building as a Guide to Action" (paper delivered at AID Conference on Institution Building and Technical Assistance, Washington, D.C., December 4, 1959, mimeo.).

3. U.S., Congress, House of Representatives, Committee on Foreign Affairs, *Foreign Assistance Act of 1968, Hearings on H.R. 15263*, 90th Cong., 2d sess., April 24, 1968 (Washington, D.C., 1968), pp. 103.

4. *Ibid.*, p. 1035.

5. *Ibid.*, p. 1050.

6. U.S., Congress, *Congressional Record*, 90th Cong., 2d sess., July 18, 1968 (Washington, D.C., 1968), p. H6968.

7. U.S. Congress, Senate, Committee on Foreign Relations, House of Representatives, Committee on Foreign Affairs, *Legislation on Foreign Relations*, 90th Cong., 2d sess. (Washington, D.C., January 1, 1969), p. 9.

8. U.S. Agency for International Development, *Population Program Assistance*, (Washington, D.C., October 1970), p. 182.

9. U.S. Congress, Senate, Committee on Government Operations, Subcommittee on Foreign Aid Expenditures, *Population Crisis, Hearings on S. 1676*, 89th Cong., 2d sess. (Washington, D.C., 1966), pt. 4, pp. 859, 867; *ibid.*, 90th Cong., 2d sess., 1968, pt. 3, pp. 623-25.

10. Comment made at meeting of AID Research Advisory Committee, November 1968.

11. AIDTO Circular Airgram X 3309, January 13, 1968, pp. 1-2.

12. Cf. *Population Crisis, Hearings on S. 1676*, 90th Cong., 2d sess., 1968, pt. 3, p. 519.

13. Reimert T. Ravenholt, "The A.I.D. Population and Family Planning Program—Goals, Scope, and Progress," *Demography*, V, 2 (1968), 564-671.

14. *Ibid.*, p. 571. Also R. T. Ravenholt, "AID's Family Planning Strategy," *Science*, CLXIII (January 10, 1969), p. 124.

15. Kingsley Davis, "Population Policy: Will Current Programs Succeed?" *Science* CLVIII (November 10, 1967), p. 124.

16. Fred Jaffe, "Family Planning and Public Policy: Is the 'Culture of Poverty' the New Cop-Out?" as reprinted in *Population Crisis, Hearings on S. 1676*, 90th Cong., 1st sess., 1967, pp. 195-202.

17. Judith Blake, "Population Policy for Americans: Is the Government Being Misled?" *Science*, CLXIV (May 2, 1964), pp. 522-29.

18. Interview with Bernard Berelson, April 1970.

19. Bernard Berelson, "Beyond Family Planning," *Studies in Family Planning*. No. 38, February 1969.

20. Charles F. Westoff and Norman B. Ryder, "Use of Oral Contraception in the United States, 1965," *Science*, CLIII (September 9, 1966), pp. 1199-205.

21. Reimert T. Ravenholt and Phyllis T. Piotrow, "Use of Oral Contraceptives in Developing Countries," *Pakistan Journal of Medical Research*, VIII (1969), p. 213.

22. Cf. Reimert T. Ravenholt *et al.*, "Oral Contraceptives: A Decade of Controversy," *International Journal of Gynecology and Obstetrics*, VIII, 6 (November 1968), 941-42.

23. AIDTO Circular Airgram XA 3538, June 19, 1968; AIDTO Circular Airgram AG 12, March 17, 1970.

24. Samuel P. Huntington, *The Common Defense* (New York: Columbia University Press, 1961), pp. 289, 307-8, 328.

25. Letter from William H. Draper, Jr., to Rutherford Poats, acting administrator, AID, May 15, 1969.

26. James G. March and Herbert A. Simon, *Organizations* (New York: John Wiley & Sons, 1958), p. 198.

27. Oscar Harkavy, "The Role of Foundations in Population Research and Planning," speech delivered at the Johns Hopkins University, June 9, 1965, p. 2.

28. Herbert A. Simon, "Birth of an Organization: The Economic Cooperation Administration," *Public Administration Review*, December 1953, p. 234.

29. *New York Times*, July 30, 1968, pp. 1, 30.

30. *New York Times*, September 1, 1968, p. 46.

31. Population Crisis Committee, *Population Crisis, A Washington Newsletter*, October 1968, p. 3. (Concerning Public Law 90-436.)

32. *New York Times*, September 7, 1968, p. 18.

33. Population Crisis Committee, *Population Crisis*, p. 6.

34. Interview with William S. Gaud, March 26, 1971.

35. U.S. President's Committee on Population and Family Planning, *Population and Family Planning: The Transition from Concern to Action* (Washington, D.C., 1968), pp. 21-26.

36. *Ibid.*, p. 36.

37. *Ibid.*, p. 12.

38. For comparison of these figures, which are found in varying forms in U.S. Bureau of the Budget, *Budget for Fiscal Year 1970, 1971: Special Analyses* (Washington, D.C., 1969, 1970), pp. 167 and 126, the best source is *Planned Parenthood, Memorandum 4.2* from the Washington office, February 18, 1969, p. 1.

CHAPTER 16

1. U.S. Congress, *Congressional Record*, 91st Cong., 1st sess. (Washington, D.C., 1969), pp. S4108-4111.

2. U.S. Congress, Senate, Committee on Government Operations, *Population Crisis, Hearings on S. 1676*, before Subcommittee on Foreign Aid Expenditures, 89th Cong., 1st sess. (Washington, D.C., 1965), pt. 1, p. 63.

3. U.S. Congress, *Congressional Record*, 91st Cong., 1st sess. (Washington, D.C., 1965), p. 43048 (April 23, 1969). For a complete list of population bills introduced in the 91st Congress, 1st sess., see Population Crisis Committee, *Population Crisis, A Washington Newsletter*, June 1969, p. 5; September 1969, p. 3; March 1970 (unpaged).

4. For a report on the task force hearings and recommendations, see U.S. Congress, *Congressional Record*, 91st Cong., 1st sess. (Washington, D.C., 1969), pp. E11014-E11018 (December 29, 1969).

5. National Association of State Universities and of Land Grant Colleges Task Force on International Developmental Assistance and International Education, John A. Hannah, chairman, *International Developmental Assistance*, January 1969 (unpaged); also speech by John Hannah to Annual Convention of State Universities and Land Grant Colleges, Chicago, Ill., November 11, 1969, p. 8.

6. *New York Times*, May 29, 1969, p. 14.

7. U.S. Agency for International Development, "Technical Assistance Bureau Aims at Stronger AID Programs in '70s," press release, September 24, 1969.

8. Letter from General William H. Draper, Jr., to Rutherford B. Poats, May 15, 1969.

9. Interview with William S. Gaud, March 26, 1971.

10. U.S. Congress, Senate, Committee on Foreign Relations, *Foreign Assistance Act, 1969, Hearings on S. 2347*, 91st Cong., 1st sess. (Washington, D.C., 1969), p$_i$ 71-72.

11. U.S. Congress, House of Representatives, Committee on Foreign Affairs, *Foreign Assistance Act of 1969, Hearings on H.R. 11792*, 91st Cong., 1st sess. (Washington, D.C., 1969), pp. 1105-7.

12. The White House, "Memorandum for Honorable William P. Rogers, Secretary of State," July 15, 1969, signed Daniel P. Moynihan.

13. *New York Times*, July 19, 1969, p. 8. Also U.S. Department of State, *Department of State Bulletin*, August 11, 1969.

CHAPTER 17

1. L. P. Chow *et al.*, "Correlates of IUD Termination in a Mass Family Planning Program," *Studies in Family Planning*, No. 24, December 1967, pp. 13-16.

2. Gavin W. Jones and W. Parker Mauldin, "Use of Oral Contraceptives," *Studies in Family Planning*, No. 24, December 1967, pp. 1-13.

3. U.S. Agency for International Development, "Conference on Direction and Support of Research in Technical Methods for Controlling Human Reproduction, Summary of Discussion," January 26, 1968, p. 15 (typewritten).

4. John Walsh, "NIH: Agency and Clients React to Retrenchment," *Science*, CLXV (September 20, 1969), p. 1331.

5. *New York Times*, November 6, 1967, p. 1.

6. David Bell, "U.S. Domestic and Foreign Policies and World Food Needs," *War on Hunger*, Vol. II (February 1968), p. 1.

7. U.S. Congress, House of Representatives, Committee on Interstate and Foreign Commerce, Subcommittee on Public Health and Welfare, *Family Planning Services*, 91st Cong., 2d sess., serial 91-70, (Washington, D.C., 1970) p. 106; also Walsh, "NIH: Agency and Clients React," pp. 1332-34.

8. AID, "Conference on Direction and Support of Research," p. 30.

9. Oscar Harkavy, "Implementing DHEW Policy on Family Planning and Population," reprinted in U.S. Congress, Senate, Committee on Government Operations, *Population Crisis, Hearings on S. 1676*, before Subcommittee on Foreign Aid Expenditures, 90th Cong., 1st sess. (Washington, D.C., 1967), pt. 1, pp. 202-7.

10. AID, "Conference on Direction and Support of Research," p. 6.

11. Letters from John Lewis to Philip R. Lee, May 9, 1968, and to William R. Gaud, May 19, 1968.

12. Letter from Chester Bowles to Philander Claxton, Jr., May 15, 1968.

13. Frances Gulick, "The Indian Family Planning Program: The Need for New Contraceptives," Staff Memorandum, U.S. AID/India, April, 1968 (mimeo.).

14. Letter from David Bell to William S. Gaud, March 19, 1968.

15. Letter from William S. Gaud to David Bell, April 16, 1968.

16. U.S. Agency for International Development, Action memorandum for the administrator from AA/WOH, Irwin Hedges, May 24, 1968.

17. Interview with Rutherford Poats, March 1971.

18. Letter from Reimert T. Ravenholt to William H. Draper, Jr., March 14, 1968. A similar definition of the ideal contraceptive appears in U.S. Agency for International Development, *Population Program Assistance* (Washington, D.C., October 1969), p. 16.

19. Letter from William S. Gaud to David Bell, April 16, 1968.

20. Luther Carter, "Contraceptive Technology: Advances Needed in Fundamental Research," *Science*, CLXVIII (May 15, 1970), pp. 805-7.

21. Accounts of the prostaglandin research are provided in "Search Widens for Better Family Planning Methods," *War on Hunger*, July 1970; also memorandum to AA/TA Joel Bernstein from R. T. Ravenholt and J. J. Speidel, "Prostaglandins,"

September 28, 1970, and attachments; also New York Academy of Sciences, *Prostaglandins* (New York, 1971).

22. AID, *Population Program Assistance*, October 1969, p. 16.

23. John Walsh, "NIH: Agency and Clients React," pp. 1332-34; also Carter, "Contraceptive Technology," pp. 805-7.

24. Robert Gillette, "Population Act: Proponents Dismayed at Funding Levels," *Science*, CLXXI (March 26, 1971), pp. 1222-24.

25. Cf. Allen L. Hammond, "Aspirin: New Perspective on Everyman's Medicine," *Science*, CLXXIV (October 1, 1971), p. 48.

26. Laurence Galton, "The New Mystery—Maybe Miracle—Drug" *New York Times Magazine*, December 5, 1971, p. 46.

27. U.S. Agency for International Development, Memorandum to the Administrator and others, Subject: "India's Population—Family Planning Program," September 6, 1969.

28. AID, *Population Program Assistance*, p. 186.

29. U.S. Agency for International Development, *Examples of Countries with Various Problems and How AID is Dealing with Them*, July 1972, pp. 1-3 (mimeo.).

30. U.S. Congress, Senate, Committee on Appropriations, *Foreign Assistance and Related Programs Appropriation Bill, 1972*, 92d Cong., 2d sess., Report 92-594 (Washington, D.C., 1972), p. 23.

31. John P. Lewis, "Population in India," in Harrison Brown and Edward Hutchings, Jr., eds., *Are Our Descendants Doomed?* (New York: Viking Press, 1970), pp. 243.

32. W. H. W. Inman and M. P. Vessey, "Investigation of Deaths from Pulmonary, Coronary and Cerebral Thrombosis and Embolism in Women of Child-Bearing Age," *British Medical Journal*, 2 (April 1968), pp. 193-99; M. P. Vessey and R. Doll, "Investigations of Relation Between Use of Oral Contraceptives and Thromboembolic Disease: A Further Report," *British Medical Journal*, 2 (June 1969), pp. 651-57; P. E. Sartwell *et al.*, "Thromboembolism and Oral Contraceptives: An Epidemiologic Case-Control Study," *American Journal of Epidemiology* XC (November 1969), pp. 365-80. See also U.S. Congress, Senate, Select Committee on Small Business, Subcommittee on Monopoly, *Competitive Problems in the Drug Industry, Oral Contraceptives*, 91st Cong., 1st sess. (Washington, D.C., 1970), Vols. 1-3.

33. Personal communication from George Wyeth, USAID; also Purchase Order Report, computer print-out, July 15, 1972. Cf. AID, *Population Program Assistance*, December 1971, pp. 29-33.

34. AID, *Population Program Assistance*, December 1971, pp. 38-40, 222-23.

35. AID, *Population Program Assistance*, October 1970, pp. 22.

36. *U.S. Foreign Assistance in the 1970's: A New Approach, Report to the President from The Task Force on International Development* (Washington, D.C., March 4, 1970), pp. 29-30.

37. *Ibid.*, pp. 16-18.

38. U.S. Congress, *Congressional Record*, 92d Cong., 2d sess. (Washington, D.C., 1972), pp. S17056-57 (October 28, 1971).

39. *Ibid.*, (November 10, 1971) pp. S18111-S18113.

40. 92d Cong., Public Law 92-226, S.2819, February 7, 1972, sec. 106, p. 3.

41. U.S. Congress, House of Representatives, *Foreign Assistance and Related Programs Appropriations Bill, 1972*, 92d Cong., 1st sess., Report 92-711 (Washington, D.C., 1971), pp. 12-14.

42. U.S. Congress, Senate, Committee on Appropriations, *Foreign Assistance and Related Programs Appropriations Bill, 1972*, 92d Cong., 2d sess., Report 92-594 (Washington, D.C., 1972), pp. 21-22.

43. U.S. Congress, House of Representatives, *Foreign Assistance Appropriations*, 92d Cong., 2d sess., Report 92-849 (Washington, D.C., 1972), p. 4.

44. U.S. Agency for International Development, "Report to the Administrator," December 13, 1971, signed Ernest Stern, Philip Birnbaum, and Thomas Arndt.

45. U.S. Agency for International Development, *Front Lines*, X, 7 (February 10, 1972), 5-8.

46. U.S. Agency for International Development, Meritorious Unit Citation to Office of Population, Technical Assistance Bureau, April 18, 1972.

CHAPTER 18

1. Durward L. Allen, "Population, Resources, and the Great Complexity," Washington, D.C., March 5, 1969 (speech delivered at the 34th North American Wildlife and Natural Resources Conference, mimeo.).

2. Kenneth Boulding, *The Meaning of the 20th Century* (New York: Harper and Row Publishers, 1963), p. 192.

3. Jean Mayer, "Toward a Non-Malthusian Population Policy" *Columbia Forum*, Summer 1969, pp. 5-13.

4. National Academy of Sciences, Committee on Resources and Man, *Resources and Man* (San Francisco: Freeman, 1969), p. 2.

5. *Ibid.*, p. 11.

6. U.S. Congress, House of Representatives, Committee on Government Operations, Subcommittee on Conservation and Natural Resources, *Effects of Population Growth on National Resources and the Environment*, 91st Cong., 1st sess. (Washington, D.C., 1969). Also, Luther J. Carter, "The Population Crisis: Rising Concern at Home," *Science*, CLXVI (November 7, 1969), pp. 722-26.

7. Lawrence Lader, *Breeding Ourselves to Death* (New York: Ballantine Books, 1971), pp. 55, 79-81.

8. *New York Times*, October 2, 1969, p. 49.

9. *Life*, LXVIII, 14 (April 17, 1970), cover and p. 33.

10. Roger Revelle, "Paul Ehrlich: New High Priest of Ecocatastrophe," *Perspectives*, III, 2 (April 1971), 65-68.

11. Frank Notestein, "Zero Population Growth: What is it?" *Perspectives*, II, 3 (June 1970), 21-22.

12. Tomas Frejka, "Reflections on the Demographic Condition Needed to Establish a U.S. Stationary Population Growth," *Population Studies*, XXII (November 1968), p. 388.

13. Larry Barnett, "Demographic Factors in Attitudes Towards Population Growth and Control," *Journal of Biosocial Science*, IV (1972), p. 9.

14. U.S. Department of Health, Education, and Welfare, National Center for Health Statistics, *Monthly Vital Statistics Report*, XX, 12 (February 28, 1972).

15. *Washington Post*, September 7, 1971, p. 1.

16. John F. Kantner, "American Attitudes on Population Policy: Recent Trends," *Studies in Family Planning*, No. 30 (May 1968), p. 6.

17. U.S. Commission on Population Growth and the American Future, "National Public Opinion Survey," to be published with *Research Reports* (forthcoming), question no. 14.

18. *Ibid.*, no. 17a.

19. *Ibid.*, no. 17b.

20. *Ibid.*, no. 17d.

21. *Ibid.*, no. 33.

22. Garrett Hardin, "The Tragedy of the Commons," *Science*, CLXII (December 13, 1968), pp. 1243-48.

23. "National Public Opinion Survey," no. 17f.

24. *Ibid.*, no. 46.

25. Larry Bumpass and Charles Westoff, "The 'Perfect Contraceptive' Population," *Science*, CLXIX (September 1970), pp. 117-82.

26. Harriet Pilpel, "Brief Survey of U.S. Population Law," *Law and Population Series*, No. 2 (Tufts University), p. 5.

27. "Washington Women's Liberation Statement on Birth Control Pills," in U.S. Congress, Senate, Select Committee on Small Business, Subcommittee on Monopoly,

Competitive Problems in the Drug Industry: Oral Contraceptives, 91st Cong., 2d sess. (Washington, 1970), pt. 17, pp. 7283-95.

28. *New York Times*, April 4, 1971.

29. *New York Times*, May 7, 1972, p. 1.

30. *New York Times*, May 14, 1971, p. 1.

31. Judith Blake, "Abortion and Public Opinion: The 1960-1970 Decade," *Science*, CLXXI (February 12, 1971), p. 541.

32. *Ibid.*, p. 544.

33. Gerald Lipson and Dianne Wolman, "Polling Americans on Birth Control and Population," *Perspectives*, IV, 1 (January 1972), 38-40.

34. *Ibid.*, p. 38.

35. U.S. Commission on Population Growth and the American Future, *Population Growth and America's Future, An Interim Report* (Washington, D.C., March, 1971), p. 47.

36. U.S. Congress, Senate, Committee on Labor and Public Welfare, Subcommittee on Health, *Family Planning and Population Research, 1970*, 91st Cong., 1st and 2d sess. (Washington, D.C., 1970), pp. 109-81.

37. U.S. Congress, *Congressional Record*, 92d Cong., 2d sess. (Washington, D.C., 1972), p. H-10276 (November 16, 1972).

38. Public Law 91-572, Sec. 1008.

39. *Population Growth and America's Future, An Interim Report*, p. 25.

40. Senate Joint Resolution 108, introduced June 2, 1971.

41. U.S. Commission on Population Growth and the American Future, *Population Growth and the American Future* (Signet spec. ed.; New York: New American Library, 1972), pp. 3-6.

42. *Ibid.*, p. 3.

43. *Ibid.*, p. 192.

44. *Ibid.*, p. 53.

45. *Ibid.*, p. 178.

46. *Ibid.*, pp. 189-90.

47. *New York Times*, May 6, p. 1.

48. Samuel P. Huntington, *The Common Defense* (New York: Columbia University Press, 1961), p. 429.

CHAPTER 19

1. John W. Halderman, "Programs of the United Nations and Associated Agencies," in *Population and Law*, Luke T. Lee and Arthur Larson, eds., (Durham, N.C.: Rule of Law Press, 1971), pp. 388-436.

2. General Assembly Resolution 2211 (XXI), December 1966.

3. United Nations Office of Public Information, *Statement by Secretary-General U Thant on Population Problems*, Press Release SG/SM/620 Rev. 1, 9 December 1966, p. 3.

4. *Ibid.*

5. *Ibid.*

6. United Nations, *Final Act of the International Conference on Human Rights* (Teheran, 1968), p. 14.

7. *New York Times*, May 19, 1966.

8. World Health Assembly 19.43, May 20, 1966; 18.49, May 21, 1965.

9. World Health Assembly 21.43, May 23, 1968.

10. United Nations General Assembly Resolution 1838 (XVII), December 1962.

11. United Nations Economic and Social Council, XXXIX, *Official Records* (E/SR.1369), July 5, 1965, p. 29; Resolution 1084 (XXXIX).

12. United Nations, *World Population: Challenge to Development*, New York, 1966 (E/Conf. 41/1).

13. Food and Agriculture Organization of the United Nations, *The State of Food and Agriculture* (Rome: 1965) pp. 1-4.

14. United Nations General Assembly Resolution 2211 (XXI), December 1966.
15. Victor Bostrom Fund Committee, *The United Nations and the Population Crisis*, No. 8, Spring 1968, p. 14.
16. *Ibid.*, p. 13.
17. Population Crisis Committee, Press Release, May 2, 1962, p. 2 (mimeo.).
18. United Nations *Aide-Memoire, Additional Financing of the Expanded United Nations Population Program*, n.d.; *A Further Note on Additional Financing of the Expanded Program of the United Nations in the Field of Population*, July 7, 1967.
19. Letter from Julia Henderson, officer-in-charge, United Nations Economic and Social Affairs, to William H. Draper, Jr., July 11, 1967, SO 314(9) and enclosures.
20. United Nations *Aide-Memoire, Additional Financing*, p. 3.
21. United Nations, *Report on the United Nations Trust Fund for Population Activities and the Role of the United Nations in Population Action Programs*, June 9, 1969 (ST/SOA/SER. r/10), para. 50.
22. *Ibid.*, para. 59.
23. *Ibid.*, para. 49.
24. Nafis Sadik, "Introduction to Joint Discussion of Donors and Recipients" in *International Assistance for Population Programs*, edited by Development Centre of the Organization of Economic Cooperation and Development, Paris, 1970, pp. 162-63.
25. Victor-Bostrom Fund Report, in *ibid.*, p. 12.
26. Letter from William H. Draper, Jr., to Paul Hoffman, April 24, 1968.
27. United Nations Economic and Social Council, Resolution 1347 (XLV), 1968.
28. United Nations, *Report on the United Nations Trust Fund*, para. 56.
29. United Nations, *International Development Strategy* (New York, 1970), para. 15.
30. United Nations Association of the USA, *World Population* (New York, 1969), p. 22.
31. United Nations, *Procedures for Providing and Utilizing the United Nations Fund for Population Activities*, May 6, 1969, p. 3 (typewritten).
32. UNDP, *United Nations Fund for Population Activities Projects Approved for Financing during 1969*, UNFPA/AB/III/2, prepared for Advisory Board February 1-2, 1971.
33. *Principles and Procedures*, Draft 12/X11/69, p. 3.
34. *Review of Major Projects*, February 10, 1972, UNFPA/AB/IV/4, p. 1.
35. UNFPA *Principles and Procedures*, pp. 12-13.
36. UNFPA, *Tentative Work Plan*, February 20, 1972, UNFPA/AB/IV/2, para. 14.
37. *Ibid.*, para. 15.
38. UNFPA, *Principles and Procedures*, p. 12.
39. United Nations Economic and Social Council, Population Commission, *Report of the Sixteenth Session*, official records, 52d sess. (November 1-12, 1971, E/5090), E/CN.9/236, Supp. 3, paras. 168-71. See also *The Feasibility of Establishing a World Population Training Institute*, report of a United Nations (UNESCO) WHO mission, ST/SOA/SER 12.12, New York, 1970.
40. For full membership, see UNFPA, *The Population Fund*, New York, 1971 (unpaged brochure).
41. United Nations Economic and Social Council, *Population Commission, Report of the Fifteenth Session*, official records, 48th sess. (November 3-14, 1969), E/4768, E/CN.9/235, Supp. 3, para. 61.
42. United Nations Economic and Social Council, *Population Commission, Report of the Sixteenth Session*, official records, 52d sess., Supp. 3 (November 1-12, 1971), E/5090, E/CN.9/263, p. 47, para. D4(d).
43. United Nations General Assembly Resolution 2815 (XXVI), December 15, 1971.
44. UNFPA, *The Proposed Committee of the UNFPA Advisory Board* (February 10, 1972), UNFPA/AB/IV/3 Rev. 2.

45. United Nations Economic and Social Council, Resolution No. 1672 (LII), *Population and Development* (June 13, 1972), para. B5(c).

46. *Ibid.*, B5(b).

47. United Nations, *A Study of the Capacity of the UN Development System* (Geneva, 1969), Vol. 1, p. iii.

48. AID, *Front Lines*, September 19, 1969, p. 3.

49. OECD, International Assistance for Population Programs, p. 169.

50. UNECOSOC, *Population and Development*, B 4.

CHAPTER 20

1. Kingsley Davis, *The Population of India and Pakistan* (Princeton: Princeton University Press, 1951), p. 34.

2. U.S. Congress, House of Representatives, Committee on Foreign Affairs, *Foreign Assistance Act of 1962*, 87th Cong. 2d sess. (April 18, 1962), p. 1108.

3. Robert A. Dahl, *Preface to A Democratic Theory* (Chicago: University of Chicago Press, 1954), p. 34.

4. Theodore Sorenson, *Decision-Making in the White House* (New York: Columbia University Press, 1963), p. 133.

5. E. Schoette, "The State of the Art in Policy Studies," in *The Study of Policy Formation*, Raymond A. Bauer and Kenneth J. Gergen, eds. (New York: Free Press, 1968), pp. 149-79.

6. Robert C. Tucker, "The Theory of Charismatic Leadership," *Daedalus*, XCVII (Summer 1968), pp. 731-56.

7. James N. Rosenau, *Public Opinion and Foreign Policy* (New York: Random House, 1961, 1970), pp. 39-41.

8. Fred I. Greenstein, *Personality and Politics: Problems of Evidence, Influence and Conceptualization* (Chicago: Markham Publishing, 1969), p. 42.

9. Allen Potter, "Attitude Groups," *Political Quarterly*, XXIX (January-March 1958), p. 72.

10. James B. Christoph, *Capital Punishment and British Politics* (Chicago: University of Chicago Press, 1962), p. 188.

11. R. Dowse and J. Peel, "The Politics of Birth Control," *Political Studies*, XIII (1958), 182.

12. Peter Marris and Martin Rein, *Dilemmas of Social Reform* (New York: Atherton Press, 1967), pp. 234-36.

13. *Ibid.*, p. 34.

14. Anthony R. Measham, *Family Planning in North Carolina: The Politics of a Lukewarm Issue* (Chapel Hill: Carolina Population Center, 1972).

15. Carl Taylor, "Five Steps in a Practical Population Policy," *International Development Review*, X, 4 (December 1968), p. 2.

16. Marris and Rein, *Dilemmas of Social Reform*, p. 211.

17. Dowse and Peel, "Politics of Birth Control," p. 196.

18. Theodore J. Lowi, *The End of Liberalism* (New York: W. W. Norton, 1969), pp. 55-84.

19. Marver H. Bernstein, *Regulating Business by Independent Commission* (Princeton: Princeton University Press, 1955), pp. 74-102.

20. Samuel J. Eldersveld, "American Interest Groups: A Survey of Research and Some Implications for Theory and Method," in *Interest Groups on Four Continents*, Henry W. Ehrmann, ed. (Pittsburgh: University of Pittsburgh Press, 1958), p. 187.

21. Sorenson, *Decision-Making*, p. 43.

22. Anthony Downs, *Inside Bureaucracy* (Santa Monica: RAND 1967), p. 134.

23. Edward Banfield, *Political Influence* (New York: Free Press, 1961), p. 27.

24. Woodrow Wilson, *Congressional Government* (Cleveland: World Publishing, 1956), p. 190.

25. U.S. Congress, Senate, Committee on Labor and Public Welfare, *Declaration of United States Policy of Population Stabilization by Voluntary Means*, 92d Cong., 1st sess., Washington, D.C., 1971.

26. John Wahlke and Heins Eulau, *The Legislative System: Explorations in Legislative Behavior* (New York: John Wiley & Sons, 1962), pp. 254-56, 266.

27. Christoph, *Capital Punishment*, p. 173.

28. *Ibid.*, p. 174.

29. Samuel P. Huntington, *The Common Defense* (New York: Columbia University Press, 1961), pp. 353-68.

SELECTED BIBLIOGRAPHY

BOOKS

American Assembly. *The Population Dilemma.* Englewood Cliffs, N.J.: Prentice-Hall, 1963.

Balfour, Marshall, *et al. Public Health and Demography in the Far East.* New York: Rockefeller Foundation, 1950.

Bauer, Raymond A., and Kenneth J. Gergen. *The Study of Policy Formation.* New York: Free Press, 1968.

_____, Ithiel de Sola Pool, and Lewis A. Dexter. *American Business and Public Policy.* New York: Atherton Press, 1963.

Behrman, S. J., Leslie Corsa, Jr., and Ronald Freedman, eds. *Fertility and Family Planning: A World View.* Ann Arbor: University of Michigan Press, 1969.

Berelson, Bernard, ed. *Family Planning and Population Programs.* Chicago: University of Chicago Press, 1966.

Brayer, Franklin T., ed. *World Population and U.S. Government Policy and Progress.* Washington, D.C.: Georgetown University Press, 1968.

Brown, Harrison, and Edward Hutchings, Jr., eds. *Are Our Descendants Doomed?* New York: Viking Press, 1971.

Callahan, Daniel P. *The Mind of the Catholic Layman.* New York: Charles Scribner's Sons, 1963.

Coale, Ansley, and Edgar M. Hoover. *Population Growth and Economic Development in Low Income Countries: A Case Study of India's Prospects.* Princeton: Princeton University Press, 1958.

Cronin, Thomas E., and Sanford D. Greenberg, eds. *The Presidential Advisory System.* New York: Harper and Row Publishers, 1969.

Davis, Kingsley. *The Population of India and Pakistan.* Princeton: Princeton University Press, 1951.

Downs, Anthony. *Inside Bureaucracy.* Santa Monica: Rand, 1967.

Ehrlich, Paul. *The Population Bomb.* New York: Ballantine Books, 1968.

Eldersveld, Samuel J. "American Interest Groups: A Survey of Research and Some Implications for Theory and Method," in *Interest Groups on Four Continents.* Henry W. Ehrmann, ed. Pittsburgh: University of Pittsburgh Press, 1958.

Eldridge, Hope T. *Population Policies: A Survey of Recent Developments.* Washington, D.C.: International Union for the Scientific Study of Population, 1954.

Fagley, Richard F. *The Population Explosion and Christian Responsibility.* New York and London: Oxford University Press, 1960.

Fenno, Richard F., Jr. *The Power of the Purse.* Boston: Little, Brown, 1966. Freedman, Ronald, Pascal K. Whelpton, and Arthur K. Campbell. *Family Planning, Sterility and Population Growth.* New York: McGraw-Hill, 1959.

Freeman, J. L. *The Political Process, Executive Bureau—Legislative Committee Relations.* New York: Doubleday, 1955.

Gardner, Richard N. *New Directions in U.S. Foreign Policy.* New York: Foreign Policy Association, 1959.

Gilpin, Robert, and Christopher Wright. *Scientists and National Policy Making.* New York: Columbia University Press, 1964.

Greenstein, Fred I. *Personality and Politics: Problems of Evidence, Influence and Conceptualization.* Chicago: Markham Publishing, 1969.

Lee, Luke T., and Arthur Larson, eds. *Population and Law.* Durham, N.C.: Rule of Law Press, 1971.

Hardin, Garrett, ed. *Population, Evolution and Birth Control.* San Francisco: W. H. Freeman, 1964.

Hauser, P. M., and Otis D. Duncan, eds. *The Study of Population: An Inventory and Appraisal. Part I, Demography as a Science.* Chicago: University of Chicago Press, 1959.

Hill, Reuben, J. Mayone Stycos, and Kurt W. Back. *The Family and Population Control.* Chapel Hill: University of North Carolina Press, 1959.

Himes, Norman. *Medical History of Contraception.* New York: Gamut Press, 1936.

Hsu, S. C. *From Taboo to National Policy: The Taiwan Family Planning up to 1970.* Taiwan: Chinese Center for International Training in Family Planning (n.d.).

Huntington, Samuel P. *The Common Defense.* New York: Columbia University Press, 1961.

Kennedy, David. *Birth Control in America: The Career of Margaret Sanger.* New Haven: Yale University Press, 1970.

Jain, Sagar, and Steven Sinding. *North Carolina Abortion Law, 1967: A Study in Legislative Process.* Monograph 2, Carolina Population Center. Chapel Hill: University of North Carolina Press, 1968.

Kiser, Clyde V., ed. *Research in Family Planning.* Princeton: Princeton University Press, 1968.

————, Wilson H. Grabill, and Arthur A. Campbell. *Trends and Variations in Fertility in the United States.* Cambridge, Mass.: Harvard University Press, 1968.

Koya, Yoshio. *Pioneering in Family Planning.* Tokyo: Japan Medical Publishers, 1967.

Lader, Lawrence. *Breeding Ourselves to Death.* New York: Ballantine Books, 1971.

Lane, Robert E. *Political Life.* New York: Free Press, 1959.

Lasswell, Harold D. *The Decision Process: Seven Categories of Functional Analysis.* College Park: Bureau of Government Research, University of Maryland, 1956.

Leibenstein, Harvey. *Economic Backwardness and Economic Growth.* New York: John Wiley & Sons, 1957.

Lenski, Gerhard. *The Religious Factor.* New York: Doubleday, 1961.

Lindblom, Charles. *The Policy-Making Process.* Englewood Cliffs, N.J.: Prentice-Hall, 1968.

Lerner, David, and Harold Lasswell. *The Policy Sciences.* Stanford: Stanford University Press, 1951.

March, J. G., and Herbert A. Simon. *Organizations.* New York: John Wiley & Sons, 1958.

Marris, Peter, and Martin Rein. *Dilemmas of Social Reform.* New York: Atherton Press, 1967.

Mason, Edward S. *Foreign Aid and Foreign Policy.* New York: Harper and Row Publishers, 1964.

Meadows, D., et al. *The Limits to Growth.* New York: Universe Books, 1972.

Measham, Anthony. *Family Planning in North Carolina: The Politics of a Lukewarm Issue.* Chapel Hill: Carolina Population Center, 1972.

Meier, Richard. *Modern Science and the Fertility Problem.* New York: John Wiley & Sons, 1959.

Milbrath, Lester. *The Washington Lobbyists.* Chicago: Rand McNally, 1963.

Myrdal, Gunnar. *Asian Drama.* 3 Volumes. New York and Toronto: Random House, 1958.

National Association of State Universities and Land Grant Colleges, Task Force on International Developmental Assistance and International Education. *International Developmental Assistance.* January, 1969.

National Academy of Sciences, National Research Council, Committee on Resources. *Resources and Man.* San Francisco: W. H. Freeman, 1969.

————, Committee on Science and Public Policy. *The Growth of World Population.* Washington, D.C.: National Academy of Sciences, 1963.

————. *The Growth of U.S. Population.* Washington, D.C.: National Academy of Sciences, 1965.

Paddock, William, and Paul Paddock. *Famine—1975!* New York: Little, Brown, 1967.

Paige, Glenn D. *The Korean Decision: June 24-30, 1950.* New York: Free Press, 1968.

Price, D. K. *Government and Science.* New York: New York University Press, 1954.

Rainwater, Lee. *Family Design.* Chicago: Aldine Publishing, 1965.

Ramney, Austin, ed. *Political Science and Public Policy.* Chicago: Markham Publishing, 1968.

Robinson, James. *Congress and Foreign Policy Making*. Homewood, Ill.: Dorsey Press, 1962.

Rock, John. *The Time Has Come: A Catholic Doctor's Proposals To End the Battle Over Birth Control*. New York: Alfred A. Knopf, 1963.

Development Centre of the Organization of Economic Cooperation. *International Assistance for Population Programmes*. Paris, 1970.

Sanger, Margaret. *Pivot of Civilization*. New York: Brentano's, 1921.

Sax, Karl. *Standing Room Only: The Challenge of Overpopulation*. Boston: Beacon Press, 1955.

Schlesinger, Arthur, Jr. *A Thousand Days*. Boston: Houghton-Mifflin, 1965.

Sheps, Mindel C., and Jeanne Claire Ridley. *Public Health and Population Change*. Pittsburgh: University of Pittsburgh Press, 1965.

Simon, H. A. *Administrative Behavior*. New York: Macmillan, 1957.

Sorenson, Theodore. *Decision-Making in the White House*. New York: Columbia University Press, 1963.

_____. *Kennedy*. New York: Harper and Row Publishers, 1965.

Stix, Regina, and Frank Notestein. *Controlled Fertility: An Evaluation of Clinic Service*. Baltimore: William & Wilkins, 1940.

Sundquist, Jas. L. *Politics and Policy*. Washington, D.C.: Brookings Institution, 1968.

Taeuber, Irene B. *The Population of Japan*. Princeton: Princeton University Press, 1958.

United Nations Association of the United States, National Policy Panel. *World Population*. New York, 1969.

United States President's Commission on National Goals. *Goals For Americans*. New York: Spectrum Books, 1960.

Vogt, William. *Road To Survival*. New York: William Sloane Associates, 1948.

Wahlke, John, *et al. The Legislative System: Exploration in Legislative Behavior*. New York: John Wiley & Sons, 1962.

Weaver, Warren, ed. *U.S. Philanthropic Foundations*. New York: Harper and Row Publishers, 1962.

Westoff, Charles, F., *et al. Family Growth in Metropolitan America*. Princeton: Princeton University Press, 1966.

_____, and L. A. Westoff. *From Now to Zero: Fertility, Contraception and Abortion in America*. Boston: Little, Brown, 1971.

_____, R. Potter, Jr., and P. C. Sagi. *The Third Child*. Princeton: Princeton University Press, 1963.

_____, and N. B. Ryder. *Reproduction in the United States, 1965*. Princeton: Princeton University Press, 1965.

Whelpton, Pascal K., Arthur A. Campbell, and John E. Patterson. *Fertility and Family Planning in the U.S.* Princeton: Princeton University Press, 1961.

White, Theodore H. *The Making of the President, 1960*. New York: Atheneum Publishers, 1961.

Wildavsky, Aaron. *The Politics of the Budgetary Process*. Boston: Little, Brown, 1964.

PERIODICALS

Agarwala, S. "Population Control in India." *Law and Contemporary Problems*, LXXI (Summer 1960), pp. 577-92.

America. "May a Catholic President Sign?" CII (December 12, 1959), pp. 353-54.

Amlund, Curtis A. "Executive-Legislative Imbalance: Truman to Kennedy." *Western Political Quarterly*, XVIII, 3 (September 1965).

B., T. R. The New Republic. December 2, 1959, p. 2.

Back, Kurt W., and Halliman Winsborough. "Population Policy: Opinions and Actions of Government." *Public Opinion Quarterly*, CXXXII, pp. 634-45.

Bachrach, Peter, and Morton Baratz. "Two Faces of Power." *American Political Science Review*, LVI (December 1962).

Barnes, Rosanna L. "Birth Control in Popular Twentieth Century Periodicals." *The Family Coordinator*, XIX (April 1970), pp. 159-64.

Berelson, Bernard. "Beyond Family Planning." *Science*, CLXIII (February 7, 1969), pp. 533-43.

Buckman, Rilma. "Social Engineering: A Study of the Birth Control Movement." *Social Forces*, XXII (May 1944), pp. 420-28.

Casey, Thomas, S. J. "Catholics and Family Planning." *American Catholic Sociological Review*, XXI (Summer 1960), pp. 125-35.

Chisholm, Brock. "Dangerous Complacency towards Biological Warfare." *The Humanist*, January-February 1960.

Cogley, John. "The Bishop's Challenge." *Commonweal*, DCLXXI (December 1959).

Congressional Quarterly Service. "Evolution of Foreign Aid 1945-65." 1966.

Cross, Robert D. "The Changing Image of Catholicism." *Yale Review*, 1959.

Davis, Judith, and Kingsley Blake. "Birth Control and Public Policy." *Commentary*, XXIX (1960).

Dowse, R., and J. Peel. "The Politics of Birth Control." *Political Studies*, XIII (1965), pp. 179-97.

Drew, Elizabeth. "The Health Syndicate." *Atlantic Monthly*, December 1967, pp. 75-81.

Dubos, Rene K. "The Crisis of Man in His Environment." *EKISTICS*, March 1969, pp. 151-54.

Easterlin, R. A. "The American Baby Boom in Historical Perspective." *American Economic Review*, December 1961.

_____. "On the Relation of Economic Factors to Recent and Projected Fertility Changes." *Demography*, III, 1 (1966).

Eisenhower, Dwight D. "Let's be Honest With Ourselves." *Saturday Evening Post*, October 26, 1963.

Erskine, Hazel Caudet. "The Polls: The Population Explosion, Birth Control and Sex Education." *Public Opinion Quarterly*, XXX, 3 (Fall 1969).

Fagley, Richard N. "A Protestant View of Population Control." *Law and Contemporary Problems*, LXXI (Summer 1960).

Finn, James. "Controversy in New York." *Commonweal*, LXVIII (September 12, 1958).

Fischman, Jerome. "The Church in Politics: The 1960 Election in Puerto Rico." *Political Quarterly*, XXVII (1965), pp. 821-39.

Freedman, R. "The Sociology of Human Fertility." *Blackwell*, XIXI, 2 (1961-62).

Freyka, Tomas. "Reflections on the Demographic Conditions Needed to Establish a U.S. Stationary Population Growth." *Population Studies*, XXII, 3 (November 1968), 379-97.

Gardner, Richard. "Toward A World Population Program." *International Organization*, XXII, 1 (1968).

Gibbons, William J., S. J. "The Birth Control Issue—What Both Sides Say." *U.S. News & World Report*, December 21, 1959.

Greene, Wade. "Federal Birth Control: Progress Without Policy." *Reporter*, November 18, 1965, pp. 35-37.

Greer, Scott. "Catholic Voters and The Democratic Party." *Public Opinion Quarterly*, XXV (1961), pp. 611-25.

Halperin, Morton H. "The Gaither Committee and the Policy Process." *World Politics*, XIII (April 1961).

Hammond, Paul Y. "Foreign Policy-Making and Administration Politics." *World Politics*, 1965, pp. 656-71.

_____. "The National Security Council as a Device for Interdepartmental Coordination." *American Political Science Review*, LIV (1960), pp. 899-910.

Harris, Louis. "A Pollster Defends the Polls." *New York Times Magazine*, November 5, 1961.

Hartman, Carl G. "Physiological Mechanisms Concerned with Conception—An Inventory of Unanswered Questions." *Perspectives in Biology and Medicine*, IV (Autumn 1960), pp. 70-90.

Haviland, Field, "Foreign Aid and the Policy Process: 1957." *American Political Science Review*, LII (September 1958), pp. 689-724.

Hill, Reuben J., *et al.* "Population Control in Puerto Rico." *Law and Contemporary Problems*, XV, 3 (Summer 1960).

Hillsman, Roger. "Congressional-Executive Relations and the Foreign Policy Consensus." *American Political Science Review*, CII (September 1962), pp. 689-724.

Holden, M. "Imperialism in Bureaucracy." *American Political Science Review*, LX (1966), pp. 943-51.

Hudson, Jac. "Birth Control Legislation." *Cleveland Marchall Law Review*, IX (1960).

Huntington, S. P. "The Marasmus of the ICC: The Commission, the Railroads, and the Public Interest." *Yale Law Journal*, LXI (1952), pp. 473-92.

Jahnige, Thomas P. "The Congressional Committee System and the Oversight Process." *Western Political Quarterly*, XXI, 2 (June 1968).

Kaufman, H. "Organization Theory and Political Theory." *American Political Science Review*, LVIII (1964), pp. 5-14.

Leiserson, A. "Scientists and the Policy Process." *American Political Science Review*, LIX (1965), pp. 408-16.

Levine, Sol, Norman Scotch, and George J. Vlasak. "Unravelling Technology and Culture in Public Health." *American Journal of Public Health*, February 1969.

Lipsky, Michael. "Protest as a Political Resource." *American Political Science Review*, XLII (December 1968), pp. 1144-46.

Lutzger, Paul. "The Behavior of Congressmen in a Committee Setting: A Research Report." *Western Political Quarterly*, XXXI (February 1969).

McLellean, Davis S., and Charles E. Woodhouse. "Business Elite and Foreign Policy." *Western Political Science Quarterly*, March 1960.

Macmahon, A. "Congressional Oversight of Administration: The Power of the Purse." *Political Science Quarterly*, LVIII (1943), pp. 161-90, 380-414.

Mainzer, Lewis. "The Scientist as Public Administrator." *Western Political Quarterly*, XXVI, pp. 814-29.

Mayer, Jean. "Toward a Non-Malthusian Population Policy." *Columbia Forum*, XII (Summer 1969), pp. 5-13.

Nelson, W. O. "Survey of Studies Relating to Vulnerable Points in the Reproductive Process." *Acta Endocrinologica*, Supp. 25, VII (1956).

Neustadt, Richard. "White House and White Hall." *The Public Interest*, Winter 1966, pp. S 9-61.

Newsweek. "Ssh! U.S. At Work." November 6, 1961.

O'Brien, John. "Let's Take Birth Control Out of Politics." *LOOK*, October 10, 1961.

"Population Control." *Law and Contemporary Problems*, XXV (Summer 1960).

Potter, Allen. "Attitude Groups." *Political Quarterly*, XXIX (January-March 1958).

Ravenholt, R. T., and P. T. Piotrow. "Use of Oral Contraceptives in Developing Countries." *Pakistan Journal of Medical Research*, VIII (1969).

_____, et al. "Use of Contraceptives: A Decade of Controversy." *International Journal of Gynecology and Obstetrics*, VIII, 6 (November 1968).

Rock, John. "We Can End the Battle Over Birth Control." *Good Housekeeping*, July 1961.

St. John-Stevas, Norman. "A Roman Catholic View of Population Control." *Law and Contemporary Problems*, LXXI (Summer 1960).

Samuel, T. T. "Development of India's Policy of Population Control." *Quarterly Review, Milbank Memorial Fund*, XLIV, 1.

Schilling, Warner. "Science, Technology and Foreign Policy." *Journal of International Affairs*, XIII, 1 (Winter 1969).

Sharkansky, Ira. "An Appropriations Subcommittee and Its Client Agencies: A Study of Supervision and Control." *American Political Science Review*, LIX, 3 (September 1969).

Sheehan, "The Birth Control Pill." *Fortune*, April 1958.

Simon, Herbert. "Birth of an Organization: The Economic Cooperation Administration." *Public Administration Review*, III (December 1953).

Smith, Peter. "The History and Future of the Legal Battle over Birth Control." *Cornell Law Quarterly*, XLIX (1964).

Solloway, Alvah. "The Legal and Political Aspects of Birth Control in the United States." *Law and Contemporary Problems*, XV (Summer 1960), pp. 600-12.

Spencer, Steven. "The Birth Control Revolution." *Saturday Evening Post*, CCXXXIX, January 15, 1960.

Spengler, Joseph. "Economic Factors in the Development of Densely Populated Areas." *Proceedings of the American Philosophical Society*, 1951.
_____."Population Threatens Prosperity." *Harvard Business Review*, January-February 1956.
_____."The World's Hunger—Malthus, 1948." *Proceedings of the Academy of Political Science*, XXIII (1949), pp. 64-67.
Stone, A. "Fertility Problems in India." *Fertility and Sterility*, May-June 1953.
Taylor, Carl. "Five Stages in a Practical Population Policy." *International Development Review*, X, 14 (December 1968).
_____."Health and Population." *Foreign Affairs*, April 1965.
Tucker, Robert C. "The Theory of Charismatic Leadership." *Daedalus*, XCVII, pp. 731-56. Proceeding of the American Academy of Arts and Sciences. (Summer 1968.)
White, Theodore H. "No. 1 American in Europe." *New York Times Magazine*, December 21, 1952.
Wilson, James A. "The Strategy of Protest." *Journal of Conflicts Resolution*, September 3, 1961.

Also, generally: *Population Bulletin, Population Index, Population Studies, Science, Studies in Family Planning, American Journal of Obstetrics and Gynecology, Demography, Medical World News, and Perspectives.*

UNITED NATIONS PUBLICATIONS

Demographic Yearbook. (E/F .69 .XIII.I) New York, 1949-69.
Determinants and Consequences of Population Trends. New York, 1953.
The Future Growth of World Population. Population Studies No. 28, New York: United Nations Department of Social and Economic Affairs, 1958.
Lorimer, Frank. *Culture and Human Fertility.* UNESCO, 1954.
Population Bulletin. (A periodical.)
Proceedings of The World Population Conference. Rome, 1954. *(Summary Reports.* New York, 1954.)
Proceedings of The World Population Conference, 1965. (E/Conf. 4113) New York, 1965.
Report of the Second Committee. Summary Records, General Assembly. A/5354, Annex 38.
The State of Food and Agriculture. United Nations Food and Agriculture Organization. Rome, 1954.
World Population Prospects As Assessed in 1963. (ST/SOA/Series A 41.) New York, 1966.
"World Population Situation." Population Commission. (E/CN.9/231). Geneva, 1969. Mimeo.

U.S. GOVERNMENT PUBLICATIONS *

Agency for International Development. "AID Loan to Turkey is First for Family Planning Effort." Press Release AID GG—107, June 21, 1966.
_____. *Assistance for Family Planning Programs in Developing Countries.* January 1967.
_____. *Office of the War on Hunger.* Manual Order 204:3. March 23, 1967.
_____. *Population Program Assistance.* 1967 through 1970.
_____. "Technical Assistance Bureau Aims at Sharper AID Programs in '70's." Press release. September 24, 1969.
Agency for International Development. *The War on Hunger.* Manual Order 1018, 4TL, 9:86. November 11, 1966.

---

*All U.S. government publications are published by the government division indicated and printed by the Government Printing Office, Washington, D.C., unless otherwise indicated.

Brown, Lester. *Increasing World Food Output: Problems and Prospects*. Department of Agriculture. Report #25. 1965.

————. *Man, Land and Food*. Department of Agriculture. Report #11. 1963.

Burdick, E. Douglas. "India's Population Problem: A Deterrent to India's Progress." Health Division, Technical Co-Operation Mission to India. September 1959. Mimeo.

Commission on Population Growth and the American Future. *Population Growth and America's Future*. Interim Report, March 1971.

Commission on Population Growth and the American Future. *Population and the American Future*. Final Report, 1972.

Congress, House of Representatives, Committee on Agriculture. *War on Hunger. Hearings on HR 14929* before the Committee. 89th Cong., 2nd sess., 1966.

Congress, House of Representatives, Committee on Appropriations, Subcommittee on Foreign Operations. *Hearings on Foreign Aid Legislation*. 86th Cong., 1st sess., through 91st Cong., 1st sess., 1959-69.

Congress, House of Representatives, Committee on Education and Labor. *Economic Opportunity Amendments of 1967*. Report No. 866. 90th Cong., 1st sess., 1966.

Congress, House of Representatives, Committee on Foreign Affairs. *Hearings on Foreign Aid Legislation*. 86th Cong., 1st sess., through 91st Cong., 1st sess., 1959-69.

Congress, Senate, Committee on Appropriations, Subcommittee on Foreign Operations. *Hearings on Foreign Aid Legislation*. 86th Cong., 1st sess., through 91st Cong., 1st sess., 1959-69.

Congress, Senate, Committee on Foreign Relations. *Hearings on Foreign Aid Legislation*. 86th Cong., 1st sess., through 91st Cong., 1st sess., 1959-69.

Congress, Senate, Committee on Government Operations. *Population Crisis. Hearings on S. 1676* before the Subcommittee on Foreign Aid Expenditures. 89th and 90th Cong., June 22, 1965-June 15, 1966.

Congress, Senate, Committee on Labor and Public Welfare. *Declaration of United States Policy of Population Stabilization by Voluntary Means*. 92d Cong., 1st sess., 1971.

Congress, Senate, Committee on Labor and Public Welfare. *Family Planning Program. Hearings* before the committee. 89th Cong., 2nd sess., 1966.

Congress, Senate, Committee on Labor and Public Welfare. *Progress Report on the Five-Year Plan for Family Planning Services and Population Research Programs Submitted by the Secretary of Health, Education, and Welfare*. 92d Cong., 2nd sess., 1972.

Congress, Senate, Committee on Labor and Public Welfare. *Report of the Secretary of Health, Education, and Welfare Submitting Five-Year Plan for Family Planning Services and Population Research Programs*. 92d Cong., 1st sess., 1971.

Congressional Record. Proceedings and debates of the Congress, 1959-69.

Department of Health, Education, and Welfare, Public Health Service. *A Survey of Research on Reproduction Related to Birth and Population Control* (as of January 1, 1963). 1963.

Department of State. Policy Planning Council. *Foreign Implications of the World Population Explosion*. Publication No. PPC-61-3.

Department of State. *Department of State Bulletin*. August 11, 1969.

Gardner, Richard N. *Population Growth: A World Problem, Statement of U.S. Policy*. Department of State, January 1963. Originally printed as UN Document X/C. 2/L.657.

President's Committee to Study the United States Military Assistance Program. *Composite Paper*. August 17, 1969.

Task Force on International Development. *U.S. Foreign Assistance for the 1970's: A New Approach*. March 4, 1970.

abortion, x, xiii, 33, 38, 107, 134-35, 137,
189, 191-94, 195-96, 197-98, 220,
226, 228
activists, xiv, 7, 9, 11, 12, 13, 15, 17-19,
34-35, 49, 55, 57, 59-62, 63, 70, 72,
86, 88, 90, 93, 97-98, 100, 112-13,
115, 118, 146, 153, 156, 158, 165,
181, 191, 194, 200, 206, 223-26, 232
Adams, Robert, 40
Adams, Robert, 110
Adams, Sherman, 36
Africa, 3-5, 19, 113, 122, 134, 147, 202,
206, 211
Agricultural Trade and Development Act
(see Food for Peace)
Agency for International Development
(AID), xii-xiii, xv-xvi, 56, 62-65, 68,
74, 76, 77-79, 80-88, 92-100, 109,
110, 113, 115, 116-17, 118-20,
121-31, 132-39, 140-41, 142, 145-54,
155-59, 160-61, 162, 165-86, 186,
198-200, 203, 204-5, 207, 209-13,
217, 218, 220, 228-30, 231; airgrams,
62, 64, 80-82, 85-86, 92-93, 93-96;
appropriations, expenditures, funding,
29, 100, 128, 146-48, 150-53, 156-57,
158-59, 160-61, 167-69, 171, 181-85,
200; Assistant Administrator for Population (proposed), 168; European Recovery Program (see Marshall Plan,
foreign aid), 36-37; International Cooperation Administration, 33-34,
45-46, 51, 62-63; International Development Institute, 184, 217; institution building, 85, 146, 148, 152-54,
165-66; Latin American Bureau (see
Alliance for Progress also) 95-96, 99,
147, 152; Near East South Asia Bureau (NESA), 94, 96, 129, 153,
178-79; overseas missions, 94, 96, 147,
147-48, 150-53, 154-55, 167; personnel levels, 99, 149-50, 166, 167, 170,
171; Population and Humanitarian Affairs Bureau, 185; Population Branch,
96, 123, 128, 147, 156; Population,
Office of, xvi, 84, 147-50, 153-55,

156, 166, 170, 184, 185; Program and
Policy Coordination Bureau, 94, 146,
148, 181, 185, 210; Population Reference and Research Branch, 82, 99;
Population Service, 128, 129, 136,
147-50, 152, 155, 156, 158, 165-66,
200; Section, 98, 148-49; Technical
Assistance Bureau, 149, 166, 170;
Technical Cooperation and Research,
93-94, 98, 99, 121-22, 127; Title X
(see foreign aid); War on Hunger, Of-
fice of, 127-28, 131, 136, 139, 140,
145, 146, 148-49, 152, 155, 158, 166,
169, 200, 210, 229
Aiken, George, 39
Albritton, Errett M., 58
Allen, Durward, 188
Alliance for Progress (see Agency for Inter-
national Development), xii, 64-65,
84-86, 88, 94-95, 152
America, 48
American Assembly, 75, 81, 95
American Birth Control Federation, 15-16
American Catholic Women's Club (Japan),
32
American Civil Liberties Union, 49
American Law Institute, 197-98
American Medical Association, 8
American Public Health Association
(APHA), 42
American Society of Newspaper Editors, 44
Anderson, Dillon, 37
Anglican Church, 11
Anti-Poverty Program (see Office of Eco-
nomic Opportunity)
Asia, 3-5, 113, 122, 134, 147, 202, 211
Asian Population Conference, 82
Association for Voluntary Sterilization, 189

Bachrach, Peter, 47
Backlund, Randall, 169
Balfour, Marshall, 14
Ball, George, 59-60, 67, 76
Ball, William, 107
Bangladesh, 180, 181
Baptists, 42

tration (ICA), 33-34, 45-46, 51, 62;
  Marshall Plan, 36, 159, 207, 230;
  Mutual Security Program, 36, 37;
  Point IV, 36, 145; Presidential Mes-
  sages, 116, 127, 166, 169; Title X,
  132-39, 147-48, 153, 167, 184, 230
France, 10
Fraser, Donald, 135
Freeman, Orville, 116, 117, 126, 127
Frejka, Tomas, 190
Fulbright, J. William, xvi, 37, 71, 76-80,
  81-82, 83, 93, 103, 118, 122, 133,
  134-36, 137, 138, 140-41, 167,
  184-85, 231
Fulton, James, 77-78, 134, 135, 146

Gallup polls (see polls)
Gamble, Clarence, 129
Gandhi, Mahatma, 34
Gardner, John, 90, 93, 98, 109, 110, 161
Gardner, Richard, 60, 63, 66-70, 80-82, 83,
  93, 94, 97, 113-15, 133, 136, 140,
  199, 203-4, 208
Gaud, William, 83, 85, 99, 110, 126-29, 131,
  135-40, 146, 150-53, 156, 157, 158,
  160, 161, 165, 167, 168, 172-73, 175,
  200, 229
Georgetown University, 84
Germany, 20, 210
Gille, Halvor, 213
Good Housekeeping, 71
Goldwater, Barry, 116
Goodwin, Richard, 89
Gordon, Lincoln, 86
Griswold v. Connecticut, 107, 225-26
Grant, James, 45
Green Revolution, 146, 166, 170, 181, 184
Gremillion, James, 84
Growth of American Families studies, 23, 92
Growth of U.S. Population, The, 92
Gruening, Ernest, xvi, 31-32, 63, 78-79, 96,
  103-12, 116, 118, 123, 125, 133, 138,
  140, 219, 230-31
Gruenther, Alfred M., 37, 39-40, 41
Gulick, Frances, 173
Guttmacher, Alan, 16, 141, 168

Haggerty, James, 41
Hamilton, Fowler, 63-64
Hammarskjold, Dag, 12, 41, 70
Hand, Argustus, 9
Hannah, John, 165-68, 169, 181, 208
Hansberger, R. V., 194
Hardin, Garrett, 191
Harkavy, Oscar, 15, 61, 110, 159, 172, 208,
  225

Harlow, Bryce, 163
Harper, Paul, 14
Harriman, Averell, 80
Hays, Wayne, xix, 134
Health, Education and Welfare, Department
  of, xi, 58, 59, 91, 95, 98, 99, 105,
  109, 110, 117, 119-21, 141-42, 159,
  161, 163, 164, 165, 169-70, 172, 173,
  175, 177, 195, 201, 222, 225, 229,
  231; appropriation, 92, 142; Chil-
  dren's Bureau, 81, 95, 98, 110; Family
  Planning and Population Research Act
  of 1970, 23, 195-96; National Center
  for Population and Family Planning
  (proposed), 164; National Institutes of
  Health (see NIH); Public Health Service
  (U.S.), 81, 98, 122
Hebrew Congregations, Union of American,
  42
Hedges, Irwin, 158
Hellman, Louis, 16, 195
Henderson, Julia, 67, 184, 201, 204, 209
HEW (see Health)
Higgins, George, 41
Hill, Lister, 120
Himes, Norman, 5
Hoffman, Paul, 206-8, 209-10, 211-12, 215
Honda, Chikao, 33
Hong Kong, 92
Hoover, Edgar, 15, 124, 202
Hornig, Donald, 89
House of Representatives, 37, 77, 84-85,
  118, 164-65, 168, 195; Agriculture
  Committee, 103, 116-17; Appropria-
  tions Committee, 109, 119-20, 138,
  142, 231; Foreign Affairs Committee,
  77, 81, 96, 103, 133-38, 146, 168,
  184-85; Republican Task Force, 164;
  Ways and Means Committee, 141
Houston, Texas, 44
Humanae Vitae, 160, 192, 219
human rights, 92, 201
Human Rights Day, 201
Humphrey, Hubert, 82, 83, 127
Huntington, Samuel P., 55, 112, 139, 155,
  198, 233

India, 14, 17, 34, 40, 46, 47, 48, 71, 76, 82,
  83, 91, 92, 93, 97, 106, 112, 114,
  122, 125, 129, 137, 147, 153, 155,
  157, 163, 171-73, 179-80, 206, 213
Indians (American), 91
Indonesia, 213, 216
International Conference on Human Rights,
  201
International Labor Organization, 211

271

Moore, Hugh, xv, 18-19, 38, 39, 40, 49-50, 61, 70-71, 89, 105, 113, 115, 129, 133-34, 223
Morgan, Thomas, xvi, 133, 134-35, 146
Moscoso, Theodoro, 64-65, 84-86
Moseman, Albert, 99, 122-23
Moss, John, 58, 231
Moynihan, Daniel (Pat), 163-69, 194

National Academy of Sciences, 13, 74, 75, 81, 85, 92, 187-89
National Catholic Welfare Conference, 41, 59, 64, 67, 106, 107, 115, 117
National Center for Family Planning Services (see also HEW), 164, 170
National Center for Health Statistics, 95, 120
National Committee for Maternal Health, 14
National Conference on Conservation, 189
National Institutes of Health (see also HEW), xvi, 16, 56-60, 75-76, 78, 89, 92, 139, 142, 152, 156-57, 161, 164-65, 171-78, 196, 225; Center for Population Research, 161, 164-65, 174, 175; National Institute of Child Health and Human Development, 142, 161, 171, 171-77; Population Institute (proposed), 164
National Security Council, 41
National Wildlife and Natural Resources Conference, 188
Nehru, Jawahrlal, 34, 42, 71
Nelson, Gaylord, 181
New York Academy of Sciences, 177
New York, 16, 17
New York Post, 16
New York Times, 13, 20, 41, 44, 70, 97
Nigeria, 181
Nixon, Richard M., x, 45, 47, 75, 150, 163-64, 165, 166-67, 168, 169, 170, 188-89, 192, 194, 197, 209, 215, 218, 227-28
North Carolina, 219
North Carolina, University of, 95, 149
Notestein, Frank, 5, 9, 12, 14, 113, 172, 189, 198, 208
Notre Dame, University of, 84, 95
Nunley, William, 60, 65
Nuveen, John, 18

O'Brien, John, 157, 71
Oettinger, Katherine, 98, 110
Office of Economic Opportunity (OEO), xi, 91, 119-21, 127, 141, 142, 151, 161, 219
O'Hara, Barrett, 77, 135-36

Olivarez, Grace, 195, 196
O'Rourke, Edward, 82
Osborn, Fairfield, 187
Osborn, Frederick, 13, 18
Owen, David, 181
Owen, Henry, 60

Packwood, Robert, xvi, 103, 185, 192, 194-96, 231
Paddock, William and Paul, 113
Pakistan, 46, 71, 92, 155, 180, 181, 205, 211, 216
Pan American Health Organization, 85
Parran, Thomas, 31
Partnership for Health Lesiglation, 141
Passman, Otto, 82, 185
Pathfinder Fund, the, 129, 153, 154
Peace Corps, 124
Peterson, Rudolph, 166, 183-85, 216
Philippines, 82, 166
Pike, James, 44, 56-57
Pilpel, Harriet, 191
Pincus, Gregory, 16
Planned Parenthood (U.S.), 7, 10, 14-15, 15-19, 25-35, 46-47, 57-58, 60, 61-62, 64, 68, 70, 75, 76, 88-89, 91-92, 94, 97, 110, 115-16, 117, 154, 155, 165, 170-78, 189, 191, 196, 226
Plimpton, T. P., 60
Poats, Rutherford, 167, 173
pollution, 187, 189, 190, 194
polls, 20-31, 50, 69, 118-20, 160, 191, 193-94
Pope John XXIII, 49, 57, 71, 108
Pope Paul VI, 128, 159, 160
Pope Pius XI, 8, 57
Population Association of America, 189-90
Population Bomb, 18, 38, 189
Population Council, 12-15, 18, 57, 58, 64, 71, 72, 92, 95, 99, 100, 113, 115, 121, 129, 137, 153, 154, 155-56, 161, 171-72, 175, 180-82, 202, 203, 205-6, 211
Population Crisis Committee, 105, 209
population explosion, 3, 43, 71, 88, 89
Population Explosion and Christian Responsibility, 49
Population Growth: A World Problem, 68
Population Institute, 164
Population Reference Bureau, 18, 38, 58
Post Office Department, 119
Presbyterian Church, United, 42
Presidential Message on Population, viii, 166, 168-69, 228
President's Committee on Population and Family Planning (1968), 158-61

273

ABOUT THE AUTHOR

PHYLLIS TILSON PIOTROW is administrator of the Population Information Program of George Washington University Medical Center. Formerly Executive Director of the Population Crisis Committee, she has been actively concerned with the development of U.S. government policy in the population field since 1965. She has served as a consultant to the United Nations on plans for World Population Year in 1974 and as an Adviser on the U.S. Delegation to the United Nations Population Commission. Prior to joining the Population Crisis Committee, she was legislative assistant to two U.S. senators.

Dr. Piotrow received her B.A. degree summa cum laude from Bryn Mawr College, her M.A. with First Class Honors from Oxford University, and her Ph.D from the Johns Hopkins University, with work in the fields of history, political science, and population dynamics.

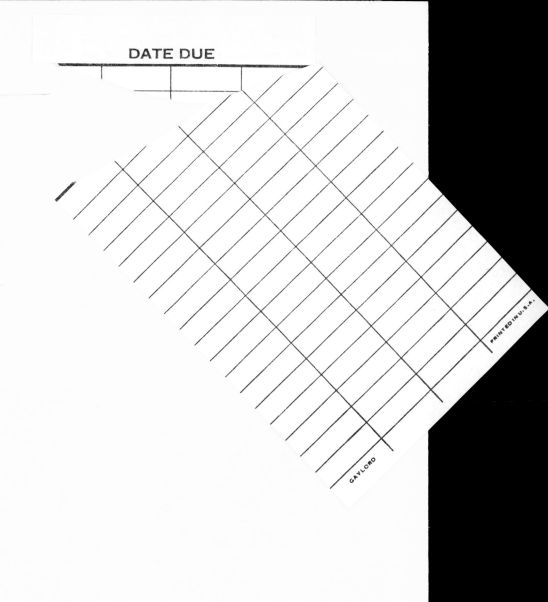

DATE DUE